Gentle Medicine

Gentle Medicine

AN A-Z OF NATURAL REMEDIES FOR COMMON AILMENTS

Angela Smyth
Consultant Editor: Dr Hilary Jones

This edition published by Limited Editions 1994

First published by Thorsons
An Imprint of HarperCollins*Publishers*
77–85 Fulham Palace Road
Hammersmith, London W6 8JB
1160 Battery Street,
San Francisco, California 94111-1213

Published by Thorsons 1994
10 8 7 6 5 4 3 2 1

© Angela Symth 1994

Angela Smyth asserts the moral right to
be identified as the author of this work

A catalogue record for this book
is available from the British Library

ISBN 0 583 31774 X

Typeset by Harper Phototypesetters Ltd,
Northampton, England
Printed and bound in Finland

Text illustrations by Chris Etheridge

About the Author

Angela Smyth is a medical journalist and author who has written extensively for health and science publications in the UK and the USA. She is a frequent contributor to the *Independent* and the *Guardian* as well as *Here's Health* and *BBC Good Health*. She is the author of *S.A.D.: Winter Depression* (Thorsons).

Consultant Editor Dr Hilary Jones is TV's best-known doctor. He contributes to a number of publications and is also a practising GP.

Consultants

Leon Chaitow, N.D., D.O. (naturopathy)
Robert Bridge R.S. Hom. (homoeopathy)
Kathryn Marsden Dip. CN, MSNC, MRNT (diet)
Helena Bridge D.O. (osteopathy/massage)
Shirley Price FISPA, MIFA (aromatherapy)
Dr Julian Kenyon (acupressure)
Anthony Attenborough (Bates method)

Contents

Note to the Reader

Before following the self help advice given in this book, readers are earnestly urged to give careful consideration to the nature of their particular health problem, and to consult a competent physician or complementary health practitioner if in any doubt. This book should not be regarded as a substitute for professional medical treatment, and whilst every care is taken to ensure the accuracy of the content, the author and the publishers cannot accept legal responsibility for any problem arising out of experimentation with the methods described.

Acknowledgements

This book would not have been possible without the help of many health professionals who donated their time and expertise in discussing the numerous remedies and treatments listed. In particular I would like to thank Leon Chaitow, N.D., D.O. for his invaluable contributions to the naturopathic recommendations outlined, Robert Bridge, R.S. Hom. for his guidance through the vastly complex world of homoeopathic self-prescribing, Kathryn Marsden for the latest research on dietary treatments, Helena Bridge, D.O. for her osteopathic expertise and creativity in putting massage down on paper, Shirley Price for her aromatherapy recommendations, Dr Julian Kenyon for his advice on acupressure, and Bates Method teacher Anthony Attenborough. My thanks also go to Janet Balaskas, founder of the Active Birth Movement, Bob King, Director of the Chicago School of Massage Therapy and the staff of the *Journal of Alternative and Complementary Medicine*.

Secondly I would like to thank members of the many self help and support groups across Britain and the USA with whom I corresponded. The service they offer is invaluable in providing the public with first hand advice, information and a support network. The names of these organizations are listed at the back of the book as sources of further reference on specific ailments.

The aim of this book is to offer its readers an informed choice of treatment, whether it be orthodox or complementary. In doing so I am greatly indebted to consultant editor Dr Hilary Jones, who alongside a busy

television schedule and a busy medical practice gave
generously of his time, bringing a delightful blend of
professionalism, practicality and open-mindedness to the
writing of the book, and demonstrating that orthodox
and complementary medicine can work together.

My thanks also go to Jane Graham-Maw and
Veronica Simpson of Thorsons for their direction and
editing, and to my agent Lisa Eveleigh. And last but not
least, I am grateful to my husband, Ian, without whose
support and encouragement the book would never have
been finished.

Angela Smyth

Preface

by Dr Hilary Jones

There has been something of a revolution in recent years concerning the nation's attitude to health, illness and treatment. I have seen this develop both as a practising GP and a television doctor and journalist and I welcome it wholeheartedly. My patients and my TV postbag convey the same message: that there is intense interest now in complementary medicine, which embraces alternative therapies in conjunction with, rather than as a substitute for, orthodox medicine.

People have become better informed and more responsible for their own well-being. They recognize not only the value of orthodox medicine, but also for the first time its limitations. No longer will they obey doctors orders without question. They realize that it is no longer satisfactory to treat symptoms merely in order to make them disappear. Instead, they expect the underlying cause of the symptoms to be accurately identified and corrected. And finally, quite rightly, they expect some say in the treatment of their own problems. They know that their lifestyle, their temperament, their relationships and their entire outlook on life are just as important as their medical history. And they are now more likely to welcome the dispensing of patiently thought-out advice than a hurriedly scribbled prescription for potent medication.

Complementary medicine is here to stay. Most conventionally trained physicians who retain open minds have accepted it. Even diehard surgeons whose former

motto was 'if in doubt, cut it out' have changed their
tune. And they have realized that a holistic approach to
their patients, treating them as whole people, not just as
a collection of body parts, can bear both physical and
psychological rewards.

Importantly, the true scientific value of
complementary medicine has been proven in carefully
structured clinical trials. Many orthodox doctors like
myself have subsequently widened the scope of the
treatments they offer their patients in their National
Health Service surgeries, and have learned new skills
such as homoeopathy, osteopathy and acupuncture.
Gentle Medicine encompasses a vast array of common
disorders from A to Z, and looks at the various
alternative treatments available for them. Prevention
quite logically comes first, followed by self help in the
form of various complementary therapies. Finally,
almost as a last resort, comes the orthodox approach, a
route which many people today will only turn to when
all else has failed. The choices are yours, and *Gentle
Medicine* offers the lot.

People have seen how psychotherapy and counselling
can offer considerable advantages over tranquillizers in
the treatment of stress. They have seen how massage,
acupuncture and osteopathy can complement
chemotherapy in the palliation of cancer, and how art
therapy and light therapy can be helpful in depression
and mental illness respectively. As as result, I believe
treatment has become more effective, less invasive, and
safer. Patients no longer want blunderbuss therapy or a
sledgehammer to crack a nut. They don't want drastic
or threatening treatment. I believe that what they are
really looking for these days is 'Gentle Medicine'.

Introduction

The last thirty years have seen significant changes in the types of treatment and health advice available. Not so long ago complementary practitioners, such as homoeopaths, massage therapists and acupuncturists were regarded disdainfully as back street quacks. Even the links between diet, exercise and good health were considered suspect. But today practitioners of complementary medicine are respectably established in hospitals and clinics, and some are the focus of government research grants. Nutritional recommendations have become part and parcel of mainstream medical practice and scientific evidence leaves little room for doubting the benefits of exercise.

During this time the emphasis in healthcare (both in orthodox and complementary medicine) has moved towards the prevention of illness and the exploration of self help through gentle, non-invasive methods. More and more people are seeking out information about how to protect themselves from life-threatening diseases, and increasing numbers are opting for complementary treatments to remedy chronic health problems.

The result has been an explosion of different attitudes, techniques and information about how to prevent, treat or deal with different ailments. A day does not go past without a new discovery being made. In writing *Gentle Medicine* my aim has been to bring together much of this varied and often conflicting information in a user-friendly reference book. The result is an encyclopaedia of more than 300 common health problems. Each entry has a varied range of preventive measures and complementary treatments, most of which can be carried out by the patient at home. The treatments were compiled in collaboration with practitioners of more than twenty of the most popular complementary therapies in use today. They range from simple dietary and exercise recommendations, to tried and tested homoeopathic and herbal remedies, and even include the more esoteric health-enhancing properties of visualization and yoga. To complete the treatment picture, Dr Hilary Jones adds orthodox medical advice for each ailment, outlining what your doctor would recommend in each case. This combination of preventive measures, complementary treatments and orthodox advice reflects the holistic nature of today's health care and provides an opportunity for informed choice of treatment.

Presenting a holistic approach is a complex task. There are well over one hundred different therapies on offer in Britain and America today. The job is further complicated by rapid changes and ongoing controversies in the fields of complementary medicine. I have not attempted to include all potential treatments for every ailment: the list would be endless. Instead I have focused on those remedies most commonly prescribed and considered by health practitioners to be the most effective and applicable to home use. Should you develop a particular interest in one or more techniques, or wish to find professional help, the Appendices provide an extensive listing of books, and the names and addresses of practitioners' organizations and associations. Addresses are also given of suppliers of equipment and remedies. In the case of more serious ailments, I include information in Appendix 2 about support groups that provide advice and contact with fellow sufferers.

Due to space limitations, this book can only provide a brief description of the symptoms and causes of each ailment. It is not in any way intended to replace a medical diagnosis, and I strongly recommend that you seek out a professional assessment of your symptoms.

Once you are aware of the nature of your ailment, *Gentle Medicine* will provide you with the means to explore different approaches to prevention and treatment. It will guide you towards the type of complementary therapy that will be most beneficial, it will empower you with the means to take control of your health, and it will offer a wealth of resources for further help, support and information.

Gentle Treatments

The range of complementary treatments available today is extensive. The ones outlined in this book are those which have been most extensively researched, and are most widely used at home. In cases where self help is not appropriate, we have added advice on where to seek professional help.

The following is a brief introduction to each type of treatment found in the book.

Acupressure

Acupressure is a massage technique which combines finger point massage with pressure to the acupuncture points lying along the meridians (channels through which *qi* or the life force of the body is thought to flow). In the same way as acupuncture (see below) is thought to stimulate the flow of *qi* through the meridians, so acupressure is thought to stimulate energy blockages which lead to disease and pain. However, because acupressure is carried out using the hands rather than needles, it is most appropriate for self help. Acupressure is best carried out using the thumb, exerting deep pressure so that the point aches a little or even feels slightly numb. It is helpful to use a circular massage movement in the direction indicated in the illustrations provided.

Acupuncture

This is obviously not a self help treatment, but is sometimes recommended as a suitable means of professional help. In the Western world acupuncture is often offered as a treatment in itself, rather than as a part of traditional Chinese medicine. Some acupuncturists may make dietary recommendations and prescribe herbs; others do not. Acupuncture, the placing of extremely thin disposable needles in points along the meridians (channels through which the *qi* or life force of the body flows), is thought to stimulate energy blockages which lead to disease. The method must be carried out by a trained practitioner (see Appendix 1 for details of where to find one). Acupuncture is a diverse system of treatment which can be applied to virtually all ailments. We have indicated conditions where we feel it would be particularly helpful.

Alexander Technique

The Alexander Technique is an educational therapy aimed at improving overall mental and physical well-being through changes in habitual posture. The technique aims to allow the body to have perfect balance and poise with minimum tension and energy usage. Though difficult at first, the Alexander Technique leads to a sense of lengthening, ease of movement, reduced muscular and mental tension and often pain relief. It can be particularly effective in helping back and neck problems and in rehabilitation following accidents.

Because lessons are required from a professional, the Alexander Technique is not a self help method. However, once learnt, the exercises and education can be used at home without a professional.

Applied Kinesiology (AK)

This is a professional diagnostic technique, which can help distinguish the location of problems and their causes. By testing different muscle groups of the body, the kinesiologist is able to identify areas of muscle weakness which indicate areas of impaired energy and function. AK practitioners believe that muscle strength and tone reflects the inner state of the organs, so AK is thought to help diagnose potential areas of disease in organs such as the heart, lungs, bowel and kidneys. The technique is particularly useful for identifying food and substance sensitivities.

Aromatherapy

The ultimate in gentle medicine, aromatherapy has its roots in the ancient use of aromatic herbs in Egypt, India, Greece and the Arab world. Knowledge of how odour can be used to stimulate, relax and heal has been passed down through the centuries and was refined in the early 20th century in France and Germany. Since then aromatherapy has become a widely practised treatment, and its use in orthodox medicine is increasing. Essential oils, obtained from plants, roots, leaves, flowers and fruit, have been shown to have powerful psychological effects: research has shown that certain oils, when inhaled, have the power to relax or stimulate. In treatment, aromatherapy can be used to relieve conditions such as depression and fatigue. Many essential oils also have antiseptic and anti-inflammatory properties.

Aromatherapy can safely be used as a self help treatment in the home. However, certain guidelines should be followed:

- use the purest oils available from reputable suppliers (see Appendix 3).
- essential oils are highly concentrated. When placed on

the skin they are nearly always diluted with a carrier oil (sunflower, safflower or almond are suitable) or an emulsified oil and water lotion. The dilution you will need is outlined in the treatment for each ailment. When making up a dilution, add the required drops of oil to the carrier oil or lotion and shake well.

- if you have a sensitive skin, it is advisable to test a little of the diluted essential oil on a small area of your skin before proceeding with treatment.
- avoid contact with the eyes.
- keep essential oils out of the reach of children.
- always close your eyes when inhaling essential oil.

Bach Flower Remedies

Flower remedies were first invented and used by Dr Edward Bach around the turn of the century. They are now extensively used in the home and are suitable for self help. The remedies are derived from wild flowers and one from pure stream water, which Dr Bach believed provide subtle energy, effective in treating emotional disharmony. The remedies are made by picking fresh flowers and placing them on the surface of a bowl of water where they are left in the sun for several hours. It is thought that the action of the sun on the flowers releases their life force or energy into the water. Each of the remedies is appropriate to specific personality traits, and is administered in liquid form. The most commonly used remedy is Rescue Remedy, a combination of five flower remedies.

Bates Method

An alternative method of dealing with eyesight problems. Bates Method teachers believe that many vision defects are due to tensions and poor functioning of the muscles controlling the lens of the eyes. The method provides exercises to strengthen these muscles. Treatment should be carried out initially under the supervision of a Bates teacher, though we have included some safe and beneficial introductory exercises in the section on eyesight problems.

Biochemic Tissue Salts

This therapy is based on the theory that the body contains 12 essential mineral salts. Imbalance or deficiency in these salts is thought to lead to disease. Biochemic tissue salts are manufactured in the same way as homoeopathic remedies in very dilute forms (see Homoeopathy below). The tissue salts are normally sold in the 6th decimal trituration (6x). They are available from pharmacists and health food stores and can safely be used in the home.

Biofeedback

Stress and anxiety bring physical responses in the body, such as increased pulse, sweating or muscle tension. With the help of a mechanism strapped to the body to monitor these effects, biofeedback helps you to know when the body is responding to stress, and allows you to develop strategies to reduce tension. As you become increasingly aware of what stress feels like, you learn to respond to its signs and prevent it occurring.

Chinese Medicine

This is a complex system of treatment which has evolved over thousands of years using diet, herbalism, acupuncture and exercise to treat a wide variety of ailments. The principle concept of traditional Chinese medicine is that disease is caused by an imbalance of the vital force or energy, also known as *qi*. The

practitioner's aim is to detect imbalances in the flow of
qi and redress them before they cause serious illness. The
practitioner of traditional Chinese medicine uses
diagnostic methods which are very different from those
of orthodox doctors. He or she observes the patient as a
whole, taking into consideration mind, body and spirit,
and not forgetting environmental concerns. Treatment
may include dietary recommendations, exercise,
acupressure or acupuncture. Like many holistic practices
Chinese Medicine is highly individual.
Recommendations are made for each person's particular
set of symptoms, rather than a collective treatment for
each ailment. In this book we have placed herbal
treatments under the general heading of Chinese
Medicine and given a separate heading for acupressure.
Acupuncture is recommended where appropriate under
the title Professional Help.

Dietary

The importance of diet in preventive medicine and
treatment is becoming increasingly acknowledged.
Practically every day, news hits the headlines regarding
something we should or should not eat or drink. Diet is
probably the area where we can make the greatest
impact on general health and vitality, the prevention of
disease and the treatment of common ailments.

The dietary advice given in this book originates from
different sources. Firstly, we have incorporated the latest
findings from nutritional research being carried out in
universities and hospitals throughout the Western world.
This work gives clinical evidence of the effects of diet
on many different diseases and syndromes. Secondly, we
have included information from naturopathic medicine, a
complementary treatment founded on the principles that
disease occurs when the body's inner force is suppressed
through incorrect diet and lifestyle. Naturopathic
treatment seeks to provide the body with the strength to

heal itself through the elimination of toxins, and the rebalancing of diet according to individual needs and lifestyle. Therapy may include a period of fasting, special diets, methods to encourage elimination, and supplementation with vitamins, minerals, amino acids or other nutrients.

Exercise

Not a therapy as such, though many who exercise regularly claim it is a 'drug'. Over the last 20 years the benefits of exercise in preventing disease and contributing to overall well-being have become increasingly recognized. Like diet, exercise is one of the most important factors in healthy living, for the following reasons:

- it prevents weight gain and helps lose excess weight, thought to contribute to disease.
- it improves blood circulation and heart function.
- it assists digestion.
- it strengthens bones, increases muscle mass and keeps joints mobile.
- it reduces stress and relieves anxiety and depression.
- it increases circulation to the brain, improving mental function and relieving fatigue.

The exercise treatments in this book range from recommendations to increase regular aerobic exercise (activity which requires increased oxygen intake and strengthens the heart, such as brisk walking, running or swimming), to specific stretches designed to strengthen specific muscle groups. Whatever your age or strength, we suggest that you start any new exercise gently, allowing yourself to gradually build up strength and stamina. We also advise you to carry out the treatment regularly. It is better to exercise little and often than to overdo it.

Herbalism

The value of plants in treating illness has been documented for some 5,000 years. Modern herbalism stems from a variety of sources, and much has been passed down through folklore and tradition. Like many of the other gentle treatments listed in this book, herbal medicine is used to provide the body with the ideal environment for health and self healing. Herbs are generally given fresh or dried, taken as infusions (herbs prepared like a tea), decoctions (herbs gently simmered in water), ointments (herbs made up into a cream), compresses (prepared herbs placed in a compress which is applied externally) or, most commonly, tinctures (alcoholic extracts). Fresh herbs can also be incorporated into the diet. Instructions on how to prepare and administer each specific herbal remedy are given with each ailment. The following rules should be adhered to when keeping and preparing herbal remedies:

- use only herbs you can identify and you know are safe.
- store herbs in an airtight glass jar. Do not refrigerate.
- use a glass or porcelain pot or saucepan to prepare remedies.
- do not exceed the recommended doses.
- during pregnancy is it not advisable to self-administer herbs without the supervision of a professional herbalist.

Herbs can be grown in the garden from seed, or plants can be obtained from specialist suppliers. Gathering herbs from the wild should be carried out with caution; they may be contaminated with car fumes or pesticides, or you may identify them wrongly. For most people the easiest access to herbal remedies is through a health food store or herbalist, some of which provide herbs by mail order (see Appendix 3).

Homoeopathy

Homoeopathy is a complete system of complementary medicine based on the principle of 'like cures like'. In other words, homoeopathic remedies which produce a set of symptoms (mental, emotional and physical) of an ailment in a healthy person, can cure those symptoms in a sick person.

Remedies are prepared from extracts of plants, minerals, and animal and human tissues or secretions, which are diluted many times and shaken vigorously. While this dilution process greatly reduces the physical presence of the original composition of the remedy, it seems to bring out other qualities which are often more powerful than the original concentrate. Despite the fact that nobody has been able to show exactly how homoeopathy works, its efficacy has been seen in clinical trials, and it is extensively used in Europe, and to a growing extent in America and Australasia.

Homoeopathic prescribing is highly individualized. Unlike orthodox drugs, where one remedy is prescribed for virtually all cases of a particular illness, homoeopaths treat the person rather than the disease. In this book we do not have the space to provide an individualized means of prescribing for every ailment. However, we have listed remedies which professional homoeopaths consider to be common to the majority of people. We recommend that you consult a professional homoeopath for individualized prescribing if you find that the treatments listed do not seem appropriate.

Where homoeopathic treatment is appropriate we list a selection of remedies which would commonly be prescribed. With each remedy a brief symptom picture is given. The remedy chosen should be the one with the description most like your symptoms. For example, when treating a child with a cold, you would look at the physical symptoms, such as a sore throat and runny nose. You would also take into consideration the mental and emotional state of the patient, whether the child is clinging and tearful, or irritable and aloof, as described in the text.

Homoeopathic remedies are available as pills, granules, tinctures and ointments. They are available in many different potencies; in this book most recommended remedies are the 6c potency, which is the most easily obtained. Treatment should be kept to a minimum; once symptoms start to improve it is not necessary to keep taking the remedy. Indeed it is only necessary to repeat the remedy if the original symptoms recur. It is not unusual, on taking a homoeopathic remedy, for symptoms to initially worsen for a few days before they get better. If this occurs, stop taking the remedy and consult a professional.

Hydrotherapy

The relaxing, rejuvenating and healing power of water has long been acknowledged. Hydrotherapy, or water therapy, has many applications; the treatments suggested in this book have the following effects:

- stimulation of blood circulation: water can provide extremes of temperature, allowing the blood vessels to constrict and dilate, stimulating blood circulation. Increased blood flow provides an injured or diseased area with additional nutrients to aid healing, and helps eliminate toxins. It also increases the flow of oxygen through the body and the brain, maintaining energy and alertness.
- to draw out heat: cold compresses (cloths soaked in cold water) are sometimes used to remove heat from inflammatory conditions.
- to provide support while exercising: the buoyancy of water provides support for weak limbs. Swimming in warm water is an effective means of strengthening weak muscles.

Hypnotherapy

The act of putting a patient into a trance to implant suggestions for self cure has been used by healers throughout the ages. Although the mechanism by which hypnotherapy operates is still unclear, the method is used today by doctors, psychotherapists and other health professionals to cure obsessive habits and relieve a number of emotional and physical disorders. It is particularly helpful in giving up smoking and dealing with substance abuse, and the relief of anxiety, phobias, depression and pain. Although methods of self hypnosis are sometimes used, we recommend that you consult a professional.

Massage

Based on the natural instinct to hold or rub an area which hurts, or to provide physical comfort through touch in times of stress, massage is a popular and effective gentle treatment and one which can easily be used in the home on yourself and others.

On a physical level massage relaxes tense, tight and knotted muscles. It stimulates blood and lymph flow through the body. Increased blood supply provides the tissues and organs with more oxygen, helping them to function better. Energy is increased, muscle and skin tone is improved. In times of injury, increased circulation facilitates healing. By increasing lymph flow, massage assists the elimination of waste materials, which can stagnate, contributing to stiffness and disease.

By relieving tense muscles and increasing blood flow, massage has a soothing effect on the central nervous system. This treatment is effective in preventing and treating stress and anxiety, and inducing deep relaxation. It is well known that stress compromises the immune system. Indirectly, massage can therefore strengthen the body's resistance to disease.

The massage treatments described in this book can be carried out with a little oil, lotion or talc unless otherwise indicated. (A vegetable oil, such as almond, sesame or safflower is suitable.) The techniques can be used on people of any age; however, the intensity of the strokes should accommodate the physical condition of the receiver, not the giver. In children, the weak and the elderly, take care not to 'over-massage'. The treatment should be felt, but should not cause pain and tension. Massage should not be used when there is acute inflammation, fever, serious heart disease, a cancerous condition (unless approved by a professional), or phlebitis. Massage should also be avoided on areas of broken skin and varicose veins.

Meditation

Meditation is taught by trained teachers. Once the technique has been learnt it can be practised alone at home to assist in achieving a state of total relaxation. Your teacher will recommend that you sit in a quiet room and fix your gaze on an object (a candle or crystal, for example). You will be taught to become aware of your breathing and to repeat your mantra (a word, chosen by yourself or your teacher, which is used as a mental focus). The object of meditation is to achieve a state of total physical relaxation and to empty the mind of all thought.

Osteopathy and Chiropractic

Both osteopaths and chiropractors are specialists in the diagnosis and treatment of mechanical disorders of joints (particularly joints of the spine). Both believe in the principle that misalignments in the vertebrae can interfere with the circulation of blood, lymph and nerve activity to vital organs, causing discomfort, and sometimes disturbing bodily functions which may result in disease. Chiropractors usually use x-rays when making a diagnosis, and treatment often involves short direct manipulations to the spine. Osteopaths tend to rely on palpatory (feeling with the hands) diagnostic techniques and use massage, heat treatment, gentle manipulation and exercise to 'ease' misalignments back into place.

Cranial Osteopathy (Craniosacral Therapy)

Cranial osteopathy is a supplementary technique used by some specialized osteopaths. Through very gentle techniques, it explores the pulse of cerebrospinal fluid in the skull and pelvic (sacral) area. It is sometimes used to treat small babies and children for a variety of problems, and is especially helpful in resolving childhood problems thought to result from a difficult birth.

Reflexology

Also known as zone therapy, this is a system of diagnosis and treatment carried out by massaging the feet. Reflexologists believe that the body is divided up into 10 energy zones which correspond to different areas of the feet. By massaging the relevant area of the foot, it is possible to bring a response in the corresponding tissues of the body. How reflexology works has not been established, yet it is thought to be helpful in treating a number of different ailments, from back pain to heart disorders. It is particularly useful in cases where the area of injury or disease cannot be touched or treated directly.

Relaxation Techniques

Stress is a natural response to fear. It prepares the body for 'fight or flight' by tensing the muscles and constricting the blood vessels. However, most of the stress we encounter today is mental anguish and does not require us to fight or flee. The body is thus left in a state of physical tension, leading to decreased energy, fatigue, and lowered immunity. Prolonged stress has been shown to be a major contributing factor to disease.

Both as a preventive measure and a treatment, relaxation is an important therapy in combating stress and anxiety and strengthening the body's resistance to disease. However, for some people relaxation is very difficult to achieve. Often, when we think we are relaxing, our muscles remain tense and we cannot 'switch off' mentally. To relax effectively, the mind should be in the present (not worrying about the past or future), barely ticking over, the body should be limp, and the breathing deep and slow. Carry out the relaxation treatments we recommend in a quiet, dimmed room where you will not be disturbed.

Visualization

Many alternative and orthodox practitioners have found that visualizing a positive scene or symbol can bring mental and physical relaxation, relieve pain, help fight disease and assist healing. To carry out visualization, you need to be in a quiet room where you will not be disturbed. Relax in a comfortable position and let your attention go to the area of your body which is injured or diseased. Focus on that area and let an image come to your mind. It may be a real-life image of the body part, or an abstract image or symbol. Allow the image to change as it will. Then start to visualize something happening to heal the body part. You may see white blood cells flowing towards it to attack disease; you may see light, energy, or warmth. Many people find that the healing image brings immediate physical or psychological relief. For those who have difficulty visualizing, autogenic training with a qualified practitioner can help. Relaxation tapes can also be beneficial.

Yoga

Hatha yoga is a movement system which strives to achieve harmony of mind and body. The system teaches postures which encourage stretching just to individual capacity. Yoga is therefore appropriate to all age groups. The postures strengthen muscles and greatly increase flexibility. Circulation and balance are also improved. Through breathing and visualization exercises, yoga induces deep relaxation and combats stress. Yoga thus helps to strengthen immunity and bring increased energy. The postures can also be used to combat specific ailments, as outlined in this book.

Of the many remedies and treatments listed in this book, we recommend you keep a supply of the following at hand for common problems and emergencies:

Dietary

- vitamin C.
- vitamin E.
- multi-vitamin and mineral supplement.
- wheatgerm (keep refrigerated).
- live yoghurt or lactobacillus acidophilus supplements.

Aromatherapy

- lavender oil to relax.
- peppermint to rejuvenate/stimulate.
- tea tree oil as an antiseptic and antifungal.
- citronella oil to repel insects.

Herbal

- mullein oil for earaches.
- meadowsweet to soothe stomach problems.
- ginger for nausea and sickness.
- valerian for anxiety, stress, insomnia.
- dandelion for constipation and urinary problems.
- aloe vera plant or juice for burns.

Homoeopathy

- Arnica 6c.
- Arnica cream.
- Aconite 6c.
- Arsenicum album 6c.
- Nux vomica 6c.
- Belladonna 6c.
- Chamomilla 6c.
- Pulsatilla 6c.
- Ledum 6c.
- Nelson's Burn ointment.

Bach Flower Remedies

- Rescue Remedy is useful in most situations, particularly injury, shock, nervous conditions and pain.

Hydrotherapy

- bowl or tubs for sitz baths.
- cotton cloths for compresses.
- an ice pack or packet of frozen peas (which can be refrozen and kept purely for hydrotherapy purposes).
- kitchen roll.
- a hot water bottle or heated pad.

Massage

- light vegetable oil (safflower, sesame, almond) or lotion.
- a tennis or squash ball for those who find it hard to massage with the fingers.

Abscess

A collection of pus in a pocket of tissue which develops when the body traps bacteria. The pus which forms is from white blood cells carried to the area to fight the infection. (See also Dental Abscess.)

Treatment

Dietary

recurrent abscesses may indicate a sluggish digestive tract and inadequate elimination. The following guidelines help detoxify the system and stimulate digestion:

- reduce intake of fatty foods, including meat, eggs and dairy products.
- reduce intake of sweet foods and refined carbohydrates (white flour and sugar).
- increase intake of fresh fruit and vegetables.

the following supplements are recommended:

- zinc: 45 mg daily.
- vitamin A: 50,000 iu daily for 2 weeks.

Aromatherapy

- tea tree oil is a useful antiseptic. Dab a solution of 2 drops to 1 cup of water on the abscess several times daily.

Herbal

- echinacea decoction helps rid the body of bacterial infections: place 2 teaspoons of the root in a cup of water, bring to the boil and simmer for 10 minutes. Drink 3 times daily.

Homoeopathy

take one tablet every hour for 4 doses and repeat if needed:
- when the abscess is very tender and causes stabbing pain: Hepar sulphuris 6c.
- in the early stage when the abscess is throbbing, red and inflamed: Belladonna 6c.

Chinese Medicine

- abscesses are thought to be caused by excessive heat in the body. Herbs are recommended to reduce heat: Chinese golden thread, dandelion or wild chrysanthemum and violet in the form of a tea.

Hydrotherapy

- prepare a hot compress by soaking sterile cotton wool in hot water. Hold it on the abscess to help expel the pus.

Orthodox

- your doctor may drain the pus from the abscess. Antibiotics are sometimes recommended to clear up further infection.

Acid Stomach

More commonly known as heartburn, this causes a burning pain in the gullet and chest, often accompanied by belching (which seems to bring relief), and sometimes a feeling of food getting stuck. Causes vary, but often include overeating, or consuming too much rich or spicy food and alcohol. Stress can also contribute. Acid stomach is common in pregnant women (see also Heartburn under Pregnancy Problems) and people who are overweight. (See also Indigestion.)

Prevention

- avoid rich, spicy food.
- eat little and often, and avoid heavy meals at night.
- take regular exercise to aid digestion — but not immediately after a meal.
- try to reduce stress.

Treatment

Dietary

- reduce intake of food, and eat little and often.
- avoid caffeine (coffee, tea, chocolate, cola), alcohol, sugar, carbonated drinks, spices and fatty foods.
- counteract acidity by eating plenty of alkaline foods: fresh fruit and vegetables (but not milk).

Herbal

- meadowsweet infusion soothes the membranes of the digestive tract: add one cup of boiling water to 1–2 teaspoons of the dried herb, infuse for 15 minutes, and drink. Take three times daily.
- ginger can be taken in capsule form or as a decoction: add 1½ teaspoons of the freshly grated root to a cup of water, simmer for 10 minutes and drink when needed.

Homoeopathy

take 1 tablet every 15 minutes for up to 4 doses and repeat if needed:

- after rich foods, with gas and rancid belching: Carbo vegetabilis 6c.
- after spicy food, caffeine, alcohol: Nux vomica 6c.
- burning pain, worse in the small hours of the morning: Arsenicum album 6c.

Chinese Medicine

- acid stomach is thought to be caused by an imbalance of the spleen and liver. Herbs recommended include ginseng, liquorice and orange peel. Acidic and 'cold' foods (bananas, grapefruit, salads, watermelon, tomatoes) should be avoided.

Exercise

- regular exercise, walking, running, swimming or cycling at least 3 times a week helps reduce weight, takes pressure off the stomach, and relieves stress. However, never exercise within 3 hours of eating.

Orthodox

- antacids, a mixture of magnesium hydroxide and aluminium hydroxide, can be bought over the counter. They should be taken 1—2 hours before meals, and last thing at night. Antacids should be taken with caution by anyone suffering from high blood pressure, kidney disease or any type of intestinal bleeding.

Acne

Pimples, blackheads and whiteheads on the face, neck or back. Acne often results from the hormonal changes of adolescence which lead to an increase in oily sebum production, and clogged pores. Acne can also occur in adults of any age, particularly premenstrual women (see Premenstrual Syndrome) and women taking the Pill. (See also Spots and Pimples.)

Treatment

Practical Advice

- avoid oil-based cosmetics.
- wash the skin well with unperfumed soap twice daily.
- do not squeeze pimples or whiteheads: it will cause scarring and spread the infection.

Dietary

- avoid fats, sugars, refined and junk foods. Eat plenty of raw fruit and vegetables, wholegrain breads and cereals, cooked dried beans, additive-free low fat dairy products, chicken and fish.
- increase intake of zinc, found in poultry, fish, organ meats, wholegrain breads and cereals. Studies have shown a daily supplement of zinc picolinate (45 mg daily) to be effective.

Herbal

- blue flag decoction: put 1 teaspoonful of dried herb into a cup of water and simmer for 10 minutes. Drink three times daily to detoxify the system.

Homoeopathy

take 1 tablet 3 times daily for up to 7 days and repeat if needed:
- initially try: Calcarea silicata 6c.
- with itchy spots: Kali bichromicum 6c.
- with red, sore, infected spots: Sulphur 6c.
- extreme sensitivity to touch: Hepar sulphuris 6c.

Orthodox

- gels and creams containing benzoyl peroxide are recommended to help unblock pores. Doctors may prescribe antibiotics to reduce infection of pores. Drugs and creams based on vitamin A reduce sebum production, but may have side effects, such as dry eyes, inflammation of the lips and reddening of the skin. Specially designed oral contraceptives may be offered to combat acne in women. Doctors sometimes recommend getting out in the sunshine or using a sun lamp for short periods.

Adenoids, Enlarged/Infected

The adenoids (two swellings above the tonsils which help in resisting infection) may be naturally bulky or may become enlarged as a result of infection. Usually this affects children aged between 5 and 7, who tend to breathe through the mouth and snore. Infection may lead to coughs, ear problems, loss of sense of smell and taste. The condition often disappears as children grow older.

Treatment

Dietary

the following guidelines help reduce congestion:
- avoid cow's milk, cream, butter, cheeses, roast peanuts, bananas and excessive sugar.
- avoid fatty and fried foods and excessive salt.
- increase intake of vitamin C to fight infection (found in citrus fruits, berries, green leafy vegetables, tomatoes, and potatoes).
- garlic also attacks infection: add to food liberally, or take 2 garlic capsules daily.

Herbal

- infusion of cleavers reduces inflammation and tones the lymphatic system: pour cup of boiling water onto 2 teaspoons of the dried herb, infuse for 15 minutes and drink 3 times daily.
- red sage gargle helps fight infection and soothes the

throat: pour a cup of boiling water onto 2 teaspoons of the leaves and infuse for 10 minutes, allow to cool and gargle 3 times daily.

Homoeopathy

1 tablet to be taken twice daily for up to 2 weeks and repeat if necessary:
- as a first resort try Agraphis nutans 6c.
- inflamed adenoids and tonsillitis, poor mental and physical development: Baryta carbonica 6c.
- inflamed adenoids, child overweight and prone to head sweats during sleep: Calcarea carbonica 6c.
- thick yellow discharge from nose and throat, tearful child: Pulsatilla 6c.

Massage

- massage gently down either side of the nose using the thumb and forefinger.

Orthodox

- very large or persistently inflamed adenoids are usually removed surgically, especially if they interfere with hearing, speech or school attendance. However, unless the problems are persistent doctors do not recommend surgery, as the adenoids are useful glands which help fight infection.

Ageing

Not an ailment but a natural process of physical and mental changes which occur as we grow older. Some believe the rate of ageing is determined by genetic makeup; others say it is a result of cumulative damage to cells. Evidence points to the fact that both are implicated, suggesting that there are ways of slowing down or even reversing the process of ageing.

Prevention/Treatment

Dietary

- studies have shown that a gradual reduction in calorie intake increases lifespan in animals. Studies on humans show that those who are overweight live shorter lives than those who are not. Reducing calorific intake means cutting out all 'empty foods' (refined carbohydrates, sugar, junk food) and eating a highly nutritious diet of wholegrain cereals, low fat protein and plenty of fruit and vegetables.
- fight free radicals — substances which enter the body and cause some of the damaging effects of ageing:
  - increase intake of vitamin C, found in fresh fruit and vegetables (eat these raw if possible).
  - increase intake of vitamin E, found in wheatgerm, seeds and seed oils.
  - increase intake of selenium, found in whole wheat, brown rice, poultry and low fat dairy produce.
  - increase intake of beta-carotene, found in green leafy, orange and yellow vegetables.
- increase intake of the amino acids cysteine and methionine, found in beans, fish, liver, brewer's yeast and nuts. Alternatively take a supplement of 250 mg daily of each (not to be taken by diabetics, and take well away from mealtimes).

Exercise

- studies have shown that exercise started early in life retards signs of ageing. Exercise helps prevent one of the western world's biggest killers, coronary heart disease. Exercise at any age helps maintain bone and muscle strength; it preserves flexibility and balance. Exercise aids circulation and the elimination of toxins, all of which help preserve healthy skin and hair.
- yoga can be carried out at any age. It is a method which stretches and tones the body and provides relaxation, another important ingredient for longevity.

Orthodox

- doctors recommend the dietary and exercise treatments listed above. Cosmetic surgery may be used to remedy the physical effects of ageing.

AIDS (Acquired Immune Deficiency Syndrome)

A deficiency in the immune system strongly thought to be caused by infection with HIV (human immunodeficiency virus), which is spread through infected blood and semen (sexual contact, sharing needles, or a mother passing the virus on to her foetus are the most common means of transmission). HIV affects certain white blood cells which are crucial for fighting disease and infection. As a result, people with AIDS fall prey to a variety of infections, from skin disorders, diarrhoea and yeast infections, to tuberculosis, neurological disorders and cancer. Early symptoms include enlarged lymph glands or unexplained weight loss and fatigue. The syndrome is fatal and as yet there is no cure. Treatment is aimed at strengthening the immune system, and dealing with the infections brought by immune deficiency.

Prevention

- practise safe sex:
  - limit sexual partners to those whose sexual history you know.
  - use a condom for oral, anal or vaginal sex.
  - hugging, mutual masturbation, kissing, body massage, body kissing and touching are safe.
- intravenous drug users should avoid sharing needles.
- if travelling in third world countries, carry a supply of disposable sterile needles in case you require medical injections.

Treatment

New discoveries about AIDS are being made every day, though as yet there is no cure for the syndrome. The following treatments are some of the current methods used as this book goes to press:

Orthodox

Antiviral drugs, such as zidovudine (AZT) and acyclovir, are prescribed, and are thought to prolong life once symptoms have started.

Other Treatments

Many different complementary therapies are being used alongside orthodox treatment of HIV and AIDS. They aim to stimulate immune function and provide antivirals to resist the infection. The ones most commonly used are listed below.

Dietary

- increase intake of beta-carotene, found in green leafy, orange and yellow vegetables.
- vitamin C stimulates immunity and is an antiviral. Naturopaths advise taking vitamin C to bowel tolerance (i.e. keep taking it until it causes diarrhoea, then cut back to find the highest tolerable level).
- increase intake of bioflavonoids, found in green leafy vegetables and the pith and rind of citrus fruits. These enhance the action of vitamin C.
- zinc is also an immune stimulator and antiviral: take 15 g of zinc picolinate daily.
- ensure your diet is as nutritious as possible: whole grains, fresh fruit and vegetables (organic if possible), lean meat, fish and dairy products are recommended. Limit intake of junk and refined foods, alcohol, nicotine and recreational drugs.

Herbal

- golden seal boosts immunity and fights microbes, such as fungal infections. It is a useful remedy for diarrhoea. Consult a herbalist for the appropriate dosage.
  caution: not to be used during pregnancy or by those with high blood pressure.

Homoeopathy

- professional homoeopathic prescribing would appear to be beneficial both to those who are HIV+ and people with AIDS.

Chinese Medicine

- Chinese herbs and acupuncture are being extensively and effectively used to treat many of the symptoms brought by AIDS (night sweats, fatigue, neuropathy, diarrhoea). Many people with HIV who take Chinese herbs claim that their overall health improves. Studies have also found Chinese medicine to be useful in relieving the side effects of orthodox drug use and radiation. The herbs commonly used are the tonic herbs: astragalus, ganoderma and ginseng; and the blood circulating herbs: salvia, millettia and peony.

Relaxation

- a diagnosis of HIV+ brings considerable mental anguish. Stress and unhappiness have been shown to weaken the immune system further.
- yoga and meditation can help people with AIDS.
- massage promotes relaxation, relieves pain and reduces muscle tension. With the right therapist, it provides intimate, caring and pleasurable physical contact.
- joining a support group, where you can share your experience of the physical and mental effects of the syndrome with others in the same situation, is highly

beneficial in dealing with stress and anguish. It also provides you with the latest information on research, treatment and methods of coping.

Alcoholism

Often alcohol becomes so much a part of daily life that we are not aware of becoming dependent on it. Anyone who abuses alcohol or drinks excessively will experience problems with physical and mental health. Personal relationships, work and finances can also suffer.

The following signs indicate if you need help in resolving alcohol abuse:

- you turn to alcohol when feeling sad or faced with a problem.
- you are sometimes unable to meet responsibilities due to heavy drinking.
- someone close to you is concerned about your drinking.
- you experience unpleasant side effects when you stop drinking.
- you drink in secret and feel guilty about it.

Treatment

Alcohol abuse is difficult to treat alone. A number of self help groups (see Appendix 2) provide treatment to sufferers and help families of alcoholics. Alternatively, you could seek help from a doctor or psychotherapist who specializes in alcohol abuse, a homoeopath or a hypnotherapist. Treatment should be aimed not only at helping you to stop drinking, but to bring you to better understanding of why you drink and help create a lifestyle where you do not need to drink. The following treatments can be used to complement professional therapy.

Dietary

nutritional deficiencies in alcoholics accentuate the other complications of alcohol abuse. Studies have shown that supplementation of the following nutrients helps accelerate alcohol detoxification and prevent liver damage:

- zinc, found in lean meat, poultry, fish, and wholegrain cereals. A supplement of 15 mg daily is recommended.
- increase intake of vitamin C, found in fresh fruit and vegetables, and E, found in wheatgerm, seed oils and nuts.
- the amino acid glutamine has been shown to be helpful in decreasing the desire to drink alcohol. 2—4 g daily is recommended (to be taken well away from mealtimes).

Herbal

- alcoholics are often deficient in GLA (gamma-linolenic acid). GLA is found in evening primrose oil which is thought to help prevent mood swings and liver damage. Take 4 capsules daily.
- in overcoming withdrawal, infusion of skullcap, motherwort, or lavender can be helpful: add a cup of water to 2 teaspoons of the herb, infuse for 15 minutes and drink 3 times daily.

Homoeopathy

- Quercus mother tincture: add 3 drops to a little water and take twice daily to reduce alcohol craving.

Chinese Medicine

- herbs would be recommended to clear heat from the body. Strong green tea is used to cool the liver and stomach. A detoxification programme would be combined with counselling and self help groups.

Bach Flower Remedies

- Agrimony is recommended for those who turn to alcohol to overcome difficult times, Aspen for those with obsessional thoughts. Olive is used for those in recovery.

Allergic Dermatitis

A rash or inflammation of the skin in reaction to a substance. The symptoms are the same as for eczema (see entry). The most common causes of allergic dermatitis are detergents (traces of which can be left in washed clothes, causing irritation), nickel (in watches, jewellery and bra straps), chemicals in rubber gloves and condoms, cosmetics, plants and some medicines. The reaction may also result from a food source.

Treatment

- the best treatment is to identify the source and avoid it.
- see Eczema for natural treatments which may be useful.

Professional Help

- applied kinesiology can be helpful in identifying unknown allergens.

Orthodox

- tests can be carried out to identify the suspected allergen by placing the substance on a patch of skin and observing the reaction over several days. Corticosteroid drugs or creams may be used to treat symptoms.

Allergies — Food

The most common food allergens are dairy produce, eggs, strawberries, fish and shellfish, cereals, and some food additives. Symptoms of food allergy include cramps, nausea, vomiting, diarrhoea, gas, migraine headaches, skin eruptions and irritations, hyperactivity, mood swings, fatigue and food cravings.

Prevention

- food allergies can sometimes develop when a child is weaned too early. Try to breast feed infants for at least the first 6 months of life; longer if possible. Introduce new foods slowly and carefully, ensuring the baby has adapted to the new food before moving on to the next one. Start with baby rice and millet. Do not give wheat or milk during the first year.

Treatment

Dietary

- the first step is to identify which foods (or drinks) upset you. The following method can be used:
  - list any foods which disagree with you or produce fatigue, skin reactions, hyperactivity, irritability, etc.
  - list foods or drink you consume every day.
  - list any foods you regularly crave.
  - list foods you would miss if unavailable.
  - list any foods you have begun to eat recently.
- any foods which appear more than once on these lists is a potential allergen.
- you can further identify food allergens by testing your pulse. Take your pulse on waking, just before each meal, 30 minutes after the meal and before going to bed. If the pulse remains constant then the foods you are eating are probably not causing an allergy. If the pulse swings up or down more than 6 beats, it is

likely that the food is causing an allergic reaction.
Work your way through the suspected foods using
this means of diagnosis.

- eliminate any food which seems suspect for at least
  2 weeks, then reintroduce it and notice whether it
  produces symptoms. Replace foods which cause
  allergic reactions with alternative foods, for example,
  soya milk, goat's milk, or non-dairy whiteners can
  replace cow's milk. After 6 months try reintroducing
  the offending food: you may find you have overcome
  your sensitivity.

Professional Help

- to reduce sensitivity to food allergies, naturopaths
  often recommend a detoxification diet. This should be
  carried out in consultation with a professional.
- if you are unable to identify what is causing your
  allergy, a kinesiologist can help by using muscle
  testing to identify which foods are producing
  weaknesses in the body.
- professional homoeopathic prescribing will boost
  general immunity and thus reduce sensitivity to
  potential allergens.

Orthodox

- doctors recommend avoidance of potential allergens.
  Look carefully at ingredients on processed foods to
  ensure they do not contain substances which will
  trigger an attack. (See also Colitis.)

Allergies – Hay Fever and Rhinitis

This is an exaggerated response of the immune system
to substances such as grass or tree pollen, spores from
moulds, house-dust mites, or animal dander (shed dead
skin and fur from pets). Symptoms include a congested,
runny nose, itchy, watery eyes, headache, drowsiness,

itchy throat and sneezing. (See also Asthma, Eczema, Hives, Allergies — Food, Allergic Dermatitis).

Prevention

- putting net curtain over windows and wearing sunglasses reduce pollen exposure.
- in hot climates, air conditioning can greatly help to provide an indoor sanction.
- ionizers help to remove pollen, dust and other airborne allergens from the atmosphere.
- special duvet and mattress covers are available which reduce irritation from dust mites.

Treatment

Dietary

- vitamin C combined with bioflavonoids acts as a natural antihistamine to control a streaming nose, or help unblock a congested one. Increase your intake of vitamin C by eating plenty of citrus fruits. Bioflavonoids are found in the rind and pulp of citrus fruits: take a piece of grapefruit or orange peel, slice it up and boil with a little water and honey for 10 minutes. Eat a piece before going to bed, and when symptoms start during the day. Alternatively, vitamin C with citrus bioflavonoids can be taken in supplement form: take 500 milligrams three times daily.
- pantothenic acid has also been shown to relieve allergy symptoms. Take a supplement of 200—500 mg of pantothenic acid and 50 mg of vitamin B complex daily.
- pollen supplements help prevent allergies, particularly hay fever: take 4—6 tablets daily for several weeks before the hay fever season.
- liquorice and beta-carotene are also helpful — if you are buying supplements over the counter, follow the

instructions on the packet; otherwise consult a
naturopath or nutritionist.

Aromatherapy

- add 1 drop of essential oil of lavender to 5 ml of
  carrier oil or lotion, store in a bottle and use to
  massage the sinuses at the sides of the nose once
  daily.
- alternatively, dilute 1 drop of essential oil of inula in
  5 ml of jojoba or sweet almond oil, and rub into the
  sinuses once daily.

Acupressure

- to relieve headaches, sneezing and itching eyes, find
  the highest spot of the muscle in the webbing
  between the thumb and index finger, rub firmly for
  one minute, then repeat on the other hand.
  - **caution:** not to be used during pregnancy.
- to strengthen the immune system find the spot on the
  top of the forearm between the two arm bones, two
  finger widths from the wrist; firmly massage this area
  with a deep circular motion of the thumb.

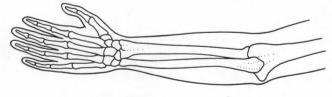

Back of hand

Exercise

- rigorous exercise can help control allergies, which are
  often aggravated by stress. Try early morning jogging,
  brisk walking or swimming.

Orthodox

- antihistamines are generally recommended. Sometimes inhaled medications, including steroids, can reverse and control allergy-induced asthma. In severe cases, or where immediate results are needed, a cortisone injection is suggested and provides relief for around 3 months.

Alopecia *see* Hair Loss

Altitude Sickness *see* Mountain Sickness

Alzheimer's Disease

A progressive illness which generally occurs after the age of 60, in which the nerve cells degenerate and the brain shrinks. Symptoms range from memory loss and forgetfulness to confusion and dementia.

Prevention

from the limited knowledge available about the causes of Alzheimer's disease, the following preventive measures have been suggested:

- avoid free radicals: cigarette smoke, pollution, radiation, and rancid fats.
- counteract the production of free radicals in the body by eating foods rich in antioxidants:
  - vitamin C, found in fruit and vegetables.
  - vitamin E, found in wheatgerm, seeds, and vegetable oils.
  - beta-carotene, found in orange and green leafy vegetables.
  - zinc and selenium, found in liver, lean meats, Cheddar cheese, lentils, wholemeal bread.

- avoid cooking in aluminium utensils.
- avoid antacids and deodorants that contain aluminium.

Treatment

People with dementia rarely ask for help themselves, and it is usually left to distraught relatives to enlist professional support. The aim of treatment is to maintain quality of life and standard of everyday function as far as possible. Drug therapy is generally kept to a minimum, but may become necessary if agitation, aggression or antisocial behaviour occur. The following herbal treatment can complement orthodox help.

Herbal

- studies have shown ginkgo biloba extract to be useful in treating this condition. Ginkgo biloba increases blood supply to the brain and increases nerve impulse transmission. The recommended dose is 40 mg, 3 times daily of ginkgo biloba extract containing 24 per cent ginkgo heterosides.

Amnesia *see* Memory Problems

Anaemia

A shortage of haemoglobin, the red pigment in blood cells which transports oxygen. The most common cause is lack of adequate dietary iron (see Iron Deficiency), although excessive loss of blood through menstruation or a stomach ulcer can contribute. Symptoms and signs of anaemia include fatigue, dizziness, breathlessness, poor concentration, recurrent colds and infections, pallor, and white eyelid linings. In children mental development can be retarded and behavioural problems can occur.

Treatment

Dietary

- increase your intake of foods rich in easily absorbed iron. Good sources are: beef, pork, lamb, organ meats, poultry, fish, cooked dried beans, dark green leafy vegetables, dried fruits. Animal products provide more easily absorbable iron than vegetable. The following chart indicates which foods are best.

Iron absorption from different foods

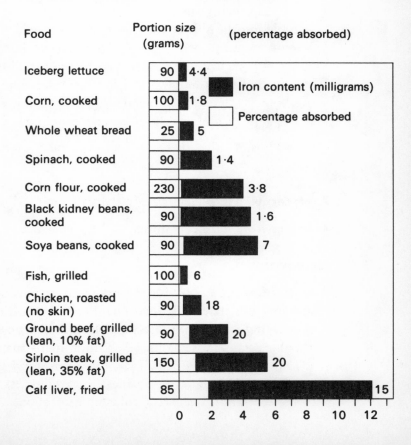

Food	Portion size (grams)	(percentage absorbed)
Iceberg lettuce	90	4·4
Corn, cooked	100	1·8
Whole wheat bread	25	5
Spinach, cooked	90	1·4
Corn flour, cooked	230	3·8
Black kidney beans, cooked	90	1·6
Soya beans, cooked	90	7
Fish, grilled	100	6
Chicken, roasted (no skin)	90	18
Ground beef, grilled (lean, 10% fat)	90	20
Sirloin steak, grilled (lean, 35% fat)	150	20
Calf liver, fried	85	15

Iron content (milligrams)

Percentage absorbed

0   2   4   6   8   10   12

- to increase iron absorption, incorporate vitamin C from citrus fruits or juices (orange, grapefruit or lemon) into your meals. Do not drink tea immediately before, during or after meals as this inhibits iron absorption.
- large doses of iron supplements may cause stomach upsets and constipation, and can be fatal in children. They could also compete with other minerals, leading to nutritional imbalances. If you have to take supplements it is advisable to take a multivitamin and mineral supplement which includes copper, iron, selenium, vitamin B2, B6, B12, folic acid, vitamin C and vitamin E.

Chinese Medicine

- aims at restoring the body's ability to absorb iron by stimulating the spleen with Return Spleen tablets, also known as gui pi wan.

Biochemic Tissue Salts

- Calc Phos, 4 times daily, helps form healthy red blood cells.
- Ferr Phos, 4 times daily, aids absorption of dietary iron.

Professional Help

- acupuncture has been shown to help anaemia.

Orthodox

- your doctor will look for the underlying cause of anaemia and treat it. If there is no apparent underlying cause, iron injections or tablets are usually given.

Anaemia, Megaloblastic

Megaloblastic anaemia is caused by a deficiency of vitamin B12 or folic acid. These are two different and chemically unrelated nutrients, but deficiency of either has the same effect — it interferes in the production of red blood cells in the bone marrow. Sometimes the body is unable to absorb these nutrients, as in Crohn's disease and coeliac disease (see entries). Symptoms include fatigue, headaches, pallor, loss of appetite, poor concentration, and a sore mouth and tongue.

Treatment

Dietary

- increase intake of vitamin B12, found in animal produce (lean meats, poultry, fish, shellfish, milk, liver, kidney, cheese and eggs). Vegans are at increased risk of vitamin B12 deficiency and should take yeast extract or vitamin supplements (2–3 mcg daily) as a precaution.
- increase intake of folic acid, found in green leafy vegetables, such as spinach, broccoli and lettuce, brewer's yeast, liver, orange juice and avocados.
- reduce intake of alcohol, which depletes stores of vitamin B12 and folic acid.

Orthodox

- injections of vitamin B12 and folic acid tablets are given to replace the deficient nutrients.

Anal Fissure

An ulcer develops from a tear in the lining of the anus, often as a result of straining to pass hard, dry motions. Symptoms include pain during bowel movements. There may also be bright blood spotting on the toilet paper.

Prevention

- avoid becoming constipated: eat plenty of fibre (wholegrain cereals, fruit, vegetables, cooked dried beans and peas), and drink at least 8 glasses of water daily. See further recommendations under Constipation.

Treatment

Practical Advice

- use soft toilet paper, or wet wipes. Wash the anal area regularly, particularly after bowel movements, to prevent infection of the broken skin.

Dietary

- in order to loosen the motions, a short-term solution is to eat prunes once a day. For long-term benefit, introduce more general fibre into your diet in the form of wholegrain cereals (but not wheat bran), fruit and raw vegetables. (See also Constipation.)
- drink at least 8 glasses of water daily.
- olive oil can be dabbed on the fissure to relieve pain and irritation.

Herbal

- dandelion decoction (dandelion coffee) is a gentle laxative: mix 2—3 teaspoons of root with one cup of water, simmer for 10 minutes and drink 3 times a day.
- for a general bowel tonic mix an infusion of 2 teaspoons of dandelion root, 2 teaspoons of yellow dock, 1 teaspoon of senna, liquorice and ginger. Take before sleeping.

Homoeopathy

take twice daily for up to 7 days and repeat if necessary:

- when it feels as if the stools tear the anus: Nitric acid 6c.
- when it feels as if the anus is full of splintered glass: Ratanhia 6c.

Hydrotherapy

- hot sitz baths are useful, in combination with a high fibre diet.

Exercise

- if you have a sedentary lifestyle, exercise is very important to maintain a healthy digestive system. Take a walk, a run or a swim at least three times a week.

Yoga

the following yoga position will help relieve constipation:
- lie on your back. Bring the right knee up to the chest, inhale and bring the head up and the chin towards the knee. Hold the position for 10 seconds; breathe out and lower the leg to the floor. Repeat with the left leg, and then with both together.

Orthodox

- liquid paraffin is sometimes recommended to soften the stools. If fissures are persistent, a procedure to enlarge the anal passage (anal dilation) is carried out. Surgery may be used to remove the ulcer. To counteract pain, a rubber or foam ring to sit on will reduce pressure on the tender area.

Anal Itching

Persistent itching around the anal area, sometimes caused by fissures (see above), haemorrhoids (see entry), discharge, eczema or a rash resulting from sweat accumulation, bad hygiene and sitting for long periods. Itching can sometimes be caused by worms, particularly in children (see entry).

Treatment

Practical Advice

- once an irritation has started and the skin becomes broken it is very difficult to heal in the anal area. To prevent further irritation, use moist wipes instead of toilet paper. Wash the anal area gently, but regularly, and always after bowel movements, and pat dry with a towel. Avoid scented soaps and talcum powder.
- allow the area to air as much as possible.
- wear cotton underwear and avoid tight trousers and nylon tights.
- irritation is sometimes a reaction to the detergent you are using to wash your clothes. Try a different brand and ensure you rinse your underwear well.
- dab the anal area with olive oil: it will soothe the itching and make bowel movements easier.

Dietary

- constipation can sometimes lead to anal irritation. To avoid constipation, introduce more fibre into your diet in the form of wholegrain cereals, fresh fruit and raw vegetables. Eat at least one large plateful of salad daily and drink at least 8 glasses of water a day. (See also entry on Constipation.)
- anal itching is sometimes thought to be caused by a candida infection of the stomach and bowel (see Fungal Infection). This can be counteracted by inserting into the rectum a plastic syringe applicator filled with live yoghurt. This should be carried out daily.

Aromatherapy

- before going to bed, run a warm bath, add 300 g of bicarbonate of soda and 5—8 drops of chamomile. Sit in the bath for at least 10 minutes to relieve irritation and promote healing.

Homoeopathy

- Paeonia 6c, twice daily for up to 7 days and repeat if needed.

Orthodox

- doctors often prescribe hydrocortisone cream for this complaint. It is effective in relieving itching and mending broken skin, but can mask the presence of infection. When used continuously it thins the skin. Therefore it should be used with caution.

Aneurysm

The abnormal and permanent ballooning of a weak artery wall due to its weakened structure and the pressure of blood flow. The weakness may be a result of disease, injury, or a congenital defect. Aneurysms can exist for years without symptoms. They cannot be reversed and therefore treatment is aimed at preventing them from becoming worse.

Treatment

Dietary

- cut down on saturated fats (red meats and dairy produce).
- increase intake of oily fish: sardines, herrings, salmon.
- eat plenty of garlic.
- sprinkle brewer's yeast on your food.
- avoid salt.

Homoeopathy

- Baryta carbonica 6c, once daily for one month helps tone and strengthen the arterial walls.

Exercise

- gentle regular exercise, such as walking or swimming, is good for this condition. However, avoid going out in very cold weather, and stop exercising immediately if you feel any pain.

Relaxation

- attending a yoga or meditation class will help improve or prevent this condition. The following relaxation routine should be carried out at least once daily:
  - lie on a firm surface, close your eyes and become aware of how your body feels. Focus your attention on each part of your body, starting with the tips of the toes, and finishing with your face and eyes; consciously try to relax every part of your body in turn. The whole procedure should take at least 10 minutes.
  - yogic breathing helps relaxation: kneel on the floor, place one hand on your stomach and the other on your chest. Inhale, allowing your stomach to bulge out, then slowly exhale, feeling your stomach deflate. Then place your hand on your chest and repeat the procedure allowing your chest to bulge and deflate. Repeat this pattern for several minutes.
  - biofeedback can help you learn to relax if you have difficulties.

Orthodox

- for life-threatening aneurysms, surgery is relatively successful in tying off the weakened area or replacing it with a synthetic graft.

Angina

A tight constricting sensation across the chest, accompanied by pain which moves up the neck and jaw and down the arms, particularly the left side. This may be accompanied by dizziness, nausea and difficulty in breathing. Such symptoms require immediate medical attention. Angina is caused by a fall in blood supply to the heart, and occurs when the demands on the heart are increased through overexertion, excitement, stress, high blood pressure or structural changes to the blood vessels supplying the heart. Angina is an early symptom of coronary heart disease (see entry).

Prevention

- do not smoke.
- reduce intake of saturated fats (red meat, full-fat dairy products, confectionery made with fat, savoury snacks containing fat, and fried foods). Eat moderate amounts of poultry, skimmed milk and low fat cheeses and spread. Use olive oil on salads and when cooking.
- try to adopt a regular exercise routine: walking and swimming are helpful.
- take measures to reduce stress (see Stress).

Treatment

Practical Advice

- stop smoking.
- if you experience angina attacks at night, tilt the head of your bed up by 3 or 4 inches to reduce the pressure of blood on your heart. If an attack still occurs at night, sit on the edge of the bed with your feet on the ground, allowing the blood to flow into your legs.

Dietary

eating the wrong foods can raise your blood pressure
and promote an attack of angina:
- reduce intake of animal fats (found in meat, dairy
  produce and eggs).
- avoid salt.
- increase intake of fibre, found in wholegrain cereals,
  fresh fruit and vegetables.
- eat fish regularly (sardines, herring, salmon, trout,
  mackerel).
- incorporate raw garlic into your diet.

Aromatherapy

- essential oil of lavender has been shown to aid
  relaxation: add 4 — 5 drops to a bath, a steam
  inhalation or put on a handkerchief.

Herbal

- infusion of hawthorn berries provides a good tonic
  for the heart and circulatory system. Pour one cup of
  water on 2 teaspoons of hawthorn berries, infuse for
  20 minutes and drink three times a day (warm or cold).

Homoeopathy

for acute attacks take:
- with fear and panic: Aconite 6c as often as required
  until symptoms are alleviated.
- when the chest feels as if it is squeezed by an iron
  band: Cactus grandiflorus 6c as often as required until
  symptoms are alleviated.

Chinese Medicine

- angina is believed to be a stagnation of the blood and
  energy in the heart. Herbal medicines such as
  cinnamon twigs, safflower, red sage root or macrosten
  onion bulb may be prescribed.

Acupressure

- symptoms can be relieved by applying deep thumb pressure to points H7, B15 and P6 (see illustration) for at least a minute.

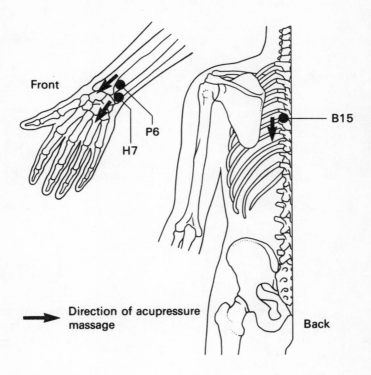

Front

P6

H7

B15

→ Direction of acupressure massage

Back

Reflexology

- heat the lung and heart areas of the foot by supporting the foot with one hand, and vigorously rubbing the areas with the other palm and/or fist.
- to relax the central nervous system, massage the points of the toes, beginning with the little toe, until you reach the big toe. With two fingers massage down the inside of the foot on the area of the spine and the tailbone. Repeat on the other foot.

Reflexology

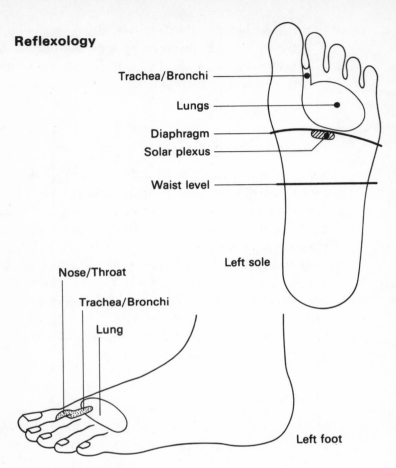

The reflex areas

Exercise

- regular, gentle exercise has been seen to improve angina. Walking is particularly good. However, consult your doctor before embarking on an exercise routine.

Orthodox

- treatment varies depending on the cause of angina. Drugs are prescribed to enlarge the blood vessels and reduce the workload of the heart muscle. Beta-blockers are sometimes given to reduce the force of the heart beat; antihypertensive drugs are sometimes given to lower high blood pressure (see Blood Pressure, High), and calcium-antagonist drugs are designed to reduce the force of the heart beat.

Ankles, Swollen

Swollen ankles result from an accumulation of excess tissue fluid. Flying, hot weather, standing for long periods, premenstrual syndrome (see entry), kidney infection (see Urinary Tract Infection), varicose veins (see entry), heart failure (see Coronary Heart Disease) thrombosis (see entry), pregnancy, and oral contraceptives can all contribute to this condition. It is also found in people with a protein or vitamin B deficiency. Very puffy ankles may be a sign of high blood pressure (see Blood Pressure, High), or pre-eclamptic toxaemia (see Pre-Eclampsia).

Treatment

Swollen ankles may be a sign of a serious internal disorder. If you suddenly notice unusual swelling, consult your doctor. Once serious problems have been ruled out, the following treatments may help.

Herbal

- parsley is a natural diuretic (it helps the body get rid of excess water). Add liberally to your food, and take an infusion 3 times daily: pour a cup of boiling water on 2 teaspoons of the leaves and infuse for 10 minutes.
  - **caution:** not to be used during pregnancy.

Hydrotherapy

- prepare two bowls of water: one with hot, but not

boiling water, the other with cold (add some ice).
Plunge your feet into first the hot, then the cold,
several times, finishing with cold. This will help
increase circulation and reduce puffiness.

Massage

massaging the feet, ankles, calves and thighs can greatly
assist in moving fluid out of the ankles. This can be
done by a professional or by a friend. Lie on your front
while your partner massages the back of the leg from
the ankle up to the knee using slow firm sweeping
motions up the calf, avoid the knee area and continue
with firm upward sweeping strokes and kneading of the
thigh muscles. Self-massage of the lower legs and ankles
can be done according to the following routine:

• sit on the floor with your knees bent. Place your
  thumbs on the outside of the shin bone and link your
  fingers around the knee. Apply pressure to the
  thumbs, moving slowly down the outside of the leg
  to the ankle bone. Then move your thumbs around to
  the inside of the ankle and massage up the leg.
  Finally place your thumbs in front of your knee and
  your fingers behind, and squeeze the calf muscle.
  Work down the back of the leg squeezing and
  releasing.

• **caution:** do not massage over varicose veins

Orthodox

• doctors recommend putting your feet up whenever
  possible. They may also suggest using elastic
  stockings. Diuretic drugs (water tablets) may be
  prescribed to eliminate excess fluid, and a low salt
  diet is often recommended.

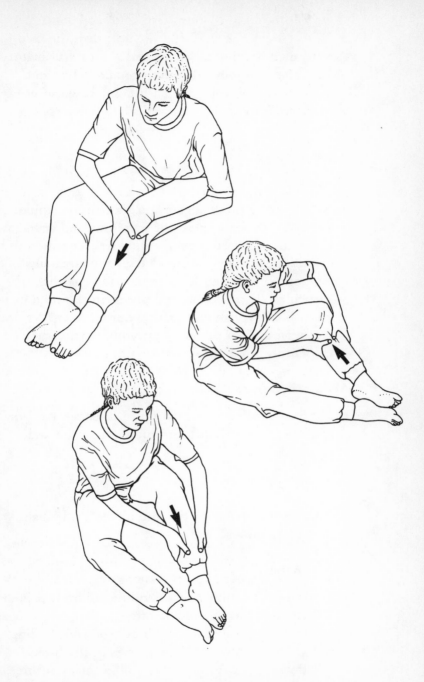

Ankylosing Spondylitis

Also known as bamboo spine, this is an inflammatory
disease affecting joints in the spine and pelvis and
sometimes the rib cage, which become fused, causing
stiffness, rigidity and pain, particularly after resting.

Treatment

Dietary

- reduce intake of all sugars and starchy foods (pasta,
  potatoes). Increase intake of pulses and vegetables.
- if you are regularly taking painkillers for this
  condition, it is advisable to increase your intake of
  vitamin C, found in fresh fruits and vegetables,
  particularly citrus fruits and juices; iron, found in red
  meat, poultry, fish and green vegetables, and vitamin
  A, found in liver, kidney, egg yolk, butter, fortified
  margarine, whole milk and cream.

Aromatherapy

- add 5—8 drops of essential oil of lavender, basil or
  rosemary to the bath to promote relaxation and
  relieve pain.

Homoeopathy

- a few drops of Arnica tincture placed in the bath will
  relieve aching and stiffness.

Hydrotherapy

- hot and cold compresses provide relief from pain and
  stiffness and can be used as often as required. Prepare
  two bowls of water, one with hot, but not boiling
  water, one with cold. If the pain is in the back, lie
  face down and have a partner fold a towel in three,
  roll it up and dip it in the hot water. Wring it out
  well, unroll it and place the towel, still folded, over

the painful area for 3 minutes. Do the same with a
second towel in the cold water. Remove the hot towel
and place the cold one on the same area for about
1 minute. Keep repeating the sequence for about
20 minutes.

Exercise

- gentle daily exercise is vital in preventing rigidity —
  swimming is particularly good.

Yoga

yoga also helps maintain mobility by providing general
stretching, and breathing exercises to open up the rib
cage. The following exercises and postures should be
carried out daily.

- kneel on the floor, place one hand on your stomach
  and the other on your chest. Inhale, allowing your
  stomach to bulge out, then slowly exhale, feeling
  your stomach deflate. Then place your hand on your
  chest and repeat the procedure allowing your chest to
  bulge and deflate. Repeat this pattern of breathing
  slowly for several minutes.

Professional Help

- osteopathy, chiropractic and massage help relieve pain
  and increase mobility. Acupuncture also helps relieve
  pain. Individual homoeopathic prescribing has shown
  good results.

Orthodox

- painkillers (aspirin, paracetamol) are offered, though
  long-term use can result in dietary deficiencies
  (bleeding of the stomach leading to loss of iron), and
  the development of ulcers. Anti-inflammatory drugs
  and steroids may also be recommended along with
  physiotherapy to help maintain flexibility.

Anorexia Nervosa

A psychological eating disorder most common in young women, where there is an obsessive fear of being fat. Symptoms include severe weight loss, restless energy, sometimes vigorous exercising, binge eating which at times is followed by deliberate vomiting (see Bulimia), fatigue, loss of menstrual periods, depression, withdrawal, and refusal to admit to being ill. Professional treatment is vital, as death from malnutrition or dehydration is possible.

The following self-treatments can be useful in conjunction with orthodox approaches aimed at helping both the sufferer and the family.

Treatment

Practical Advice

- try to talk to someone outside your family and immediate circle of friends. Some support groups and women's centres (see Appendices) have telephone counselling lines which can provide immediate help and advice.
- emotional support is important in treating this illness. Try to find a counsellor, therapist, friend or relative who you can trust to talk with and express your feelings.
- becoming involved in creative activities helps express inner feelings, allowing parts of yourself that want to emerge and be recognized come out. Painting, listening to music, dancing, going to the theatre or cinema, gardening, doing pottery, photography or cooking are all activities which could help.
- writing a journal of your thoughts and feelings permits you to have a private place to be honest with yourself about what is happening at an inner level.

Chinese Medicine

- professional treatment is necessary and would attempt to strengthen the digestive system and spleen and improve the capacity to absorb food which is sometimes lost after long periods of starvation. Nutrients prescribed to increase the appetite include rice and wheat sprouts, radish seeds or loganberries.

Massage

- receiving a regular massage from a therapist or learning to give massages and receive them from friends or family is a very good way to relax and unwind. It will also help you to feel more nurtured and comfortable with your body. Massage can be very healing, and can put you in touch with feelings from the past which may resolve psychological problems.

Orthodox

- careful assessment is made of the patient and her family, since the family can play an important role in the cause and treatment of this disorder. Specialized treatment is carried out in hospitals and clinics where the patient is encouraged to eat and receives counselling and therapeutic support.

Anxiety

An emotional state ranging from mild unease to intense fear, often characterized by a sense of impending doom. Physical symptoms can include palpitations, throbbing or stabbing pains, breathing difficulties, headaches, neck and back pain, restless trembling hands, fatigue, diarrhoea, upset stomach, and depression.

Treatment

Long-term anxiety is psychologically draining and can compromise the immune system, making you more susceptible to infection and disease. Counselling or psychotherapy can greatly assist in getting to the root of the cause of your anxiety. A simple chat with your doctor or health practitioner can also help. The following treatments help resolve short-term anxiety.

Dietary

- avoid caffeine (coffee, chocolate, cola, tea).
- a deficiency in vitamin B complex can increase symptoms of stress. To ensure adequate intake, a vitamin B complex supplement should be taken once daily.

Aromatherapy

- essential oil of lavender has been shown in studies to relieve anxiety: a few drops can be used in steam inhalations, a bath or simply sprinkle 2 drops on a tissue or handkerchief and inhale it from time to time. Regular treatment from a professional is extremely relaxing.
- for severe anxiety add one drop of valerian oil to a steam inhalation or bath.

Herbal

- valerian is one of the most useful herbs taken to reduce tension and anxiety. Pour a cup of boiling water over 1–2 teaspoons of the root and let it infuse for 15 minutes. Drink when needed.

Chinese Medicine

- traditional doctors see anxiety as a weakness of energy in the liver and spleen. They recommend Chinese angelica and ginseng.

Bach Flower Remedies

• Aspen or Rescue Remedy are useful.

Massage

• stress and anxiety produce rigid and painful muscles, particularly in the neck and shoulders. A regular massage from a therapist, friend or partner relaxes these muscles, and in turn relieves anxiety. The best way to carry out a quick neck and shoulder massage is for you to kneel with your arms and head supported on a chair or table. Your partner should firmly squeeze and stroke the muscles of shoulders and neck either side of the spine working upwards and outwards.

Relaxation

• attending a yoga or meditation class will help improve or prevent anxiety. The following relaxation routine should be carried out at least once a day:
  • lie on a firm surface, close your eyes and become aware of how your body feels. Focus your attention on each part of your body, starting with the tips of the toes, and finishing with your face and eyes; consciously try to relax every part of your body in turn. The whole procedure should take at least 10 minutes.
• anxiety is often caused by hyperventilation, and can be helped by yogic breathing: kneel on the floor, place one hand on your stomach and the other on your chest. Inhale for about two seconds, allowing your stomach to bulge out, then slowly exhale for about four to eight seconds, feeling your stomach deflate. Then place your hand on your chest and repeat the procedure allowing your chest to bulge and deflate. Repeat this pattern for several minutes.
• biofeedback can help you learn to relax if you have difficulties.

Orthodox

- tranquillizers, such as Valium, are often prescribed, though long-term use can lead to over-reliance and serious side effects. Counselling is sometimes recommended.

Appendicitis

Acute inflammation of the appendix, a small tube branching off the large intestine. Symptoms include loss of appetite, stomach ache around the navel, shifting to sharp pain in lower right of the belly, nausea, fever, and sometimes constipation or diarrhoea. This condition requires immediate medical attention and hospital admission.

Treatment

Orthodox

- in the early stages after admission to hospital a fluid-only diet is recommended. It rests the inflamed bowel, and if surgery does follow, you will avoid having to wait before receiving a general anaesthetic. Once advanced inflammation is present, surgical removal of the appendix (appendectomy) is the only recommended treatment. If this is delayed the appendix may burst, leaking infected contents into the stomach which leads to life-threatening infection of the lining of the abdomen.

Homoeopathy

- after surgery the wound should be kept clean by bathing with a solution of Hypericum and Calendula (4 drops of each to a cup of warm water; retailed as Hypercal by Nelson's).
- to relieve bruising and pain and to prevent infection

of the wound: Arnica 6c, twice daily for up to 10 days.
- to relieve nausea or vomiting after the anaesthetic: Phosphorus 6c, 3 times a day for 3 days.

Bach Flower Remedies

- take Rescue Remedy to diminish the fear of an operation and to aid recovery.

Arteriosclerosis

The artery walls, which are usually elastic, become hardened with age and hamper the heart's ability to pump blood through the body. This condition greatly contributes to coronary heart disease (see entry), and leads to high blood pressure and increased likelihood of strokes and heart attacks.

Prevention

- do not smoke.
- avoid saturated fats (see dietary guidelines below).
- take regular exercise.

Treatment

Practical Advice

- smoking accelerates the process of arteriosclerosis by making the blood more 'sticky' and likely to clot around the arteries. Stopping smoking is the first step in treatment of this disease.

Dietary

making the following changes to your diet can prevent and reverse the illness to a significant degree:
- avoid saturated fats, found in red meats, fatty dairy products, shortening and margarine, coconut and

palm oils used in snack foods, and eggs.
- substitute red meat for fish or poultry.
- increase intake of fibre, particularly fruit and vegetables, cooked dried beans and oat bran.
- eat a diet which is rich in wholegrain cereals, fresh fruit and vegetables, avoid refined and junk foods.
- reduce intake of salt and sugar.
- supplementation with vitamin E has been shown to help circulatory problems: take between 150 and 200 mg daily.
- incorporate plenty of garlic into your diet.

Massage

- regular massage from a therapist, friend or family member can greatly assist in relaxation, helping to lower blood pressure.

Exercise

- regular, gentle exercise, such as daily walking, swimming or gentle running or cycling, is helpful in treating this condition.

Relaxation

- attending a yoga or meditation class will help improve or prevent this condition. The following relaxation routine should be carried out at least once daily:
  - lie on a firm surface, close your eyes and become aware of how your body feels. Focus your attention on each part of your body, starting with the tips of the toes, and finishing with your face and eyes; consciously try to relax every part of your body in turn. The whole procedure should take at least 10 minutes.
- yogic breathing helps relaxation: kneel on the floor, place one hand on your stomach and the other on your chest. Inhale for two seconds, allowing your stomach to bulge out, then slowly exhale for four to

eight seconds, feeling your stomach deflate. Then place your hand on your chest and repeat the procedure allowing your chest to bulge and deflate. Repeat this pattern for several minutes.
- biofeedback can help you learn to relax if you have difficulties.

Orthodox

- your doctor can detect arteriosclerosis by feeling the firmness of the arteries, by listening to blood flow with a stethoscope, or by examination of the blood vessels at the back of the eye. It is likely that the dietary, relaxation and exercise treatments listed above will be recommended.

Arthritis

Arthritis brings inflammation in one, several or many joints of the body, leading to pain, redness, swelling and stiffness around the joint, and sometimes symptoms in other more distant parts of the body. There are different types of arthritis, which have specific causes, symptoms and treatments. The following are the most common types.

- symptoms caused by wear and tear or degeneration of the joints, also known as osteoarthritis (see entry).
- symptoms caused when the immune system acts against and damages joints and surrounding tissues causing general inflammation of all structures of the body, including the joints. This is the most common type of arthritis, known as rheumatoid arthritis (see entry).
- arthritis of the spine, where the joints linking the vertebrae become inflamed and the bones fuse; the hips may also be affected. This is known as ankylosing spondylitis (see entry).

- when uric acid, one of the body's waste products, accumulates in the joints causing inflammation; this is known as gout (see entry).
- by examining the symptoms and signs, your health professional can tell which type of arthritis you may have. Fluid may be drawn from the joint for analysis or x-rays may be taken to assess the damage to the joint. For treatment see specific entries.

Astigmatism *see* Eyesight Problems

Asthma

Recurrent attacks of breathlessness and wheezing, a dry cough and a feeling of tightness in the chest, which often begins at night. A bad attack causes sweating, rapid heart beat, and extreme gasping for breath which can be fatal. Asthma occurs when the airways in the lungs go into spasm as a result of an allergy, air irritants, lung infection or stress. Severe attacks require professional treatment. The following self help tips can complement professional help.

Prevention

- avoid cigarette smoke and wood-burning fires.
- if you suddenly go out into cold weather, cover your mouth and nose with a scarf.
- remove potential allergens from the indoor environment (see Allergies — Hay Fever and Rhinitis).
- aspirin can sometimes trigger an attack, so avoid it if you are sensitive.

Treatment

Dietary

* avoid potential food allergens (milk, eggs, nuts and seafood), processed foods and food additives, such as monosodium glutamate (621) and sodium metabisulphite (E223), found in beer and wine and some dried fruits. Avoid the yellow colouring agent tartrazine (Yellow 5; E102).
* studies have shown that following a strict vegetarian diet reduces incidence and severity of asthma.
* studies have shown that people taking 100 mg per day of vitamin B6 noticed a reduction in the frequency and severity of asthma attacks. Vitamin B6 is found in wheatgerm, brewer's yeast, poultry, fish, cooked dried beans and peas and peanuts.

Aromatherapy

* atlas cedarwood, eucalyptus and peppermint help ease breathing when placed on a tissue and inhaled.

Herbal

* elecampane infusion: add 1 teaspoon of the shredded root to one cup of cold water, let it stand for 10 hours, strain, heat and take hot 3 times daily.

Homoeopathy

* if very restless and anxious: Arsenicum album 6c as required.
* symptoms worse in late evening and night, made worse by cold weather; symptoms come on very suddenly and are accompanied by great anxiety: Aconite 6c as required.
* symptoms worse between 3 and 5 a.m., aggravated by damp weather: Natrum sulphuricum 6c as required.
* professional treatment will help to reduce the frequency and severity of the attacks.

Chinese Medicine

- treatment should be carried out by a professional, who would offer herbs, such as ephedra and bitter almond seed to calm wheezing attacks, and acupuncture to treat the lungs, kidney or spleen.

Reflexology

- massage the area between the big toe and the second toe on both feet.
- massage the top of the foot, spreading the toes apart and loosening the toe ligaments.

Acupressure

- reach with your right hand over your shoulder to press firmly on point B13 (see illustration). Take 5 long deep breaths then release and repeat with the left hand.
- make fists and place on your chest with thumbs

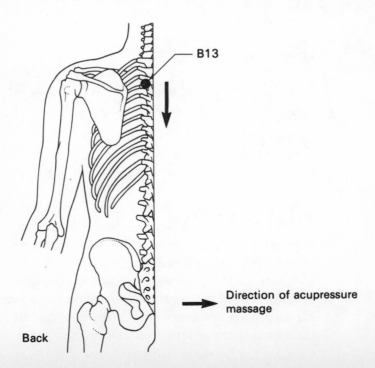

B13

Direction of acupressure massage

Back

pointing upwards. Place your thumbs on the muscles that run below the collarbone. You will probably feel a sensitive spot. Press firmly and breathe deeply for 2 minutes.

Yoga

do the following sequence of exercises when an attack starts. Try to relax and clear your mind of everything as you do the movements.

* sit on the floor with the seat of a chair facing you. Let your head, chest, and arms drop forward towards the seat of the chair. Inhale and let your head fall back, exhale and let your head fall forward. Repeat 5 times. Let your head fall back and forwards while inhaling and exhaling, this time chanting 'AH' as you come forward exhaling.
* kneel on the floor, sitting on your heels. Move your head back and forth as above, 5 times. Then clasp your hands behind you and lean forward, if possible until your head touches your knees or the floor. Repeat several times.

Orthodox

* drugs are usually prescribed: sodium cromoglycate is designed to prevent asthma and needs to be taken continuously. Inhaled corticosteroid drugs reverse the spasm in the air tubes and are known as reverse inhalers.

Atherosclerosis

A gradual clogging up of the insides of the artery walls by fatty plaque deposits, which restrict blood flow, leading to high blood pressure and increased likelihood of stroke or heart attack. This condition is more common in men than women, and in those who smoke, are overweight, or lead a sedentary lifestyle.

Prevention

- see dietary recommendations below.
- take aerobic exercise (such as brisk walking, cycling or swimming) at least 3 times a week.
- take measures to reduce stress (see entry).

Treatment

Dietary

atherosclerosis is rare in countries where a diet low in fat and high in fibre is consumed. The first steps in treating this disorder should therefore be dietary:

- avoid saturated fats, found in red meats, fatty dairy products, eggs, shortening, coconut and palm oils used in snack foods.
- substitute red meat for fish and poultry.
- use olive oil for cooking and dressings, replace butter with polyunsaturated margarine.
- increase intake of fibre, particularly fruit and vegetables, cooked dried beans and oat bran.
- reduce intake of salt and sugar.
- eat a diet which is rich in wholegrain cereals, fresh fruit and vegetables. Avoid refined and junk foods.
- increase intake of citrus fruits, tomatoes, potatoes, strawberries and spinach, rich in vitamin C, which has been shown to help prevent the buildup of harmful cholesterol.

Exercise

- exercise helps protect the body from harmful cholesterol. Regular walking, running, swimming, cycling or aerobics is the best. However, check with your doctor before starting a new exercise programme.

Orthodox

- anticoagulant drugs such as aspirin are prescribed to reduce clots forming in the blood, and have been shown to be useful in people who have already had a stroke or a heart attack. Vasodilator drugs are designed to open up the arteries, but are not very effective and do not resolve the degeneration of the artery walls. Different types of surgery can widen the arteries or replace damaged areas with vein or synthetic grafts (see Coronary Heart Disease and Aneurysm).

Athlete's Foot *see* Fungal Infection

Backache

This can describe pain anywhere from the base of the skull to the tail bone. The following self-assessment chart provides some indication of the many different causes and symptoms. (For lower back pain, see separate entry.)

1. soft-tissue/musculo-skeletal backache:
   - trouble arises from the muscles, joints and ligaments running along the spine. Lifting, straining or bad posture (prolonged driving or sitting at a desk) is often a cause.
2. 'slipped disc' backache:
   - trouble arises from a backward movement of the cartilaginous 'disc' which sits between each vertebra of the spine and the next one. The disc pushes against nerves in the spinal cord and commonly produces referred pain down the back of the leg (sciatica, see entry). Lifting with a bent back or awkward twisting is often responsible. See also entry on Slipped Disc.
3. inflammatory and pathological backache:
   - these make up the minority of backaches, but are the most serious. Infections in the bones themselves, tumours and degenerative disorders such as arthritis may all be responsible. The back pain may be the first sign of a problem arising in the back, or it may equally represent the first symptom of distant disease somewhere else in the body.

Making a Diagnosis

did the pain come on suddenly? Likely to be 1.

was it triggered by exertion/lifting? Likely to be 1.

do you feel generally unwell/tired? Likely to be 3.

is the pain worse on coughing? Likely to be 2.

does the pain radiate down the leg? Likely to be 2.

is the pain and stiffness worse in the morning? Likely to
be 1 or 2.

is the pain worse bending forwards? Likely to be 2.

is the pain worse leaning backwards? Likely to be 1.

is the small of the back completely straight? Likely
to be 1 or 2.

Treatment

Severe or prolonged cases of backache require
professional help. The following self help treatments can
be used once the likelihood of a severe 'slipped disc' or
the pathological causes of backache have been ruled out.

Hydrotherapy

- hot and cold treatments are very helpful for this
  condition and can be carried out as often as required.
  Prepare two bowls of water, one hot, one cold. Fold
  two towels in three and dip one in the hot water,
  wring it out tightly and place over the painful area
  for 3 minutes. Then do the same with the cold for
  1 minute. Keep repeating the procedure for about
  20 minutes.

Massage

- it is difficult to massage your own back, but
  treatment from a professional therapist, a friend or
  family member can provide much relief if the
  backache is muscular in origin. Lie on your front on
  a firm surface, or sit leaning over the back of a chair.
  Your partner should use deep stroking movements
  (effleurage) up the muscles on either side of the spine,

and small circular strokes with the tips of the fingers (petrissage) around areas of tension (shoulder blades and buttocks).

Acupressure

- use firm pressure for at least one minute on the points illustrated.

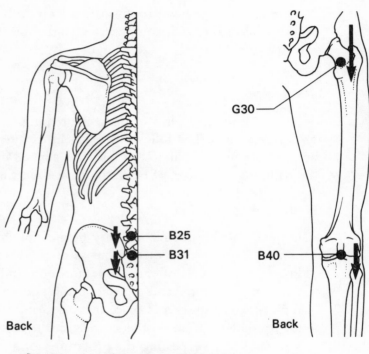

➤ Direction of acupressure massage

Exercise

- exercise is helpful in some cases of backache. However, it is not advised if it makes the pain worse. Swimming, gentle stretching or yoga strengthen the back muscles without straining, and are very helpful as a preventive measure.
- the following exercises help relieve stiffness and muscular pain by 'massaging' the whole of the spine:

- sit on a yoga mat or carpet with your legs bent and arms grasped around your knees. Slowly rock backwards and forwards so that your whole spine touches the floor.
- lie on your back with legs straight and arms stretched out to the sides. Bend your left leg and place the foot on the outside of your right knee. Keep your shoulders flat on the ground. Lower your left knee towards the ground. Hold the position and release. Repeat with the other leg.

Relaxation

- use a firm mattress for resting.
- support the knees and hips when lying flat by placing a small cushion or pillow under the small of the back or under the knees.
- lie on your side if you have pain in the leg(s).
- place a small pillow under the neck for neck and shoulder pain.
- try to let go of the tension in your body by carrying out the following routine.
  - close your eyes and be aware of your body. Focus on relaxing each part, starting with the tips of your

toes and finishing with your face and eyes. The
whole procedure should take about 10 minutes.

Professional Help

- an osteopath or chiropractor is specialized in
  diagnosing and treating such problems. An
  acupuncturist can often relieve severe back pain. The
  Alexander Technique is useful for backache resulting
  from poor posture and once the initial pain has gone,
  will help prevent a recurrence.

Orthodox

- anti-inflammatory drugs or muscle relaxants may be
  prescribed, along with physiotherapy. Traction,
  wearing a collar or surgical corset may also be
  recommended. As a final resort, surgery may be
  carried out.

Bad Breath

Generally caused by poor oral hygiene, though smoking
and eating strong-smelling foods can contribute. Some
believe that a yeast infection of the digestive tract can
also result in bad breath.

Treatment

Practical Advice

- plaque buildup is often the cause of bad breath. The
  mouth produces plaque every day, and the only way
  to get rid of it is by flossing and brushing the teeth
  every day. Most cases of bad breath disappear if the
  following routine is carried out morning and evening:
  1. using at least 5 inches/12 cm of floss, wrap each
     end around a finger from each hand. Starting with
     the top right back tooth, wiggle the middle area of

the floss between each tooth gently up and down several times. The aim is to remove plaque, not just bits of food caught between the teeth. Work all the way around the mouth.

2. brush the teeth with gentle circular movements.
3. gently brush the top of the tongue.
4. rinse several times with cold water.
5. if desired, use a mouth rinse.

Dietary

- sugar promotes the production of plaque, so is best avoided.
- coffee, alcohol and smoking all contribute to bad breath.
- chewing parsley or drinking fenugreek or peppermint tea will sweeten the breath after a meal.
- to combat yeast infections, eat plenty of live yoghurt, or take supplements of *Lactobacillus acidophilus*. Take 1 teaspoon of the powder, 1 teaspoon of *Bifidobacteria* powder, and ½ teaspoon of *Lactobacillus bulgaricus* (available from health food stores) in a glass of spring water, 3 times daily.

Herbal

- for inflamed or bleeding gums, add 2 teaspoons of red sage leaves to half a litre of water, bring to the boil and leave to stand covered for 15 minutes. Strain and use as a mouth rinse several times a day.
  - **caution:** not to be used during pregnancy.
- echinacea decoction can be used as an everyday mouthwash: add 2 teaspoons of echinacea root to one cup of water, simmer for 10 minutes and allow to cool.
- the Indian practice of chewing cardamom seeds after a meal has been shown to prevent tooth decay, and associated bad breath.

Homoeopathy

3 times daily for 7 days:
- sour smelling breath, particularly in the morning and after meals or drinking alcohol: Nux vomica 6c.
- breath smells of onions: Petroselinum 6c.

Chinese Medicine

- giant hyssop and peppermint tea are prescribed to help detoxify the intestines; radish seeds and oriental worm root to aid digestion.

Orthodox

- regular dental treatment includes professional cleaning, aimed at avoiding tooth and gum decay.

Balanitis

Inflammation of the head of the penis and sometimes the foreskin. The area is itchy, red and sometimes moist. Balanitis can be caused by the irritation of a nappy or damp clothing, a bacterial or yeast infection, injury, irritation from chemicals in clothing, condoms or spermicide. The condition is most common in men with diabetes (see entry), as sugar in the urine encourages the microbes to multiply.

Treatment

Practical Advice

- in babies, balanitis is treated by more frequent changing of nappies (diapers), and keeping the penis clean and dry. You may find that using disposable nappies is contributing to the problem. Alternatively, it could be a soap or detergent you are using to clean the baby or the nappies.

- in adults it is advisable to see a doctor for a checkup, as the symptoms of balanitis are similar to other more serious diseases.
- once a diagnosis is confirmed, the following gentle treatments may help.
  - always wear cotton underwear.
  - try changing your detergent to see if the condition is improved, always rinse underwear thoroughly.
  - avoid scented soaps and talc.
  - use hypo-allergenic condoms and spermicides.
  - if your doctor confirms a yeast infection as the cause of balanitis, it is advisable that any sexual partners are also checked out, as the infection may be passed back and forth between you.

Dietary

- if balanitis is caused by a yeast infection, increase your intake of live natural, unsweetened yoghurt (at least one small carton daily).
- decrease intake of foods containing sugars and yeast (this includes fruit and alcohol).
- take ½ a teaspoon of *Lactobacillus acidophilus* in a glass of water 3 times daily, with 1 teaspoon of *Bifidobacteria* powder, and ½ teaspoon of *Lactobacillus bulgaricus* (available from health food stores) in a glass of spring water, 3 times daily. This restores healthy bacteria to the body and helps fight yeast infections.

Aromatherapy

- wash the penis regularly with a solution of tea tree oil. This is an effective antiseptic and antifungal agent. Dilute 4 drops of essential oil of tea tree in a basin of warm water.

Herbal

- after cleaning and drying thoroughly, apply aloe vera gel.

Orthodox

- your doctor will prescribe an antibiotic cream and, if the problem is recurrent, may recommend circumcision.

Baldness *see* Hair Loss

Bamboo Spine *see* Ankylosing Spondylitis

Bed Wetting

Around 10 per cent of children still wet the bed at the age of 5, and some continue up to the age of 16 or later. In most cases bed wetting indicates that the nervous system is not yet mature enough to control the bladder. Sometimes it results from stress or anxiety. In cases where children above the age of 4 have difficulty with daytime as well as night-time bladder control, consult a professional, as this could be a sign of bladder infection or an anatomical abnormality of the kidney.

Treatment

Practical Advice

- bed wetting in young children is perfectly normal, and most children outgrow it with time. To avoid worrying the child, change the sheets without fuss; it is not advisable to praise children if they have a dry night, or punish them when they are wet, as this emphasizes the problem and can lead to stress and anxiety which may make things worse.
- withholding drinks in the evening is not helpful; neither is 'lifting' the child during the night to empty their bladder.
- to avoid embarrassment in older children, leave out

dry nightwear and sheets so that they can change themselves. This will also help them feel in control of the situation.

Aromatherapy

• massage the child's stomach with 2 drops of essential oil of cypress added to 8—10 ml of carrier oil or lotion.

Homoeopathy

to be taken at bedtime for up to 1 week, repeat if needed:
• bed wetting during dreams of urination: Equisetum 6c.
• bed wetting during first sleep; difficulty in urinating after urine has been forcibly retained: Causticum 6c.

Bach Flower Remedies

• Cherry Plum has been shown to be useful in treating this condition.

Acupressure

• apply deep thumb pressure to the points illustrated overleaf two or three times weekly.

Professional Help

• hypnotherapy can be effective in resolving stubborn cases of bed wetting.

Orthodox

• drug therapy using Tofranil (an antidepressant) or anti-diuretic hormones (which suppress the urge to urinate) is sometimes recommended, but is only effective throughout the duration of the therapy. If bed wetting continues after the age of seven, some parents use an alarm, which sets off a bell the minute

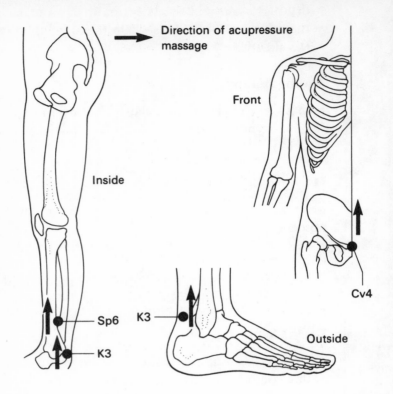

the bed becomes damp, training the child to wake up and go to the toilet.

Bedsores

Ulcers which develop on the skin as a result of spending long periods in bed or immobile. They start as tender red areas, and develop into deep sores which can become seriously infected and are difficult to heal.

Prevention

- bedridden patients should be turned regularly to distribute the pressure around the body.
- use a fleece lining or an 'egg box' foam mattress on the bed to relieve pressure.

- if possible, use a water bed.
- regular massage for bedridden patients improves circulation and prevents sores developing.

Treatment

Practical Advice

- studies have shown the effectiveness in using sugar or honey to encourage bedsores to heal: pack the sore tightly with granulated sugar or honey, and cover with an airtight dressing. Reapply each day.

Dietary

people who develop bedsores are generally in a weakened state and good nutrition is very important to resist infection and promote healing.
- eat a wholefood diet with plenty of protein, fruit and vegetables.
- take the following supplements:
  - vitamin C: 2–6 g daily.
  - vitamin B complex: 50 mg twice daily.
  - vitamin A: 50,000 iu daily.
  - zinc: 25–50 mg daily.

Aromatherapy

- a solution of water with 2 drops of essential oil of tea tree can be used to clean the sore, to encourage healing, and prevent infection.

Homoeopathy

- Calendula 6c: take 3 times daily for up to 7 days and repeat if needed.

Orthodox

- doctors recommend that immobile or bedridden patients are regularly turned, to redistribute weight on different areas of the body. Regular washing also helps prevent sores. Once the sores have developed antibiotics are given, and a cushioned dressing is used. Plastic surgery is carried out in extreme cases.

Bee Stings *see* Insect Bites and Stings

Belching

The noisy return of air from the stomach to the mouth. This may result from eating or drinking too quickly, or the nervous habit of swallowing air. With indigestion or acid stomach, belching can relieve discomfort. In pregnancy it sometimes helps relieve nausea and heartburn. (See also Acid Stomach; Flatulence; Indigestion; Pregnancy Problems.)

Prevention

a close friend or partner may be able to tell you if you have a tendency to swallow air. Once you are aware of the habit, it will be easier to control it.
• avoid carbonated drinks and beer.
• always eat with your mouth closed.
• don't chew gum.
• do not drink straight from the can or bottle.
• eat slowly.
• exercise regularly.

Treatment

Herbal

• fennel, peppermint or vervain infusion aids digestion: pour a cup of boiling water on a teaspoon of the dried herb and leave to infuse for 5 minutes before drinking. Make when required.
• sucking a strong peppermint sweet helps.

- ginger infusion helps relieve the need to belch: pour a cup of boiling water on 1 teaspoon of freshly grated root and leave to infuse for 5 minutes and drink when needed.

Homoeopathy

take every 30 minutes for up to 5 doses:
- if belching relieves pain or discomfort: Carbo vegetabilis 6c.
- if belching does not relieve discomfort: China 6c.

Orthodox

- your doctor may recommend antacids to help aid digestion.

Black Eye

Injury to the eye area which damages the many small blood vessels beneath the skin, causing them to leak blood which collects in the loose transparent skin around the eye. If vision is affected seek professional attention.

Treatment

Practical Advice

- don't apply pressure to the eye or surrounding area.
- avoid aspirin, which prevents the blood from clotting.
- don't blow your nose hard, as it may rupture the blood vessels and increase the bleeding.

Homoeopathy

- Arnica 6c, every hour for up to 4 doses. Repeat next day if necessary. Arnica cream applied around the eye will help reduce bruising as long as the skin is unbroken.

- if the bruising is slow to clear: Ledum 6c, 3 times daily for 4 days.
- if the bones around the eye are very sore: Symphytum 6c, 3 times daily for up to 4 days.

Hydrotherapy

- immediately place a cold compress (a cloth soaked in ice cold water and wrung out), or an ice pack (a pack of frozen peas wrapped in kitchen roll) on the affected eye for 5 minutes. The cold constricts the blood vessels and decreases the bleeding which makes the eye go black. If there is swelling, repeat every 10 minutes through the day.

Orthodox

- treatment as above.

Blackhead

Blackheads develop when plugs of oil block the outlet of sebaceous glands surfacing through pores on the skin. On exposure to the air, the oil blackens due to oxidation and remains in the pores of the skin. Blackheads generally occur on the face, chest, shoulders, and back.

Treatment

Practical Advice

- avoid harsh soaps and drying creams. Instead use a mild oil in water emulsion cleanser which can be applied by hand and wiped off with tissues before rinsing the face with water. Avoid alcohol–containing tonics and skin fresheners.
- use a water in oil moisturizer.

Dietary

- avoid fatty and fried food.
- increase intake of green vegetables, particularly raw ones.
- increase intake of vitamin B complex, found in wholegrain breads and cereals, liver, or brewer's yeast (1 tablespoon added to water or fruit juice 3 times daily). A face mask of brewer's yeast and yoghurt, used 3 times a week for 15 minutes on freshly cleansed skin, helps to calm overactive oil glands.

Aromatherapy

- dilute 5 drops each of atlas cedarwood and juniper berry in half a cup of spring water and use as a skin freshener throughout the day.

Hydrotherapy

- blackheads that are not inflamed can be removed by steaming the skin over a bowl of hot water, or applying a hot compress: soak a clean cloth in hot water to which 2 teaspoons of bicarbonate of soda have been added (this helps open up the pores), wring out the cloth and apply to the blackheads. With a clean tissue, gently squeeze out the oily plugs. Never use your nails to do this. Finish by applying a small amount of antiseptic cream, or a solution of water and essential oil of tea tree (2 drops to 1 cup of water).

Orthodox

- doctors recommend avoiding make up altogether, or changing to a non-oil based brand. They advise cleansing the skin well morning and night, using a mild soap, and rinsing well with water afterwards. Exposure to moderate amounts of sunlight is recommended and low dose tetracycline antibiotics are often prescribed.

Bladder Stones

Hard salt collections which tend to congregate at the
exit of the bladder causing at times severe abdominal
pain, a frequent urge to urinate, pain during urination
and occasionally traces of blood in the urine. This
condition is not common, but men are more susceptible,
particularly those who have lived for any time in warm
climates.

Treatment

Herbal

• stone root is used in the prevention and treatment of
  bladder stones. Make a decoction using 1–3
  teaspoons of dried root, add to one cup of water,
  simmer for 15 minutes. Drink three times daily.

Chinese Medicine

• star fruit promotes urination and relieves the
  discomfort of kidney stones: boil 3 fresh fruit with
  2 teaspoons of honey; eat the fruit and drink the juice
  once daily.

Hydrotherapy

• drink plenty of fluids to help reduce urine
  concentrations. If the kidneys are painful, apply a
  warm water bottle to the painful area.

Professional Help

• professional homoeopathic treatment can be extremely
  helpful in this condition.

Orthodox

• surgery to remove or break up the stones, so that
  they can be excreted.

Blister

A pocket of fluid in the outer layer of skin which results from damage to the flesh, e.g. burns (see entry), friction, or disease (eczema or chicken pox sometimes manifest as blisters).

Prevention (Friction Blisters)

• use petroleum jelly on areas of skin likely to be rubbed by unfamiliar clothing or shoes.
• wear thick cotton socks for sports.
• use talcum powder on the feet.
• if you are planning a walking trip, toughen up the skin on your feet by rubbing surgical spirit on areas vulnerable to blisters twice daily.

Treatment

Practical Advice

• it is best to let a blister heal on its own. However, if it is causing pressure or pain, or if it is likely to burst through further friction, you can puncture it with a sterilized needle (daubed in alcohol or held in a flame), and drain out the fluid, trying to leave the skin intact. During the day, cover it with a sterile dressing or sticking plaster/band aid. Remove the dressing at night to let the blister dry out.

Aromatherapy

• add two drops of essential oil of Roman chamomile to half a cup of water and use as an antiseptic when the dressing is changed.

Homoeopathy

• bathe punctured blisters in a solution of Hypericum and Calendula (Hypercal).

- for red, swollen and itchy blisters: Rhus toxicodendron 6c, every 4 hours until symptoms are alleviated.
- Nelson's Burn Ointment eases the pain and encourages healing.

Orthodox

- if the blister becomes infected and does not heal on its own it may require professional draining, antiseptic cream and antibiotics to prevent the infection spreading.

Blood Poisoning *see* Septicaemia

Blood Pressure, High

High blood pressure occurs when there is an increase in the force of blood flow against the artery and heart walls. Smoking, obesity, too much alcohol, stress, and heart conditions are contributing factors. There are no obvious symptoms of high blood pressure, but the condition can lead to stroke, heart attack, kidney failure, and sometimes damage to the eyes.

Treatment

Dietary

- studies show that following a vegetarian diet can significantly lower or even eliminate high blood pressure. If you decide to become a vegetarian, ensure that you replace meat with sufficient vegetable protein, such as soya, cooked dried beans, nuts, seeds, and wholegrain cereals.
- reduce intake of animal fat (meat, eggs, butter, cream), sugar and salt.

- increase intake of fibre, found in wholegrain breads and cereals, vegetables and fruit.
- increase intake of potassium, found in fish, orange juice, bananas, potatoes, avocados, lima beans, tomatoes, apricots, peaches.
- increase intake of calcium, found in low fat milk, yoghurt and cheese, sesame seeds, chick peas, spinach and broccoli.
- increase intake of magnesium, found in nuts, cooked dried beans and peas, soya beans, dark green leafy vegetables, seafood, and milk.

Aromatherapy

- lavender has been shown in studies to aid relaxation (see Relaxation below). Add a few drops to the bath and relax in the soothing odour. A professional aromatherapy treatment is very therapeutic.

Chinese Medicine

- Chinese herbs are effective in treating high blood pressure. Treatment should be carried out by a professional; herbs such as chrysanthemum flowers, peony root and astragalus are likely to be prescribed.

Herbal

- see Angina page 48.

Massage

- regular massage can greatly help relieve stress. Go to a qualified therapist or teach yourself and a friend to do it, then exchange treatments.

Acupressure

- applying deep pressure to the points illustrated, three or four times a week, may be helpful.

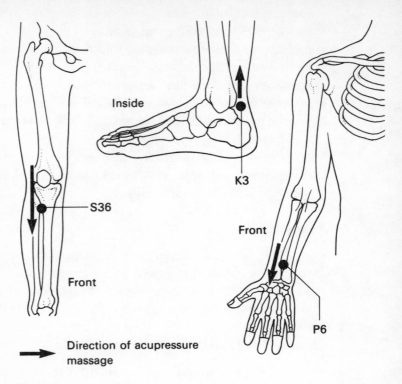

Direction of acupressure
massage

Exercise

- regular non-competitive exercise is vital in treating this condition. Walking, gentle swimming or cycling are all beneficial activities. However, consult your health professional before embarking on a new exercise routine.

Relaxation/Stress Relief

- stress is one of the principal causes of high blood pressure. Learning to identify what arouses anger, anxiety and other types of emotional stress in your professional and personal life is one of the first steps in treatment. Consider the following questions when you think about resolving stress:
  - are you always in a hurry?
  - do you always work to deadlines?
  - do you snatch meals and eat quickly?

- do you get less than 7 hours' sleep each night?
- do you participate in competitive sports?
- do you often have conflict in your personal relationships?
- sometimes stress relief is simply a question of easing work commitments and getting more sleep. For some people however, help is required to make necessary lifestyle changes: professional counselling, family or group therapy can be helpful.
- biofeedback can help you learn to relax if you have difficulties.

Yoga

- attending a yoga class will provide relaxation and stretching, while improving your breathing, vital to good circulation. The following routine should be carried out once daily:
  - lie on a firm surface, close your eyes and become aware of how your body feels. Focus your attention on each part of your body, starting with the tips of the toes, and finishing with your face and eyes; consciously try to relax every part of your body in turn. The whole procedure should take at least 10 minutes.
- yogic breathing helps relaxation: kneel on the floor; place one hand on your stomach and the other on your chest. Inhale, allowing your stomach to bulge out, then slowly exhale, feeling your stomach deflate. Then place your hand on your chest and repeat the procedure, allowing your chest to bulge and deflate. Repeat this pattern for several minutes.

Professional Help

- homoeopathy can treat high blood pressure successfully, but a personal prescription must be made, taking account of the individual's physical and emotional situation. Therefore, professional treatment is recommended.

Orthodox

- doctors advise stopping smoking, cutting down
  consumption of alcohol, animal fats and salt, and
  losing weight. Drugs such as beta-blockers (which
  lower the heart rate), diuretics (which encourage the
  excretion of urine), or vasodilators (which enlarge the
  blood vessels) may be recommended.

Blood Sugar, Low

Also known as hypoglycemia, this is an abnormally low
level of sugar in the blood. The condition can occur in
diabetics (see entry on Diabetes) when they take too
much insulin, skip meals, or unexpected activity uses up
their stores of sugar. It can also occur in non-diabetics
as a result of eating too many sugary snacks, which
causes blood levels to rise and fall dramatically.
Symptoms include weakness, shakiness, sweating,
fatigue, headaches, irritability, confusion, and in severe
cases, coma in diabetics.

Treatment

Dietary

- for emergency short-term relief of symptoms, suck a
  boiled sweet, eat a teaspoonful of honey or drink a
  glass of milk to boost low blood sugar.
- for long-term relief, avoid sugar in any form (this
  includes cakes, desserts, sweetened drinks and
  breakfast cereals). Instead eat plenty of protein (fish,
  poultry, cheese, eggs, milk), fresh vegetables and fruit,
  beans, lentils, peas, brown rice and wholegrain bread
  and pasta. Avoid alcohol, tea and coffee. Eat little and
  often (four to six meals daily). Do not miss meals,
  especially breakfast.
- chromium helps to normalize blood sugar

metabolism. It is found in wholegrain breads and cereals, pork, kidney, molasses, lean meats and cheeses. One of the best sources is brewer's yeast: take 1 dessertspoon in water or fruit juice daily.

Orthodox

- doctors have only recently begun to recognize the symptoms of low blood sugar. Treatment includes dietary adjustment and ensuring the patient is not suffering from the very rare insulin secreting tumour.

Body Odour

The smell caused when stale sweat comes into contact with bacteria on the skin. In some cases body odour can be caused by excessive sweating, dietary problems or medication.

Treatment

Practical Advice

- the most effective way to prevent body odour is to wash all over at least once a day, and to use an underarm deodorant or antiperspirant. Deodorants work by restricting the action of bacteria on the skin; antiperspirants reduce the volume of perspiration that is released through the skin (the latter are not favoured by natural practitioners as they interfere with the natural elimination process of sweating). Dusting the body with sodium bicarbonate is a more natural, while effective, deodorant.
- in warm weather wear loose clothing made from natural fabrics (cotton, linen, wool). Change clothing worn next to the skin daily.
- sometimes body odour can be caused by fungal infections (see entry).

Dietary

improper diet and deficiencies in certain vitamins and
minerals can sometimes contribute to this condition:

- excess fat can sometimes be a cause of body odour,
  particularly saturated fats found in meat and dairy
  produce.
- avoid foods which contain saturated fats or which list
  vegetable oil as one of the ingredients, but fail to
  mention the type of oil. Replace saturated fats with
  sunflower seed oil, polyunsaturated margarine, and
  olive oil.
- deficiency of zinc is sometimes related to excessive
  perspiration: take 20—30 mg of chelated zinc daily.

Aromatherapy

- mix 6 drops of essential oil of lavender in 1 pint of
  distilled water and keep in the bathroom. Dab onto
  areas of the body which perspire easily.

Orthodox

- excessive perspiration, also known as hyperhydrosis, is
  treated by applying aluminium chloride preparations
  to the affected areas.

Boils

An inflamed, pus-filled lump on the skin, which usually
results from a bacterial infection. Common sites are the
back of the neck, armpits, groin and buttocks. Recurrent
boils could be a sign of inadequate diet or an early
symptom of diabetes.

Treatment

Dietary

- zinc deficiency may lead to boils. To increase intake of zinc eat plenty of poultry, fish, liver, butter/lima beans, pork, wheatgerm, and wholegrain breads and cereals.
- naturopaths believe that boils are the body's way of cleansing itself of impurities. They also suggest that overindulgence in saturated fats (meat and dairy produce) may encourage boils. They recommend a purification diet for 7 days, consisting of fruit juices, fresh fruit (particularly citrus) and vegetables (particularly green), along with plenty of mineral water.
- constipation can sometimes cause boils (see entry).

Aromatherapy

- essential oil of tea tree: dab on boils 4—6 times daily.

Herbal

- garlic is an effective antiseptic, helping to detoxify the body. Incorporate the raw herb into your diet as much as possible.

Homoeopathy

every hour for up to 4 doses and repeat if needed:
- hot, red and throbbing: Belladonna 6c.
- extremely sensitive, lancing pains: Hepar sulphuris 6c.
- where the boil is slow to come to a head: Silicea 6c.
- where other remedies have been tried without success: Myristica 6c.

Chinese Medicine

- herbs are recommended to reduce heat in the body, thought to cause boils: Chinese golden thread, dandelion or wild chrysanthemum and violet are given in the form of a tea.

Biochemic Tissue Salts

- Calc Sulph, 4 times daily.

Hydrotherapy

- an Epsom salts bath stimulates circulation and encourages elimination through the skin: dissolve 1 lb of Epsom salts, available from pharmacies, in a hot bath and lie in it for 10—20 minutes before going to bed. This bath should not be taken more than twice weekly, and is not recommended for people who are weak or frail.

Orthodox

- large boils are lanced, and antibiotics prescribed to clear up the infection. Doctors advise against squeezing boils, as this increases the risk of spreading the infection.

Breast Feeding Problems

Babies benefit from receiving only breast milk for at least the first 6 months of life, and preferably for the first year. Learning how to breast feed properly can make the experience much more comfortable and fulfilling for both mother and baby. La Leche League (see Appendix 2) is an international support group providing information and advice about breast feeding. The following gentle treatments are recommended for commonly experienced problems.

Insufficient Milk Production

- ensure you are getting an adequate diet. Eat plenty of wholegrain cereals, fruit, vegetables and lean proteins,

with plenty of fluids (especially apple and grape
juice).
- herbal: goat's rue infusion has been shown to increase
  milk production by up to 50 per cent: pour a cup of
  boiling water onto 1 teaspoon of the dried leaves,
  infuse for 10 minutes and drink twice daily.
- dandelion root is also helpful: use 1 teaspoon per cup
  of water, bring to the boil, simmer for 10 minutes
  and drink three times daily.
- feed your baby regularly, because the glands needs
  stimulation to produce milk.
- stress can sometimes suppress milk supply. Talking to
  a supportive friend or relative can help relieve
  anxiety; yoga, meditation, massage or aromatherapy
  help relieve tension.
- the homoeopathic remedy, Agnus castus 6c, can be
  taken 4 times daily for up to 3 days.

Breast Engorgement/Too Much Milk

- if the breasts become painfully swollen with milk,
  expressing the excess provides relief.
- if engorgement is accompanied by feelings of
  sensitivity and tearfulness: Pulsatilla 6c, every 4 hours
  until breasts feel more comfortable.
- if engorgement is accompanied by sensitivity to the
  cold and experiencing cold sweats: Calcarea carbonica
  6c, every 4 hours until breasts feel more comfortable.

Painful Nipples

- La Leche League advises making sure the nipple is
  completely in the baby's mouth, so that it does not
  move about, causing irritation.
- expose your nipples to the air as much as possible to
  let them dry naturally.
- allow a drop of milk to remain on the nipples after
  feeding, it helps to heal cracks.
- after the feed, bathe the nipples in Arnica solution

(10 drops of tincture to ½ pint of water), dry
thoroughly and apply Calendula cream.
- nipples inflamed and tender: Chamomilla 6c, every 4
  hours for up to 6 doses.
- nipples cracked and excessively sore: Castor equi 6c
  every 4 hours for up to 6 doses.

See also the entry on Mastitis for more specific details.

Breast Lump

A breast lump may be due to a cyst (also known as
fibrocystic disease), thickening of the milk glands (fibro-
adenoma), a benign growth, or cancer. Symptoms
include lumps, hard or tender areas, changes in nipple
shape, skin colour, shape or hang of breast, and
puckering of the skin. Pain is rare. More than eighty per
cent of breast lumps are not cancerous; however, they
should all be examined by a doctor.

Prevention

The dietary guidelines given below help prevent breast
lumps.

Treatment

Practical Advice

- wear a supportive bra.
- examine your breasts after every period.

Dietary

- breast pain and lumps are alleviated in some people
  by increasing intake of vitamin A (found in liver,
  kidney, egg yolk, and low fat dairy products), and
  beta-carotene (found in dark green, dark yellow and
  orange vegetables: broccoli, spinach, carrots, apricots,
  peaches).

- vitamin E aids absorption of vitamin A (vitamin E is found in vegetable oils, seeds, wheatgerm, nuts, avocados, wholegrain breads and cereals, spinach, broccoli, asparagus, dried prunes). Alternatively, try a course of vitamin E supplements: 200 mg daily. (Check with your doctor first if suffering from high blood pressure.)
- women with low levels of selenium are at greater risk for fibrocystic breast disease. Selenium is found in whole wheat and rice, oatmeal, poultry, low fat dairy produce, lean meats, organ meat, fish and seafood.
- evening primrose oil supplements have been shown to help reduce breast lumps: take 500 mg twice daily.
- breast lumps thrive in fat. Adopt a diet that is low in fat, and high in fibre (whole grains, vegetables, fruit and beans). This will allow more oestrogen to be excreted, causing less hormonal stimulation in the breasts.
- if you are overweight, try to reduce your weight.
- reduce intake of caffeine (coffee, tea, chocolate, cola).

Exercise

- exercise stimulates blood circulation to the breasts, helping to clear toxins. Regular walking, swimming, running, racquet sports or aerobics are all useful activities.

Orthodox

- routine breast examinations should be carried out by a doctor or nurse, perhaps when you go for a cervical smear test. Cysts are usually drained of fluid. Other lumps are usually surgically removed.

Breast Tenderness

Tender or sore breasts, often accompanied by a feeling of heaviness or being swollen, are common in most women just before menstruation (see Premenstrual Syndrome), during pregnancy, or while breast feeding. If none of these causes can explain the tenderness, it is advisable to consult your doctor for an examination.

Prevention – for Premenstrual Breast Tenderness

Dietary

- reduce intake of alcohol.
- reduce intake of salt.
- eat a wholefood diet, with plenty of fresh fruit and vegetables and low fat protein.
- reduce intake of coffee.

Aromatherapy

- 6—8 drops of geranium oil can be used in the bath, or in a massage (15 drops in 50 ml bland carrier oil).

Herbal

- eat plenty of fresh, chopped parsley. This helps the body expel excess water.

Massage

- professional massage helps increase the circulation of the blood and lymph and prevents the buildup of toxins in the body. It may help in reducing breast tenderness if carried out a few days before tenderness is due to begin.

Exercise

- take regular vigorous exercise, such as brisk walking, running, swimming, dancing, aerobics, or racquet sports.

Relaxation

- reduce stress as much as possible, particularly in the week before your period. Attending a yoga or meditation class will help.
- ensure you get enough sleep and time for yourself.

Treatment – For Tenderness While Breast Feeding

- prepare your breasts while pregnant by massaging them with a little almond oil after a bath or shower. Avoid using soap on your nipples. Wear a cotton bra.
- if you are overproducing milk, expel a little from time to time.
- ensure you have the nipple completely in the baby's mouth: this will prevent the nipples from being tugged and moved about, causing tenderness.
- rub a little breast milk into the nipple after feeding, to help heal any cracks. Allow the nipples to dry well. Apply Calendula cream if they are still sore.

Orthodox

- treatment depends on the cause of tenderness. Diuretics (drugs to encourage the excretion of water from the body) may be recommended for premenstrual women.

Breech Baby

When a baby is in a breech position, the head lies beneath the mother's ribs, while the buttocks lie above the pelvis. Many babies turn themselves before birth; some remain in the breech position and are born without problems. However, if the baby is still in the breech position 4 weeks before the birth, it is advisable to try turn it with the techniques outlined below.

Prevention

- gentle exercise, such as regular walking for at least an hour a day, may help encourage the baby's head to go down.

Treatment

Homoeopathy

- Pulsatilla 200c, one tablet daily for 3 days, in addition to the other techniques described, may be helpful.

Massage

- before you attempt to turn the baby, consult your doctor or midwife on how the baby is lying and how he/she is likely to turn.
- lie on your back, placing several pillows under your hips, so that they are higher than your head. Relax and breathe deeply. Gently massage your stomach for about 10 minutes. Use gentle circular strokes in the direction that the baby is likely to turn. Mentally, try to communicate with your baby, encouraging her/him to turn. Repeat the exercise morning and night. It will probably take around two weeks for the baby to turn. At this point you will feel a change, and should stop the exercises and have a checkup immediately to confirm the baby's position.

Professional Help

- Chinese medicine can be helpful. Moxibustion, where a burning stick of mugwort is used to warm acupuncture points, is successful in turning a baby in many cases.

Orthodox

- your doctor may try to turn the baby before delivery. If this is not possible, an episiotomy is usually performed to widen the opening of the vagina, and forceps are used to ease the baby's delivery.

Broken Bones *see* Fractures

Bronchitis

Inflammation of the airways that connect the windpipe to the lungs. Symptoms include a persistent phlegm-producing cough and breathlessness. Acute bronchitis can last from a few days to two weeks, and usually results from a virus. It can be dangerous in the elderly and in those with heart disease. Chronic bronchitis can last for months and is usually caused by smoking and environmental pollution.

Treatment

Aromatherapy

- inhalations help clear chest congestion: add a few drops of both essential oil of eucalyptus and sweet thyme to a bowl of steaming water, sit with your face over the bowl, eyes closed, with a towel over your head and the bowl and inhale the steam vapour deeply.

Herbal

- elecampane infusion: pour a cup of cold water onto 1 teaspoon of the shredded root. Let it stand for 10 hours. Heat and sip a cupful hot 3 times daily.
- for irritating coughs, wild cherry bark infusion: pour a cup of boiling water on 1 teaspoon of dried bark, brew for 15 minutes, drink 3 times a day or as needed.

Homoeopathy

to be taken 3 times daily for up to 4 days:
- early symptoms accompanied by fever, tight chest, tickling cough, thirst: Aconite 6c.
- with loose white sputum, rattling cough and irritability: Kali bichromicum 6c.
- with loss of voice, burning throat, cough and thirst: Phosphorus 6c.

Chinese Medicine

- treatment would be aimed at preventing an attack by improving lung energy through herbs such as plantain seed, balloon flower root, honeysuckle flowers, skullcap root or gardenia fruit.

Orthodox

- cough medicines are prescribed, and inhalant drugs to open up the airways. Smokers are advised to stop immediately, and to avoid places where other people smoke to cut down on passive smoking. Antibiotics are used to eradicate secondary infection with bacteria; they can be life-saving in the frail and the elderly.

Bruises

A discoloured area under the skin which results from a knock or injury which damages minute blood capillaries, causing bleeding under the skin. Bruising occurs very easily in some diseases, such as haemophilia, where a blood clotting agent is absent. (See also Black Eye.)

Treatment for Bruises in Non-Haemophiliacs

Dietary

- if you tend to bruise easily, increasing your intake of vitamin C, bioflavonoids and zinc may help, as these nutrients strengthen the integrity of the capillaries. Vitamin C and bioflavonoids are found in citrus fruits (juice, fruit and pith), green peppers and buckwheat. Zinc is found in meat, Cheddar cheese, lentils, haricot beans, wholemeal bread and eggs.

Herbal

- bathe the bruise with a cold solution of witch hazel, available in most pharmacies.

Homoeopathy

- Arnica ointment is very effective when applied immediately to a bump or a bruise. Any household with children should have a tube handy. It should not, however, be applied to broken skin.
- Arnica 6c: take every hour after the injury for up to 6 doses; and 3 times daily the next day if pain continues.

Bach Flower Remedies

- Rescue Remedy cream is useful in relieving bruises. The drops help overcome shock.

Hydrotherapy

- make an ice pack by wrapping a packet of frozen peas in a kitchen towel. Hold the pack on the bruise for 10 minutes to reduce swelling and pain.

Orthodox

- when bruises are due to injury, treatment usually involves bathing the area in cold water or applying a cold compress. Haemophiliacs are treated with factor VIII, a blood protein which helps the blood to clot.

Bulimia

Bulimia is an illness where bouts of excessive eating are typically followed by self-induced vomiting, often carried out in secret. Women between the ages of 15 and 30 are the most common sufferers, and like those who suffer from anorexia nervosa (see entry), they have an obsessive fear of being fat, which is what prompts the vomiting. Some sufferers also use laxatives to expel food quickly. Bulimia may result in significant weight loss (though not always). If vomiting occurs frequently it can lead to dehydration, weakness and cramping. Sufferers are often depressed and sometimes suicidal. Professional treatment is essential, as this is an illness which requires psychological as well as physical support. The self help advice given in the entry on Anorexia Nervosa applies to bulimia also and can be useful in conjunction with orthodox approaches aimed at helping both the sufferer and the family.

Orthodox

- treatment is similar to that of anorexia and is best carried out in a hospital or specialized centre. It involves monitoring and regulating eating habits and counselling or psychotherapy. Antidepressants may also be prescribed.

Bunion

A painful, inflamed, fluid-filled area at the side of the big toe where it joins the foot. The toe joint abnormally projects outwards, pushing the big toe over or under the other toes. Bunions often result from wearing narrow or pointed high-heeled shoes, although they can also be an inherited condition. The bunion forms when the projecting joint rubs against shoes, causing irritation and inflammation.

Treatment

Hydrotherapy

• prepare an ice pack by wrapping a packet of frozen peas in kitchen paper. Place on the bunion for 10 minutes while sitting with the leg elevated. Remove for 10 minutes then repeat. Carry out this procedure several times morning and night.

Reflexology

ask a partner or friend to carry out the following technique:
• have the sufferer sitting with their feet up, soles facing you. Place one hand on top of the foot to support it. Place the fingers of the other hand on top of the fingers supporting the foot, and the thumb underneath the big toe. Massage deeply with the thumb around the sole of the big toe, and beneath the bunion.

Orthodox

• your doctor will recommend wearing soft, comfortable shoes. A special toe pad or corrective sock may be used to straighten the big toe. Chiropodists use a number of techniques to pad and protect the tender area. Some bunions require surgery to remove the inflamed tissue, or to rebuild the joint.

Burns

Burns and scalds can be caused by heat, friction or chemicals. Large burns (anything bigger than the palm of the hand) can lead to loss of body fluid, and require immediate medical attention.

Treatment

Aromatherapy

- after holding the burn under cold water, apply essential oil of lavender, cover with a sterile dressing if necessary and repeat the application every 24 hours.

Herbal

- the juice of the aloe vera plant is renowned for reducing pain, preventing infection, and promoting the healing of burns. Keep a plant in the house. Remove a leaf, taking care to avoid the thorns, slit it open and place on the skin allowing the juice to reach the burn.
- honey is a good healing agent. Spread a thin layer on the burn and cover with a dressing. Repeat every 2 or 3 days.

Homoeopathy

the following remedies can be of great help in reducing pain and shock. They should be taken every 30 minutes for up to 4 doses:

- immediately after the burn to relieve pain: Cantharis 6c.
- for shock, fear and restlessness: Aconite 6c.
- Nelson's burn ointment is also effective, as is Urtical (a mixture of Urtica urens and Calendula).

Bach Flower Remedies

- take 4 drops of Rescue Remedy immediately.

Hydrotherapy

- if the skin is not broken, immediately immerse the burn in cold water for at least ten minutes. Add Hypericum and Calendula tinctures (10 drops of each) to the water to relieve pain. (Do not put butter or oil on the burn.) If the injured person is to be taken to hospital, wrap the burnt area in a clean cloth soaked in cold water.
- if the skin is broken apply a sterile, non-fluffy dressing to prevent infection.

Orthodox

- severe burns are dressed. Painkillers and antihistamines may be given along with antibiotics if there is infection.

C

Calf Cramps

Spasmodic calf cramps may occur for a number of different reasons: wearing uncomfortable or high-heeled shoes, sudden strenuous exercise, or dietary deficiencies. More constant calf pain with redness and puffiness could be a sign of deep vein thrombosis (see entry) which needs immediate medical attention.

Treatment

Dietary

- increasing your intake of calcium may help avoid calf cramps. Good sources of calcium are: milk, cheese and yoghurt, dark green leafy vegetables, broccoli, canned fish, cooked dried beans and peas, almond butter and sesame products.
- vitamin D is essential for the absorption of calcium. It builds up in the skin on exposure to the sun, and is found in vitamin D-fortified milk, liver, egg yolk, cod liver oil and fish.
- for night calf cramps, vitamin E supplements have been found to help. Increase your vitamin E intake by eating wheatgerm, sunflower seeds, soya beans, olive oil, eggs and parsley. Alternatively, take a 300 iu vitamin E supplement daily.

Homoeopathy

- Cuprum metallicum 6c, sucked slowly when cramp

occurs, helps relieve the spasm and ache which follows.

Massage

- massage stimulates circulation in the veins of the legs:
- sit on a flat surface and bend your knees. Using the heel of both hands, massage the muscles of the back of the calves, starting in the middle and working outwards.
- then, using the thumbs, make small circular movements to soften the muscles all over the backs of the calves.
- these techniques can also be done in the bath with soap lather on your hands.

Acupressure

- acupressure can be useful in relieving the symptoms. Apply deep pressure to the points illustrated.

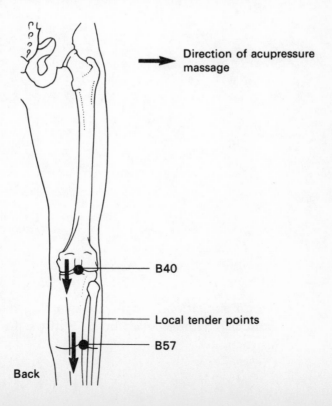

Exercise

- regular walking, cycling or swimming helps prevent cramps.
- to stretch the calf muscles during a cramp, stand facing the wall with your feet together about 2—4 feet from the wall. Place your forearms flat on the wall and lean forward, keeping your heels fixed on the floor. You should feel a stretch in the back of the calves. Move the feet back or forward to adjust the stretch.

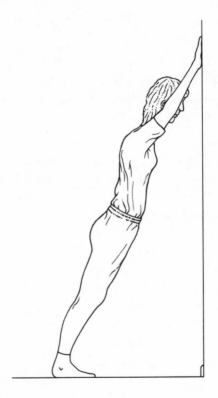

Yoga

- the sun salutation is useful for general stretching, particularly the legs (see under Stiffness for instructions).

Orthodox

- doctors recommend stretching and massaging the muscles involved. If the cramps occur at night, a drug containing calcium or quinine may be prescribed to prevent painful disturbances.

Cancer

This is a general term given to the unrestrained growth of cells in a organ or tissues which interferes with the normal functioning of the body. The most common cancer sites are the lungs, breasts, intestines, skin, stomach and the pancreas. Symptoms vary according to the type of cancer, though the following list shows common early signs and symptoms which warrant a checkup with your doctor:

rapid weight loss without an obvious cause.
a sore which fails to heal within 3 weeks.
a mole which itches, bleeds or grows.
severe headaches.
difficulty swallowing.
continuous hoarseness.
persistent abdominal pain.
change in size or shape of testicles.
change or lump in breast.
discharge or bleeding from the nipple.
vaginal bleeding or spotting between periods.
repeatedly coughing up blood.

Prevention

There is no single cause for cancer; however, the following guidelines have been identified as precautionary practices.

- avoid cigarette smoke.
- avoid exposing the skin to strong sunlight.

- as many as 70 per cent of cancers are thought to be diet-related: eat a diet rich in fibre (fresh fruit and vegetables, especially broccoli, Brussels sprouts and cauliflower, wholegrain cereals, dried cooked beans and peas); limit intake of fat, meat, sugar and alcohol; eat foods rich in beta-carotene (green leafy and orange vegetables), vitamin C (fresh fruit and vegetables), selenium (seafood, brewer's yeast, wholegrain cereals), and vitamin E (seeds, nuts and wheatgerm).
- avoid additives in food.
- avoid nitrates, found in processed meats (bacon, sausage).
- avoid contaminated or mouldy foods, particularly peanuts.
- avoid being overweight, as fat appears to promote cancer.
- take regular exercise and avoid excessive stress (see entry on Stress).
- carry out regular examinations/screening for breast, cervical and intestinal cancer. Early detection allows a greater chance of effective treatment.

Treatment

Orthodox

- surgery, radiation (X-rays or internal implants) and/or chemotherapy (drugs which kill cancer) are the common orthodox treatments. They can be very effective for some types of cancer and less so for others. All have significant side effects, and it is advisable to seek out as much information as possible about what can realistically be expected from the treatment, regarding side effects, recurrences and survival rates. Getting a second or third opinion, and talking to other people with cancer or joining a support group is helpful in making treatment decisions.

Other Therapies

A number of complementary treatments are used for cancer, some of which are now offered in orthodox establishments. The principal objective of these methods is to prepare the body and the mind to fight the disease and live in a positive way. The following approaches give some idea of the treatments you are likely to encounter.

Dietary

- based on the assumption that the patient with cancer is physically exhausted, dietary treatment aims at restoring energy. The basic premise is to enjoy all foods and drink (including alcohol, if you like) in moderation, while increasing intake of foods which provide the highest nutritional value.
- eat as much fresh food as possible, particularly organic produce.
- avoid processed foods.
- reduce animal fat (dairy products, meat).
- eat plenty of wholegrain cereals and fresh fruit and vegetables.

Homoeopathy

- trials are being carried out in hospitals in Europe using homoeopathy to treat some types of cancer. Consult the national homoeopathic organizations (see Appendix 1) for further information.

Massage

- regular massage promotes relaxation and eases pain. It helps release pent-up emotions, and provides therapeutic physical contact, which people with cancer are often lacking. Look for an experienced massage therapist with whom you feel comfortable and who you can trust.

Relaxation

- meditation, yoga, breathing exercises and visualization have all been found to be useful in relieving the discomfort, anxiety, stress and depression associated with cancer. Achieving a relaxed state helps relieve pain and is thought to aid the healing process.

Reflexology

- reflexology has also been shown to be helpful. It is not as intimate as massage, yet can provide similar effects.

Talking Therapy

- counselling, group therapy and psychotherapy are used to help release tension, aid relaxation and ease anxiety. All help prepare the body to fight the disease and improve quality of life.
- research has shown that cancer patients who attend support groups have a higher incidence of survival than those who do not (see Appendix 2 for further information).

Carpal Tunnel Syndrome

Numbness, tingling and pain in the thumb, index and middle fingers, which causes weakness and pain when writing, typing, gripping, or other activities which involve repetitive use of the wrists and hands. The condition is caused by pressure on the nerve where it passes from the wrist into the hand via the 'carpal tunnel'. Symptoms usually get worse at night and may affect one or both hands. The condition appears for no obvious reason, typically in middle-aged women, or women who are pregnant or taking the Pill.

Treatment

Practical Advice

- rest the hands as much as possible.
- take regular breaks from repetitive hand work. Try to do the exercises listed overleaf every 30 minutes.
- vitamin B6 deficiency has been linked to carpal tunnel syndrome. Studies show that taking a daily supplement of 100 mg of vitamin B6 daily, with a vitamin B complex, helps relieve symptoms after a period of 6—12 weeks.
- excessive protein intake, oral contraceptives and some food additives and drugs inhibit the body's uptake of vitamin B6. Reduce intake of protein to 50 grams daily, avoid yellow dyes in foods, and if possible, find an alternative means of contraception.

Homoeopathy

to be taken 3 times daily for up to 2 weeks:
- symptoms relieved by heat and rubbing: Magnesia phosphorica 6c.
- tendons feel contracted, loss of grip and sensation: Causticum 6c.

Hydrotherapy

- prepare an ice pack by wrapping a bag of frozen peas in kitchen towel, place it on the wrist for 10 minutes, then take it off for 10 minutes. Repeat 4 times. Carry out this procedure morning and night.

Acupressure

- place your left thumb in the centre of the back of the wrist, two and a half fingers' width from the crease joining the wrist to the hand. Put your fingers around the other side of the wrist. Apply firm pressure to these points (see illustration overleaf) for one minute. Repeat on the other wrist.

- place your left thumb on the centre of the back of the wrist at the point where the hand joins the wrist. The fingers of the left hand should be directly behind on the inside of the wrist. Apply firm pressure for 1 minute and repeat on the other side.

Exercise

do the following exercises at least 4 times daily to relieve numbness and tingling:
- clench your fists, then spread your fingers out. Repeat 20 times.
- circle the hands, rotating from the wrist, for about 2 minutes.
- then do the same exercise with your hands above your head. This relieves tension in the arms and neck.

Professional Help

- osteopathy, chiropractic, massage and acupuncture are effective treatments for this condition.

Orthodox

- a corticosteroid injection may be given to relieve pain. Diuretics (drugs to expel water from the system) are sometimes used if fluid retention is the cause. As a final resort surgery may be carried out, to sever the thick fibrous band which presses on the nerve in the carpal tunnel.

Cataract

The gradual loss of transparency of the lens of the eye, resulting in cloudy or distorted vision. Cataracts are most common in the elderly, though they can also occur in newborn babies as a result of infection.

Treatment

Dietary

naturopaths believe that cataracts result from free radical damage to the proteins in the lens. They recommend a high intake of antioxidants to combat free radicals:

- increase intake of vitamin C, found in fresh fruit and vegetables, particularly citrus fruits (oranges, grapefruit, lemons), Brussels sprouts, strawberries and broccoli. Studies have shown that taking 1 g of vitamin C daily brings a reduction in cataract development.
- increase intake of selenium, found in wholegrain cereals, brown rice and oatmeal.
- increase intake of vitamin E, found in vegetable oils, wheatgerm and nuts.
- increase intake of beta-carotene, found in yellow, orange and green leafy vegetables.
- avoid free radicals: cigarette smoke, air pollution, and rancid fats.

Homoeopathy

- Cineraria maritima mother tincture diluted 1:50 and used as an eyebath: twice a day for 3 weeks.

Chinese Medicine

- hachimijiogan is a common remedy used to treat this condition in China and Japan. It is a combination of different herbs which has been shown to be effective in both preventing and treating cataracts. Professional treatment is advised.

Orthodox

- once a cataract has developed there is no way of reversing it. The lens is surgically removed and replaced by an artificial one. The results of surgery are usually good.

Celiac Disease *see* Coeliac Disease

Cellulite

Puckered areas of fatty flesh, often referred to as 'orange peel skin'. Cellulite generally occurs around the tops of the thighs, hips, buttocks and upper arms, and is more common in women than men. Nobody really knows what causes cellulite, yet many theories abound on how it can be treated.

Treatment

Dietary

cellulite is thought by some to be caused by a buildup of toxins in the body, resulting from eating the wrong food, living in a polluted environment and suffering from poor elimination. The following dietary recommendations may help:
- do not smoke.
- avoid caffeine (coffee, tea, chocolate, cola) and alcohol;

instead, drink plenty of mineral water and dilute fruit juices.

- some naturopaths advise a detoxification programme, where only raw food is eaten for several weeks.
- constipation may contribute to cellulite (see entry for treatment).

Aromatherapy

- a good blend to use is 4 drops each of juniper berry and rosemary, and 3 drops each of cypress and patchouli, in 1 fl oz/30 ml of carrier oil or lotion. This should be massaged into the cellulite twice daily in a circular motion.

Herbal

- fresh parsley is a rich source of vitamin C, a good detoxicant, and a diuretic (it helps the body eliminate water). Eat plenty of the herb, raw in salads.
- **caution:** not to be used during pregnancy.

Hydrotherapy

- in France a popular treatment for cellulite is directing powerful jets of alternating hot and cold water on the body. You can do the same with a strong shower hose directing the water against the problem area for 5–10 minutes each day. Finish up with a cold spray.

Massage

- deep massage stimulates the circulation and the elimination of waste products and excess water thought to cause cellulite. Regular massage from a professional therapist may help eliminate cellulite.
- self-massage should be carried out carefully. Ensure you use oil or a talc. Begin with light upward strokes, increasing the pressure gradually. Daily massage with a massage glove or brush in the shower or bath is also helpful.

Exercise

- cellulite seems to afflict those who lead a sedentary life. A regular exercise programme which incorporates at least 30 minutes of aerobic exercise (such as walking, cycling or swimming), 3 times a week, is necessary in dealing with this problem.

Orthodox

- doctors recommend moderate weight reduction (see Obesity), regular exercise and a healthy diet. Cosmetic surgery, known as liposuction, introduces a long thin hollow tube into the fatty area and sucks out the excess fatty tissue. The technique holds some risks and only provides temporary relief.

Cervical Erosion

This is a common ailment in women of childbearing age. It manifests as a reddish sore on the cervix or neck of the womb, beside the cervical opening, which results from hormonal changes during or after pregnancy, or taking the Pill. It can also be caused by using an IUD or the friction of intercourse. Symptoms include white discharge with an unpleasant odour, and sometimes a bloody discharge. A cervical smear test (Pap smear) will confirm diagnosis.

Treatment

Herbal

- golden seal infusion used as a douche: add a cup of boiling water to 1 teaspoon of the herb, infuse for 15 minutes, strain and allow to cool. Use in a sterile douche daily for 3 or 4 weeks. (Golden seal stains, so take care of clothing.)

Hydrotherapy

- hot and cold sitz baths can be used to stimulate blood circulation to the cervix and encourage healing. Use a bath and a tub or large bowl of water, fill one with hot water (105—115°F/40—46°C). Spend 30 seconds in the hot, then 3 seconds in the cold. Repeat 3 times, finishing with the cold. Ensure you wrap up well afterwards. Carry out this treatment every other day.

Orthodox

- in cases producing severe symptoms, heat or freezing treatments are used to cauterize the area of erosion.

Chapped Skin

Rough, sore or cracked skin on areas that have been left wet and exposed to the wind or cold. Chapping usually occurs on the hands, face or lips, when the natural oils which keep the skin soft are depleted.

Treatment

Practical Advice

- to prevent chapped hands, wear gloves when doing household chores, and avoid immersing hands in water as much as possible.
- always dry hands thoroughly and apply a rich lanolin-based hand cream.
- if the skin on the face is chapped, always apply moisturizer before going outside.
- in winter, place bowls of water around the house to counteract the dry air caused by central heating, which draws moisture out of your skin.
- for chapped lips, always apply a lip salve before going outside during the winter; apply sunscreen in summer.

Dietary

- continuously chapped skin may indicate a dietary deficiency. Ensure you incorporate plenty of fatty acids in your diet by eating sufficient vegetable oil (olive, sunflower, or safflower).
- increase intake of vitamin D, obtained by exposure to sunlight, and vitamin A, found in cod liver oil, egg yolk, mackerel and liver, carrots and carrot juice.
- vitamin E oil or cream rubbed into the skin can also help.

Aromatherapy

- once a week steam the face over a basin of hot water to which 2 drops of geranium have been added. Then add 2 drops of either chamomile, patchouli or lavender (or one drop each of the last two) to 10 ml carrier oil or lotion and massage into the skin.

Homoeopathy

take 3 times daily for up to 4 days, repeat if necessary:
- deep cracks with a watery discharge: Petroleum 6c.
- cracks and chapping with the formation of a yellow crust: Graphites 6c.
- cracks in the middle of the lips from exposure to sea air: Natrum muriaticum 6c.

Orthodox

- doctors recommend the practical advice above.

Chicken Pox

A very infectious disease spread by the shingles or chicken pox virus. Symptoms include fever, rash (blisters which turn into scabs), and fatigue. The disease is common in children, and it can be serious in adults, particularly the elderly.

Treatment
Dietary

- you may not feel like eating solid foods, but do ensure you get plenty of fluids, particularly fruit and vegetable juices, rich in vitamin C (orange, grapefruit, lemon). When you feel ready, move on to broths, soups and solid steamed vegetables and fresh fruit until your appetite is back to normal.

Aromatherapy

- essential oil of peppermint soothes the rash: add 1 drop of the oil to a litre of water, apply regularly to the spots.

Homoeopathy

- if you or your child has been in contact with chicken pox or shingles: Rhus toxicodendron 6c, twice daily for 10 days, as a preventive measure.
- remedies for children during the illness: to be taken 4 times daily for up to 5 days:
  - in peevish child who resents being held: Antimonium tartaricum 6c.
  - in whining child who won't be left alone: Pulsatilla 6c.
  - in feverish, restless child: Rhus toxicodendron 6c.

Chinese Medicine

- teas made from safflowers, honeysuckle flowers or cimicifuga tube are recommended.

Bach Flower Remedies

- to relieve the rash: Chicory, Hornbeam or Cherry Plum.

Hydrotherapy

- apply cool, wet towels to soothe the rash.
- soak in a lukewarm bath to which a handful of oatmeal or baking soda has been added. This is particularly helpful to relieve discomfort before sleeping.

Orthodox

- doctors prescribe calamine lotion to relieve the discomfort of the rash, dab it on whenever needed. Paracetamol is sometimes given to reduce fever.

Chilblains

Painful and itchy swellings, which generally occur on the hands, feet or ears in response to the cold. They are generally a result of poor circulation, which can be aggravated by smoking.

Treatment

Aromatherapy

- essential oil of black pepper or rosemary stimulates blood circulation. Massage the feet with 2—4 drops of essential oil in 10 ml of carrier oil or lotion. Alternatively, dab the oil neat on the chilblain.

Herbal

- if the skin is not cut or cracked, dust cayenne powder on the chilblains to stimulate blood circulation.
- if the skin is broken, rub in Calendula ointment to promote healing.

Homoeopathy

to be taken every 30 minutes for up to 6 doses:

- for red, swollen chilblains that burn and itch: Agaricus 6c.
- Nelson's Tamus ointment is effective when applied to the chilblains.

Chinese Medicine

- bad circulation is seen as a deficiency in yang *qi*. Cinnamon twigs, red sage, dried ginger and angelica would be recommended.

Hydrotherapy

- for chilblains on the feet, plunge the feet for 30 seconds first in a bowl of hot water then in cold. Repeat for 15 minutes, to stimulate circulation.

Massage

- regular massage helps improve circulation and prevent chilblains.

Folk Remedies

- add a tablespoon of honey to a tablespoon of glycerine, mix with an egg white and a little flour to make a paste. Spread this over the chilblains and leave for 24 hours.

Orthodox

- doctors advise wearing several thin layers of clothing to trap heat and protect from the cold. Sometimes creams containing menthol and camphor can be useful.

Chlamydia

Chlamydia is one of the most common sexually transmitted diseases. In men it produces burning on urination, discharge from the penis and swelling of the testicles, which may lead to infertility. Women may experience early symptoms of vaginal discharge, soreness or bleeding after intercourse, stinging or burning when passing water. When left untreated, chlamydia can lead to pelvic inflammatory disease (see entry) and infertility. It has also been linked to miscarriage, ectopic pregnancy, premature birth and eye infections in newborn babies.

Prevention

- using a condom helps prevent transmission of the bacteria from one partner to another.
- if your partner has symptoms it is advisable to have a checkup as chlamydia can be symptomless in women.
- women who are planning a pregnancy are advised to have a chlamydia test.

Treatment

Orthodox

- due to the risks of infertility or miscarriage brought by this condition, treatment with antibiotics is recommended. Metronidazole, chlorhexidine pessaries, tetracycline, or erythromycin (if you are pregnant) are usually prescribed. The treatments below can be used as an adjunct to orthodox treatment, helping to strengthen the immune system and restore the body to good health after medication.

Dietary

- by strengthening your immunity you can help the body fight this infection. Eat a wholefood diet with plenty of low fat protein, fruit and vegetables.
- supplementation with vitamin E (200 iu daily) and zinc (15 mg daily) has been shown to bring increased resistance to chlamydia.
- to build healthy intestinal flora after antibiotics, eat

plenty of 'live' yoghurt. Alternatively, take 1 teaspoon of *Lactobacillus acidophilus* 1 teaspoon of *Bifidobacteria* powder, and ½ teaspoon of *Lactobacillus bulgaricus* (available from health food stores) in a glass of spring water, 3 times daily.

Aromatherapy

• use 1 drop of essential oil of tea tree in a water douche.

Professional Help

• homoeopathy and Chinese medicine are helpful.

Cholesterol, High

Normal blood cholesterol is considered to be between 3.6 and 7.3 mmol (millimols) per litre (140–280 mg/dl). Excess cholesterol (which usually accumulates as a result of eating the wrong foods) circulates in the blood, and can deposit in fatty layers in arteries, clogging them up (atherosclerosis, see entry) and contributing to the risk of heart disease (see Coronary Heart Disease).

Prevention/Treatment

Dietary

• reduce intake of animal fats (meat, dairy produce and eggs). Avoid red meat, eat moderate amounts of poultry, skimmed milk and low fat cheeses and spread.
• replace saturated fats with polyunsaturated ones.
• avoid full-fat dairy products, ice cream, confectionery made with fat, savoury snacks containing fat, and fried foods.
• increase intake of wholegrain bread and cereals, fruit and vegetables, cooked dried beans and peas, fruit juices and mineral water.

- use olive oil — which contains monounsaturated fats — for cooking. Avoid products containing coconut or palm oil.
- oat bran and rice bran have been shown to reduce cholesterol. The recommended daily intake is ½ cup per day cooked as cereal, or incorporated into your meals.
- eat moderate amounts of nuts and avocados. These contain monounsaturated fat, which is thought to help lower cholesterol.
- try to replace the meat content of your diet with fish, particularly salmon, tuna, trout, mackerel and sardines. Fish oil has been shown to reduce cholesterol.

Herbal

- raw garlic has been shown to reduce harmful blood fats. Use it raw in salads and make garlic bread. Eating it with parsley helps eliminate the lingering odour.

Exercise

- aerobic exercise helps lower cholesterol levels. Any activity which raises the pulse and respiration rate significantly for more than 20 minutes is most effective. Jogging, swimming, skipping, and brisk walking are all good.

Relaxation

- studies have shown that simple relaxation can lower cholesterol levels. Learning to meditate, or attending a yoga class, will help you achieve deep relaxation. The following daily routine will also help:
  - lie on a firm surface, close your eyes and be aware of how your body feels. Focus your attention on each part of your body, starting with your face and eyes. Consciously try to relax every part in turn.

The whole procedure should take at least 10 minutes.
- relaxation tapes and biofeedback are helpful if you find it hard to relax.

Orthodox

- a low fat, high fibre diet is recommended. In severe cases, drugs are prescribed to lower the fat content of the blood.

Chronic Fatigue Syndrome *see* ME

Cirrhosis

A liver disease caused by cell damage and the gradual buildup of scarred tissue, which prevents the liver from functioning normally to remove toxins from the blood. Heavy alcohol consumption is the most common cause. Symptoms include jaundice (yellowish tinge of the whites of the eyes and skin), fever, loss of body hair, swelling of the stomach and ankles, breast enlargement, drowsiness and confusion. Cirrhosis is a life-threatening disease and all treatment should be carried out in collaboration with your doctor.

Treatment

Dietary

- avoid alcohol.
- reduce intake of salt.
- increase intake of fibre, found in wholegrain breads and cereals, fresh fruit and vegetables, cooked dried beans and peas, dried fruit and oat bran.
- reduce intake of fats. Eat only low fat protein, such as poultry, fish, soya, nuts and beans. Drink only skimmed milk or soya milk.

- increase intake of vitamin A, found in liver, orange and dark yellow and dark green vegetables.
- increase intake of zinc, found in lean meat, poultry, fish and wholegrain cereals.
- increase intake of magnesium, found in nuts, cooked dried beans and peas, wholegrain breads and cereals, soya beans and dark green leafy vegetables.
- increase intake of selenium, found in brown rice, oatmeal, poultry and lean meat.
- a multivitamin and mineral supplement may be required to ensure adequate intake of vital nutrients to help repair liver tissue damage.
- the amino acid cystine helps protect the liver against the damage caused by alcohol: 1 g, 3 times daily taken with vitamin C.
  - **caution**: not to be used by diabetics.

Herbal

skilled treatment from a professional is advised. The following remedies have been shown to protect the liver against damage caused by alcohol.
- evening primrose oil: 3 x 500 mg capsules, 3 times daily.
- milk thistle: grind and use 1 teaspoon in an infusion 3 times daily.
- dandelion root: make a decoction by adding 1 teaspoon to a cup of water, bringing to the boil and simmering for 10 minutes; take 3 times daily.

Bach Flower Remedies

- these may help where alcoholism is a problem (see entry).

Professional Help

- acupuncture can stimulate healing of the liver.
- individual homoeopathic treatment can be helpful.

Orthodox

- the damage to the liver in alcoholic cirrhosis is irreversible, but progression of the disease may be halted by complete abstinence from alcohol. In other types of cirrhosis, orthodox medical treatment focuses on the cause of the symptoms.

Coeliac Disease

A disease most often found in small children, where the small intestine is unable to digest and absorb food as a result of sensitivity to gluten, a protein found in wheat, rye and other grains. Symptoms include diarrhoea, failure to gain weight, bloated stomach, and fatigue. In adults it can bring symptoms of depression, mood swings, fatigue, infertility, constipation, and skin eruptions.

Prevention

- some believe that coeliac disease may be related to early weaning of infants to cereals. They recommend breast feeding at least to the age of four months and then limiting cereal intake to baby rice and millet. Avoid wheat products for at least the first year.
- allergy to milk and other foods may also be related to this disorder (for more information on diagnosis and treatment, see Allergies — Food).

Treatment

- avoid all foods containing gluten. This means you should exclude all grains except brown rice, millet and corn. Use corn tortillas for sandwiches and rice cakes for crackers. Most commercially prepared foods contain gluten, so avoid prepared foods.
- eat plenty of rice, low fat meats, fish, dairy products,

vegetables, fruit and corn.
- take a multivitamin and mineral supplement daily.

Herbal

- the protein-digesting enzyme from papaya, called papain, has been shown to digest wheat gluten and make it harmless to coeliac patients. Taking papain supplements may help.
- in some, coeliac disease brings an inflamed and irritable intestine. Slippery elm can help soothe the mucous membranes of the stomach: take ¼ teaspoon of the ground powder in warm water 4 times daily.

Professional Help

- applied kinesiology is a method of muscle testing which may be used to identify if gluten is causing the problem.

Orthodox

- to ensure that gluten is the culprit, a sample of the cells of the small intestine is removed and examined microscopically. A lifelong gluten-free diet is the recommended treatment.

Colds

A viral infection which leads to inflammation of the membranes lining the nose and throat, resulting in a stuffy, runny nose, sore throat and sometimes a headache. The virus is caught by breathing in infected droplets from someone else's sneeze or cough, or touching an infected area.

Prevention

The weaker your immune system, the less able you are to resist the many strains of cold infection.

Complementary treatment usually aims at strengthening the immune system in an attempt to prevent colds.

Poor nutrition is one of the most frequent causes of a malfunctioning immune system. A low fat, high fibre diet, comprising plenty of wholegrain cereals, green, orange and yellow vegetables and fruit, moderate amounts of fish or poultry, and low fat dairy produce, should provide sufficient vitamins and minerals to nourish the immune system. A multivitamin and mineral supplement, and a vitamin C supplement (500 mg, 2 times daily) should be added when immunity is low, i.e. during and immediately after a cold.

Treatment

Dietary

- when you have a cold, drink plenty of mineral water, and juice to replace fluid loss through your streaming nose. Eat extra citrus fruit (oranges, lemons, grapefruit), or take vitamin C supplements (500 mg 3 times daily) to fight infection.

Aromatherapy

- tea tree and lemon essential oils combat infection: use a drop of each in steam inhalations.
- if the chest is congested, steam inhalation with essential oil of eucalyptus or peppermint is beneficial (add 1–2 drops to a basin of steaming water, cover the head and basin with a towel and inhale deeply). If you suffer from asthma, avoid steam inhalations; instead, inhale from a few drops on a tissue.

Herbal

- ginger promotes perspiration and soothes the throat. Pour a cup of boiling water on to 1 teaspoon of peeled and shredded fresh root, let it infuse for 5 minutes, add honey if you like and drink whenever needed.

Homoeopathy

to be taken every 2 hours for up to 4 doses:

- feeling tired, shivery, with aching limbs: Gelsemium 6c.
- feeling irritable, nose runs during the day, but congested at night: Nux vomica 6c.
- thick, greenish mucus, stabbing pains in ears and throat, irritable, chilly: Hepar sulphuris 6c.
- frequent sneezing with burning nasal discharge, streaming eyes, better in open air: Allium cepa 6c.
- hot and cold, offensive sweats, metallic taste: Mercurius solubilis 6c.

Orthodox

- generally no treatment is given, as colds usually clear up without medication within a week or two. Sometimes mild painkillers, antihistamines or decongestants are given. Antibiotics are useless against viruses and should only be prescribed if secondary bacterial infection has occurred.

Cold Sores

A blister or clump of blisters around the mouth, which erupt into a sore. They are caused by the herpes simplex virus (see Herpes, Genital) which lies dormant, and is activated by sudden exposure to hot or cold weather, exposure to direct sunlight or viral infections. Low immunity and stress may trigger an eruption.

Treatment

Practical Advice

- keep the sore clean and dry to prevent infection with bacteria.
- your toothbrush may carry the virus. Once the blister

has formed, change your toothbrush. Change it again once the attack has cleared up.
- use a potent sunblock lip salve to protect from the harmful effects of sunlight.

Dietary

- studies have shown that the amino acid L-lysine may help reduce the frequency and severity of cold sores. L-lysine is found in kidney beans, split peas, corn and wheat.
- the herpes simplex virus thrives off arginine, found in nuts, chocolate and seeds, so avoid these foods.
- a diet which incorporates wholegrain cereals, low fat dairy produce and meat, fish, and plenty of vegetables and fruit is essential to resist infection.

Aromatherapy

- geranium oil applied externally to cold sores every hour reduces pain and accelerates healing. You could also try eucalyptus.

Homoeopathy

take 1 tablet, 3 times daily as soon as the blisters start to develop. Continue dosage for up to 4 days:
- deep cracks in dry, burning lips with several blisters, or when provoked by sea air: Natrum muriaticum 6c.
- when not provoked by sea air: Rhus toxicodendron 6c.

Orthodox

- idoxuridine and acyclovir are two commonly used antiviral medications which can be applied to the affected areas as soon as symptoms begin. They will not cure the outbreak on the lips, but will reduce the duration and severity of the attack.

Colic

A baby with colic cries or screams excessively, often
drawing up his/her legs and passing wind. Colic is
generally worse in the evening, and is not eased by the
usual means of comforting — holding, feeding or nappy
(diaper) changing. Colic usually occurs in the third or
fourth week of life, and clears up by the twelfth. It is
thought to be due to intestinal spasm. If the baby is sick
between bouts of colic, or has diarrhoea, constipation or
a fever, consult your doctor.

Treatment

Dietary

- if the baby is being breast fed, it is possible that
  something the mother is eating is causing the colic.
  Cow's milk may be a culprit, in which case cutting
  out dairy produce is worth trying. To ensure
  alternative calcium intake, eat plenty of green leafy
  vegetables, chickpeas, canned fish, cooked dried peas
  and beans. Other foods which may provoke colic in
  breast fed babies are: caffeine (coffee, tea, cola,
  chocolate) wheat, citrus fruit, strawberries and spices.
- ensure that your baby eats slowly.
- if the baby is weaned, avoid bananas, yogurt, lettuce
  and gassy foods such as turnips, green peppers and
  beans.
- some children have difficulty digesting cow's milk;
  instead give soya or goat's milk.

Homoeopathy

to be taken when required by breast feeding mother, or
crushed and put into baby's milk:
- fractious and inconsolable, quietened by being carried
  around: Chamomilla 6c.
- better in the open air and soothed by gentle rocking:
  Pulsatilla 6c.

- colic improved by arching back: Dioscorea 6c.
- gurgling sound as fluid goes down, clenches thumbs and toes: Cuprum metallicum 6c.

Massage

- lay the child on his/her back, and using almond oil massage the abdomen in a clockwise direction using two or three fingers. Gently massaging the back can also help.

Acupressure

- apply deep thumb pressure to the points illustrated.

Relaxation

- anxiety and tension in the mother can sometimes be the cause of a colicky baby. This is a stressful period, so it is important that you get support and help from family or friends and if possible take time off from the baby to do something which helps relieve tension: a yoga class or regular exercise may help.

Professional Help

- craniosacral osteopaths use very gentle treatments which unwind uncomfortable strain patterns in the baby's connective tissue, thought to be caused by the physical stress of birth or pre-natal positioning. This treatment can begin at about 3 weeks after birth, but it should only be carried out by osteopaths with specific craniosacral training (see Appendix 1).

Orthodox

- doctors no longer prescribe medication for small babies with colic. They advise against overfeeding, and recommend rhythmic, soothing activities. Colicky babies are sometimes calmed by 'white noise', continuous vibratory noises, such as the drone of a vacuum cleaner, a washing machine or drier, or a fan.

Alternatively, wrap the baby up in a shawl or blanket so that movement of limbs is restricted, and walk around the house with him/her. A warm water bottle, wrapped in a towel and placed on the baby's stomach, may also help.

Colitis

Inflammation of the large intestine, causing diarrhoea, abdominal pain, and sometimes mucus and blood in the stools. The cause of colitis is unknown, though its prevalence in industrialized nations suggests it may result from lack of fibre in the Western diet.

Treatment

Dietary

- food allergies may sometimes be the cause of colitis. The most common food allergens are milk products, cereals (wheat, oats, barley, rye) and caffeine (coffee, tea, cola, chocolate). To see if you are allergic to a food, eliminate it from your diet for at least two weeks, and notice if symptoms are improved (see also Allergies — Food).
- adopt a high fibre diet, provided by whole grains (or brown rice if you are allergic to other grains), and plenty of fruit, vegetables, and lean protein.

Herbal

- garlic supports the growth of natural bacterial flora in the intestines, while killing infection. Use copiously in cooking, and chop and spread it raw on bread. Garlic capsules (3 capsules, 3 times daily) can be taken if you do not like the taste or smell of fresh garlic.
- slippery elm helps soothe the irritated mucous membranes of the intestine: add ¼ teaspoon to a glass of warm water and take 4 times daily.

Homoeopathy

take hourly for up to 6 doses and repeat if necessary:

- where there is a lot of blood and mucus in the faeces and the feeling that the bowel is not completely emptied: Mercurius corrosivus 6c.
- profuse diarrhoea accompanied by burning and colicky stomach, restlessness, anxiety and chilliness: Arsenicum album 6c.
- greenish painless diarrhoea with gurgling and stomach cramps, worse early morning: Podophyllum 6c.

Acupressure

- using the thumb, apply deep pressure to the points illustrated for at least a minute, three or four times a week.

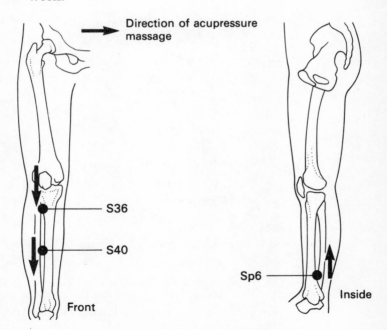

Direction of acupressure massage

S36

S40

Front

Sp6

Inside

Exercise

- the following exercises strengthen the muscles of the abdomen and help reduce distension. Try to do the

exercises at least twice daily. Start gently, and
gradually build up strength:

- lie on your back, slowly lift your straight legs
  12 inches/30 cm off the ground, lower and relax.
  Repeat 5—10 times.
- in the same position lift the legs until they are
  vertical, then open the legs apart and bring them
  together. Repeat 5—10 times.

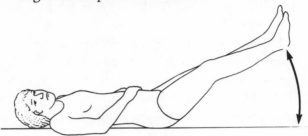

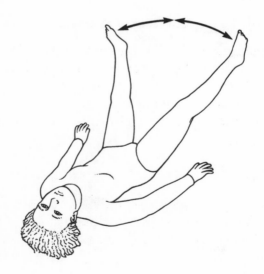

- sit ups also strengthen abdominal muscles. (Don't
  anchor your feet, and only sit half-way up.)

Orthodox

- as this disease can be mistaken for many others,
  diagnosis is made by examination of the rectum and

colon through a viewing tube (sigmoidoscopy).
Treatment is with steroid drugs, and in severe cases,
surgical removal of part of the intestine.

Conjunctivitis

In this condition, also known as pinkeye, the delicate
lining covering the outer eye and eyelid becomes
inflamed, generally due to bacteria or a virus which gets
rubbed into the eye. Sometimes the condition can be
triggered by allergies or environmental irritants, such as
smoke or chlorine from a swimming pool. Symptoms
include yellow discharge from the eye on waking, and
red, itchy eyes.

Treatment

Practical Advice

- conjunctivitis is very infectious, so ensure that you do
  not share towels, bedding or clothes. Wash your
  hands frequently.
- to soothe red, itching eyes, lie down and place a cool
  moist tea bag on each closed eye for about 10
  minutes.

Herbal

- wash the eye with Eyebright tea. Add one teaspoon
  of the herb to a cup of boiling water, allow to cool
  and strain. With an eye cup, use the solution to rinse
  the eye.

Homoeopathy

to be taken hourly for up to 4 doses and repeat if
needed:
- gritty sensation in the eye, which is worse in a
  warm atmosphere and very bloodshot: Argentum
  nitricum 6c.

- burning sensation, swollen puffy lids, better for cool bathing: Apis 6c.
- itching eyes with thick yellow discharge: Pulsatilla 6c.
- bathe the eyes several times a day in a solution of 10 drops of Euphrasia mother tincture and 1 teaspoon of salt to half a pint of warm water.

Chinese Medicine

- chrysanthemum tea is very beneficial. For children aged 4 and over, take 1 sachet in water, 3 times daily; for babies take 1 teaspoon of crystals in water, 3 times daily.

Orthodox

- use warm water to wash the eyes gently. If infection is the cause, antibiotic eye drops or ointment are prescribed. Allergic conjunctivitis is helped by antihistamine or allergy-arresting sodium cromoglycate drops (Opticrom).

Constipation

Irregular, infrequent or difficult bowel movement is generally caused by the wrong food, or lack of fluid or exercise. Stress and irregular bowel habits can also play a role. See your doctor if you have a sudden change in bowel habits which lasts more than a few days.

Treatment

Practical Advice

- never resist the urge to go to the toilet, and make a regular habit of trying to defecate once a day, to get the body into the rhythm of regular elimination.
- avoid over-the-counter laxatives: they weaken the digestive muscles, ultimately worsening the condition.

Dietary

- introduce more fibre into your diet (wholemeal bread, pasta, brown rice, unpeeled fruit and vegetables).
- drink at least 6 glasses of water per day. A warm glass on waking can stimulate bowel movement.
- constipation in children is often related to excess milk. Try reducing milk intake, replacing it with water, fresh fruits and juices, lots of green and root vegetables and wholegrain foods.

Bach Flower Remedies

- Walnut, Holly and Larch are all useful.

Herbal

- see Anal Fissure page 42.

Massage

- lie down, and oil hands lightly. Place one hand over the other, and with the fingers flat begin pressing about 1 inch into the abdomen at (1) (see illustration). Make small slow circles. Move up a little, and repeat. Continue up the left side, across above the navel, and down the right side. Make large slow sweeping

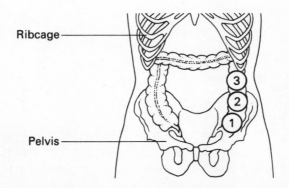

movements along the path just covered, going in the
reverse order. Repeat the whole procedure several
times, then go to the toilet. The massage should help
loosen the bowels.

Acupressure

- with your right thumb and index finger press firmly
  on the webbing between your left finger and thumb
  (see illustration) for 1 minute. Switch sides and repeat.

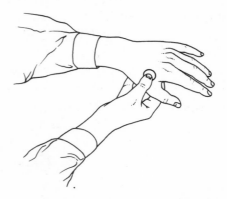

- lie on your back and place all of your fingertips
  directly between your navel and your pubic bone.
  Press in one inch; maintain the pressure for 30
  seconds, while breathing, then release.
- press firmly on the point Liver 2 on the top of the
  foot (see illustration).

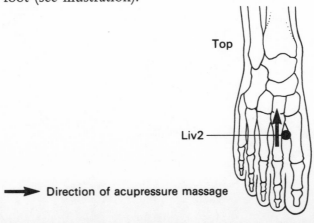

Top

Liv2

➡ Direction of acupressure massage

Exercise

- constipation is more common in those who are sedentary. Regular exercise, such as walking, jogging, cycling or swimming, helps improve bowel function.

Yoga

- every morning start the day with 2 glasses of lukewarm water, then do the following movements:
- the half shoulder stand: lie on your back and raise your legs as you inhale. Exhale, bringing your hips off the ground, bend your knees if you want to and place your hand under your hips to support yourself. While in this position take 10 breaths quickly in and out, letting your abdomen move in and out rhythmically with the breathing. Bend your legs and slowly lower your feet and hips to the ground.

Orthodox

- doctors recommend establishing a regular routine for going to the toilet. For some, a regular routine may be once a day, for others it may be once a week. Glycerin suppositories may be prescribed to help soften the motions.

Coronary Heart Disease

Malfunctioning of the heart due to narrowing or blockage of the arteries supplying the heart muscle. Heart disease brings chest pain during overexertion, stress or anxiety (see Angina). It may result in a heart attack, where shortage of oxygen causes damage to part of the heart muscle.

Prevention/Treatment

Although coronary heart disease does not generally show symptoms until after middle age, its foundations are laid early in life. The following measures implemented early in life have been shown to help prevent this condition. They can also be useful in controlling the disease.

Practical Advice

- do not smoke.

Dietary

- if you are overweight, try to lose weight, or at least avoid putting on more weight. Research shows that excess weight puts significant pressure on the heart and increases blood cholesterol levels.
- eat plenty of wholegrain cereals, fruit and vegetables, cooked dried beans and peas.
- instead of red meat and dairy produce, eat more

poultry, fish (especially oily fish, such as mackerel and salmon), and vegetable proteins.
- reduce intake of eggs, full fat dairy products, cakes, pastries and biscuits, and salt.
- cook with olive oil rather than butter or meat fat.
- eat a handful of nuts daily.

Herbal

- research from Thailand shows that hot red peppers help prevent the formation of blood clots. Introduce chilli or capsicum into your diet.
- onions and garlic also help reduce blood clotting. Use these herbs liberally in your meals or take 3 garlic capsules 3 times daily.
- fresh ginger added to the diet helps reduce the stickiness of blood platelets and reduce clotting.

Exercise

- aerobic exercise (brisk walking, jogging or an exercise class) for 20—30 minutes, 3 times a week should be a minimum for everyone, as it strengthens the heart, opens the arteries and burns off excess cholesterol.

Relaxation

stress relief is important in prevention and treatment:
- yoga and meditation help reduce stress and induce relaxation.
- massage and aromatherapy are effective methods of relaxing mentally and physically.
- biofeedback is a useful tool if you are unable to relax.

Orthodox

- drugs are prescribed to improve blood flow and reduce the work of the heart. Surgery may be recommended to bypass a diseased artery. Angioplasty is a method used which passes a type of balloon through the narrowed part of the artery to stretch it and enlarge the volume, allowing for easier blood flow.

Cough

A reflex which occurs to clear the chest airways of mucus, phlegm or irritant. Coughing is often a symptom of a common cold (see Colds). It may also be a sign of whooping cough, asthma or croup (see entries). Coughs which persist for more than a month may be bronchitis (see entry). Any unusual cough, with or without phlegm, persisting for longer than 7—10 days should be checked out by the doctor.

Treatment

Aromatherapy

- massage essential oil of eucalyptus and sandalwood or frankincense into the chest and back.
- if there is a lot of mucus, massage essential oil of myrrh on to chest and back, and drop a little on the pillow at night.
- if there are breathing difficulties: essential oil of frankincense: place a little on a tissue or handkerchief and inhale regularly.

Homoeopathy

for early symptoms, once hourly for up to 5 doses; for persistent symptoms, twice daily for 4 days:
- cough with hoarseness, much rattling in the chest, difficulty breathing: Antimonium tartaricum 6c.
- painful dry bouts of coughing, which are worse with slightest movement, patient thirsty: Bryonia 6c.
- tickling in throat, paroxysmal bouts of coughing as soon as one lies down: Drosera 6c.
- hollow crowing cough like a saw going through wood: Spongia 6c.

- machine-gun cough culminating in vomiting of mucus: Corallium rubrum 6c.
- barking cough with fever after getting chilled: Aconite 6c.
- tickling cough set off by the least draught of cold air: Rumex crispus 6c.

Acupressure

- during a fit of coughing the muscles in the upper back can go into spasm. To relieve coughing, apply pressure to the point between the shoulder blade and the spine at the level of the heart.

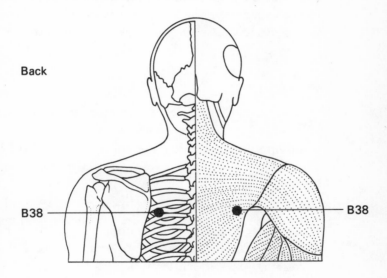

Back

B38 — B38

Orthodox

- antihistamine cough remedies may be prescribed if the patient has trouble sleeping, since one of their side effects is drowsiness. Cough suppressants are not recommended, for they prevent the body from expelling mucus or phlegm.

Cramp

A painful muscle spasm which results from excessive
contraction of the muscle fibres. Cramps usually occur
during or after exercise due to a buildup of lactic acid in
the muscles. They can also result from repetitive action
(writer's cramp), or being in an awkward position.
Night cramps may be caused by poor circulation. (See
also Calf Cramps.)

Prevention

- do at least 15 minutes of warm-up stretches before
  exercising.
- start exercising slowly and gradually build up
  exertion.

Treatment

Practical Advice

- moving and stretching the affected part relieves
  spasm.

Dietary

- if you are susceptible to cramp, increase your intake
  of calcium. Good sources are milk, cheese and
  yoghurt, dark green leafy vegetables, broccoli, canned
  fish, and sesame products (tahini, halva).
- increase intake of vitamin D, essential for the
  absorption of calcium. The vitamin builds up in the
  skin on exposure to sunshine, and is found in
  vitamin-fortified milk, liver, egg yolk and fish.
- vitamin E supplements have been shown to help night
  cramps: take 300 iu daily.

Homoeopathy

- Cuprum metallicum 6c, sucked slowly when cramp

occurs, helps relieve spasm and the ache which follows.

Hydrotherapy

- a hot shower increases circulation and brings relief.

Massage

- massage quickly relieves cramp by stimulating blood circulation and flushing out lactic acid. It also prevents the muscles becoming stiff later. Gently knead the affected muscles or ask a friend or partner to do it.

Orthodox

- massage is recommended. For frequent night cramps, a calcium-containing drug or quinine may be prescribed. If a cramp lasts for longer than an hour, consult your doctor.

Crohn's Disease

Recurrent attacks of inflammation of the gastrointestinal system, causing pain, fever, diarrhoea and weight loss. In between attacks, the inflamed tissue heals, leaving scars, which can obstruct the intestine and reduce nutrient absorption. Inflammation may also occur in the eyes and joints, and the skin may be affected by eczema.

Treatment

To be carried out in consultation with a professional.

Dietary

- many find that Crohn's disease, like colitis, can be relieved by eliminating foods which produce an allergic reaction. The most common ones are dairy

produce and grains (wheat, oats, barley, rye and corn).
Try eliminating these foods for at least 2 weeks to see
if symptoms improve. (See also Allergies — Food for
further information.)
- Crohn's disease is often accompanied by deficiency in
the following nutrients: vitamin A (found in liver,
kidney, egg yolk, butter, whole milk cheese, and cod
liver oil); beta-carotene (found in dark green, orange
and yellow fruits and vegetables), vitamin D (obtained
through exposure of the skin to sunlight, and eating
fortified milk, egg yolk, cod liver oil and fish).
- take a vitamin B complex supplement once daily.

Aromatherapy

- essential oil of lavender has been shown to induce
relaxation and relieve stress. Use it in steam
inhalations, a diffuser, a bath, or sprinkled on a
handkerchief. Compresses placed on the abdomen,
using water with a few drops of Roman and German
chamomile, are also useful.

Stress Relief

- Crohn's disease is made worse by stress. Learning
yoga or meditation can help you to counteract stress.
Hypnotherapy, autogenic training and biofeedback
can also help. Regular massage and exercise is also
beneficial.

Orthodox

- sulphasalazine, a combination of anti-inflammatory
agents, may be given to relieve the inflammation. It
sometimes causes nausea, headaches and abdominal
pain. Corticosteroid drugs are also used to reduce
inflammation. Side effects may be swelling, high
blood pressure, diabetes, or peptic ulcer.

Croup

Inflammation and narrowing of the air passages in children as a result of infection or obstruction. The symptoms are a barking cough, hoarseness, and stridor (a wheezing, grunting noise when the child inhales).

Treatment

Practical Advice

- provide as much humidity in the child's room as possible, by means of a humidifier or by placing bowls of water near radiators. During a severe attack of coughing, take the child to a steamy bathroom: the humidity will help relieve the attack. Stay with the child and try to keep him/her calm.

Herbal

- elecampane infusion is helpful in expelling phlegm and soothing the voice box and lungs: pour a cup of cold water onto 1 teaspoon of the shredded root, let it stand overnight, heat up and drink hot three times daily.

Homoeopathy

- night coughing, if the child is breathless and panicked: give one dose of Aconite 6c, and another 30 minutes later if the child is still awake.
- for a very dry, barking cough, which sounds like sawing wood: Spongia 6c, one dose, and another 30 minutes later.

Orthodox

- most cases of croup are mild and pass quickly. If the infection persists, antibiotics are prescribed. If the child is unable to breathe, or is turning blue, obtain medical help immediately.

Cuts and Scratches

Mild cuts and scratches heal quickly on their own provided they are kept clean, and the patient is healthy. Deep, penetrating cuts, particularly those contaminated by soil, may contain tetanus spores, so full immunization against tetanus is vital. The following treatments are some tips to soothe pain, ensure cleanliness and speed healing of small wounds.

Treatment

Practical Advice

- wash the broken skin with warm soap and water and remove all debris. To stop bleeding put a clean absorbent cloth over the cut and apply pressure. Elevate the wound if possible. Once the bleeding has stopped, apply a plastic or gauze bandage.

Aromatherapy

- essential oil of tea tree is a powerful antiseptic, while geranium helps to heal. Add a few drops of each to the water when washing a wound.

Homoeopathy

- Calendula ointment prevents the formation of sepsis and helps to soothe grazes and wounds.
- take Ledum 6c hourly for six doses if concerned about the risk of tetanus infection.

Bach Flower Remedies

- Rescue Remedy helps relieve the shock of a injury.

Folk Remedies

- Sugar accelerates healing and helps prevent scarring: pack a cleaned cut or wound with granulated white

sugar and cover with gauze. Rinse and repeat four
times a day.

Cystitis

A condition commonly found in women, which causes
inflammation of the inner lining of the bladder, usually
due to a bacterial infection. Antibiotics, oral
contraceptives, stress, diet and bruising during
intercourse can also cause inflammation of the bladder.
Symptoms of cystitis include a frequent or constant urge
to pass urine with little success. When urine is passed it
is accompanied by burning or stinging pain. Sometimes
the urine has blood in it. There may also be fever,
chilliness and stomach pain.

Treatment – To Relieve Discomfort

Dietary

- drink lots of water (at least 8 glasses daily), to flush
  the infection out of the bladder.
- drink sugar-free cranberry juice twice daily, or eat the
  fresh cooked fruit. Cranberries acidify the urine, and
  prevent the growth of bacteria.
- avoid tea, coffee and alcohol.
- take 1 g of vitamin C daily until symptoms are
  relieved.

Herbal

- yarrow infusion: pour a cup of boiling water onto
  1 teaspoon of the dried herb, leave to infuse for 15
  minutes. Drink warm at least three times daily.

Homoeopathy

to be taken every 30 minutes for up to 5 doses and
repeated if necessary:

- urine feels like scalding water; violently painful: Cantharis 6c.
- burning pain at the end of urination and afterwards: Sarsaparilla 6c.
- stinging pains better from cold bathing: Apis 6c.
- violently painful with blood in the urine: Mercurius corrosivus 6c.
- cystitis after sex, pain eased by urinating: Staphysagria 6c.
- where cystitis is recurrent, professional treatment will reduce the frequency and the severity of the episodes.

Hydrotherapy/Aromatherapy

- take a warm bath, add a few drops of essential oil of lavender, juniper or sandalwood to the water for further relief.
- massage the tummy and lower back with 5 drops of one of the above oils diluted in 20-25 ml carrier oil or lotion.
- rest with a warm water bottle over the abdomen.

Preventing Recurrent Attacks

Practical Advice

- do not delay the urge to urinate.
- after passing water or bowel movements always wipe from front to back, not the other way round.
- shower before intercourse (both partners).
- ensure sufficient lubrication before intercourse: use KY jelly if necessary.
- empty the bladder soon after intercourse.
- avoid douches, vaginal deodorants and powders.

Orthodox

- antibiotics are generally given to alleviate the infection. They provide quick relief, but often promote an attack of thrush (see entry) because as they kill off healthy bacteria as well as the harmful ones. If you take antibiotics, ensure you eat plenty of unsweetened 'live' yoghurt to restore healthy bacteria to the digestive system.

Dandruff

Can manifest as a dry, flaky scalp, or itchy, waxy scales
which stick to the hair and cause severe irritation. Dry
dandruff usually indicates insufficient brushing (which
usually removes the flakes), poor circulation of the scalp,
or the use of alkaline products which irritate the scalp.
Waxy dandruff may result from overactivity of the
sebaceous, oil producing glands, or from dietary
deficiencies. It may also be a symptom of a fungal
infection. Severe dandruff could be due to psoriasis (see
entry).

Treatment

Practical Advice

- brush your hair well every day with a natural bristle
  brush.
- avoid harsh dyes, and scented hair products.

Dietary

- dandruff may result from food allergies. See Allergies
  — Food.
- increase intake of vitamin A, found in liver, kidney,
  egg yolk, butter, whole milk and cream, cod liver oil.
- take a vitamin B complex supplement: 50 mg twice
  daily.
- cut down on sugar.
- some naturopaths believe that excess consumption of
  citrus fruits and juices (orange, lemon, grapefruit)

contributes to dandruff. Limit intake of these fruits; instead eat plenty of bananas, avocados, and raw and cooked vegetables.

- increase intake of zinc, found in lean meat, poultry, fish and organ meats.
- massage vitamin E oil directly into the scalp at night for 2—3 weeks.
- take a supplement of evening primrose oil, 500 mg, 6 times daily.

Aromatherapy

- for greasy dandruff, apply the following mixture to the scalp and leave on overnight: 4 drops of essential oil of cedarwood mixed with 2 drops of juniper or lemon in 10 ml carrier oil. Shampoo thoroughly in the morning and rinse. Repeat this procedure 3 times a week until symptoms are relieved.

Herbal

- infuse 30 g each of fresh or dried rosemary and sage in half a litre of water for 24 hours, use as a hair rinse daily.

Massage

- with the tips of your fingers, rub firmly in circular movements all over the scalp, as if washing the hair. Try to move the loose skin of the scalp back and forth. Pick up clumps of hair and tug a little. This will improve circulation of the scalp.

Orthodox

- your doctor will probably recommend a medicated shampoo, containing zinc pyrithione or selenium sulphide, for flaky dandruff. Shampoos containing coal tar or selenium sulphide are better for waxy dandruff. Ensure the shampoo is allowed to soak into the scalp for at least 5 minutes before rinsing.

Deafness

Hearing loss can be complete or partial, and can result from a number of different causes: ear blockage, disease, injury, degeneration of the hearing mechanism brought by loud noise or old age. In children deafness may be caused by ear infections (see Earache).

Prevention

One of the most common causes of hearing loss is exposure to loud noise. Always protect your ears with ear plugs when exposed to noisy machinery, music or gunfire.

Treatment

Practical Advice

- if you are having unusual hearing problems, check with your doctor that you do not have a buildup of excess ear wax: this causes temporary deafness but is easily treated (see Tinnitus for details).

Chinese Medicine

- acupuncture is often used in China to treat deafness, particularly when it occurs following an infection. Herbs may be prescribed to clear the infection, such as peppermint, thorowax root, plantain seed, and chrysanthemum flowers. In the elderly, a kidney tonic may be prescribed.

Professional Help

- cranial osteopathy can be effective in treating deafness which occurs after a head injury.

Orthodox

- deafness caused by infection is treated by an operation

to drain the middle ear. Wax is successfully removed by syringing. Hearing aids are recommended for those with permanent deafness.

Deep Vein Thrombosis

The clotting of blood in the deep-lying veins of the legs which inhibits the return of blood to the heart. (The same condition can occur in the superficial veins of the legs and is known as thrombophlebitis — see entry). It is generally caused by sluggish circulation due to sitting or lying for long periods. Pregnant women and women taking the Pill are more susceptible. Symptoms include pain, tenderness, swelling and discoloration of the leg, sometimes with ulceration of the skin. This is a serious complaint and treatment should be carried out in consultation with your doctor.

Prevention

- the risk of developing this condition is greatly reduced by getting people up out of bed as soon as possible after childbirth or surgery.
- if you are immobilized for long periods, try to keep the blood circulating by wiggling the toes and flexing ankles and knees.
- massage is very helpful in stimulating circulation of the veins of the legs. However, avoid massaging directly on varicose veins.
- do not smoke.
- avoid taking the Pill.
- do not sit for long periods without getting up to move your legs. When travelling, get up and walk about every 30 minutes.
- put your feet up when resting.
- wear support hosiery.

Treatment

Herbal

- hawthorn infusion stimulates the blood circulation: pour a cup of boiling water over 2 teaspoons of the berries and infuse for 20 minutes. Drink 3 times daily.
- incorporate plenty of raw garlic into your diet, or take 3 garlic capsules 3 times daily.
- ginger is also helpful in stimulating circulation. Add to your meals or make an infusion by adding a cup of boiling water to 1 teaspoon of the peeled, grated root, infuse for 15 minutes and drink 3 times daily.

Homoeopathy

to be taken every hour for up to 3 doses and repeated if necessary:
- if accompanied by varicose veins, bruised and sore: Hamamelis 6c.
- after injury, feels and looks bruised, cannot bear touch: Arnica 6c.
- unbearable bursting pain, must keep leg raised: Vipera 6c.

Hydrotherapy

- contrasting temperatures help stimulate sluggish circulation. Spray the legs first with cold water then hot for 5 minutes each. Repeat several times morning and evening.

Exercise

- exercise keeps the blood moving around the body, stopping stagnation and the formation of clots. Daily walking or swimming is helpful in preventing and treating this condition.

Orthodox

- small clots are generally left alone to break up spontaneously. Thrombolytic drugs are prescribed to dissolve larger clots. In severe cases the clot is surgically removed.

Dental Abscess

Bacteria invade a cavity in the root of a decaying or dead tooth, pus forms and creates a very tender throbbing abscess.

Treatment

Aromatherapy

- essential oil of cloves is a good painkiller: add 10 drops to 10 ml of carrier oil and apply directly.
- add a drop of each of tea tree and geranium essential oils to a glass of warm water and use as a gargle.

Herbal

- mouthwash: add 2 teaspoons of red sage leaves to half a litre of water, bring to the boil and leave covered for 15 minutes. Gargle with the warm solution for 5–10 minutes several times a day.
- golden seal is effective in attacking the bacteria associated with abscesses. It also stimulates the immune system and reduces inflammation: take 2–4 ml of the tincture in water 3 times daily.
- **caution:** not to be used during pregnancy or by those with high blood pressure.

Homoeopathy

1 dose every hour for 3 doses and repeat if needed:
- foul taste and offensive breath, profuse salivation,

pains worse at night: Mercurius solubilis 6c.
- hot and throbbing, pain relieved by clenching teeth: Belladonna 6c.
- teeth and gums excessively painful and made worse by cold drinks: Hepar sulphuris 6c.
- to promote discharge of the abscess, with sticking pains and the sensation of a hair on the tongue: Silicea 6c.

Orthodox

- if the abscess is large, antibiotics are given to prevent the spread of infection throughout the body. Once sterilized by a full course of antibiotics, the abscess is then drained, cleaned and the tooth filled, or removed.

Denture Problems

These problems can range from having a very sore mouth to experiencing difficulty talking, or even keeping the dentures in place. The following tips will help you to get used to the dentures, and ensure healthy gums.

Practical Advice

- break yourself in to dentures gradually. Don't try to wear them all the time; give your gums frequent rests.
- eat soft foods until your mouth is used to the dentures.
- to get used to talking with dentures, practise reading out loud in private. It may take a little time to habituate yourself, but practice makes perfect.
- even with dentures, you still need to clean your mouth regularly. Use a very soft brush over the gums, followed by a mouthwash (see below).
- a dental adhesive (available over the counter in

chemists) may be useful to hold the dentures in place while you are getting used to them.

Aromatherapy

- essential oil of lavender helps soothe sore gums, while tea tree is a good antiseptic: add 2 drops of each to a glass of warm water and use as a mouth rinse morning and night.

Herbal

- red sage mouthwash is effective in soothing inflamed or bleeding gums. Pour a cup of boiling water onto 2 teaspoons of leaves, allow to infuse for 15 minutes, and use as a mouth rinse as required.

Orthodox

- consult your dentist if you are suffering long-term discomfort: ill-fitting dentures, gum ulcers or an infection are common problems which can be remedied.

Depression

Depression affects people in different ways. Common symptoms include intense misery, negativity and self-doubt, tearfulness, guilt and bouts of crying, lethargy, difficulty sleeping, loss of appetite, loss of sex drive, constipation, and headaches.

Treatment

Practical Advice

- depression is a physiological and psychological illness which cannot be treated alone. One of the first steps is to seek out a trusted friend, relative or health professional with whom you can share your feelings and get advice on how to cope. Some doctors' practices have counsellors. Alternatively a self help group (see Appendix 2) may be able to offer support or recommend professional help.

- try to avoid spending long periods alone, even though you may not feel like socializing. Seek out new activities and people with whom you can share your feelings.

Dietary

- depression can sometimes result from nutritional allergies (see Allergies — Food) or deficiencies.
- avoid junk food and sugar and increase your intake of wholegrain cereals, vegetables, fruit, lean meats, low fat dairy products and fish. Take a multivitamin and mineral supplement daily.
- the amino acid tryptophan has been found to relieve depression. Natural sources include turkey, chicken, fish, cooked dried beans and peas, brewer's yeast, peanut butter, nuts and soya beans. Ensure a plentiful intake of these foods, and eat them with a carbohydrate (potatoes, pasta, rice), which facilitates the brain's uptake of tryptophan.
  - **NB:** you may have heard that synthetic drugs containing tryptophan have been withdrawn from the market. Natural food sources such as those given above are, however, completely safe.
- the amino acid D,L-phenylalanine (DLPA) has been shown to relieve depression. 100—500 mg are recommended daily.
  - **caution:** not to be taken by those with high blood pressure.

Aromatherapy

essential oil of clary sage is both a powerful relaxant and mentally uplifting. It eases mental fatigue and depression and helps bring good sleep.

- put 2—3 drops into a bowl of steaming water and

inhale, or inhale 4—6 drops from a tissue.
- add 5—6 drops to a bath.
- place 1—2 drops on the edge of the pillow.

Bach Flower Remedies

- use together or separately as needed:
Rescue Remedy, Sweet Chestnut, Mustard. (All the remedies may be of use, depending on the particular case, but these three are specifically for depression.)

Exercise

- exercise diverts the mind and alleviates mental stress. It also increases blood flow to the brain. Studies have shown that jogging for 30 minutes 3 times a week is as effective as psychotherapy in treating depression. Establish a routine of regular exercise (walking, jogging, swimming, or playing a sport) for 30 minutes at least 3 times weekly. Start gradually, building up to a more energetic pace as you go on. If you can find someone to exercise with, it will encourage you and provide more pleasure.

Professional Help

- studies have shown that some people with depression have a particular strain pattern which can be corrected by craniosacral osteopathy. This is often the case in depression which follows a shock to the system, such as childbirth, or chronic pain of a structural nature.

Orthodox

- your doctor may suggest counselling or psychotherapy. A course of drugs may also be prescribed, such as tricyclic antidepressants. These can be very effective; however, they are not without side effects. Discuss the potential effects and the expected duration of antidepressant medication with your doctor.

Dermatitis *see* Allergic Dermatitis; Eczema

Diabetes

Also known as sugar diabetes, or diabetes mellitus, this is a condition where the body produces very little or no insulin, the hormone needed to transform carbohydrates into energy. Consequently, sugar accumulates in the blood. Symptoms include the constant need to urinate, thirst, recurrent infections, fatigue and weight loss. There are two types of diabetes: insulin dependent diabetes (IDD) usually begins in childhood and requires regular intake of insulin; non-insulin dependent diabetes (NDD) typically begins later in life. All treatments should be carried out in collaboration with your doctor.

Treatment

Dietary

professional dietary treatment from a registered dietitian or a naturopath is recommended, and can be effective in treating diabetes. In mild cases of non-insulin dependent diabetes, the following dietary recommendations may help:

- 50—60 per cent of your diet should be high fibre wholegrain complex carbohydrates (wholemeal bread, rice, pasta, oatmeal, bran and other unrefined cereals).
- replace red meats with fish and chicken. Eat soya bean products as often as possible.
- eat plenty of beans, peas and root vegetables.
- replace full fat milk products with skimmed milk products.
- cut out all foods containing sugar.
- avoid all sweet fruits and juices.
- eat plenty of vegetables (raw when possible), especially cucumbers, garlic, soya beans and tofu, avocado, Jerusalem artichokes, and Brussels sprouts.

- cut out alcohol and caffeine (coffee, tea, cola, chocolate).
- take 2 tablespoons of brewer's yeast daily. This contains chromium, which helps to normalize blood sugar metabolism.
- research studies show olive oil to be helpful. Incorporate into your diet as much as possible.

Herbal

- onion and garlic have been shown to lower blood sugar levels significantly. Eat as much cooked and raw garlic as possible, or take 3—6 garlic capsules daily.
- fenugreek seed is known to have anti-diabetic effects and should be liberally incorporated into your diet.

Chinese Medicine

- diabetes has been documented in Chinese literature in ancient medical texts. Lilyturf root, grassy privet, lotus seed and Chinese yam are generally recommended. Insulin dependent diabetics may find help with professional treatment.

Exercise

- regular exercise is very important in treating diabetes. It reduces the need for insulin injections, it prevents the accumulation of cholesterol and limits weight gain. Aerobic exercise (swimming, brisk walking, jogging, or bicycling) 3 times weekly for 30 minutes is a good routine.

Orthodox

- for insulin dependent diabetics, regular injections of insulin are essential. Your doctor will also make dietary recommendations.

Diaper Rash *see* Nappy Rash

Diarrhoea

A food intolerance, a virus, or a bacteria may cause
diarrhoea. It may also result from a change of diet or
anxiety. If diarrhoea is accompanied by vomiting and
lasts for more than 24 hours, consult your doctor.

Prevention

• when travelling abroad, particularly in hot countries
  where refrigeration is lacking, avoid eating meat,
  dairy produce, raw fish and ice cream. Ensure you
  peel all fruit and eat only cooked vegetables. Drink
  only bottled drinks or boiled water and avoid ice
  cubes in drinks. Eat plenty of unsweetened yoghurt
  containing acidophilus (i.e. 'live' yoghurt) before the
  trip to ensure healthy bacteria in the digestive system.

Treatment

Dietary

• diarrhoea is one of the most common symptoms of
  food allergy (see Allergies — Food).
• during an attack, do not eat solids. To replace lost salt
  and water and to avoid dehydration (this is
  particularly important in infants and the elderly) add
  a teaspoon of salt and 2 dessertspoons of sugar to 1
  litre (2 pints) of boiled water and a half a litre (1 pint)
  of orange or lemon juice. Drink half a litre of the
  mixture per hour until symptoms subside.
• grated apple which has been left to go brown is an
  effective folk remedy to settle the stomach.
• live yoghurt which contains *Lactobacillus acidophilus*
  should be taken as a preventative measure and is an
  effective treatment for diarrhoea. Alternatively, take
  ½ teaspoon of *Lactobacillus acidophilus*, with 1 teaspoon
  of *Bifidobacteria* powder, and ½ teaspoon of
  Lactobacillus bulgaricus (available from health food
  stores) in a glass of spring water, 3 times daily.

Herbal

- golden seal infusion: pour a cup of boiling water onto 2 teaspoons of the dried root, leave to infuse for 15 minutes. Drink 3 times daily.
- **caution:** not to be used during pregnancy or by those with high blood pressure.

Homoeopathy

to be taken every 30 minutes for up to 4 doses and repeat if necessary:
- profuse diarrhoea accompanied by burning and colicky stomach, restlessness, anxiety and chilliness: Arsenicum album 6c.
- vomiting and diarrhoea with profuse cold sweats: Veratrum album 6c.
- after rich foods, stomach feels like a stone, thirstless: Pulsatilla 6c.
- after stimulants (coffee, alcohol, spices) diarrhoea alternating with fruitless urging: Nux vomica 6c.

Chinese Medicine

- for acute diarrhoea, dandelion, golden thread or skull cap root would be recommended.

Acupressure

- see illustration on page 174.

Orthodox

- diarrhoea is nature's way of getting rid of harmful bacteria or an infection, so antidiarrhoea drugs are no longer recommended, as they may prolong the problem. Recurrent, persistent or bloody diarrhoea should be investigated by your doctor.

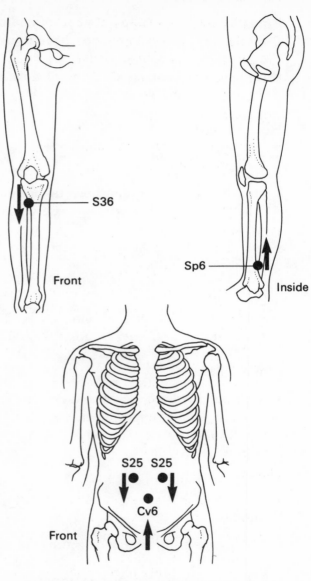

Direction of acupressure massage

Diverticulitis

The inflammation of small finger-like bulges (see Diverticulosis) of the lining of the intestines which causes pain in the lower left side of the abdomen, constipation and sometimes fever.

Prevention

- constipation is often the underlying cause (see entry for prevention).

Treatment

Dietary

- initially, low bulk foods may be required while the bowel is very inflamed and sensitive. However, it is important to incorporate more fibre into the diet gradually to help soften the motions and prevent constipation, which makes the condition worse. Gradually increase intake of cooked vegetables, brown rice and pasta, and later raw vegetables and fruit and any other whole grain cereals.
- drink at least 6 glasses of water daily.
- avoid foods with pips and seeds which may lodge in the diverticula.

Herbal

- garlic helps combat infection: incorporate liberally into your diet, or take 3—6 capsules daily.
- decoction of slippery elm helps soothe the inflamed diverticula: add 1 teaspoon of the powder to half a cup of water, bring to the boil and simmer for 15 minutes. Drink three times daily.

Massage

- using a light vegetable oil, gently massage your lower abdomen with circular strokes in a clockwise direction for several minutes before rising in the morning. Follow this with a glass of warm water or herbal tea.

Orthodox

- antibiotics are often prescribed to remedy the infection. Antispasmodic drugs may also be given to reduce pain.

Diverticulosis

This is one of the most common causes of stomach pain in anyone over the age of 60. Small pouches, known as diverticula, develop in the bowel tube in areas where there is muscle weakness. Spasm occurs in the intestine around the diverticula, leading to bloating, pain in the lower abdomen, constipation or diarrhoea or both alternately. The pouches or sacs may get clogged up with debris from the gut and become infected, leading to diverticulitis (see entry above).

Treatment

Practical Advice

- diverticulosis is often caused by irregular bowel movements and constipation. Try to establish a regular routine for passing motions, and don't delay or ignore the urge to go to the toilet when you need to (see Constipation).

Dietary

- avoid refined foods (white flour, rice, and other processed cereals).
- gradually increase intake of fibre, found in wholegrain cereals, vegetables, fruit and cooked dried beans and peas.
- drink at least 6 glasses of water daily.

- avoid pips and seeds which may lodge in the diverticula.

Herbal

- raw garlic helps combat infection. Eat a clove 3 times daily, chopped in food or made into garlic bread. Alternatively take 3–6 garlic capsules daily.
- decoction of slippery elm helps soothe the sensitive or inflamed mucous membrane of the digestive tract: add 1 teaspoon of the powder to half a cup of water, bring to the boil and simmer for 15 minutes. Drink 3 times daily.

Massage

- using a light vegetable oil, gently massage your lower abdomen with circular strokes in a clockwise direction for several minutes before rising in the morning. Follow this with a glass of warm water or herb tea.

Orthodox

- investigations may be carried out by your doctor using a simple barium X-ray or sigmoidoscopy (the passing of a hollow telescope into the back passage) to make a diagnosis. Antispasmodic drugs may be prescribed to ease stomach pain. Antibiotics will be given for severe pain and fever caused by infection.

Dizziness

A sense of being unbalanced and spinning. It may be a mild, brief symptom, or a more prolonged attack of vertigo, which usually brings nausea, sweating or fainting. The following chart lists the principal causes of dizziness:

- a fall in blood pressure on rising from a lying or

sitting position too quickly.
- fatigue (see entry).
- stress (see entry).
- anaemia (see entry).
- low blood sugar (see Blood Sugar, Low).
- Ménière's disease (see entry).
- brain haemorrhage or tumour.
- phobias (see entry).
- side effects of drugs.

Treatment

Severe, prolonged or recurrent dizziness should be reported to your doctor. The following treatments will help brief spells:

Practical Advice

- sit down, put your head between your knees and breathe deeply.

Dietary

- if living in a hot climate, take vitamin B complex supplements and extra salt to help prevent recurrent attacks.

Homoeopathy

take 2 doses 10 minutes apart and repeat if necessary:
- worse on rising from a seat, better for keeping absolutely still: Bryonia 6c.
- made worse by loud noise: Theridion 6c.
- feeling trembly and dizzy, head feels heavy: Gelsemium 6c.
- room seems to turn in a circle, sees stars before the eyes: Cyclamen 6c.

Chinese Medicine

- treatment will depend a lot on the cause, but

mulberry fruit, Chinese angelica, wolfberry and
dasdrodia tube are common herbal remedies.

Acupressure

- pinch hard between your eyebrows with the index
  finger and thumb.

Professional Help

- sometimes spinal misalignments can result in
  dizziness. It may be worth seeing an osteopath or
  chiropractor to check whether this is the cause. If so,
  treatment involving massage and adjustments to the
  spine may help.

Orthodox

- treatment is aimed at resolving the cause of dizziness.
  If the condition is caused by a disorder of the inner
  ear, antiemetic or antihistamine drugs may be
  prescribed.

Dysentery

A severe intestinal infection caused by bacteria or
parasitic amoebae. Symptoms include diarrhoea, which
can quickly lead to dehydration; fever and abdominal
pain.

Treatment

Practical Advice

- always wash your hands after going to the toilet, and
  before touching another person or preparing food.

Dietary

- replacement of salts and fluid lost through diarrhoea
  is essential to prevent dehydration (see Diarrhoea).

Add a teaspoon of salt and 2 dessertspoons of sugar
to 1 litre (2 pints) of boiled water and half a litre
(1 pint) of orange or lemon juice. Drink half a litre
of the mixture per hour until symptoms subside.
- when symptoms have subsided, introduce small
  quantities of wholegrain solids and vegetables.
- ensure adequate intake of potassium, found in
  potatoes, avocados, bananas, apricots, orange juice,
  cooked dried beans and peas.
- take a vitamin B complex supplement daily.

Homoeopathy

one dose every 10 minutes for up to 6 doses and repeat
if necessary:
- burning in the rectum and anus with involuntary
  evacuations: Aloe 6c.
- exhausting diarrhoea with cold sweats and vomiting:
  Veratrum album 6c.
- feverish and anxious with burning pain in stomach,
  better for warmth: Arsenicum album 6c.
- greenish painless diarrhoea with gurgling and
  stomach cramps, worse early morning: Podophyllum
  6c.

Herbal

- decoction of slippery elm or marshmallow soothes an
  inflamed digestive system: add a teaspoon of chopped
  marshmallow root or slippery elm powder to a cup of
  water and boil for 15 minutes. Drink 3 times daily.

Chinese Medicine

- dysentery is considered to be caused by heat and
  damp poison in the intestine. Treatment with
  anemone, white peony root and golden thread is
  recommended.

Orthodox

- antibiotics are prescribed if bacteria is the cause.
  Amoebic dysentery is eradicated by a course of the
  amoebicide metronidazole or a derivative.

Dysmenorrhoea *see* Period Pain

E

Earache and Ear Infections

Earache can be caused by a number of mechanical and pressure-related problems, by a bacterial or viral infection resulting from a cold or sore throat, or by a buildup of ear wax. Earaches often start at night, and can be accompanied by fever. They can lead to severe infection and permanent ear damage and should always be investigated by a doctor.

Prevention

- research has shown that children who are breast fed experience fewer ear infections than children who are not.

Treatment

Dietary

- recurrent earaches can sometime be resolved by eliminating dairy products from the diet. Use goat's milk products in place of cow's milk.

Herbal

- essential oil of St John's Wort: 2 drops in each ear.

Homoeopathy

to be taken every 15 minutes for up to 4 doses and
repeat if necessary:
- in the early stages of infection with sudden onset,
  feverish restlessness and painful sensitivity to noise:
  Aconite 6c.
- throbbing and stitching pains, external ear is red and
  hot, children become wild-eyed and delirious:
  Belladonna 6c.
- inconsolable and furious from the pain, cannot be
  soothed, pain worse from cold air and draughts:
  Chamomilla 6c.

Bach Flower Remedies

- if a child is panicked and frightened: Rescue Remedy.

Hydrotherapy

- for immediate pain relief hold a warm hot water
  bottle wrapped in a towel to the ear.

Acupressure

for earaches caused by sensitivity to cold, or change in
air or water pressure, which are not infected:
- press firmly with 3 fingers on the area directly in
  front of the ears for 3 minutes.
- place your middle fingers in the hollows behind the
  ear lobes; hold lightly for 2 minutes while breathing
  deeply.
- apply firm pressure to the point between the inside of
  the ankle bone and the Achilles tendon (see illustration
  overleaf). Hold for one minute each side.

Professional Help

- recurrent earaches may be resolved by cranial
  osteopathy, particularly when they have started after

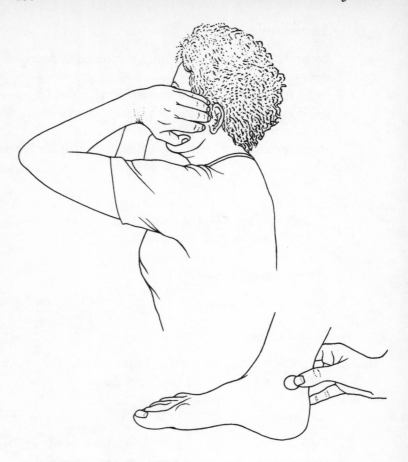

an injury, bumps to the head or spine, which can affect the drainage of the ears.

Orthodox

- inflammation or infection in the ear canal itself can be very painful and your doctor will recommend cleaning and antibiotics. Eardrum tension or the presence of infected fluid behind it also requires pain relief and antibiotics.

Eczema

Inflammation of the skin (often in creases: elbows, knees, and armpits) accompanied by itchiness, redness and sometimes the formation of blisters, scales or scabs. Eczema may result from a number of underlying factors: dietary problems, emotional stress, chemical irritants, or allergies (see Allergic Dermatitis).

Prevention

- avoid harsh detergents and soaps. Eczema can sometimes be caused by metal in jewellery or bra straps. For hand eczema, wear plastic or cotton gloves for all household and garden work.

Treatment

Dietary

- increase intake of vitamin A, found in liver, kidney, egg yolk, butter, whole milk and cream, cod liver oil.
- take a B complex supplement daily.
- increase intake of niacin, found in lean meat, fish, cooked dried beans and peas, peanut butter.
- remove potential food allergens (dairy products, wheat, corn, soya beans, all food and drink preservatives, colorants and additives. Cow's milk can be replaced by goat's or soya milk. See also Allergies — Food).
- to relieve inflammation, vitamin C and bioflavonoids act as a natural antihistamine: they can be taken in supplement form, or you can eat the fruit, pulp and rind of organic citrus fruits. Shred the peel and simmer gently in a little water and sugar until soft.

Herbal

- evening primrose oil has been shown to be successful in relieving the itching related to eczema: take 4—6

500 mg capsules twice daily (children 2—4 capsules
twice daily). This treatment may take 3—6 months to
show any effects.

Homoeopathy

eczema requires professional treatment although the
following remedies may be helpful to alleviate
symptoms temporarily. To be taken once daily for up to
7 days:
- with burning, red, hot and itching skin: Sulphur 6c.
- skin cracked with thick yellow oozing discharge:
  Graphites 6c.
- deep cracks in skin with a watery discharge:
  Petroleum 6c.

Chinese Medicine

- medical trials carried out at Great Ormond Street
  Hospital, London, have shown Chinese herbs to be
  very beneficial in treating eczema. Chinese doctors
  recommend individual prescribing, as eczema can
  result from a number of different causes. Some of the
  herbs used are oriental wormwood, Chinese gentian,
  peony root and rumania.

Acupressure

- massaging the illustrated points several times a week,
  using deep pressure, may help.

Relaxation

- eczema can sometimes be made worse by stress.
- take daily exercise (walking, swimming, jogging).
- set time aside each day for relaxation (see Stress).
- take a daily bath to which 2 drops of essential oil of
  lavender are added.

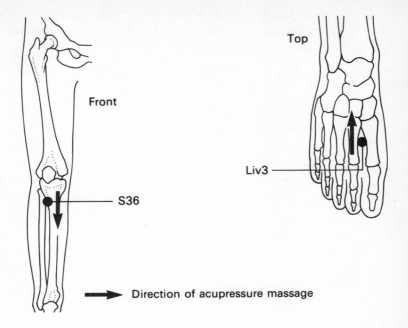

Direction of acupressure massage

Orthodox

- short-term therapy with steroid creams is recommended. However, the condition often returns and constant use of these creams can lead to thinning of the skin.

Ejaculation Problems

Conditions in which ejaculation either occurs too soon (premature ejaculation), does not occur at all (inhibited ejaculation), or when the ejaculate is forced backwards into the bladder (retrograde ejaculation).

Premature Ejaculation

A common problem, particularly in young men in new relationships. It is often due to incomplete control of the ejaculatory impulse, anxiety, or being unaware of techniques which can delay orgasm and the need to prolong sex to fulfil a partner. If premature ejaculation happens often, it can lead to dissatisfaction for both partners, resulting in loss of sex drive.

Practical Advice

- the squeeze technique: this is a form of biofeedback which allows the development of control over what is normally an automatic function. Either partner gently squeezes the head of the penis between the thumb and finger when the man is about to ejaculate, until the urge to climax has passed. This can be done several times, and ejaculatory control will gradually become automatic.
- another method is for both partners to stop thrusting a moment before ejaculation. Again, if this technique is practised routinely, automatic control is gradually achieved.

Relaxation

- stress and anxiety can sometimes make ejaculatory control even more difficult. Try to relax during lovemaking and focus more on giving each other pleasure than on penetration itself.

Professional Help

- homoeopathic remedies have been found to be helpful but an effective prescription necessitates an understanding of the individual's emotional and physical situation, so professional treatment is recommended.

Inhibited Ejaculation

A rare condition, where erection is normal, but ejaculation does not occur. It may result from taking medication, or be a symptom of an underlying disorder, such as diabetes, so discuss the problem with your doctor.

Retrograde Ejaculation

Here the valve at the base of the bladder fails to close during ejaculation. It can result from a neurological disease or from surgery on the bladder, prostate or pelvis. Avoid going to the toilet just before intercourse — having a full bladder can sometimes help resolve the problem.

Emphysema

In emphysema the air sacs deep in the lungs become damaged due to smoking or air pollution. They enlarge and burst, reducing the area which absorbs oxygen. Symptoms include difficulty breathing, and consequently limited exertion and expansion of the chest, and chest infections.

Treatment

To be carried out in consultation with your doctor.

Aromatherapy

- massage the chest with 20 ml light vegetable oil mixed with 2 drops of each of the following essential oils: Atlas cedarwood, peppermint, or eucalyptus.

Homoeopathy

take twice daily for 7 days; repeat if necessary:
- great rattling and suffocative wheezing but unable to produce phlegm: Antimonium tartaricum 6c.
- worse for cloudy days, warm rooms and early morning: Ammonium carbonicum 6c.
- worse for cold air and draughts and in the late evening: Hepar sulphuris 6c.

Hydrotherapy/Aromatherapy

• steam inhalations help the body to expel phlegm
when the chest is congested. Fill a basin with boiling
water, add 3 drops of essential oil of eucalyptus.
Keeping the eyes closed, put your head over the basin
with a towel over you to trap the steam and inhale
deeply for 2—5 minutes.

Reflexology

• the lung area is on the upper surface of both feet, just
below the toes, stretching from the second to fourth
toes. Gently massaging this area facilitates breathing.

Exercise

• studies have shown that daily bicycling (stationary or
outdoors) can greatly relieve the symptoms of
emphysema. Walking and swimming are also very
good. Exercise should be gentle to begin with,
building up exertion gradually. Try to breathe deeply
while exercising. Ideally such exercise should be
practised for 5 minutes three times daily.

Yoga

attending a class will help educate you to breathe better.
The following movements aid expansion of the chest
and should be done as often as is comfortable:
• arm rotation: place your fingertips on your shoulders,
inhale and bring your elbows together in front of
you. Lift them as high as possible, then bring them
back to your sides in a circle exhaling (see
illustration).
• while sitting on a stool or standing, stretch out your
arms in a breaststroke action, bringing the arms back
behind you with fingers clasped behind your buttocks
and shoulders pulled back. Inhale and lift your arms
up as far as possible. Exhale and lower the arms.

Orthodox

- regular courses of antibiotics are recommended for repeated chest infections. Bronchodilator drugs may be given to open up the remaining healthy airways linking the windpipe to the lungs. Corticosteroid drugs are sometimes given to reduce inflammation of the lungs and dispel phlegm. Oxygen therapy is usually necessary in the later stages of the disease.

Endometriosis

Fragments of the lining of the uterus, which is shed during menstruation, lodge elsewhere in the pelvic cavity, in areas of the reproductive and sometimes the digestive system. They respond to the menstrual cycle and bleed, causing cysts of varying sizes to build up. Symptoms include heavy periods, often with abdominal or back pain (generally most severe toward the end of the period), painful intercourse, and sometimes, constipation or diarrhoea. Endometriosis can be a cause of infertility.

Treatment

Practical Advice

- tampons can sometimes inhibit menstrual flow; sanitary towels may be more comfortable.
- if sexual intercourse is painful, use a lubricant, such as KY jelly; if you are trying to get pregnant, egg white is a good lubricant, and is said to help sperm motility.

Dietary

- cramps are caused by the production of prostaglandins which activate the uterine muscles. Oily fish, such as sardines, salmon or mackerel, contain natural anti-prostaglandins, which help reduce cramps. Alternatively take fish oil supplements or cod liver oil.
- the British Endometriosis Society recommends the following dietary supplements:
  - vitamin B6, 100 mg daily, with 25—50 mg of vitamin B complex daily.
  - calcium and magnesium improve muscle tone and reduces the pain of cramps: take a multimineral supplement containing them daily.
  - vitamin E naturally balances oestrogen and has an important part to play in the management of hormone levels. It helps keep scar tissue soft and flexible, reducing the pain caused by adhesions. Take 400—600 iu daily. (Consult your doctor first if you suffer from high blood pressure.)

Biochemic Tissue Salts

take 4 tablets dissolved on the tongue twice daily for 2 weeks.
- for premenstrual syndrome and depression: Kali Phos.
- for heavy periods: Kali Phos and Silica.
- for painful periods: Mag Phos.

Acupressure

- to relieve cramps, press firmly on the point which is located on the inside leg, 2 inches above the ankle bone.

Visualization

- sit or lie quietly and start breathing down into your stomach. Relax each part of your body in turn. Visualize yourself in pleasant surroundings. Then visualize the weak confused endometriosis cells, lost in the wrong place, and the strong purposeful army of white blood cells flooding in to attack the endometriosis. Imagine the scar tissue disintegrating and the internal organs pink and healthy. Carry out this procedure at least twice a day.

Professional Help

- endometriosis responds well to individual homoeopathic prescribing.

Orthodox

- regular examinations rarely show up endometriosis. Surgery must be carried out and a laparoscopy (insertion of a scope into the abdomen to take a look). The Pill or other drugs, such as danazol, inhibit ovulation and thereby prevent the changes which occur in the second half of the menstrual cycle and lead to bleeding at period times.

Epilepsy

Excessive electrical discharge from nerve cells in the brain leads to seizures which may be partial, where consciousness is maintained, or general, where consciousness is lost.

Treatment

To be carried out in collaboration with a doctor.

Practical Advice

• allergy to chemicals, pesticides, or certain foods (peanuts and tea, for example) has been seen to trigger epileptic attacks. See Allergies — Food for further information on the identification and treatment of food allergies, or consult a naturopath, applied kinesiologist or clinical ecologist.

Dietary

• some studies show that vitamin D and vitamin B6 deficiency can prompt epileptic attacks. Vitamin D is obtained through exposure to sunlight and eating fish or drinking fortified milk. Supplements of both these vitamins should only be taken under the supervision of your doctor.
• magnesium, zinc and calcium have all been found to have anticonvulsant properties. In studies a magnesium supplement of 450 mg daily successfully controlled attacks. Adequate intake of zinc and calcium can be maintained by a daily multivitamin and mineral supplement.
• low blood sugar may also be a causative factor. See Blood Sugar, Low.
• the amino acid taurine has been shown to help control seizures: 50 mg to 1 g daily are recommended.

Exercise

• exercise is beneficial, providing the condition is stable. Walking, swimming or gentle aerobics are good activities.

Professional Help

- fits which start after a head injury may be helped by cranial osteopathy.

Orthodox

- anticonvulsants and sedatives are usually prescribed to maintain the minimum level of drug in the bloodstream sufficient to control the seizures. Some cases of epilepsy can be treated by the surgical removal of part of the brain.

Episiotomy

A cut made in the skin and muscles between the vagina and the anus, to enlarge the vaginal opening during childbirth. Until relatively recently, episiotomies were performed routinely in order to avoid natural tearing and, it was thought, to prevent damage to the baby's head. Current research shows that the procedure is only necessary in rare cases of foetal distress. Studies show that natural tears generally heal quicker than surgical ones, which cut through deeper layers of tissue and can take a long time to heal.

Prevention

- during pregnancy practise pelvic floor exercises: while lying, sitting or standing, tighten and release the muscles which control urine flow ten times. Do this as many times as possible every day.
- in the last 6 weeks of pregnancy, massage the perineum (the area between the vagina and the anus) and the outer vaginal area with olive oil.
- upright births: crouching, kneeling, squatting, standing or being on all fours when giving birth helps prevent or minimize tearing and the need for an

episiotomy. Lying or sitting puts more strain on the perineum.

- do not rush or push forcefully in the second stage of birth. Follow your own instinct to deliver your child, pushing when you need to and as hard as you need to. Giving yourself time allows the perineum to expand, preventing tears.
- avoid the use of disinfectant to wash the vagina, as this washes away natural lubrication and dries up the skin.
- apply a hot towel or nappy (diaper) to the perineum. This brings blood to the area and relaxes the tissues.
- when you feel the baby's head, ease the tissues of the perineum, or massage them with a little oil. Use your own hands to help the baby out.

Treatment After an Episiotomy or a Tear

Stitching is generally required after a tear, and always after an episiotomy. The following remedies help speed healing and reduce discomfort.

Aromatherapy

- to aid healing and avoid infection, take a daily bath to which 2 drops of essential oil of both cypress and lavender have been added.

Homoeopathy

- apply Calendula cream locally, as often as needed.
- after surgical incision where there is great sensitivity: Staphysagria 6c 3 times a day for up to 7 days.

Exercise

the following stretches will help bring blood to the perineum, to promote healing.
- lie on your stomach on the floor, tighten and relax the pelvic floor muscles (the muscles which control

urination) ten times, repeat as often as possible.
- in the same position, lift one leg and tighten the pelvic floor muscles, then do the same with the other leg. Repeat on each side 10 times.

Orthodox

- doctors recommend keeping the area as clean as possible after an episiotomy, to prevent infection. Measures should also be taken to avoid constipation and straining.

Eyesight Problems

Problems with eyesight can be treated in different ways. Orthodox medicine nearly always corrects defective sight with glasses or contact lenses, though some new surgical techniques with lasers are now being used to correct the eyes themselves. The Bates Method is a complementary technique, which re-educates the eyesight through exercises. This is generally done through individual sessions with a Bates teacher. Below are some techniques a teacher would use to help common eye problems such as shortsightedness, longsightedness, presbyopia (old-age sight), and astigmatism.

- daily relaxation: palming. Sit at a chair with your elbows on a table or desk. Cover the eyes with the palms of your hands for at least 10 minutes daily. It may be helpful to listen to the radio while doing this, to allow you to forget about your eyes and relax.
- get into the habit of only using your glasses when you really need them. Leave them off as often as possible, but do not strain your eyes. However, always put the glasses on when driving or using machinery or tools.
- make a point of looking at things which interest you and which give you pleasure (flowers, children, water,

etc.). The aim of this exercise is to amplify your appreciation of sight.

- become aware of your whole range of vision. Sports, particularly racquet games, help with this.
- head swing: hold your forefinger in front of your eyes, about 6–10 inches from your face, and move it from the left to the right shoulder following it with your eyes; your neck should be loose and the head should follow the finger around. Focus on the finger, but be aware of the moving background behind.
- do the same exercise, but now focus entirely on what is behind the finger. This generally gives awareness of a doubled finger in front of the background.
- follow an imaginary finger, letting your eyes rest as far in your line of vision as they want to.

These exercises can be carried out frequently for up to half a minute each.

If You Have Difficulty Reading

- try reading the different print sizes in a newspaper. First start with the large headlines, then move on to the smaller bold print and finally the ordinary text.
- use a postcard or ruler to separate the lines.
- read a paragraph, then visualize its contents (the place, the people, the events), then read the next paragraph.
- scan a paragraph looking for words you recognize. Then scan it again looking for words with tails (p, q, y). Piecing the paragraph together in a jigsaw fashion may make reading easier.

For Tired Eyes

- ensure you are getting adequate sleep.
- lighting which is too bright or too dim can cause eye strain. Fluorescent lighting is often harsh on the eyes. Replace any flickering lights.
- if working at a visual display unit, take a 5 minute break every hour. Try to glance up and across the

room or look out of the window at regular intervals to change your range of focus.

Homoeopathy

• some remedies such as Euphrasia or Ruta graveolens may be useful — consult a practitioner.

Massage

• never massage the eyes, but you can very gently soothe the areas above and below the eyes.

To Soothe Aching Eyes

• make a pot of tea with two tea bags. Leave until it is cold, then place a tea bag on each eyelid, lie back and relax. A piece of freshly cut cucumber over the eyes has a similar soothing and refreshing effect.

Acupressure

• place your thumbs on the upper part of the eye socket near the bridge of the nose. Press upwards and breathe deeply for 1 minute.
• place your index finger in the centre of your cheeks, below the lower ridge of your eyes. Place your middle fingers directly underneath, below the cheekbone. Apply light pressure, close the eyes and breathe deeply for 1 minute.

Orthodox

• it is advisable to have a checkup with an optician or ophthalmologist to exclude serious eye conditions, such as cataracts or glaucoma (see entries). The assessment will also identify the need for glasses or contact lenses.

Facial Pain

May be caused by injury, infection (for example sinusitis: see entry), teeth and/or jaw problems, or a nerve disorder (trigeminal neuralgia is the most common type, producing a sharp, knife-like pain). Sometimes facial pain may come from a disease or injury to another area of the body, or may have no apparent cause.

Treatment

There are many factors which may lead to facial pain. It is advisable to consult a professional to rule out serious disorders.

The following self help techniques provide some immediate relief.

Massage

thorough, slow neck, scalp and face massage while lying down is very beneficial:
- place your fingertips together in a line on the middle of your forehead, resting your thumbs on your temples. Draw your fingertips outwards across the forehead. Repeat several times, then gradually move your fingers higher up your forehead and into the scalp. Continue this procedure across the scalp, always starting from the middle and working outwards (see illustration).
- massage the whole of the scalp as if washing your hair, for about one minute.

- work across the scalp gently tugging at your hair from the roots.
- placing your middle and fourth finger on your temples, and your thumb under your jaw, gently massage in the temples in circular motions.
- move your fingers to just above your ears and repeat the procedure. Continue massaging down in front of the ears and top of the jawbone.
- using the same two fingers, massage the area just below your cheekbones. Work your way along the edge of the cheekbones to the ears using very small circular movements, then massage down the upper edge of the jawbone into the chin.
- massage around the chin and the mouth.
- finally, hook the fingers of both hands over the corresponding shoulder, and sink the fingers into the large muscle running along the shoulder blades. Press down deeply for about 1 minute. Stroke the muscles of the neck from the top and side of the neck down and out to the shoulder joint.

Relaxation

- facial pain is often a result of tension — gritting the teeth, or smiling through difficult situations — and muscle spasm. Yoga, meditation and biofeedback are methods which help to reduce tension.

Professional Help

- facial pain resulting from stress, tension or a history of head or spinal injury can be greatly helped by osteopathy, particularly craniosacral techniques, or chiropractic. Acupuncture can also be very effective.

Orthodox

- treatment depends on the cause. Sinusitis is treated with antibiotics; teeth problems with dentistry; trigeminal neuralgia with the anticonvulsant carbamazepine.

Fainting

Temporary loss of consciousness due to lack of sufficient blood reaching the brain. It is often caused by pain, shock, fear, hunger or lack of oxygen. Recurrent fainting may be a sign of a more serious illness, and should be reported to your doctor.

Treatment

Practical Advice

- if a person faints do not make them sit up. Lying down allows the blood to return to the brain. Providing the patient is breathing normally, raise the feet slightly and allow them to remain lying for 15 minutes after regaining consciousness. If they do not regain consciousness after a few minutes, call emergency medical help immediately and if they are not breathing, give artificial respiration.
- if a person is feeling faint, with symptoms of dizziness, nausea, weakness or profuse sweating, they should sit on a chair with the head between the knees. Clothing should be loose and they should be kept cool. Give them some water to drink and open the windows to allow them more oxygen.

Bach Flower Remedies

- 4 drops of Rescue Remedy should be taken once the person starts to come round.

Acupressure

the following points stimulate the body to rebalance and rejuvenate. They can be helpful if you are feeling faint, or used to revive someone who has fainted:
- press firmly between the base of your nose and your upper lip, applying pressure for 1 minute.
- make fists and rub them against your lower back for 1 minute.
- rub between the groove of the big toe and second toe for 30 seconds.

Orthodox

- repeated attacks of fainting require medical investigation. Treatment will be aimed at resolving the cause.

Fallen Arches *see* Flat Feet

Fatigue

Tiredness that is not relieved by a few good nights' sleep may be due to anaemia (see entry); ME (see entry); glandular fever (see entry); depression (see entry); grief; anxiety (see entry); dietary deficiencies; toxicities derived from polluted food, smoking, drinking, or medication; or lack of fresh air and exercise. It can also be one of the very early signs of pregnancy, or a symptom of an underlying illness. If fatigue is persistent and is not relieved by some of the recommendations below, consult your doctor.

Treatment

Practical Advice

- ensure at least 8 hours' sleep a night. (If you are unable to sleep, see Insomnia). Get into a routine of going to bed early and getting up early.
- set yourself goals each day — but make them attainable ones. Knowing you are in control of your activities will help you achieve them without getting overtired.
- involve yourself in active activities in the evening, such as reading, sewing, knitting, playing a game, drawing, etc., rather than watching television.

Dietary

- low blood sugar is a common cause of fatigue which manifests mid morning or afternoon. See Blood Sugar, Low for treatment.
- iron deficiency is also a common cause of fatigue. See the dietary section under Anaemia for easily absorbed iron-rich foods.
- ensure you start the day with a nutritious breakfast.
- eat a wholefood diet which incorporates plenty of fresh fruit and vegetables, lean protein and low fat produce. Eat a number of small meals spread throughout the day rather than one huge blow-out daily.
- ensure adequate intake of complex carbohydrates (bread, potatoes, pasta, rice). Avoid 'empty carbohydrates', found in sugar (soft drinks, chocolate, cakes, etc.).
- avoid alcohol.

Aromatherapy

- essential oil of peppermint is stimulating and strengthening. Place 2 drops in a bath with 4—6 drops rosemary, or place on a tissue and inhale.

Homoeopathy

- Arnica 6c, every 10 minutes for 3 doses, taken at night, will help you switch off from the day's exertion, and improve quality of sleep.

Bach Flower Remedies

- olive: take several times a day for 4–7 days.

Exercise

- for nonspecific fatigue, which is not related to a viral infection, moderate exercise will help you sleep better and boost energy. Any aerobic exercise which works up a sweat is beneficial.

Relaxation

- fatigue is often caused by an ongoing concern or stress. If you know what is worrying you, try to discuss it with someone you trust and respect. If the problem cannot be resolved immediately, set aside some time each day when you will not think about it, or decide to give yourself a break from it and address the problem in a week or a month's time. Professional psychotherapy or counselling can help resolve issues which cause ongoing anxiety or stress.
- learning meditation or biofeedback will help you become aware of stresses in your life and how to deal with them.
- massage is an excellent way of relaxing, and is very restorative.

Yoga

yoga is an incredibly energizing activity. It enhances your breathing, allowing more oxygen into the system, it improves blood circulation by stretching the muscles, and it relaxes the mind. Attending a class regularly will help relieve fatigue. The following routine should be carried out first thing in the morning:

- stand with feet apart and arms outstretched to the side. Swing both arms as far as you can to your right, turning your head and shoulders, then back to the left. Repeat this movement 5 times.
- let your arms, head and trunk drop down to the floor in front of you. Inhale and gradually lift your trunk and head, and reach up as high as you can with your arms. Remain in the stretch for a few seconds, exhale and repeat.

Orthodox

- fatigue is one of the most common ailments reported to doctors. A routine checkup will probably be required to rule out serious illness. Treatment is aimed at relieving the cause of the problem.

Feeding Problems in Children

These problems are usually experienced by the parents, rather than by the children themselves. Parents tend to worry about the amount of food their child does not eat, rather than what they do. They have fixed ideas about how much they should and should not eat, and become a little obsessed about 'normal' weights and 'normal' growth. Feeding problems usually begin at the age of about 6 months, when weaning from milk to solids takes place.

Practical Advice

- generally, children should be encouraged to experiment with new foods without being 'forced' to eat certain things. Some toddlers tend to play slowly with their food, others are happy to be spoon fed by the parents.
- a good piece of advice is never to allow your child to

see that you are concerned over what and how much they eat. Once they see a chink in your defences, they are likely to play on it for the sake of gaining attention. Any parent worried about true nutritional deficiency, food allergy or failure to grow properly should consult a health professional.

- children generally know what kinds of foods are good for them, though they do not know what is bad for them. If a child repeatedly refuses a food it is likely that it does not agree with him/her. Some restraint should be exercised, however, if the child constantly demands sweet and sugary foods and junk food and drink.

Homoeopathy

- feeding problems respond well to individualized prescribing.

Feet, Aching

Fallen arches (see Flat Feet) or varicose veins (see entry) can cause aching feet, as can walking or standing for long periods. Ill-fitting shoes, corns, calluses and bunions (see entry) can all contribute.

Prevention

- being overweight puts more strain on the feet; try to maintain your recommended weight.
- avoid wearing high-heeled or ill-fitting shoes for long periods. Alternate with well-fitting, flat-heeled shoes, and periods of going barefoot.

Treatment

Practical Advice

- go barefoot when you are at home.

- put your feet up whenever possible.
- try not to stand for long periods without taking regular breaks.
- wear support tights for varicose veins (see entry).
- use shock absorbing insoles in shoes, especially if you are pregnant or suffering from arthritis of the knees, hips or spine.

Aromatherapy

- add six drops of essential oil of both eucalyptus and rosemary to a bowl of hot water. Soak your feet in it for 5–10 minutes. Then alternate, running hot and cold water (30 seconds of each) over your feet to improve circulation. Finish up with cold water. If you like, replace two of the drops with 2 of peppermint essential oil.

Massage

- sit on the floor and bend your knee, so your left foot is flat on the floor. Place the fingers of both hands under the foot and your thumbs on top below the ankle. Use your thumbs to press down and out from the ankle bones to the toes; try to run your hands between the bones of the feet rather than on them.
- still using the thumbs, use small circular motions to massage the area just above the toes.
- take hold of the big toe with thumb and fingers, circle the toe several times and gently pull it away from you. Repeat with the other toes.
- turn your foot over to one side and massage the ball of the foot underneath, using the thumbs.
- use a foot roller to massage under the feet.

Professional Help

- foot pain can be helped by professional osteopathy, reflexology, or chiropractic.

Orthodox

- treatment would address the cause of the pain. In the UK chiropodists are specialized in dealing with feet problems; in the USA a podiatrist may help.

Fever

Fever is defined as a body temperature over 37° Celsius (98.6° Fahrenheit) measured by mouth, and may be accompanied by shivering, thirst, and hot skin.

It is generally a sign of the body fighting infection, though it can also result from overexposure to heat or cold, or, in children, a result of a shock or emotional disturbance. If fever lasts longer than three days, consult your doctor. In children consult your doctor immediately if your child has any of the following symptoms:

- a temperature of over 40° C/104° F.
- becomes vague and confused.
- starts to twitch.

Treatment

Practitioners of complementary medicine consider fevers to be more of a sign of healing than a symptom of disease. In children fever often restores balance, making them feel much better afterwards.

Dietary

- eat the minimum, drink plenty of fluids. Lemon and honey with warm water prevents dehydration and provides energy.
- fever leaves the body exhausted; once the temperature has gone down, build strength with plenty of vegetables, given as soups, fresh fruit and juices, and later wholegrain cereals and lean protein.

Herbal

- catmint infusion reduces body temperature: pour a
  cup of boiling water onto 1 teaspoon of the dried
  herb, infuse for 15 minutes, and drink 3 times daily.

Homoeopathy

to be taken every 15 minutes for 4 doses and repeat if
needed:
- sudden fever after getting chilled, worse around
  midnight, frightened: Aconite 6c.
- hot, flushed skin and bright staring eyes, delirious,
  hot head with cold limbs: Belladonna 6c.
- cold to the touch but complains of burning pains,
  wants small amounts to drink at frequent intervals,
  restless and anxious: Arsenicum album 6c.

Bach Flower Remedies

- Rescue Remedy is helpful, particularly if the fever
  results from a shock, or the child is frightened. Place
  2 drops under the tongue.

Hydrotherapy

- apply cold wet compresses or sponge down the skin
  with tepid or cool water to reduce heat.

Orthodox

- doctors generally recommend paracetamol or aspirin
  for adults and children over 12 years.

Fibrillation

Fibrillation is one of the most common types of
irregular heart beat. It is seen in 5—10 per cent of all
people over the age of 65. Symptoms may be totally
absent, and the condition is discovered at routine

examination, though occasionally palpitations, shortness of breath and faintness occur. These symptoms may also indicate thyroid disorders (see Hyperthyroidism and Goitre), which need to be ruled out. Diagnosis is generally made by taking an electrocardiogram (ECG).

Treatment

Practical Advice

the following techniques can help reduce palpitations:
- hold your breath.
- slowly drink a glass of water.
- bathe your face in cold water.
- pinch your nostrils and blow through your nose.

Dietary

- reduce intake of caffeine (coffee, tea, chocolate, cola); sugar, spices.
- stop smoking.
- avoid alcohol.
- take magnesium (as part of a multimineral supplement); 50—100 mg daily.

Massage

- regular massage from a friend, partner or therapist is also helpful in promoting relaxation and taking pressure off the heart.

Exercise

- gentle walking or swimming is good for this condition.

Relaxation

- learning to meditate, attending a yoga class or practising biofeedback will all help you to relax, and prevent this condition from worsening. The following routine should be carried out at least once daily:

- lie on a firm surface, close your eyes and become aware of how your body feels. Focus your attention on each part of your body, starting with the tips of the toes and finishing with your face and eyes. Consciously try to relax every part in turn. The whole procedure should take at least 10 minutes.
- if anxiety prevents you from relaxing, try to find a friend or professional you can talk to and resolve the problems. Counselling or psychotherapy may help.

Professional Help

- acupuncture can be helpful in restoring the heart's rhythm to normal.

Orthodox

- drugs are usually prescribed to regulate the heart beat. Sometimes electric shock treatment is given to regulate the heart, or surgery may be performed to insert an artificial pacemaker.

Fibroids

Non-cancerous growths in the womb. They often produce no symptoms, but as they grow may cause heavy and long menstrual periods, painful intercourse, and bladder or bowel pressure. Sometimes fibroids can cause infertility.

Treatment

Practical Advice

- the growth of fibroids appears to be related to hormonal imbalance, particularly the overproduction of oestrogen. Coming off the Pill or hormone replacement therapy (both of which provide synthetic oestrogen) may help prevent further growth.

Dietary

- reduce intake of animal fat and increase intake of fibre. This helps reduce the production of oestrogen and restore hormonal balance.
- increase intake of vitamin C and bioflavonoids (found in the skin, peel and outer layer of fruits and vegetables, such as citrus fruits, and in leafy vegetables and red onions).
- increase intake of vitamin E (found in wheatgerm, vegetable oils, seeds and nuts).
- increase intake of vitamin A (found in liver, kidney, egg yolk, butter, fortified margarine and milk).

Visualization

- lie or sit in a relaxed position and a quiet atmosphere. Let your attention go to the area of the fibroids, focus your attention on them and experience how they feel. Try to create an image of the fibroids (it can be what you think they really look like or an abstract); keep focusing on that image, allowing it to change and evolve. Then try to form an image of something which could be done to make the fibroids reduce in size. Finally visualize what the womb looks like without the fibroids.
- if you find you are unable to do visualization alone, a practitioner of autogenic training or a counsellor, psychologist or psychotherapist can teach you.

Professional Help

- fibroids respond well to professional homoeopathic treatment.
- acupuncture can also be effective.

Orthodox

- small fibroids tend to cause no problems and often disappear after the menopause. Those which cause problems are removed surgically, an operation which may or may not involve a hysterectomy (removal of the womb).

Fibrositis

Pain and stiffness in the muscles and ligaments around joints, most commonly in the neck and shoulder area. This can be caused by overuse, or injury. Most commonly it is a result of bad posture and tension in the body.

Treatment

Aromatherapy

• taking a bath to which 4 drops of essential oil of lavender have been added relieves pain and reduces inflammation. Add essential oil of lavender to your massage oil for further effect.

Homoeopathy

every 30 minutes for 4 doses and repeat if necessary:
• stiffness and pain after unaccustomed physical exertion: Arnica 6c.
• stiffness after rest, improved by continued motion: Rhus toxicodendron 6c.
• stiffness and discomfort that worsens with continued motion: Bryonia 6c.

Hydrotherapy

• take a bag of frozen peas, wrap it in a cloth and apply to the painful area for 10 minutes. Follow this with 10 minutes of heat provided by a hot water bottle wrapped in a towel. Repeat. Carry out treatment twice daily.

Massage

- turn your neck slightly to one side. Take hold of the large muscle (the sternocleidomastoid) which runs from the base of the skull to the collar bone, hold it with fingers and thumb and squeeze firmly up and down the muscle. Turn your head the other way and repeat on the other side.

Acupressure

- lie on your front. Ask a partner to place the pads of their thumbs on either side of your spine, and apply gentle pressure, starting at the top vertebrae and working down each one. Pressure should be applied by leaning a little weight over the thumbs.

Meditation

- learning to meditate will help relieve tension, and make you aware of situations or positions which cause you to tense the muscles.

Yoga

- gently lift your shoulders up as high as you can. Hold the position for 5 seconds, then release. Repeat 5 times, morning and evening.

- circle your shoulders forward 5 times and backwards 5 times. Repeat morning and evening.
- stand facing a wall with your feet about 2–3 feet away from the wall. Place the palms of your hands on the wall just above your head. Keeping your arms and legs straight, and without moving your feet or hands, let your head and chest fall forward between your arms. Hold the position for as long as is comfortable. You should feel a stretch in the arms and shoulders. Do this exercise whenever you experience shoulder pain or stiffness.

Professional Help

- massage, osteopathy or chiropractic will all help. The Alexander Technique is helpful in correcting postural problems which often lead to fibrositis.
- acupuncture can be effective in reducing pain.

Orthodox

- painkillers and physiotherapy may be recommended.

Flat Feet

The absence of arches in the feet, which means the sole rests flat on the ground. This may be because the arch never developed, or it may be due to fallen arches as a result of weight gain, lack of exercise, wearing badly-fitting shoes, or weak muscles in the feet. Flat feet may result in aches and pains in the feet, calves and legs.

Treatment

Massage

- this is best carried out by an experienced massage therapist, a physiotherapist, osteopath or reflexologist. Treatment should concentrate on the Achilles tendon, the calves and upper legs as well as the feet.

Exercise

- stand on a hard floor, rise up onto the toes and jump into the air. Repeat 20 times morning and night.
- rock heel to toe for 3 minutes.
- while sitting, scrunch the toes up inside your shoes, allowing the foot to arch. Repeat 10 times, 10 times daily.
- practise picking up things with your toes: for example, a squash ball or a marble.

Professional Help

- osteopathy is helpful for adults. Craniosacral osteopathy can correct problems in babies and children.

Orthodox

- surgery is sometimes used to correct the bones of the feet in children. In adults, arch supports for the shoes are often recommended.

Flatulence

Also known as wind, this is the buildup of excessive air in the intestine which occurs through nervous swallowing, or gulping food and drink. Some foods, when they ferment, also produce an accumulation of gas in the intestine. Symptoms include stomach pain and a swollen belly.

Treatment

Dietary

- for those who are lactose intolerant (see Lactose Intolerance), milk can cause excessive gas. Replacing cow's milk with goat's milk or soya drinks may help.
- reduce intake of fibre, particularly beans and peas.

- reduce intake of fermented foods: cheese, soya, alcohol.
- charcoal tablets provide immediate relief by absorbing gas.
- reduce intake of carbonated drinks.
- the Hay diet may help: it recommends avoiding mixing protein and carbohydrate at the same meal (see Appendix 4).
- eat fruit *before* meals — not as a dessert or with other food.

Herbal

- infusion of sweet flag: pour a cup of boiling water on 2 teaspoons of the dried herb, infuse for 10 minutes. Drink half a cup before meals.
- ginger infusion: pour a cup of boiling water onto 1 teaspoon of grated fresh root of ginger, infuse for 5 minutes. Drink whenever needed.

Homoeopathy

to be taken every 30 minutes for up to 4 doses:
- stomach feels constantly full of gas: Argentum nitricum 6c.
- burning discomfort with some fluid reflux in the throat: Arsenicum album 6c.
- painful stuck gas, made worse by onions and garlic: Lycopodium 6c.

Chinese Medicine

- flatulence is thought to be caused by stagnation of stomach energy. Chinese doctors recommend magnolia bark, orange or lemon peel.

Reflexology

- apply pressure to the stomach point, located on the soles of both feet, above the mid line, below the ball of the foot.

- apply pressure to the large intestine point, located on the soles of both feet in the area over the lower tarsal bones.

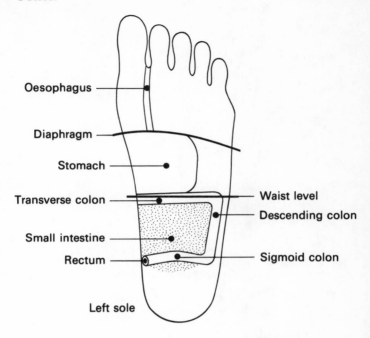

Oesophagus

Diaphragm

Stomach

Transverse colon — Waist level

— Descending colon

Small intestine

Rectum — Sigmoid colon

Left sole

Exercise

- regular exercise stimulates the digestion and promotes the reabsorption and expulsion of gas. Do not exercise within 2 hours after eating.

Yoga

the shoulder stand can help relieve the pain and discomfort of flatulence:

- lie on your back and raise your legs as you inhale, bending your knees if necessary. Exhale and lift your hips off the floor. Support them with your hands, resting your weight on your elbows. Exhale and lift your legs as high as you are able to do comfortably. Hold the position while breathing normally for several minutes, then gradually reverse the process, bringing your legs down. See illustration.

Orthodox

- usually, dietary adjustment is all that is necessary. Doctors advise reducing fibre intake. Charcoal tablets are sometimes recommended.

Flu

Caused by the influenza virus, this produces multiple symptoms including fever, headache, joint pains and a stuffy or runny nose.

Treatment

Dietary

- eat and drink plenty of vitamin C-rich foods: fresh fruits and vegetables, especially citrus fruits,

blackcurrants, Brussels sprouts and strawberries.
- increase intake of zinc, found in lean meat, fish, wholegrain breads and cereals.

Aromatherapy

- if others around you have flu, gargle daily with 1 drop of tea tree and 1 drop of lemon in a glass of warm water. Stir well before each mouthful.
- to treat flu, gargle with 2 drops of tea tree and 2 drops of geranium in a glass of warm water. Stir well before each mouthful.
- if your nose is blocked or the chest is congested, inhalations using eucalyptus or peppermint are helpful.

Herbal

- boneset infusion is one of the best remedies for flu, relieving aches and fever and clearing congestion: pour a cup of boiling water on 2 teaspoons of the dried herb and infuse for 15 minutes. Drink as hot as possible several times daily.

Homoeopathy

every hour for 3 doses, repeat if needed:
- tired and aching, apathetic, irritable, with a heavy headache and aching, heavy limbs and chills up and down the spine: Gelsemium 6c.
- with intense aching in the bones: Eupatorium perfoliatum 6c.
- chilly and very sensitive to draughts, restless and wants to stretch: Rhus toxicodendron 6c.
- heavy and aching, foul breath and diarrhoea, confused and bewildered: Baptisia 6c.

Orthodox

- aspirin or paracetamol may be recommended to relieve aches and pains, but should never be given to children under 12. For those who become chronically ill with flu (the elderly, the disabled and the immune compromised) complications may arise which require antibiotics.

Fluid Retention

Water retention may be caused by heart problems (see Coronary Heart Disease), kidney infection (see Urinary Tract Infection), premenstrual syndrome (see entry), varicose veins (see entry) or drugs. Sometimes there is no apparent cause. Symptoms include increased weight, swollen areas of the body, particularly the ankles and lower back.

Treatment

The cause of fluid retention should be investigated, and treatment carried out accordingly. In many cases, however, the underlying cause is not remediable and the following measures may help the body to excrete excess water, and make you more comfortable.

Practical Advice

- water retention in pregnancy is common and should not be a cause for concern. Lying down with your feet raised several times a day helps. Gentle exercise, such as swimming or walking, is also helpful. Reduce intake of refined carbohydrates and get as much rest as possible.
- avoid tight clothing and shoes.
- put your feet up whenever possible.

Dietary

- reduce salt intake: salt causes the body to retain water.
- eat plenty of potassium-rich foods — fresh fruit, vegetables, salads and juices.

Aromatherapy

- add 6 drops of lavender to a warm bath.
- dilute 10 drops lavender in 5 teaspoons (1 fl oz/30 ml) of carrier oil or lotion. Massage the abdomen using firm clockwise circles, massage the backs of the calves and thighs in an upward direction, and the lower back.

Herbal

- parsley is an effective diuretic (it helps the body to excrete water). Eat plenty of the raw herb or make a parsley infusion: pour a cup of boiling water onto 2 teaspoons of the chopped herb, infuse for 10 minutes in a closed container. Drink 3 times daily.
  - **caution:** not to be used during pregnancy.
- eat dandelion leaves in salads or drink dandelion 'coffee'.

Massage

- massage helps increase blood and lymph flow, and prevents the stagnation or pooling of blood in the legs and ankles. Always massage towards the heart.

Acupressure

- lie on your back on the floor. Place all your fingers between the top of the pubic bone and the navel. Press 1—2 inches into the abdomen while taking deep breaths. Hold for 1 minute.
- lying on the floor, bend the knees and bring the right foot onto the left thigh. With the right thumb, press on the inside leg where the tibia indents, just below the knee. With the left thumb, press on the point three inches above the ankle bone. Hold for one minute then do the same on the left leg.

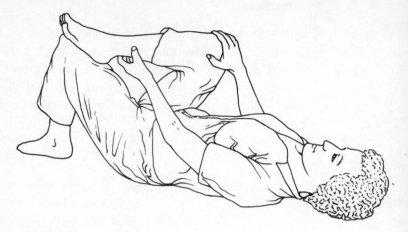

Exercise

- muscular activity helps pump blood in the veins back to the heart, which encourages elimination of waste and prevents the blood pooling in the limbs. Walking, running, cycling, swimming, dancing or aerobics are all good.

Orthodox

- diuretic drugs, in oral or injectable form, are effective in eradicating all but the most resistant forms of fluid retention. However, they should be used with caution, especially if you are taking other medication.

Food Poisoning

Usually occurs within 48 hours of consuming food or drinks contaminated by bacteria, a virus or chemical toxin. Salmonella, listeria and streptococcus are some common contaminants. Symptoms include stomach pain, vomiting and diarrhoea.

Prevention

- food poisoning or 'traveller's tummy' can be prevented by ensuring the stomach has a rich supply of healthy bacteria to fight infections: take 1 teaspoon of high potency *Lactobacillus acidophilus*, 1 teaspoon of *Bifidobacteria* powder, and ½ teaspoon of *Lactobacillus bulgaricus* (available from health food stores) in a glass of spring water, 3 times daily. Supplement this with plenty of 'live' yoghurt. While away continue to take the acidophilus mixture in a glass of water before meals. If you get symptoms of food poisoning, increase the dosage to 1 teaspoon hourly in water until symptoms subside.
- when travelling in third world countries drink only boiled or sterilized water. Avoid eating food which is not freshly cooked, or which is inadequately heated. Avoid meat, raw vegetables, unpeeled fruit, fruit juices (unless bottled) and ice in drinks (it is usually made with tap water).
- contaminants are often stored and activated in prepared food which is inadequately reheated. Avoid prepared, chilled and frozen foods.
- buy organic meat and free-range eggs, and be sure to cook them thoroughly.
- wash fruit and vegetables thoroughly.
- avoid eating raw fish or meat.

Treatment

Vomiting and diarrhoea, though unpleasant, are the body's natural way of eliminating the poison from the body as quickly as possible. Therefore, do not attempt to suppress them unless advised by a professional. The following remedies help calm the stomach, restore strength after the attack and prevent recurrences.

Practical Advice

- be sure to wash your hands thoroughly after going to the toilet, and before touching food, to prevent passing on the infection to others.

Dietary

- during the attack do not eat solids. To replace lost salt and water (this is particularly important in children and the elderly) add a teaspoon of salt and a dessertspoon of sugar or honey to one litre of boiled water and half a litre of orange or lemon juice. Drink half a litre of the mixture per hour until symptoms subside.
- once the diarrhoea and vomiting have subsided eat plain wholemeal foods, and vegetables. Bananas help settle the stomach. Live yoghurt and acidophilus powder (see above) help restore the protective bacteria in the stomach.
- take the acidophilus mixture given above in a glass of water 3 times daily for several weeks after the attack.

Herbal

- meadowsweet infusion soothes the irritated mucous membranes of the digestive system: pour a cup of boiling water on 2 teaspoons of the dried herb, infuse for 15 minutes and drink 3 times daily.

Homoeopathy

one dose every 10 minutes for up to 6 doses and repeat if necessary:
- profuse diarrhoea accompanied by burning and colicky stomach, restlessness, anxiety and chilliness: Arsenicum album 6c.
- vomiting and diarrhoea with profuse cold sweats: Veratrum album 6c.
- after stimulants (coffee, alcohol, spices) alternating with fruitless urging: Nux vomica 6c.

- burning in the rectum and anus with involuntary evacuations: Aloe 6c.
- greenish painless diarrhoea with gurgling and stomach cramps, worse early morning: Podophyllum 6c.

Orthodox

- in persistent and extreme cases drugs are recommended to alleviate exhaustion from diarrhoea and vomiting.

Foot Odour

Smelly feet often result from athlete's foot. If your feet are itchy, particularly between the toes, or if the skin is crumbling or broken, see entry on Fungal Infection. Heavy perspiration is the other major cause of foot odour. People who spend a lot of time on their feet are more susceptible.

Treatment

Practical Advice

- wash your feet often, several times a day if possible. Use warm water and soap and clean well between the toes. Dry thoroughly. Dust feet with sodium bicarbonate.
- wear cotton socks, and change them several times a day if necessary.
- do not wear the same shoes every day. Give them a chance to dry out and air. Dust the insides with sodium bicarbonate.
- wear leather shoes, never rubber, plastic or canvas. Wear open sandals when possible.

Dietary

- increasing intake of zinc and magnesium sometimes

helps alleviate foot odour. These minerals are found in wholegrain breads and cereals, poultry, fish and organ meats, nuts, cooked dried beans and peas and dark green leafy vegetables.

Aromatherapy

- dilute 10 drops of essential oil of cypress (or 8 of cypress and 2 of peppermint) in 5 teaspoons (1 fl oz/30 ml) of carrier oil or lotion. Massage into the feet morning and night to reduce perspiration and act as a natural deodorant.

Orthodox

- daily application of aluminium chloride lotion drastically reduces sweating and may be effective in reducing foot odour. Sweating can be prevented altogether by surgically cutting the autonomic nerves to the feet, but this operation is rarely carried out today.

Fractures

A break in a bone, generally caused by a fall. The bone usually breaks horizontally, but it can also fracture lengthwise, diagonally, or in a spiral. Women with osteoporosis (see entry) are more susceptible to fractures than others.

Treatment

A person with a suspected fracture should be taken to hospital immediately. If they cannot walk, call an ambulance. While awaiting medical care, prepare an ice pack by filling a plastic bag with ice or wrapping a packet of frozen peas in kitchen roll and placing it on the fracture to reduce swelling. Do not try to move the broken bone or push it back in place.

Dietary

to help build new bone cells:
- increase your intake of calcium: add non fat milk to sauces, milkshakes, casseroles, and soups, eat plenty of pulses, leafy green vegetables, and yoghurt.
- increase intake of phosphorus, found in red meat, organ meats, poultry, fish and eggs.
- increase intake of magnesium, found in nuts, cooked dried beans and peas, wholegrain breads and cereals, dark green leafy vegetables and seafood.
- increase intake of vitamin A, found in eggs, liver, butter, milk and cod liver oil.

Homoeopathy

- for shock following a fracture: Arnica 6c, every 10 minutes up to 3 doses.
- for bruising around fracture: Arnica 6c, 3 times daily for 3 days and repeat if needed.
- to aid bone repair: Symphytum 6c, twice daily for 2 weeks.

Bach Flower Remedies

- Rescue Remedy is useful in treating shock.

Professional Help

- osteopathy and chiropractic help restore muscle and ligament activity after a fracture. Physiotherapy and massage can also help.

Orthodox

- after initial pain relief or anaesthetic, x-rays are taken, the broken bones are put back in position and immobilized by means of a bandage, sling or plaster to allow healing, which may take between 2 weeks and 6 months, depending on the age of the patient and the bone broken.

Frostbite

Damage to the tissues caused by very low temperatures.
Symptoms include pins and needles, followed by
numbness. The skin becomes white and hard and later
red and swollen, blisters may form and, in severe cases,
black areas may appear.

Treatment

Practical Advice

frostbite is often accompanied by hypothermia (see
entry); both require medical attention. While waiting for
help carry out the following first aid techniques:
- shelter from the cold and cover the head and body
  with extra clothing; drink warm drinks, not alcohol.
- do not rub the frostbitten area.
- do not burst blisters.
- do not attempt to walk on a frostbitten foot or move
  the affected area.
- remove restrictive jewellery.
- gradually warm the frostbitten area by covering with
  clothing; place hands under armpits; feet under
  armpits of a companion; do not expose to direct heat.
- if warm water is available, immerse the affected area
  for several minutes, then cover with a sterile dressing.
  Keep the area warm afterwards to prevent refreezing.

Orthodox

- emergency treatment in hospital is required in severe
  cases.

Frozen Shoulder

Restricted movement and pain in the shoulder joint
which may be caused by torn muscle fibres and
inflammation. The surrounding 'capsule' or covering of

the joint itself becomes irritated. An obvious symptom of frozen shoulder is pain which occurs when lifting the arm sideways, making tasks such as brushing hair or dressing difficult.

Treatment

Hydrotherapy

- make an ice pack by wrapping ice cubes or a packet of frozen peas in kitchen towel. Prepare a hot water bottle and wrap a towel around it. Hold the ice pack over the area of pain for 3 minutes, followed by the hot water bottle for 3 minutes. Repeat the procedure 3 times and carry out several times daily.
- gentle swimming in warm water is a good way to loosen the shoulder and allow for more movement. Some hospitals have swimming pools in their physiotherapy units.

Massage

- if your right shoulder is affected, support the left elbow with your right hand, and pass the left hand over the affected shoulder. Starting close to the neck, squeeze the large muscle which passes over the shoulder blade. Try to lift the muscle as you squeeze, working all the way down to the shoulder. Repeat several times. If the left shoulder is affected, reverse the process.
- with elbow still supported, use your fingertips to stroke firmly down from the side of the top of the neck all the way along the shoulder to the shoulder joint. Repeat the procedure several times.

Acupressure

- make a fist and gently pound on the tops of your shoulders, from the joint, up to your neck.
- curve your fingers and hook them over the top of your shoulders. Feel for the area of tension and allow

your thumb to sink into it. Press firmly for 1 minute
then relax.

Exercise

- place a rolled towel under the affected armpit, and use
  the free arm to pull the elbow into the side of the
  body. This levers the upper arm, stretching the
  capsule of the shoulder joint.

Professional Help

- self treatment of frozen shoulder is very slow, and can
  be greatly aided by professional help from an
  osteopath or chiropractor. Acupuncture is helpful in
  relieving pain. The Alexander Technique will help if
  the problem is caused by postural problems.

Orthodox

- painkillers, anti-inflammatory drugs or the injection
  of steroids directly into the joint are prescribed.
  Physiotherapy is generally recommended.

Fungal Infection

Fungal infections usually affect the skin, though they
can spread to other internal organs. Common examples
are athlete's foot, causing itchiness on the feet and
between the toes, jock itch, affecting the skin around the
groin, thrush (see entry), yeast infections of the mouth
and vagina (see Oral Thrush and Vaginal Irritation),
ringworm, where disc-like shapes appear on the skin,
and dandruff (see entry). Nails can also be affected. The
infection is caused by the multiplication and spread of
common fungal organisms (usually *Candida albicans* or
tinea) which commonly cause redness, inflammation and
itching. When the nails are affected, they typically turn
white and crumbly. Fungal infections are more likely to

occur in those whose immunity is low, particularly after taking antibiotics which kill off the natural bacteria which prevent their multiplication. They can also occur when the acid/alkali balance of the body is upset by inappropriate diet, cosmetics, hormonal imbalances or other drugs.

Prevention

- to prevent athlete's foot, do not share or borrow shoes, socks or towels. Change socks and towels daily. Wear cotton socks and leather shoes.

Treatment

Practical Advice

- fungal infections thrive in damp moist environments. Wear cotton underwear to allow the skin to 'breathe', wash frequently and dry yourself thoroughly.
- ringworm: to prevent reinfection, wash all clothes thoroughly after treatment; if scalp is infected replace all brushes, combs and headgear. The infection is sometimes spread through pets: a vet can diagnose and treat infected animals.

Dietary

- enhance immunity by eating plenty of lightly cooked green, yellow and orange vegetables, wholegrain cereals, lean meat or fish.
- to discourage the multiplication of *Candida albicans*, avoid the following foods for at least one month: all sugar, including cakes and pastries, raw fresh and dried fruits and alcohol. Also avoid mushrooms, blue cheese, soy sauce and other yeast-containing foods.
- incorporate plenty of olive oil into your diet; this helps fight *Candida albicans*.
- live yoghurt helps restore healthy bacteria to the gut which is essential in fighting fungal infections. Eat at

least one 5 oz carton of plain, live unsweetened
yoghurt daily.
- avoid coffee and tea, instead drink mineral water,
  rooibos tea and other herbal teas.
- take supplements of *Lactobacillus acidophilus*:
  ½—1 teaspoon of high potency acidophilus powder
  and ½ teaspoon of bifidobacteria powder (both
  available from health food stores) in a glass of
  spring water two or three times daily.

Aromatherapy

- tea tree oil is very effective in combating fungal
  infections of the skin. Add 5 drops to the bath, or
  bathe the affected area with a solution made up of
  2 drops of peppermint and 4 of German chamomile
  added to a basin of water to relieve itching and
  redness. Dermasorb is an effective antifungal cream
  which contains tea tree oil but no drugs.

Herbal

- garlic is an effective antifungal agent: use liberally in
  cooking or take 3—6 capsules a day.
- caprylic acid, an extract of coconut, is a powerful
  antifungal agent available from health food stores:
  take 3 capsules with each meal.
- for athlete's foot: soak feet regularly for at least 30
  minutes in a strong infusion of golden seal root: add
  a cup of boiling water to 3 teaspoons of the
  powdered herb and infuse for 15 minutes. Dry feet
  well and powder with arrowroot or powdered golden
  seal root. Calendula cream may be used if cracks have
  formed.

Biochemic Tissue Salts

- Silica, 4 times daily.

Orthodox

- antifungal agents are prescribed in cream, tablet, vaginal pessary, oral solution or impregnated tampon form. Treatment is effective within a matter of days, but fungal infections have a tendency to recur; therefore, it is important to raise immunity with the help of the treatments above to prevent further infection.

Gallstones

Lumps of solid matter (mainly cholesterol) found in the gallbladder. Occasionally a stone exits from the gallbladder, blocking the flow of bile and leading to inflammation of the gallbladder, known as cholecystitis. Symptoms include pain in the upper right abdomen and sometimes between the shoulder blades, nausea, indigestion, and jaundice — yellowing of the whites of the eyes, the skin and the urine.

Prevention

- increase intake of fibre, found in wholegrain cereals, fresh fruit and vegetables, oat bran, cooked dried beans and peas.
- reduce intake of fat (except olive oil, which may be helpful), particularly saturated fat, found in animal products.
- a vegetarian diet has been shown to help prevent gallstones.

Treatment

Dietary

- reduce intake of all fats except olive oil. Do not eat fried food.
- a little alcohol each day (not more than 2 units) is thought to reduce levels of bile salts. (One unit is ½ pint of beer, a single measure of spirits or one glass of wine.)

- increase intake of fibre, particularly oat bran and guar gum.
- drink 6—8 glasses of water daily.

Herbal

- balmony is an ancient North American Indian remedy. When combined with fringetree it is an effective gallstone treatment: pour 2 cups of boiling water on 2 teaspoons of each dried herb, infuse for 15 minutes and drink 3 times daily.

Chinese Medicine

- small gallstones are dissolved with herbs such as lysimachia, pyrrosia leaf and rhubarb.

Professional Help

- food allergies may contribute to gallstones. Some naturopaths recommend an elimination diet, carried out under the supervision of a practitioner.
- professional homoeopathic treatment can help reduce the frequency and severity of attacks.

Orthodox

- when the stones are small, drugs to dissolve them may be used. Surgery is the more common treatment, which removes the stones or the whole gallbladder if necessary.

Ganglion

A cyst which develops in a joint or tendon sheath. The most common site is the back of the wrist joint, the knee or around the ankles. It may be soft or firm and is usually painless unless caught from time to time by the tendons which move against it.

Treatment

Any newly formed lump should be checked out by your doctor.

Homoeopathy

• Ruta graveolens 50M, take 1 dose.

Massage

• using the pads of your fingers and thumb, massage over the top of and around the ganglion, using gentle pressure. When carried out every morning and evening, this treatment will often make the ganglion disappear over time.

Orthodox

• early treatment used to be to hit a ganglion with a big family Bible and later with a large and heavy medical text book! While hardly a 'gentle' treatment, this was often an effective means of temporarily removing the ganglion. However, it frequently returns since the 'shell' of the cyst remains behind and closes over the resulting hole. Doctors now recommend leaving ganglions alone as they often disappear with time. Surgery is sometimes used to remove them, usually if they are cosmetically unattractive or are interfering with tendon function. A trigger finger is such an example, where one finger gets stuck down in the bent position and the ganglion prevents its being straightened without active help.

Gangrene

The death of an area of flesh due to lack of sufficient blood. The flesh becomes painful, then numb, and the skin and tissue turn black. If bacterial infection sets in it can spread to other areas, causing death to surrounding tissue. People with diabetes, arteriosclerosis, and thrombosis are more susceptible to gangrene. All treatment should be carried out in collaboration with your doctor.

Treatment

Treatment of gangrene consists of improving blood circulation to the affected area and preventing infection.

Practical Advice

- stop smoking, as it inhibits the circulation and makes the condition worse.
- keep warm. This opens up the blood vessels, encouraging circulation of blood.
- an area of the body vulnerable to gangrene should be in a postural position which encourages blood circulation. For example, a pre-gangrenous foot may be better hanging down off the side of the bed.

Dietary

- research in Canada has shown good results using vitamin E to accelerate healing in difficult wounds. The study gave patients a daily dose of 800 iu of vitamin E orally, and saturated the wound with vitamin E oil.

Massage

- massage certainly helps increase circulation and hence speeds the healing process. For this condition it is best carried out by a professional therapist.

Orthodox

- surgery is carried out to bypass or remove blockages in major arteries to restore circulation. Antibiotics are given to prevent infection. Diabetes must be under

close supervision to prevent circulatory problems
resulting in gangrene.

Gastritis

Inflammation of the delicate lining of the stomach, often
due to irritation from drugs (often aspirin), alcohol,
certain foods, tobacco, bacterial infection, peptic ulcers
(see entry) or stress. Acid stomach (see entry) can also
be a contributing factor. Symptoms include upper
stomach ache, particularly after eating, nausea and
vomiting.

Treatment

Practical Advice

* stop smoking.

Dietary

* reduce alcohol, caffeine (tea, coffee, coke, cocoa),
  carbonated drinks, curry and spicy food.
* increase intake of non-citrus fruits, raw vegetables and
  bland foods, such as brown rice, potatoes and pasta,
  and 'live' yoghurt.
* decrease intake of refined carbohydrates such as white
  bread and rice: these cause a rapid secretion of gastric
  acid which is buffered by the protein content of
  wholegrain carbohydrates.

Herbal

* golden seal infusion is an effective tonic for irritated
  mucous membranes of the digestive system: pour a
  cup of boiling water on ½ teaspoon of the powdered
  herb, infuse for 10 minutes and drink three times
  daily.

Homoeopathy

every 30 minutes for up to 4 doses; repeat if necessary:
- burning pains and vomiting, better temporarily for cold drinks: Phosphorus 6c.
- stomach feels like a stone and is very sensitive to touch: Bryonia 6c.
- stomach feels like a knot, acid reflux and hiccups: Nux vomica 6c.
- pain is better from eating but starts again 2 hours later: Anacardium 6c.

Relaxation

- do not eat when in a hurry. Try to take meals in a relaxed state and chew food thoroughly.
- biofeedback, yoga, meditation and autogenic training are helpful in relieving the stress associated with this condition.
- non-competitive exercise helps relieve stress: walking, swimming and running are all good.
- massage and aromatherapy also help with relaxation.

Orthodox

- doctors diagnose gastritis by examining the stomach lining through a gastroscope (a tube passed through the mouth into the stomach). Paracetamol or acetaminophen is recommended rather than aspirin for pain relief. Drugs may be recommended to reduce acid production and heal the stomach lining.

Gastroenteritis

Inflammation of the stomach and intestine, usually caused by a virus, bacteria or toxin in contaminated food or water, or an allergic reaction. Symptoms include nausea, vomiting and diarrhoea, stomach pain and cramp, generally lasting up to 48 hours. In infants and the elderly, seek medical advice.

Treatment

Dietary

* do not eat during the attack, but drink plenty of fluids. Water should be mixed with sugar or honey and salt (1 dessertspoon of sugar/honey, 1 teaspoon of salt to every litre of water), to avoid dehydration.
* once the diarrhoea and vomiting have subsided, eat plain wholegrain foods and vegetables. Bananas help settle the stomach. Live yoghurt helps restore protective bacteria to the stomach.
* a supplement of high potency acidophilus powder should be taken: 1 teaspoonful, along with 1 teaspoon of *Bifidobacteria* powder, and ½ teaspoon of *Lactobacillus bulgaricus* (available from health food stores) in a glass of spring water, 3 times daily.

Herbal

* meadowsweet infusion reduces acidity in the stomach, soothes the mucous membranes and reduces nausea: pour a cup of boiling water on 2 teaspoons of the dried herb, infuse for 15 minutes, and drink 3 times daily.
* after the attack, decoction of slippery elm will help soothe the digestive tract: add 1 part of the powdered bark to 8 parts of water and mix well. Tablets are also available.

Homoeopathy

one dose every 10 minutes for up to 6 doses and repeat if necessary:
* profuse diarrhoea accompanied by burning and colicky stomach, restlessness, anxiety and chilliness: Arsenicum album 6c.

- vomiting and diarrhoea with profuse cold sweats: Veratrum album 6c.
- after stimulants (coffee, alcohol, spices) alternating with fruitless urging: Nux vomica 6c.
- burning in the rectum and anus with uncontrollable diarrhoea: Aloe 6c.
- greenish painless diarrhoea with gurgling and stomach cramps, worse early morning: Podophyllum 6c.

Orthodox

- the microbiological cause of the condition should be identified. Antibiotics are not generally recommended, as they kill off 'healthy' gut bacteria. They should only be used in extreme cases of infection.

German Measles *see* Rubella

Giardiasis

An infection of the small intestine by the parasite *Giardia lamblia* which is passed through food or water or direct hand or mouth contact. It is common in tropical countries and, more recently, in developed countries where it spreads among people in institutions, particularly preschool children. Symptoms include violent, foul-smelling diarrhoea and gas, abdominal discomfort and nausea. Children with giardiasis tend to eat poorly, are tired, miserable and lose weight. Stools will be loose and smelly.

Prevention

- always wash hands thoroughly before handling food or eating and dry hands on disposable towels, air blowers or personal towels.

- in tropical countries consume only well-cooked food and bottled or boiled water.
- ensuring children have a good supply of healthy gut bacteria helps them resist infections such as giardiasis. Children under 5 ½ stone (77 pounds/35 kilos) can take ¼ teaspoon of acidophilus 3 times daily, with ¼ teaspoon of *Bifidobacteria* powder, in a glass of water.

Treatment

Antibiotics (see below) are required to rid the body of the parasite. The following self help measures complement orthodox treatment.

Dietary

- to avoid dehydration (particularly important in children and the elderly), mix a teaspoon of salt with ½ litre of boiled water, and a dessert spoon of sugar. Drink ½ litre hourly until symptoms subside.
- grated apple left to brown helps settle the stomach.

Herbal

- golden seal infusion also helps settle the system: pour a cup of boiling water on 2 teaspoons of the dried root, infuse for 15 minutes and drink 3 times daily.
- **caution:** not to be used during pregnancy or by those with high blood pressure.

Homoeopathy

one dose every 10 minutes for up to 6 doses and repeat if necessary:
- profuse diarrhoea accompanied by burning and colicky stomach, restlessness, anxiety and chilliness: Arsenicum album 6c.
- vomiting and diarrhoea with profuse cold sweats: Veratrum album 6c.
- after stimulants (coffee, alcohol, spices) alternating

with fruitless urging: Nux vomica 6c.
- burning in the rectum and anus with uncontrollable diarrhoea: Aloe 6c.
- greenish painless diarrhoea with gurgling and stomach cramps, worse early morning: Podophyllum 6c.

Orthodox

- antibiotics, such as metronidazole, are given either in a single dose or over 3 days. Sometimes a second or third dose is necessary to rid the body of the parasite. Ensure you eat plenty of 'live' yoghurt during and after taking antibiotics, to restore healthy intestinal flora which may be impaired by antibiotics. It is also advisable to take high potency acidophilus powder: 1 teaspoonful, along with 1 teaspoon of *Bifidobacteria* powder, and ½ teaspoon of *Lactobacillus bulgaricus* (available from health food stores) in a glass of spring water, 3 times daily.

Gingivitis

Inflammation and infection of the gums, often due to a buildup of plaque around the base of the teeth. Gums become red, swollen and tender and bleed easily.

Treatment

Practical Advice

good flossing and brushing is the best means of preventing and treating gingivitis. The following routine should be implemented morning and night:
- using at least 5 inches of dental floss, wrap each end around a finger from each hand. Starting with the top right back tooth, wiggle the middle area of the floss between each tooth gently up and down several times. The aim is to remove plaque, not just bits of food

caught between the teeth. Work all the way around
the mouth.
- brush teeth, gently.
- brush tongue.
- rinse mouth several times with cold water.
- use a mouth rinse.
- also brush teeth after meals.

Dietary

- eat plenty of raw vegetables and fruit.
- increase intake of vitamin C (found in citrus fruits).
- chewing cardamom seeds has been shown to prevent
  gum decay.

Herbal

- for inflamed or bleeding gums add 2 teaspoons of red
  sage leaves to half a litre of water. Bring to the boil
  and leave to stand covered for 15 minutes. Use as a
  mouth rinse several times a day.
  - **caution**: not to be used during pregnancy.
- myrrh tincture is an effective anti-microbial: add
  1—4 drops in a cup of warm water and rinse the
  mouth with the mixture 3 times daily.
- **caution:** not to be used during pregnancy.

Homoeopathy

twice daily for up to 5 days. Repeat if necessary:
- tender bleeding gums with metallic taste and profuse
  salivation: Mercurius solubilis 6c.
- gums bleed from slight touch and bleeding is slow to
  stop: Phosphorus 6c.

Orthodox

- regular visits to the dentist should include
  professional cleaning and removal of plaque. Your
  dentist may recommend an antibacterial mouthwash.

Glandular Fever

Also known as infectious mononucleosis, this is caused by the Epstein Barr virus. It is common in the 10—25 year old age group and is generally transmitted through saliva, hence it is also known as the 'kissing disease'. Symptoms include exhaustion, fever, sore throat, muscular aches and pains and swollen lymph glands, particularly in the neck.

Treatment

Practical Advice

- rest is very important in treating this condition. You may feel tired for 2 or 3 months after recovery, so take it easy to prevent a relapse.
- alcohol and smoking should be avoided.

Dietary

- a wholefood diet with plenty of fresh fruit and vegetables is vital to build resistance. If you cannot eat easily, take freshly squeezed fruit juices and vegetable soups.
- take 500 mg of vitamin C 3 times daily.
- take a 50 mg vitamin B complex supplement 3 times daily.
- to boost immunity after an attack, eat a wholefood diet rich in fruit and vegetables, with a high intake of foods rich in the following nutrients:
  - vitamin A, found in liver, kidney, egg yolk, low fat dairy products, cod liver oil.
  - beta-carotene, found in dark green, yellow and orange vegetables and fruits.
  - vitamin E, found in vegetable oils, seeds, wheatgerm and nuts.
  - vitamin C, found in vegetables and fruit.
  - the B vitamins, particularly vitamin B6, found in

    lean meat, wheatgerm, brewer's yeast, fish, soya
    beans, peas, peanuts.
- copper, iron, zinc, selenium, found in lean meats,
  poultry, fish, wholewheat bread, brown rice and
  oatmeal.

Herbal

- tincture of myrrh helps fight infection. Take 1—4 ml
  of the tincture in a cup of warm water 3 times daily.

Homoeopathy

three times daily for up to 7 days. Repeat if needed:
- sleepy and stupefied, dark mottled rash, purplish
  throat with ulcers on the tonsils: Ailanthus 6c.
- profuse offensive sweats, painfully swollen neck
  glands, exhausted and shaky: Mercurius solubilis 6c.
- sensation of a hot ball in the throat with pain darting
  into the ears on swallowing, generalized aching:
  Phytolacca 6c.
- in addition there are a number of remedies which are
  extremely helpful when the patient experiences a
  permanent impairment in their level of health or
  general energy after recovering form the acute phase.
  Consult a professional homoeopath.

Chinese Medicine

- Chinese doctors treat this condition by eliminating
  heat in the blood, liver and stomach. Red peony,
  dyers' woad leaf, honeysuckle, forsythia fruit,
  chrysanthemum flowers and dandelions would be
  prescribed. Individual treatment is recommended.

Orthodox

- doctors recommend rest and plenty of warm drinks.
  Most people recover after 4—6 weeks without
  medication.

Glaucoma

A condition in which fluid builds up in the eye, causing an increase in pressure which can damage delicate tissues and lead to gradual vision loss. Symptoms include an aching or throbbing pain in and above the eye, gradual loss of peripheral vision, and the perception of rainbow rings around lights.

Treatment

To be carried out in collaboration with your doctor/ophthalmologist.

Dietary

- the most documented treatment of glaucoma by natural means is through supplementation with vitamin C. The quantities involved are larger than those contained in most supplements so you are advised to carry out this treatment under the supervision of a naturopath.
- increase intake of bioflavonoids, which improve integrity of the blood capillaries and strengthen the tissues of the eye. Bioflavonoids are found in the skin, peel and outer layer of fruits and vegetables, such as citrus fruits (try to obtain organic fruits if you intend to eat the peel), leafy vegetables, red onions, beetroot and the blue or red pigment in berries.
- reduce intake of alcohol and caffeine which can interfere with blood circulation to the eye.
- increase vitamin A-rich foods such as liver, kidney, egg yolk, butter, cheese, dairy products, cod liver oil.
- do not smoke.

Hydrotherapy

- prepare a bowl of hot water and one of ice cold water. Soak a face cloth in the hot water and wring out, place on the eyes for 2–3 minutes, remove, and do the same with the cold; alternate hot and cold 3 times to stimulate circulation to the eyes.

Reflexology

- massage the reflex to the eye, found at the base of the second and third toes, just below where they join the sole of the left foot.

The reflex areas

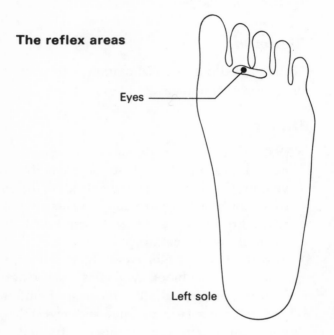

Eyes ————

Left sole

Professional Help

- the Bates Method may help this condition.
- cranial osteopathy helps reduce stagnation around the eyes and can be helpful.

Orthodox

- eye drops or drugs to reduce the rate of fluid production in the eye or to increase its outflow are generally recommended. Laser surgery may be used to open up the channels through which excess fluid can be drained away.

Glue Ear

Glue ear usually results from persistent ear infections, colds or chest complaints. It commonly brings a discharge of thick yellow mucus from the ear. The middle ear is 'glued up' and restricts hearing. It may be triggered by cold weather or swimming. See also Earache.

Prevention

- research shows that fewer ear infections occur in children who are breast fed.

Treatment

Dietary

- the build up of mucus in the ear may result from food allergies. See Allergies — Food to test for common allergens and how to avoid them.
- certain foods are thought to affect mucus production. The following should be avoided: cow's milk products (replace with goat's milk or soya milk), roast peanuts, excessive sugar.
- foods which reduce mucus include garlic, onions, watercress, parsley and celery. Try to encourage a wholefood diet with plenty of fresh fruit and vegetables, grains and lean meat or fish.

Herbal

- to reduce mucus, golden seal is an effective remedy: take 2—4 ml of the tincture in water 3 times daily. This is a long-term treatment which could take 3—4 months to produce results.

Homoeopathy

- professional help is recommended, although the

remedies listed for earache may be helpful in the short term.

Bach Flower Remedies

- Passion Flower and Rescue Remedy can help a child who is frightened or panicked by the pain: give 2 drops of each under the tongue.

Biochemic Tissue Salts

take 4 times daily for 1 week and repeat if necessary:
- if there is thick mucus: Kali Mur.
- intense pain: Ferr Phos.

Hydrotherapy

- a warm hot water bottle, protected by a towel or cover, can be held against the ear to provide relief.

Acupressure

- for acute pain: gently massage down the outside of the child's arm, from the elbow to the wrist, massaging between the two bones which make up the arm. Repeat 20 times on both arms.

Professional Help

- cranial osteopaths use techniques to improve drainage in the ears.
- acupuncture may also help.

Orthodox

- if the pressure of mucus builds up, surgery may be recommended to pierce the eardrum and allow the pus to drain out. A grommet is generally inserted to leave the hole open to drain future fluid and allow the lining of the middle ear cavity to dry out. The operation may weaken the ear drum, and you should not swim or bathe without wearing moulded ear plugs.

Goitre

Enlargement of the thyroid gland at the front of the neck, which may be caused by lack of adequate dietary iodine. The gland is unable to produce enough thyroxine, so becomes enlarged in an attempt to increase production. Goitre can also develop when the gland becomes overactive or underactive (see Hyperthyroidism and Hypothyroidism). Symptoms include feeling hot, palpitations, irritability, weight loss, disturbed menstrual periods and sometimes bulging eyes.

Treatment

Consultation with your doctor is important to determine the cause of the goitre, as treatment will vary accordingly. The recommendations below are for goitre caused by iodine deficiency. See also Hyperthyroidism and Hypothyroidism for other treatments.

Dietary

- increase intake of iodine, found in fresh saltwater shellfish and seafood, iodized salt, and foods grown on iodine-rich soil.
- some foods can inhibit intake of iodine; if you are deficient, avoid foods such as cabbage, soya beans, turnips, mustard, cassava root, peanuts, pine nuts and millet.

Herbal

- bugleweed is used to treat overactive thyroid gland, especially when symptoms include tight chest or nervous palpitations. Pour a cup of boiling water over 1 teaspoon of the dried herb, infuse for 15 minutes, drink 3 times daily.
- bladderwrack, a common seaweed, has been shown to help goitre caused by an underactive thyroid gland: pour a cup of boiling water onto 3 teaspoons of the

dried herb and infuse for 10 minutes, drink 3 times daily.

Orthodox

• drugs can usually correct thyroid function, but surgery may be required if individual areas of gland are separately affected or if a large goitre causes pressure symptoms in the neck.

Gonorrhoea *see* Sexually Transmitted Diseases

Gout

A buildup of uric acid crystals in the joints, especially the big toe, which becomes red, inflamed and very painful. Gout is often an inherited condition, though it may also result from kidney malfunction, blood disorders, overindulgence in rich food and alcohol, or some drugs.

Treatment

Dietary

• reduce intake of foods which stimulate the production of uric acid: fatty fish, anchovies, shellfish, meat and meat stock, caffeine (coffee, tea, cola, chocolate).
• cherries have been found to relieve symptoms. Eat at least half a pound daily if available.
• take 1 g of vitamin C daily.
• drink plenty of water.
• avoid alcohol, which increases uric acid production.
• charcoal tablets can help reduce uric acid levels: take 1 tablet 4 times daily.

Herbal

- celery seed increases the elimination of uric acid: pour a cup of water on 2 teaspoons of crushed seeds, infuse for 15 minutes and drink 3 times daily.

Homoeopathy

to be taken every 15 minutes for up to 4 doses and repeated if necessary:
- joint feels cold but is alleviated by cold bathing: Ledum 6c.
- joint very painful, especially at night, patient very irritable and sensitive to rudeness: Colchicum 6c.
- joint feels bruised, terrified of being approached in case the toe is touched: Arnica 6c.
- Urtica urens tincture, 3 drops in a little water twice daily will help to eliminate uric acid.

Hydrotherapy

- apply an ice pack to the painful area: wrap ice cubes or a bag of frozen peas in kitchen paper and hold on the joint for 3—5 minutes at regular intervals.

Reflexology

- massage of the area affected by gout will be painful, therefore reflexologists direct treatment at the 'zone related area', that is, a corresponding area in the body which links up to the reflexes of the affected area. In the case of gout, massage would be carried out on the hands and fingers on the same side as the affected foot.

Orthodox

- non-steroidal anti-inflammatory drugs are given to relieve pain and inflammation.

Graves' Disease *see* Hyperthyroidism

Groin Strain

Pain and stiffness in the groin, due to overstretching
muscles on the inside of the thigh. Groin strain is
usually brought on by sudden exertion. To distinguish it
from other ailments, attempt to bring the knee up to the
stomach: this activates the strained muscles and
intensifies the pain.

Prevention

the following yoga stretches provide good warm up
exercises to be carried out before exercising and can
greatly assist in preventing groin strain:
- stand with feet together, legs straight. Clasp hands
  behind your back and bend from the waist forward.
  Come up and repeat several times.
- in the same position, bend forward, then bend one
  knee slightly, straighten, then bend the other knee.
  Repeat several times.
- place hands on hips, spread legs apart to shoulder
  width, turn the right foot 90 degrees to the right and
  the left foot slightly inwards to the right. Keeping
  your body facing forward, move your trunk down
  towards the right leg. Hold for as long as is
  comfortable, then repeat on the other side (see
  opposite, top).
- with the legs in the same position as above and hands
  on hips, bend your right knee so that the thigh is
  parallel to the floor and the back leg is fully
  extended. Hold for as long as is comfortable, then
  repeat on the other leg (see opposite, bottom).

Treatment

Aromatherapy

- essential oil of sweet marjoram and rosemary help dull the pain: add 3 drops of each to a warm bath and soak in it.

Hydrotherapy

- immediately after the injury, place an ice pack on the affected area: wrap a packet of frozen peas in kitchen paper, and place on the muscle for 10 minutes. Remove for 10 minutes and repeat.

Professional Help

- massage, osteopathy or chiropractic will all help.

Orthodox

- physiotherapy and rest is recommended.

Haemorrhoids

Also known as piles, these are swollen, protruding veins around the anus. They are a type of varicose vein which can lie inside the rectum or outside. Symptoms and signs include itching and pain and sometimes bleeding when motions are passed. Haemorrhoids often occur in pregnancy or as a result of constipation or lifting a heavy object.

Any continuous bleeding from the anus warrants a medical checkup.

Prevention

- haemorrhoids are rarely seen in countries where a high fibre, unrefined diet is the norm. Increasing intake of fibre by eating wholegrain cereals, fruit, vegetables, and low fat protein will help prevent haemorrhoids.

Treatment

Practical Advice

- try to establish a regular routine to empty the bowels, and never resist or delay the urge to go to the toilet.
- use soft toilet paper or moist wipes to avoid irritating the haemorrhoids. Always wash and dry the area carefully after a bowel movement, finishing any wash or spray with cold water.
- haemorrhoids in pregnancy: These occur due to the

increasing pressure of the uterus on the vessels which
drain the haemorrhoidal veins. To relieve the pressure,
lie on your left side for 20 minutes every 2—4 hours.

Dietary

the following recommendations will help relieve
constipation, the major cause of haemorrhoids:
- drink at least 8 glasses of water per day.
- introduce more fibre into your diet, found in bran,
  oats, wholegrain breads and cereals, vegetables and
  fruits, cooked dried beans and peas.
- avoid coffee, strong spices, beer and cola, as these can
  increase irritation.

Herbal

- daub the haemorrhoids with witch hazel solution
  (particularly good if they have a tendency to bleed).
- pilewort ointment: simmer 2 tablespoons of fresh or
  dried herb in 200 g of Vaseline for 10 minutes, strain
  and pour liquid into a container. Apply to
  haemorrhoids at least 2 times daily. (You may like to
  keep an old pan specifically for herbal preparations.)

Homoeopathy

3 times daily for up to 4 days and repeat if necessary:
- feels like splinters of broken glass in the rectum on
  passing a stool: Ratanhia 6c.
- bruised and sore with a congested bursting feeling:
  Hamamelis 6c.
- sensation of a ball in the rectum, tendency to
  prolapse, worse during pregnancy: Sepia 6c.
- hot, burning and itching, worse from getting
  overheated: Sulphur 6c.

Hydrotherapy

- sit in a warm bath to which 4 drops of both essential

oil of peppermint and cypress have been added, with 2 tablespoons of bicarbonate of soda.

Massage

to help relieve constipation the following routine should be carried out first thing in the morning, before eating:

- lie down and oil hands lightly. Place one hand over the other, keeping the fingers flat begin by pressing down about 1 inch into the abdomen at in the left corner at 1 (see diagram). Make small slow circles. Move up a little and repeat. Continue with the same procedure up the left side, across above the umbilicus (including the corners under ribcage), and down the right side. Then make large slow sweeping strokes along the path just covered, but going in the reverse direction. Repeat several times.

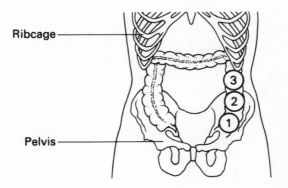

Orthodox

- rectal suppositories and creams containing corticosteroid and painkilling drugs are given to relieve discomfort. Haemorrhoids are sometimes removed surgically, or may be injected with a sclerosing agent which effectively seals them off and allows them to shrivel up naturally.

Hair, Dry

Some people are born with dry brittle hair, as a result of having few oil glands in the scalp. Providing you follow the practical advice below, your hair should remain in good condition. In some cases dry hair may result from a dietary deficiency, and occasionally it is one of the first signs of thyroid problems (see Goitre, Hyperthyroidism, Hypothyroidism). A simple blood test to measure blood thyroxine levels can rule this cause out. Excessive cosmetic treatments and blow drying can also contribute to dry hair.

Treatment

Practical Advice

- avoid excessive use of cosmetics on the hair.
- use a mild shampoo, once or twice weekly.
- avoid blow drying, hot rollers, or curling tongs.
- avoid excessive bleaching, tinting and perming.
- as an alternative to chemical dyes and hair tints, use natural herbal dyes such as henna, which strengthen the hair and give shine.

Dietary

- deficiencies of the following nutrients can cause dry, brittle hair:
  - protein, found in lean meats, fish, cheese, cooked dried beans, soya beans.
  - vitamin A, found in liver, kidney, egg yolk, butter, cheese, milk.
  - vitamin B12, found in lean meats, poultry, fish, shellfish, milk, organ meats, cheese and eggs.
  - vitamin C, found in fresh fruit and vegetables.
  - iron, found in red meat, dried fruits, dark green leafy vegetables, fish, wholegrain breads and cereals.
  - zinc, found in oysters, lean meat, poultry, fish,

organ meats, wholegrain bread and cereals.
- increase intake of fatty acids found in seeds and nuts.
- a multivitamin and mineral supplement will help remedy any deficiencies.

Orthodox

- your doctor may refer you to a dermatologist.

Hair, Excessive

Excessive hair growth is usually hereditary in origin. At times, however, it can result from a hormonal imbalance which produces growth in male patterns on the face, chest and legs of women (also known as hirsutism). This commonly occurs at puberty or menopause, or when an adrenal gland tumour develops. Excessive hair growth can also result from taking certain drugs, also referred to as hypertrichosis.

Treatment

Cosmetic

- in cases where hair growth is a hereditary characteristic, treatment is purely cosmetic. The following are some of the common methods used to remove or disguise excess body hair.

Bleaching
- if hair is very dark it can be bleached using commercially prepared bleaches, or mixing ½ cup of 20 volume peroxide to a paste with soap flakes, with 2 teaspoons of ammonia. Mix well, spread on hair for 10—15 minutes, then wash off. Repeat every few days until hairs are colourless. Repeat each month. If facial hair is to be bleached, use a specially prepared cosmetic bleach, and test on a small area of skin first.

Shaving

- removal of hair with hand or electric razor. It leaves a hard stubble and has to be repeated at least twice weekly. It is not advised on the face.

Cream Depilatories

- removal of hair with a chemical cream which dissolves the hair. The effect is much like shaving. It is advisable to test the cream on a small area of skin, as the products are harsh and may be problematic on sensitive skins.

Waxing

- placing on the skin cold or warm wax which sticks to the hair. When the wax is pulled off, the hairs come with it, pulled out by the roots. The method can be uncomfortable (much like removing a sticking plaster/band aid from the skin). Regrowth is slower than shaving or depilation, and does not produce a stubble. Waxing can be carried out in a professional beauty salon, or with home waxing kits. It is advisable to have facial hair removed professionally, at least the first time.

Sugaring

- a method similar to waxing, widely practised in Arabic countries. A sugar paste is made which is spread on the skin and pulled off along with the hair.

Plucking

- excess hair is plucked using sterilized tweezers. Can be appropriate for small areas of hair, particularly the eyebrows.

Electrolysis

- this allows for permanent hair removal and is the most popular method for removing excess facial hair. A needle is inserted into the hair follicle and an electric current passed through to cauterize the hair root. The procedure must be repeated several times to stop hair growth. It should be carried out by an expert, as scarring can occur.

Professional Help

- homoeopathic treatment can be helpful.

Orthodox

- in cases where hormonal imbalances are the cause of excessive hair growth, anti-androgen medications are prescribed. A particular brand of oral contraceptive pill, Dianette, is also often used.

Hair, Greasy

Oily, greasy hair can be a result of large or numerous oil glands in the scalp, or the production of excessive oil due to hormonal disturbances (particularly during adolescence). Diet can also play a part.

Treatment

Practical Advice

- wash your hair often with a mild shampoo, every day if necessary.
- when washing the hair, use a final rinse made up of the juice of one lemon in a pint of warm water. This helps close up the hair follicles which produce oil.
- use oil-free conditioners.

Dietary

- reduce intake of fats and fried food.
- increase intake of fresh vegetables and fruit, wholegrain cereals and low fat protein.
- avoid coffee, tea, chocolate and cola drinks.

Hair Loss

Loss or absence of hair, also known as alopecia or balding, is a hereditary and unavoidable condition in some adult men. In young people and women, temporary thinning of the hair may be a result of severe stress or shock. It may also be a side effect of medication or the result of a dietary deficiency or hormonal imbalance.

Treatment

Dietary

Hair loss resulting from stress, trauma, shock or long-term illness can be helped by the following dietary recommendations:

- increase intake of vitamin C, found in fresh fruit and vegetables, particularly citrus fruits and juices, parsley, broccoli, green pepper and blackcurrants.
- take a vitamin B complex supplement daily.
- take brewer's yeast: 1 tablespoon in a glass of water 3 times daily.
- increase intake of protein, found in meat, fish, liver, wheatgerm, dried cooked beans and peas, tofu, cheese, milk, and eggs.

Homoeopathy

to be taken morning and night for up to 1 month:

- hair loss after pregnancy: Lycopodium 6c.
- hair loss after grief or extreme emotion, accompanied

by exhaustion and indifference: Phosphoric acid 6c.
- hair loss during the menopause with hot sweaty flushes and heavy bleeding: Sepia 6c.

Chinese Medicine

- Chinese doctors believe that hair is nourished by the blood, and thus influenced by the condition of the liver and kidney. Treatment is aimed at toning these organs using fleeceflower root, wolfberry fruit or mulberry fruit.
- acupuncture may also be recommended.

Professional Help

- homoeopathy may help.

Orthodox

- if you are taking medication, ask your doctor about its potential side effects, and look for alternatives if it causes hair loss. The Pill, anti-coagulants, diet pills, and thyroid medications can all contribute to hair loss.
- hair growth can be encouraged by a relatively new treatment called minoxidil liquid. Transplantation techniques, though limited in their ability to restore thick hair, are also sometimes carried out.

Halitosis *see* Bad Breath

Hangover

Symptoms of headache, nausea, dizziness and depression after drinking excessive amounts of alcohol. Many of the effects result from dehydration and can be avoided by drinking large quantities of water before going to bed.

Prevention

- do not drink on an empty stomach.
- take a B complex vitamin supplement before drinking.
- take 6—8 capsules of evening primrose oil before drinking.
- don't mix different drinks.
- eat while you drink.
- drink plenty of water to avoid dehydration.

Treatment

Practical Advice

- go out and get some fresh air.
- do not resort to the 'hair of the dog'. Trying to remedy a hangover with further alcohol only compounds the problem and sets up a dangerous habit of continuous drinking.

Dietary

- eating carbohydrate helps relieve the symptoms of hangover. A good remedy is banana milk shake: 1 banana whipped in ½ glass of milk with 2 tablespoons of honey. The banana provides potassium lost through alcohol consumption, the milk reduces stomach acidity and honey raises lowered blood sugar.

Herbal

- willow bark is a safe natural source of salicylates, the active ingredient found in aspirin. Take a decoction first thing to relieve a headache: pour a cup of water onto 2 teaspoons of the bark, simmer for 10 minutes and drink hot.

Homoeopathy

take 1 tablet every 30 minutes for up to 6 doses and repeat if needed:

- dizzy from bright lights, nauseous but unable to vomit, angry and aggressive: Nux vomica 6c.
- thirsty for large quantities of cold water, splitting headache aggravated by the slightest movement, wants to be left in peace: Bryonia 6c.
- hot, sweaty and smelly with early morning diarrhoea: Sulphur 6c.

Hay Fever *see* Allergies — Hay Fever and Rhinitis

Heartburn *see* Acid Stomach; Indigestion

Headache

Most headaches result from strain and tension in the neck, facial or head muscles, resulting from stress and/or poor posture. A headache can sometimes be a reaction to hunger, caffeine withdrawal, too much sleep, a stuffy room, noise, an allergy (see entries on Allergies), sinusitis (see entry), low blood sugar (see Blood Sugar, Low) or weather changes. Persistent headaches which have no obvious cause or headaches which wake people in the night or come and go in sudden attacks are symptoms which require medical investigation. (See also Migraine.)

Prevention

- eat regular meals.
- get enough sleep.
- take measures to avoid stress.
- get plenty of fresh air and exercise (see below).
- avoid excessive coffee or alcohol consumption.

Treatment

Aromatherapy

• tension headaches respond well to aromatherapy,
  particularly essential oil of lavender, known for its
  relaxing properties. Place 1 or 2 drops of essential oil
  of lavender on the tips of your fingers, and massage
  in circular motion across your temples, around the
  hollows at the sides of the eyes, behind your ears, and
  across the back of your neck. Caution: do not let
  your fingers go too near your eyes.
• for headaches of menstrual origin use sweet marjoram
  for the above massage.
• relax in a warm bath to which 3 drops each of sweet
  marjoram, Roman chamomile and lavender have been
  added.

Herbal

• valerian infusion is a sedative which helps reduce
  tension and anxiety. Pour a cup of boiling water onto
  2 teaspoons of the root and infuse for 15 minutes.
  Drink before going to bed.
• feverfew (*Tanacetum parthenium*) has been shown in
  clinical trials to be as effective as a painkiller. Use as a
  preventive measure. Take two or three small leaves
  daily, chopped up in food (a sprinkling of sugar helps
  to disguise the bitter taste). Feverfew tablets are
  available from pharmacies and health food shops —
  follow the dosage instructions on the packaging. The
  results may take 2—3 months to become apparent.

Homoeopathy

every 30 minutes for up to 4 doses and repeat if needed:
• throbbing and hammering, especially at the temples,
  sensitive to draughts on the head: Belladonna 6c.

- pain aggravated by the smallest movement, headaches accompanied by constipation: Bryonia 6c.
- head feels enlarged: Argentum nitricum 6c.
- sensation of a tight band spreading from base of skull to forehead, better from passing urine: Gelsemium 6c.
- sensation of a nail boring down into the head, hypersensitive to noise: Coffea 6c.
- (see also Migraine).

Massage

- massage can relieve tension in the muscles of the scalp, neck and face. Using the fingertips, briskly massage the whole of the scalp, as if you were washing the hair. Then gently pull the hair all around the head.

Acupressure

- massaging the points illustrated overleaf can help to relieve pain.

Exercise

- regular walking, jogging or swimming helps prevent tension in the neck and shoulder muscles.
- the following exercise sequence is a good preventive measure, and will help overcome a headache by relaxing the neck and head muscles:
  - while sitting, inhale and tip your head back looking up at the ceiling. Don't tip it back too far — this can compress the cervical spine and make matters worse. Exhale and bring the head down so that your chin rests on your chest. Repeat this twice.
  - exhale and turn your head to look over your right shoulder, keeping your chin level. Inhale as you turn back, looking straight ahead. Exhale as you look over the left shoulder. Inhale as you look

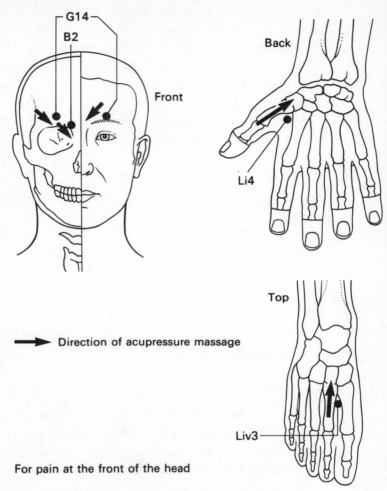

For pain at the front of the head

➤ Direction of acupressure massage

straight ahead. Repeat twice on each side.
- bring your chin down to your chest, slowly circle
  your head to the right, drop it back, and bring it
  to the left, and back down to your chest. Repeat in
  the other direction.

Professional Help

- if headaches are an ongoing problem it is worth
  consulting an osteopath or chiropractor to investigate
  spinal misalignments which lead to nerve pressure or
  muscular tension.

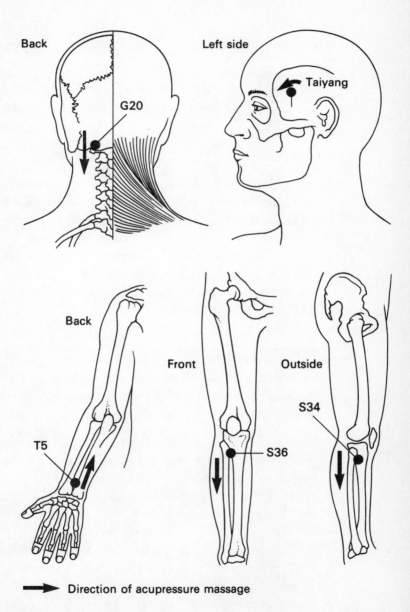

Direction of acupressure massage

For pain at the side of the head

- for headaches related to postural problems, i.e. sitting or standing in awkward positions, the Alexander Technique may be helpful.

Orthodox

- mild painkillers and rest are recommended for single, short-term headaches. For recurrent headaches, the cause must be identified and treated accordingly.

Heatstroke

Fatigue, fainting, dizziness, nausea, extreme sweating and headaches resulting from extreme heat are common signs of heat exhaustion. If left untreated this can develop into heatstroke, a life-threatening illness where the body becomes seriously overheated. Symptoms of heatstroke include shallow breathing, hot, dry skin and a rapid and weak pulse. The condition requires immediate medical attention.

Prevention

Heat exhaustion and heatstroke can be avoided by acclimatizing gradually to high temperatures. The following measures should be adopted.

- limit the time spent outside to short periods, and gradually build up your exposure to the heat over a period of two weeks.
- avoid direct sunlight; keep to the shade.
- avoid strenuous exercise.
- take frequent cool baths or showers.
- drink plenty of fluids, particularly a dilute salt and sugar solution (1 pint of water with ¼ teaspoon each of salt and sugar).
- wear light, loose clothing and protect your head with a hat or scarf.
- eat a light diet with plenty of vegetables and fruit and avoid alcohol and caffeine.

Treatment

For heat exhaustion, lie in a cool place, and sip a solution of salt water.

First Aid

- a person who does not start to recover from heat exhaustion within 30 minutes and who has difficulty walking or becomes unconscious requires emergency medical attention. Move the victim to a cool, shady area and remove clothing. Wrap him/her in a cool, wet sheet or towel, or splash cool water on them. If he/she is conscious, give a solution of salt water.

Homoeopathy

every 15 minutes for up to 4 doses and repeat if necessary:
- hot red face, throbbing headache: Belladonna 6c.
- hot red face, throbbing headache and loss of sense of direction: Glonoine 6c.

Orthodox

- severe cases are admitted to hospital for supervised oral or intravenous hydration.

Hepatitis

Inflammation of the liver, often due to a viral infection. There are two types: hepatitis A (infectious hepatitis) which is spread by infected motions passed from hand to mouth, infected water or food; hepatitis B (serum hepatitis) spread by infected blood or body fluids. Symptoms include jaundice (yellowing of the skin), fever, severe fatigue, nausea, vomiting, headaches and aching muscles. The condition can sometimes lead to irreversible liver damage and death — therefore, self help

treatments should be carried out in consultation with
your doctor or other health professional.

Prevention

- the hepatitis A vaccine is recommended for all close
  contacts of patients with the illness, to offer
  protection against outbreaks in households or
  institutions.
- the hepatitis B vaccine is recommended for intimate
  contacts of sufferers of acute hepatitis B, and sexual
  contacts of highly infectious carriers.

Treatment

Dietary

- naturopaths use a number of dietary measures to treat
  hepatitis. Since these often require taking large doses
  of vitamins, it is advisable to carry out treatment
  under the supervision of a professional. The following
  recommendations may be made:
- avoid alcohol, reduce intake of saturated fats, fried
  food, refined carbohydrates (white flour and sugar).
  Increase intake of fibre (wholegrain cereals, fruit and
  vegetables, cooked dried beans and peas) which
  encourage the elimination of bile acids and toxins
  which accumulate in the liver and gallbladder.
- some studies have shown large doses of vitamin C
  improved viral hepatitis. Naturopaths recommend
  between 10 and 50 g daily or to bowel tolerance (i.e.
  if you start to get diarrhoea, lower the dose).
- vitamins B12 and folic acid have been shown to
  reduce recovery time. The B vitamins should be taken
  together in a daily vitamin B complex supplement.

Herbal

- dandelion is a well-recognized liver remedy: put 3
  teaspoons of the root into one cup of water, simmer

for 15 minutes. Drink 3 times daily. Dandelion leaves
can also be eaten raw in salad.

- milk thistle is said to promote the regeneration of
diseased liver cells: make an infusion by pouring a
cup of water on 1 teaspoonful of the bruised seeds,
allow to stand for 10 minutes and drink 3 times daily.
- globe artichoke stimulates the elimination of bile from
the body, an important factor in the treatment of
hepatitis: eat the fresh vegetable as often as possible.

Chinese Medicine

- traditional Chinese doctors would use acupuncture
and herbs such as oriental wormwood and gardenia
fruit to treat this condition.

Orthodox

- doctors recommend bed rest and abstinence from
alcohol for at least 6 months. Steroid drugs may be
prescribed to prevent further damage to the liver.

Hernia

Part of an organ, usually the intestine, protrudes
through a weak area of the abdominal wall. The first
sign is a bulge in the abdominal wall, the groin or
scrotum, the thigh, or the navel. Hernias are often a
result of a congenital weakness in the abdominal wall.
Sometimes they are caused by lifting or straining. If you
find a tender bulge, consult your doctor. (For hiatus
hernia, see entry.)

Prevention

Practical Advice

- learn to lift correctly: bend at the knees, not from the
waist.

Dietary

- avoid being overweight.

Exercise

strengthen the stomach muscles with the following
exercises:
- lie on your back and bend your knees, leaving your
  feet flat on the floor. Lift your buttocks and lower
  back off the floor, leaving your feet and shoulders on
  the floor supporting the weight. Lower yourself
  gently. Repeat 10 times daily.

Treatment

If you suspect a hernia, consult your doctor. He or she
may try to push the hernia back and offer a supportive
garment worn temporarily to hold it in place. Hernias
which cannot be pushed back are removed or
repositioned surgically.

Post-Treatment

Do not lift any heavy objects for at least 3 months.

Biochemic Tissue Salts

- Calc Fluor: three times daily to improve tissue tone.

Herpes, Genital

A virus which is usually transmitted through sexual
contact and brings an itching, burning, painful rash of
small blisters in the genital area. The blisters burst,
leaving small ulcers, which take around 2 weeks to heal.
Other symptoms include swollen glands, fever and
headache. Women often find urination painful.
Sometimes there are also sores around the mouth.

Treatment

The herpes virus remains in the body and may become active when you are run down or under stress. Exposure to bright sunlight, menstruation and injury can also trigger the virus. The following treatments will help reduce severity of the attack.

Practical Advice

- do not have intercourse when you or your partner has an attack of herpes.
- do not share towels, sponges or lipsticks.
- ensure you wash your hands well after touching the genital area during an attack.
- to help prevent further attacks, keep your immune system healthy: eat sensibly, exercise regularly and use stress reduction techniques (see entry on Stress).
- avoid exposing the blisters to sunlight, as this can activate the virus.

Dietary

the amino acids arginine and lysine have been found to influence the incidence of herpes attacks:
- reduce intake of arginine, found in nuts, carob, chocolate, gelatin, coconut, oats, wholemeal and white flour, peanuts, soya beans and wheatgerm.
- increase intake of lysine, found in fish, shrimps, prawns, chicken, lamb, milk, cheese, beans, brewers' yeast, beansprouts, fruit and vegetables.
- take 1.5 g lysine daily as a preventative measure. Increase the dose to 3 g daily during an attack.
- take 1 g of vitamin C with bioflavonoids daily during an attack.

Hydrotherapy

- during an attack, take frequent warm baths with 3 tablespoons of salt added.

Professional Help

- homoeopathic treatment can help to reduce the frequency and severity of the attacks.

Orthodox

- antiviral medication, such as acyclovir, is given as a cream to reduce the duration and severity of the attack. Tablets are occasionally used to prevent recurrent attacks.

Hiatus Hernia

Part of the stomach protrudes up into the chest, causing acid reflux from the stomach to the oesophagus, heartburn and pains in the chest. Hiatus hernia often occurs in the obese and those who smoke.

Treatment

Practical Advice

- to prevent regurgitation of food during the night and heartburn, raise the head of the bed slightly: place a brick under the legs or wedge the mattress using foam rubber or a bolster.

Dietary

- avoid being overweight.
- eat small meals, slowly; do not eat late at night.
- do not lie down or bend over immediately after eating.
- avoid fatty and spicy foods, alcohol and cigarettes.
- substitute coffee, tea and cola with vegetable juices and herb teas, and do not drink during meals.
- the Hay diet (food combining) improves digestion and therefore reduces reflux. It is described in several

books including *Food Combining for Health* by Doris Grant and Jean Joice (Thorsons).

Herbal

- decoction of slippery elm: mix 1 part of powdered bark to 8 parts water, simmer for 10 minutes and drink half a cup 3 times daily.

Biochemic Tissue Salts

- Calc Fluor enhances elasticity. Take 3 times daily for 7 days and repeat if necessary.

Exercise

to strengthen stomach muscles:
- lie on your back with your knees bent and feet flat on the floor. Lift your buttocks and lower back off the floor, leaving your feet and shoulders on the floor supporting the weight. Lower yourself gently. Repeat 10 times daily.

Professional Help

- responds well to homoeopathy and osteopathy.

Orthodox

- antacids are recommended. Surgery may be carried out to return the hernia to the stomach.

Hiccups

A sudden contraction of the diaphragm, which allows air to rush suddenly into the lungs, causing the vocal cords to close suddenly. Generally hiccups is not serious, though often uncomfortable. Occasionally prolonged hiccups can result from irritation of the diaphragm or the nerves which supply it as a result of pneumonia, stomach problems, alcoholism or hepatitis. Prolonged

attacks can be exhausting and surgery may be
recommended.

Treatment

everyone has their own popular remedy for short bouts
of hiccups; the following are a few of the most tried
and tested ones.
- breathe into a paper bag.
- eat a teaspoon of sugar.
- squirt lemon juice into the back of the throat.
- suck a wedge of lemon.
- for babies, give water with sugar or honey added.

Chinese Medicine

- ginger rhubarb and berilla stems are commonly
  prescribed. Persistent cases are treated with
  acupuncture.

High Blood Pressure *see* Blood Pressure, High

Hives

Also known as urticaria or nettlerash, this is a skin
condition which brings itchy lumps (whitish with a red
inflamed area around them). It is often triggered by an
allergic reaction to food (see Allergies — Food),
additives, drugs, particularly aspirin, insect bites or
stress. If the eyes, lips or throat are affected, seek
medical attention, as breathing may be impaired.

Treatment

Finding the source of the hives and avoiding it is the
best cure. To relieve the attack the following remedies
are helpful.

Dietary

- possible food triggers may be strawberries, shellfish, tomatoes, chocolate, eggs, wheat, nuts, food additives, milk. Try excluding each of these from your diet one by one to see if symptoms are relieved.

Herbal

- for hives brought on by anxiety or stress, valerian infusion: pour a cup of boiling water onto 2 teaspoons of the root and infuse for 10 minutes. Drink during periods of stress.
- aloe vera gel soothes the rash.

Homoeopathy

every 15 minutes for up to 4 doses and repeat if necessary:
- stinging itchy rash especially if triggered by shellfish: Urtica urens 6c.
- burning and itching rash after getting wet: Rhus toxicodendron 6c.
- dusky pink rash with swelling of lips, eyelids or throat: Apis 6c.

Hydrotherapy

use one of the following:
- add 3 tablespoons of sodium bicarbonate to a bath, to relieve itching.
- add 5 tablespoons of oatmeal to the bath to soothe the rash.
- add a cupful of vinegar to the bath water — this restores the skin's pH. Alternatively, apply a diluted solution to affected areas with cotton wool.

Orthodox

- calamine lotion to relieve itching, along with antihistamine drugs. In severe cases where the lips, tongue and eye are affected, and difficulty breathing (also known as anaphylactic shock), urgent hospital treatment is necessary.

Housemaid's Knee

Inflammation of the pocket of tissue covering the kneecap, usually as a result of prolonged kneeling or a blow to the knee. The pocket fills with fluid and the kneecap becomes swollen, red and painful.

Treatment

Practical Advice

When the knee is very painful, rest is the best treatment, try to elevate the leg as much as possible and do not kneel.

Herbal

* a comfrey poultice eases the pain: place a handful of fresh or dried comfrey leaves in a saucepan, cover with water and bring to the boil. Remove from the heat and place the leaves between 2 pieces of gauze. Allow to cool slightly, then place on the knee. It should be hot but not burning. When the poultice cools maintain the warmth by putting a hot water bottle on top.

Homoeopathy

* Ruta graveolens 6c, 3 times daily for up to 7 days. Apply Ruta cream locally.

Hydrotherapy

* hot and cold treatment increases circulation to the area, relieves inflammation and removes toxins. Prepare an ice pack: take a bag of frozen peas and wrap kitchen towel around it. Prepare a hot water

bottle and wrap a towel around it. Place first the ice pack on the knee for 10 minutes, then the hot water bottle, alternate several times. Carry out this procedure morning and night.

Massage

- massaging the muscles above and below the knee joint will help encourage circulation and remove toxins from the area. This should be carried out by an experienced professional.

Exercise

once the pain and inflammation has subsided, exercise is very important to mobilize the joint:
- Sitting on an upright chair, raise and straighten your right leg and push your heel away from you, then bend it fully. Repeat 5 times.
- Sitting raise your right leg and circle it clockwise 5 times then anti-clockwise 5 times. Repeat.
- do these exercises as often as is possible and comfortable.
- swimming is also very beneficial.

Orthodox

- rest and painkillers are recommended. Antibiotics may be prescribed if infection is present within the fluid or on the skin surface. Elastic support bandages discourage further buildup of fluid.

Hyperactivity

A disorder in infants and children, manifested by abnormally overactive and restless behaviour.
Hyperactive babies are fidgety and cry incessantly, they often have eczema, and feed poorly. Hyperactive children typically rock the cot, bang their heads and are difficult. In school they are disruptive, unable to keep

still, with a tendency to throw things, a short attention span, poor co-ordination and tearfulness.

Dietary

- research has shown a clear link between certain foods, additives and hyperactivity. Avoid food and drink from the following list:
  - junk and processed foods.
  - all foods and drinks with synthetic colouring, flavouring and additives. Tartrazine, E102, is especially suspect.
  - all aspirin preparations and artificially flavoured vitamin pills. Remember, many children's medicines have artificial colours and flavourings, these should be avoided if possible.
  - sugar and foods and drinks that contain sugar.
- some children may have allergies to milk, corn, wheat and eggs. See Allergies — Food.
- a strictly wholefood diet which includes plenty of lean meat and fish and fresh fruit and vegetables is recommended for hyperactive children.
- tap water can sometimes contain ingredients which cause hyperactivity. Drink only bottled spring water.
- zinc supplements have been shown to be beneficial.

Herbal

- research has shown that hyperactive children are often deficient in essential fatty acids. These can be replenished by supplementation with evening primrose oil. Studies have shown that three 500 mg capsules of Efamol evening primrose oil taken morning and evening for 6—8 weeks, dropping back to 500 mg morning and evening, brings an improvement. Rubbing the oil into the skin can also help.

Professional Help

- homoeopathy and/or cranial osteopathy have been found to be helpful. Applied kinesiology can help identify specific sensitivities.

Orthodox

- stimulant drugs, such as amphetamines, are used to motivate the part of the brain which suppresses excess activity. The drugs also suppress appetite, thus reducing growth in children and can cause nausea and abdominal pain. Psychotherapy and assessment for special educational needs may be necessary.

Hypertension *see* Blood Pressure, High

Hyperthyroidism

Overactivity of the thyroid gland and subsequently excessive production of thyroid hormones. The most common form of hyperthyroidism is Graves' disease, an auto-immune disorder in which the body produces antibodies which stimulate the production of thyroid hormones. Symptoms include weight loss, increased appetite, sweating and heat, bulging eyes and sometimes tremors. It is most common in middle-aged women.

Treatment

Professional help is recommended for this condition. Some of the remedies which may be offered are listed below.

Dietary

- a natural wholefood diet is recommended. Eat plenty

of onions, seafood and vegetables grown organically
on iodine-rich soil.

Herbal

- bugleweed is recommended, particularly if the
condition brings palpitations and tight chest: pour a
cup of boiling water on a teaspoon of the herb, infuse
for 15 minutes and drink 3 times daily.

Chinese Medicine

- the condition is thought to be caused by heat in the
liver. Marine plants and seaweed are prescribed.
Acupuncture can be helpful.

Professional Help

- professional homoeopathic treatment may help.

Orthodox

- drugs are recommended to inhibit the production of
thyroid hormones. Surgery may be carried out to
remove part of the thyroid gland.

Hypoglycaemia *see* Blood Sugar, Low

Hypothermia

An abnormal fall in body temperature to 35° C (95° F)
or below. Symptoms include shivering, slow pulse,
pallor, lack of energy, drowsiness, and confusion, which
may lead to lowered heart and breathing rate and loss of
consciousness. The condition is common in elderly
people living alone in poorly heated homes. The
condition requires immediate medical attention.

Prevention

- to prevent hypothermia in the elderly, ensure accommodation is heated to at least 18° C (65° F). Warm clothing should be worn (including a hat if temperatures are low). It is important to eat hot food and drink warm drinks several times daily.
- when walking or climbing in cold isolated locations, always carry survival bags lined with space blankets.

Treatment

First Aid

- cover the victim's head, give him/her warm drinks, but no alcohol. Do not rub the skin or expose the victim to direct heat (e.g. hot water) as this may cause death. Instead gradually warm the victim by moving to a warm place if possible and covering with blankets and giving him/her hot drinks. Contact your doctor immediately. If you are outside, get into a sleeping bag with the person to transfer your body heat.

Orthodox

- treatment varies depending on the age of the victim. Gradual warming with heat-reflecting materials is used. In severe cases patients are admitted to intensive care, where methods of warming the blood are carried out.

Hypothyroidism

Underactivity of the thyroid gland, leading to insufficient production of thyroid hormones which regulate metabolism. Symptoms include lack of energy, muscle weakness, dry skin and hair, weight gain, and recurrent infections. Sometimes the thyroid gland enlarges, producing a lump at the front of the neck (known as goitre). Hypothyroidism in children results in delayed development. Medical diagnosis is made through a blood test. A diagnosis can also be made by taking your temperature for three consecutive mornings: if it is below 36.4° C (97.6° F), consult your doctor.

Treatment

Professional help is recommended for this condition. Some of the remedies you may encounter are listed below.

Dietary

- treatment consists of supplementing the diet with natural thyroid hormones fabricated from iodine and the amino acid tyrosine:
- increase intake of iodine, found in seafood, seaweed, kelp, and saltwater fish. Use iodized salt.
- avoid foods which inhibit the uptake of iodine: turnips, cabbage, soya beans, peanuts, pine nuts, mustard.
- take supplements of the amino acid tyrosine: 250 mg daily.
- increase intake of the following nutrients:
  - vitamin A, found in liver, kidney, egg yolk, butter, fortified margarine, cheese and cream, cod liver oil.
  - vitamin C, found in fresh fruit and vegetables.
  - vitamin E, found in seeds and seed oils, nuts, wheatgerm.
  - riboflavin, found in milk products, liver, green leafy vegetables, mushrooms.
  - niacin, found in lean meat, chicken, fish, dried cooked beans.
  - pyridoxine, found in lean meat, wheatgerm, brewer's yeast.
  - zinc, found in lean meat, oysters, poultry, fish, organ meats, wholegrain cereals.

Herbal

- bladderwrack helps regulate thyroid function. It can be taken in tablet form or as an infusion: pour a cup of boiling water on 2 teaspoons of the herb, infuse for 10 minutes and drink 3 times daily.

Exercise

- aerobic exercise stimulates the production of thyroid hormones. Brisk walking, running, swimming or cycling should be carried out for at least 15 minutes daily.

Orthodox

- treatment consists of replacing the deficient hormones with thyroxine. Treatment is usually for life. A goitre may be surgically removed.

Impetigo

A contagious bacterial skin infection common in children. Symptoms include reddened skin and blisters which burst leaving a yellow crusty appearance, usually around the nose and mouth. When babies are affected, seek medical attention.

Treatment

Practical Advice

- change bed linen daily; do not share towels, face cloths or clothes which may spread infection.

Dietary

- avoid all fruit and sugar, eat plenty of raw and cooked green, yellow and orange vegetables, wholegrain bread and cereals, vegetable protein, or fish and poultry.

Aromatherapy

- essential oil of tea tree is an effective antibacterial agent, available as an oil or ointment. Apply at night.

Herbal

- bathe the blisters with marigold solution to resist infection and aid healing: add 5 drops of marigold tincture to ½ pint of cooled boiled water.

Homoeopathy

to be taken three times daily for 3 days and repeat if necessary:

- cracked and scabby nostrils, yellow crust on the chin, whitewashed tongue: Antimonium crudum 6c.
- thick brown crusts on the face with thick yellow discharge from the eyes: Dulcamara 6c.
- when the rash is on the scalp, and blisters ooze pus: Mezereum 6c.

Orthodox

- antibiotic tablets and ointment are usually prescribed. Children should stay away from others until the infection clears.

Impotence

The inability to achieve or maintain an erection can result from a number of causes: stress, fatigue, anxiety, guilt, depression, drugs or alcohol. About 10 per cent of cases are caused by physical or structural problems, such as diabetes, or spinal cord disorders. An erection may take longer to achieve, or occur less frequently as men get older, due to changes in circulation, or lowered levels of the male sex hormone, testosterone.

Treatment

Dietary

- avoid alcohol, drugs and caffeine. These constrict the blood vessels, and inhibit blood flow needed to achieve an erection.

Aromatherapy

- essential oils of clary sage, sandalwood and ylang

ylang are renowned for encouraging relaxation and feelings of sensuality. Try adding 2 drops of each to 20 ml of your massage oil, or bath.

Chinese Medicine

• Chinese doctors believe that too much anxiety can bring an energy stagnation in the liver. Treatment varies depending on the patient, but Sextone and cibot root are often prescribed.

Massage

• learning how to massage each other can be pleasurable and erotic. It is relaxing for the giver and the receiver, it slows down lovemaking and helps open up both partners to communication.

Acupressure

• acupressure is useful in some cases — see illustration for points to use.

Exercise

• moderate exercise helps you to relax while boosting energy levels; it also increases physical awareness and stimulates sexuality.
• if you are already exercising, don't overdo it. Too much activity can leave you exhausted and reduce stimulation; moderation is the key.

Relaxation

• general stress and anxiety often inhibit sex drive. Being uptight about daily activities or events or nervous about your 'performance' diverts blood away from the sexual organs.
• to relieve general stress and anxiety a yoga or meditation class may help you learn to unwind and relax. Exercise is also a good method as it usually energizes at the same time as relieving stress.

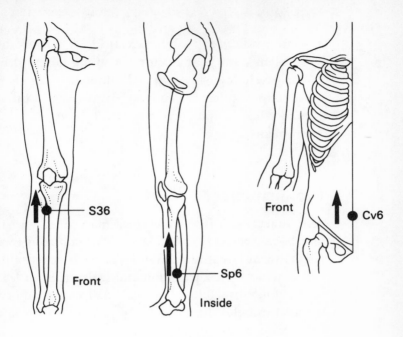

Direction of acupressure massage

Aromatherapy or massage are good methods of relaxation. Self-hypnosis and relaxation tapes can also help. Using one of these techniques before you go to bed will help clear your mind of concerns.

- anxiety about relationships or sex can sometimes be resolved by talking with your partner at a time when you are not trying to 'perform'. Explaining your concerns honestly without feeling guilty helps dispel anxiety.
- sexual anxiety which is not relieved by the above may be helped by psychosexual counselling. This is usually carried out with both partners, who are encouraged to relearn their sexual experience together, and explore what is causing the stress in their sexual relationship. Specific exercises may be recommended to break the vicious circle of performance related anxiety.

Orthodox

- some medications inhibit erection, so discuss this problem with your doctor if you are taking drugs. For psychologically induced impotence, sex therapy is sometimes offered. Penile implants may be offered to men whose impotence is caused by structural problems or disease.

Incontinence, Faecal

Temporary loss of bowel control may occur with diarrhoea (see entry). Regular lack of control generally results from faecal impaction — faeces blocked in the bowel which cause irritation and inflammation leading to the uncontrollable release of small pieces. Injury to the anal muscles during surgery or childbirth can also be a cause, as can dementia or paralysis.

Treatment For Blocked Bowel

Dietary

- try to avoid becoming constipated by gradually increasing your intake of fibre. Eat more wholegrain cereals (bread, rice, pasta), dried cooked beans, fresh fruit and vegetables. Prunes, figs, and oatmeal are particularly high in fibre.
- drink at least 6 glasses of water a day.

Herbal

- for a sluggish bowel, herbalist Simon Mills recommends the following mixture: 4 teaspoons of psyllium, 2 teaspoons of chamomile flowers and 1 teaspoon of alder buckthorn bark. Powder the mixture and take 1 teaspoon daily.
- a powerful laxative to be used only on a short-term basis is decoction of senna: put 1 teaspoon of the

dried bark (powdered or broken up) into a saucepan, add one cup of water, bring to the boil and simmer for 15 minutes. Strain and drink 3 times daily.

Homoeopathy

3 times daily for 4 days and repeat if needed:
- incontinence after coughing or sneezing with loss of sensation in the rectum: Causticum 6c.
- incontinence when passing urine or wind: Aloe 6c.

Acupressure

- lie on your back, with your knees bent. Place all fingertips on the midpoint of the chest where the ribs meet, press firmly down for 30 seconds, then move the hand down half-way to the navel, press for 30 seconds, then move down to mid-way between the navel and the pubic bone, press down firmly for a further 30 seconds while breathing deeply.

Exercise

- take a 30-minute walk each day, jog or swim 3 times a week.

Yoga

- rapid abdominal breathing helps activate the digestive system: exhale forcibly using the abdomen, then inhale by relaxing it. Repeat 10 times, allowing the abdomen to go in and out rhythmically; then relax for 20 seconds and do 10 more. To make this more effective, carry it out while doing the half shoulder stand: lie on your back and raise your legs, bending your knees if necessary. Support your hips with your hands, letting your elbows rest on the floor. Lift your legs up to the vertical position. Carry out the breathing exercise above, then let your legs unroll and return to the floor.

Orthodox

- glycerin or laxative suppositories may be
  recommended to relieve constipation. Enemas may be
  used to empty the bowel.

Incontinence, Urinary

The inability to control urination can be due to injury,
disease, or weakness of the muscles controlling the
bladder. In men it may also be a symptom of prostate
problems (see Prostate, Enlarged). Early signs are leaking
urine when coughing, lifting or laughing. Lack of
urinary control may occur after childbirth as a result of
weakened pelvic floor muscles.

Treatment

Practical Advice

- some drugs affect bladder control, particularly those prescribed for high blood pressure. Ask your doctor about the potential effects of any drugs you may be taking, and if they are causing incontinence, ask for alternatives.
- if you are affected by stinging or burning sensations during urination, the incontinence may be caused by cystitis, which can be easily treated (see entry).
- keep the genital area clean and dry. Wash after going to the toilet. Avoid using scented soaps, talcs and deodorants in the genital area. Wear cotton underwear, and avoid tight clothing and nylon.
- only go to the toilet when your bladder is full. Do not get into a habit of precautionary trips which prevent the bladder from filling up and working properly. Drink at least 2 litres of fluid over the course of the day. This will ensure regular use of the bladder muscles.

Dietary

- excess weight puts pressure on the muscles controlling the bladder. If you are overweight it will be difficult to overcome urinary incontinence, so try to lose the extra pounds by following the dietary advice in the section on Obesity.
- straining due to constipation weakens bladder muscles. Introduce more fibre into your diet and follow the recommendations in the section on Constipation.

Homoeopathy

3 times daily for 4 days and repeat if needed:
- involuntary urination from coughing, sneezing or laughing or after forcible retention: Causticum 6c.

- involuntary urination when lying down or after getting the feet wet: Pulsatilla 6c.

Chinese Medicine

- golden lock tea is generally recommended for this condition.

Acupressure

- massaging the points illustrated several times a week may be helpful.

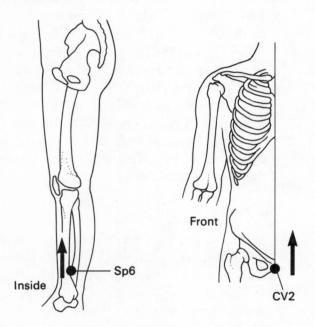

Inside   Sp6   Front   CV2

➤ Direction of acupressure massage

Exercise

- the muscles which need to be exercised are the pelvic floor muscles which control urination. To locate the muscles, try stopping the flow when you next go to the toilet. Then try tightening (contracting) and relaxing the muscles when you are not urinating. Every day, practise tightening and relaxing these muscles (when not urinating). At first they will feel weak, so start with just a few contractions, but do them frequently (at least 5 contractions 10 times daily); gradually build up to 10 contractions 10 times daily or more. You can contract and relax your pelvic floor muscles while sitting, lying or standing, while working, cooking or watching television. Progress will be slow, but if you follow this routine regularly, the muscles will strengthen. Once or twice a week check your progress by stopping the flow when you urinate: after 6 or 8 weeks of exercise you should find stopping the flow will be easier.

Orthodox

- for women your doctor may recommend hormone replacement therapy if the bladder outlet muscle has weakened as a result of the menopause. Physiotherapy may also be advised: the therapist may use mild electrical stimulation to produce pelvic floor contractions, or may suggest internal weight training, whereby weighted balls are held in the vagina to strengthen and tone the muscles.

Indigestion

A general term for discomfort brought by eating. Symptoms include stomach pain, acid in the gullet (see Acid Stomach), nausea and gas. It is often caused by eating too much or too quickly, or by eating rich or spicy food. Stress may also be a contributing factor.

Prevention

Dietary

- eat small meals regularly.
- eat slowly and in a relaxed manner and chew the food thoroughly.

- avoid highly spiced or rich foods.
- limit fluid intake during meals, but drink plenty of water between meals.
- replace refined carbohydrates with wholegrain carbohydrates (wholemeal bread, brown rice and pasta).
- reduce sugar intake.
- eat plenty of green vegetables.
- boil or grill food rather than frying it, and avoid sauces.
- avoid eating fruit with or after meals. Keep it separate.
- some people have found the Hay diet helpful (see Appendix 4).

Treatment

Aromatherapy

- lie or sit and massage the abdomen with a teaspoonful (5 ml) of carrier oil containing 1 drop of essential oil of peppermint or ginger (or 2 drops in 10 ml). Always massage in a clockwise direction.

Herbal

- meadowsweet infusion protects and soothes the mucous membranes of the stomach, reduces acidity and relieves nausea: pour a cup of boiling water onto 2 teaspoons of the dried herb, infuse for 15 minutes and drink 3 times daily.

Homoeopathy

take 1 tablet every 15 minutes for up to 4 doses and repeat if needed:
- after rich foods, with gas and rancid belching: Carbo vegetabilis 6c.
- after spicy food, stimulants, alcohol: Nux vomica 6c.
- burning pain, worse in the small hours of the morning: Arsenicum album 6c.

- stomach keeps filling up with gas, explosive belching and flatulence, worse from sweets and nervousness: Argentum nitricum 6c.
- intolerant of pulses, onions and garlic and large meals in general, flatulence gets obstructed and becomes painful: Lycopodium 6c.

Chinese Medicine

- hawthorn berry, wheat and rice sprouts can be taken to relieve discomfort.

Relaxation

- set aside a regular time for eating and try to clear your mind of concerns before you sit down. Do not read or watch television while eating, and try not to think about or discuss problems or worries, concentrate on thorough chewing and enjoyment of the meal.
- try to find time for the following routine once a day. Lie on a firm surface, close your eyes and be aware of how your body feels. Focus your attention on each part of your body, starting with your face and eyes; consciously try to relax every part in turn. The whole routine should take at least 10 minutes.

Reflexology

- massage the area relating to the stomach, found on both soles of the feet, above the midline in the arch (see diagram overleaf).

Orthodox

- antacids may be recommended for temporary relief, but should not be used long term. If indigestion lasts for more than a few days and especially if you feel generally unwell, consult your doctor.

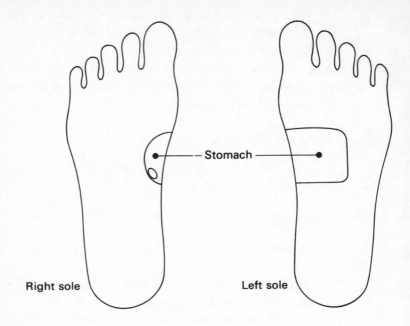

Right sole   Left sole

Infection

Bacteria, viruses or fungi invade and spread through the body producing a wide range of symptoms and illnesses. Features of infection include inflammation, fever, joint aches, redness and pus; they are a natural manifestation of the immune system's fight against the disease.

Treatment

Practical Advice

- if possible keep drugs to a minimum. Drugs often suppress the formation of white blood cells which are vital for fighting infection. Antibiotics alter the natural flora of the body, making it more susceptible to infection.
- limit intake of alcohol, nicotine, chemicals and food additives, which also impair immunity.
- get plenty of rest.

Dietary

the following antioxidants help boost immunity and resist infection:

- vitamin C, found in blackcurrants, parsley, broccoli, green peppers, strawberries, oranges and tomatoes.
- vitamin E, found in wheatgerm, seeds and seed oils, margarines, and egg yolk.
- beta-carotene, found in green leafy vegetables and yellow vegetables and fruit.
- vitamin B complex: take 1 supplement daily.
- selenium, found in wholemeal flour, mackerel, pork, eggs and cheese.
- zinc, found in oysters, liver, meat, Cheddar cheese, beans and lentils.
- magnesium, found in Brazil nuts, wholemeal flour, plain chocolate, lentils, parsley.
- avoid sugar, including that found in fruit and fruit juices.

Relaxation

- stress has been shown to reduce the body's immunity to infection. Taking adequate exercise, and participating in yoga or meditation can help reduce the stress of everyday life. If you are anxious or stressed for reasons which seem beyond your control, it may be advisable to seek professional help from a psychologist, psychotherapist or counsellor.

Orthodox

- any fever produced by infection requires an explanation. The cause could be anything from a common cold, through to a chest infection, malaria or AIDS. So unexplained fever after 24—48 hours should be assessed by a doctor.

Infertility

You or your partner may be considered infertile if you
have been having unprotected intercourse for a year and
have not been able to conceive. This does not
necessarily mean you cannot have a child, but it may
mean you need help in establishing optimal conditions
for fertilization. The most common causes of infertility
are inadequate healthy sperm production by the man, or
failure to ovulate in the woman. However, there are a
number of other possible causes, and finding the reason
for infertility is the first step to treatment.

Treatment

Practical Advice

- the most likely days or nights you will conceive are
  the 13th, 14th and 15th days before your next
  menstrual period. Record the dates of your period and
  time intercourse during the fertile period.
- abstaining from intercourse for a day or two before
  these dates ensures a healthy sperm count during the
  fertile period.
- sperm need to be kept cool, so men should avoid
  tight clothing, hot baths and jacuzzis.
- the best position to conceive is with the man on top.
  After ejaculation, the woman should remain lying
  down for at least 30 minutes.
- do not use KY jelly, as this may inhibit sperm
  movement. It is said that egg white is a good
  alternative lubricant which encourages sperm
  movement.
- do not douche after intercourse.

Dietary

- eat a balanced diet of wholegrain cereals, fresh fruit
  and vegetables, lean protein, cooked dried beans and
  peas, and vegetable oils.

- increase intake of vitamin E, found in wheatgerm, nuts, vegetable oils and seeds.
- stop smoking and drinking caffeine (coffee, tea, chocolate and cola) as these can interfere with ovulation and sperm production.
- avoid alcohol completely, since even small amounts can render susceptible males infertile.
- try to obtain your normal weight. Being under- or overweight can sometimes interfere with conception. Eat sensibly, however: this is not the time to crash diet. See recommendations for weight loss in the section on Obesity.
- supplementation with vitamin B6 has been shown to reduce birth defects. The recommended daily intake for women who would like to conceive is 0.4 mg.

Exercise

- do not over-exercise: studies show that intensive training can reduce sperm count in men and suppress ovulation in women. Reduce your schedule, and change your activities to more gentle relaxing exercise.

Relaxation

- stress can affect the ability to conceive in one or both partners.
- attending a relaxation, yoga or meditation class will help encourage relaxation.
- having a regular massage, acupressure, or aromatherapy session will also help.
- take up a hobby or sport which you enjoy and which engages your whole attention.
- take time out to do nothing in particular (read, take a bath, go for a walk, listen to music).
- if problems are bothering you, talk about them. A counsellor or psychotherapist may be able to help if you are unable to discuss problems with friends or family.

- do not take on additional responsibilities at this time. Learn how to say 'no'.

Professional Help

- Chinese medicine and homoeopathy are known to be effective.

Orthodox

- if the above recommendations do not lead to a pregnancy, your doctor may advise an examination of both partners to rule out any physical causes of infertility. For men who produce inadequate sperm, artificial insemination by a donor may be an option; for women, drugs may be given to stimulate ovulation, or surgery may be carried out to clear blocked fallopian tubes. If none of these results in conception, in vitro fertilization may be the final option.

Inflammatory Bowel Disease

A general term for inflammatory disorders affecting the small and large intestine. Crohn's disease and colitis (see entries) are examples of inflammatory bowel disease. The cause of these diseases is unknown, but many suspect they are triggered by food allergies. Symptoms include diarrhoea, stomach pain and sometimes blood and mucus in the motions.

Treatment

Dietary

- the most common food allergens are milk products, cereals (wheat, oats, barley, rye and corn), caffeine (coffee, tea, cola, chocolate). To find out if you are allergic to a food, eliminate each of these foods, one by one, from your diet for at least 2 weeks. Notice if symptoms are improved. After 2 weeks reintroduce the food and notice if symptoms reappear. If you see a change in symptoms it is likely you have discovered an allergy and should avoid the food.

- increase intake of fibre, found in whole grain cereals, if you are allergic to cereals, eat plenty of fruit and raw vegetables.
- eat plenty of 'live' yoghurt to promote the growth of 'friendly' bowel bacteria. Supplements of *Lactobacillus acidophilus*, available in health food stores, will activate bowel bacteria, essential for healthy digestion. Take 1 teaspoon of *Lactobacillus acidophilus*, 1 teaspoon of *Bifidobacteria* powder, and ½ teaspoon of *Lactobacillus bulgaricus* (available from health food stores) in a glass of spring water, 3 times daily.

Herbal

- garlic supports the growth of natural beneficial bacteria in the colon, and kills infection. Use garlic copiously in cooking. Garlic capsules (3 capsules, 3 times daily) can be taken as an alternative to the fresh herb.

Homoeopathy

to be taken every 15 minutes for 4 doses and repeat if necessary:
- sudden spasms with ineffectual urge to move bowels: Nux vomica 6c.
- colic with exhausting diarrhoea and much gas; voiding gas provides little relief: China 6c.
- colic, bending double and hard massage brings relief: Colocynth 6c.
- rumbling and gurgling after rich food: Pulsatilla 6c.

Orthodox

- anti-inflammatory drugs may be given to relieve the swelling.

Influenza *see* Flu

Ingrown Hair

Sometimes hairs grow down under the skin, causing inflammation and pimples. This often occurs in people with very curly hair, and is more common on areas which are shaved, particularly facial or pubic hair.

Prevention

- the major cause of ingrown hairs is shaving; allowing the hair to grow may be an alternative to ingrown hairs.
- for women wishing to remove unwanted hair, waxing is an alternative to shaving which tends not to produce ingrown hairs. Warm or cool wax is placed on the skin, allowed to stick to the hairs, and then pulled off taking the hairs with it. Waxing is done in a professional beauty salons, or with home kits.
- ingrown hair often results from shaving too closely. Using an electric razor does not give as close a shave, but it may prevent ingrown hairs. If you prefer a wet shave, gently brush the skin with a wet loofah first to remove dead cells. Soak the area to be shaved in water for at least 10 minutes to soften the hair. Place shaving foam or gel on the area and leave it on for a few minutes to soak in. Use a single-bladed razor and do not shave too closely. Place a hot face cloth over the area for a few minutes after shaving. Finish off with a creamy lotion or aftershave, to keep the hairs soft.

Treatment

Practical Advice

- if a hair is obviously ingrown, place a hot face cloth over the area for 5 minutes, and ease out the hair with sterilized tweezers (place them in boiling water to sterilize them). Dab the open pore with hydrogen peroxide or essential oil of tea tree to prevent infection. If you cannot see the hair, keep the hot cloth on the area until it emerges.

Orthodox

- your doctor would ease out the hair with the above method.

Ingrown Toenail

The edges of one or both sides of the toenail (usually that of the big toe) press into the adjacent flesh leading to pain, infection and inflammation.

Prevention

Ingrown toenails often result from incorrect nail cutting, stubbing your toe, or dropping something on it.

- when cutting nails, soak the feet first to soften the nails. Cut the nail straight across, never in an oval shape. Do not cut too short: your nail should cover the toe to protect it. File down sharp edges with an emery board.
- wear protective shoes when walking on rough ground or lifting.

Treatment

Practical Advice

- soak the foot in a warm solution of water and antiseptic or a warm marigold solution (5 drops of marigold tincture to 1 litre of water) to soften and cleanse the nail. Dry and insert a thin strand of sterile cotton wool in between the nail and the flesh. This will lift the nail away from the flesh and help it to grow out. Change the cotton every day.
- wear open-toed sandals, or soft, comfortable shoes. Tight or pointed shoes will press the nail in further.

Orthodox

- antibiotics are given to treat the infection. Minor surgery under local anesthetic removes the edge or all of the nail, enabling the inflamed skin to settle down and heal before the new nail grows in about 9 months' time. This is often the only way to allow healing, since inflammation cannot be relieved while pressure from the nail is present.

Insect Bites and Stings

Insect bites, such as fly and mosquito bites, can spread infection and disease, as well as being itchy and tiresome. Bee and wasp stings are painful and can cause allergic reactions in some people. Avoiding bites and stings is the best measure, with the help of natural repellent.

Prevention

Practical Advice

- mosquitoes often come out at night. If you are sitting out in the evening, wear light clothing which covers

the skin, particularly the wrists, arms and ankles. Place mosquito screens over windows, and use a mosquito net around your bed. Insect repellents such as sprays or slow release coils help keep the mosquitoes away.
- do not wear scented toiletries outside.
- wear light clothes; dark ones attract insects.
- rubbing cider vinegar on your skin is also an effective insect repellent.

Dietary

- take thiamine (vitamin B1) to prevent bites. Large amounts of thiamine are excreted through the body and give off an odour which repels insects. Take a 100 mg tablet 3 times daily.
- daily doses of zinc also help repel insects. Take at least 60 mg daily.
- eating garlic has a similar effect.

Aromatherapy

- essential oil of eucalyptus is a natural insect repellent. Make up a solution by adding 5 drops of the essential oil to a cup of water and dab on the exposed areas of the body.
- essential oil of citronella is also effective.

Homoeopathy

- Ledum 6c taken twice daily helps prevent mosquito bites.

Treatment

Practical Advice

- a bee leaves its sting in the flesh and it should be gently scraped out with a sterile knife or needle. Take care not to push it further in, and do not suck it out. If the sting is in the mouth or throat, rinse the mouth

with iced water, suck ice cubes, and seek medical help immediately.
- bee stings are acidic and can be neutralized by dabbing a solution of bicarbonate of soda and water on the sting (2 teaspoons to 1 cup of water.)
- wasp stings are alkaline and can be neutralized by dabbling vinegar or lemon juice on the sting.
- wash insect bites thoroughly with soap and water. Try not to scratch, as this may cause them to become infected.
- to relieve the itching dissolve 1 teaspoon of baking soda in a cup of water, soak a piece of cloth in the solution and bathe the bites.

Aromatherapy

- rub a drop each of tea tree and or lavender oil into the bites, and repeat every hour until the irritation stops.

Herbal

- dab tincture of witch hazel on mosquito bites.

Homoeopathy

- dab Pyrethrum tincture on the sting.
- when an allergic reaction to a bee sting occurs: Apis 6c every 10 minutes until professional help can be obtained.

Bach Flower Remedies

- Rescue Remedy is useful, especially for children.

Biochemic Tissue Salts

- Nat Mur: crush the tablet and apply locally.

Orthodox

- calamine lotion is a harmless remedy which will

soothe the skin and relieve itching. For those who experience large swellings after being bitten, some doctors recommend wetting the skin and rubbing an aspirin over the bite to control inflammation. Antihistamine drugs are recommended for an allergic reaction. Antibiotics are given for infected bites. Severe allergic reactions with swelling of the lips, tongue and throat, accompanied by breathing problems, are a medical emergency, so consult a professional immediately.

Insomnia

Difficulty sleeping. Most people with insomnia have problems getting to sleep or staying asleep. The cause is often anxiety, though insomnia can also result from illness, pain, depression, environmental factors, lack of exercise, and drugs.

Treatment

Practical Advice

- establish a bed time and a rising time and stick to it. Do not oversleep in the morning.
- avoid daytime and evening napping: do not allow yourself to sleep until you get to bed.
- do evening activities which allow you to relax without falling asleep: an evening walk, talking with someone, playing a game or doing gentle household chores are good; television may send you to sleep before bedtime.
- ensure comfortable, quiet sleeping conditions. Make sure the bedroom is adequately heated and aired.
- resolve problems before going to sleep. If you are lying awake worrying, put the light on and write down what is worrying you. Promise yourself that you will deal with the issues in the morning when you are fresh.

Dietary

- eat your evening meal at least two hours before retiring.
- avoid caffeine (coffee, tea, chocolate, cola), tobacco, and alcohol.

Aromatherapy

- lavender is known to help relaxation. Add 5 drops of essential oil of lavender to a bath, and soak in it before retiring.
- put 3 drops of lavender on a tissue to inhale.

Herbal

- valerian tea is a natural sedative: pour a cup of boiling water over 2 teaspoons of the root, infuse for 15 minutes, and drink before going to bed.
- passiflora is also excellent — if you are buying supplements over the counter, follow the instructions on the packet; otherwise consult a medical herbalist.

Homoeopathy

- Coffea 6c, every 30 minutes when feeling hyped up, wide awake, or sensitive to every little noise.
- Arnica 6c, every 30 minutes when unable to sleep through overexhaustion.

Chinese Medicine

- herbs which are often recommended are fleeceflower stem, poria, and wild jujube seeds which do not sedate, but have a beneficial effect on the nervous system.

Exercise

- regular aerobic exercise — walking, jogging or

swimming — helps relieve tension and anxiety, and relaxes the body, permitting better sleep.

Acupressure

- regular massage of the points illustrated can be very helpful in treating insomnia.

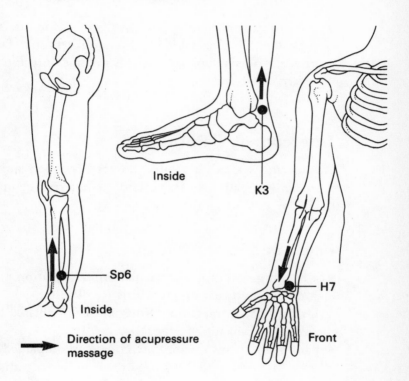

Inside

K3

Sp6

Inside

→ Direction of acupressure massage

H7

Front

Relaxation

- do the following routine before retiring or once you are in bed:
  - lie on a firm surface, close your eyes and become aware of how your body feels. Focus your attention on each part of your body, starting with the tips of the toes and finishing with the face and eyes; consciously try to relax every part in turn. The whole procedure should take at least 10 minutes.
- problems concerning work, unemployment, financial

worries, domestic hassles, ill health or workaholism
are often connected to insomnia. Identifying and
solving these problems will help improve your
sleeping pattern. Sometimes writing down a list of
concerns and worries can be enough to improve sleep.

Orthodox

• solving the problem which is causing insomnia is the
first step. Sleeping tablets or tranquillizers may be
prescribed as a short-term measure, but only for
severe cases, and as a last resort.

Intercourse, Painful

Pain during sexual intercourse affects both men and
women. The pain may be around the external genitals,
or, in the case of women, internal.

Causes in Men

• a burning sensation on ejaculation or urination
suggests urethritis or prostatitis (see Prostatitis,
Urinary Tract Infection; 'Nonspecific Urethritis' under
Sexually Transmitted Diseases).
• pain in the penis during intercourse accompanied by
redness, swelling, lumps or sores may be balanitis (see
entry), herpes (see entry) or another sexually
transmitted disease (see entry).
• soreness or irritation of the penis after intercourse
may result from a reaction to a spermicide or
lubrication, or an allergy to rubber if using a
condom. There are many different brands on the
market so try using different products. Non-allergenic
condoms are also available.

Causes in Women

- if you are starting a first or new relationship you may feel sore and bruised. Using a lubricant such as KY jelly can help avoid this. To relieve bruising, soak in a warm bath, to which 5 drops of essential oil of either lavender or clary sage has been added. Take the homoeopathic remedy Arnica 6c once hourly.
- if you have recently given birth you may be sore, especially if you have had an episiotomy (see entry). Wait at least 10 days before having sexual intercourse. Pelvic floor exercises can help tone up the vaginal muscles: contract and relax the muscles controlling urination 5 or 10 times at least 3 times a day. Arnica 6c taken twice daily for up to 2 weeks relieves bruising. Calendula cream or tincture solution or vitamin E oil applied to the stitches promotes healing.
- pain, itching and irritation accompanied by unusual vaginal discharge may be a sign of thrush or of trichomoniasis (see entries).
- if you are urinating more often than usual, or experiencing a burning feeling when you pass water, an inflamed bladder may be contributing to the discomfort (see Cystitis).
- if you have reached the age of menopause, hormonal changes may result in your vagina being tighter and drier than before (see Menopausal Problems). Using a lubricant, such as KY jelly, could solve this problem.
- if intercourse and the use of tampons are difficult or impossible, the cause may be a spasm of the muscles surrounding the vaginal entrance (see Vaginismus).
- if you feel internal shooting pain during penetration and your periods have become more painful you may have endometriosis (see entry) or cervical erosion (see entry). Experimenting with different positions for intercourse may lead to more comfortable sex. Consult your doctor if you suspect one of these may be the cause of pain.

Practical Advice

- sometimes soreness in either partner can be due to
  anxiety, inadequate foreplay, lack of lubrication or too
  forceful penetration. Taking more time to make love,
  and discussing sexual practices and problems openly
  with your partner can help overcome problems.
  Sexual counselling may be useful to facilitate such
  discussion.

Intermittent Claudication

Pain in the calves, resulting from a blockage of blood
flow in the arteries due to atherosclerosis (see entry).
The pain often starts after walking a short distance,
forcing you to stop frequently for rests. In extreme cases
blood clots form in the arteries, leading to death of an
area of tissue, gangrene and possible amputation. If you
suspect you have intermittent claudication, consult your
doctor.

Treatment

Practical Advice

- stop smoking. This is the most effective way to
  prevent or halt this condition.
- excess weight may contribute to the ailment, so try to
  maintain your normal weight (see recommendations
  for weight loss in the section on Obesity).

Dietary

- studies have shown great improvement by combining
  walking with vitamin E supplementation. Take
  300—400 iu daily.
- intermittent claudication is a sign of arterial disease,
  therefore high cholesterol foods, such as red meat and
  dairy products should be avoided, and intake of high

fibre wholegrain cereals and fresh fruit and vegetables should be increased.
- increase intake of magnesium, found in nuts, cooked dried beans and peas, whole grain breads and cereals, soya beans, dark green leafy vegetables, milk and seafood.

Herbal

- hawthorn infusion is a good tonic for the circulatory system: pour a cup of boiling water on 2 teaspoons of the berries, infuse for 20 minutes, drink 3 times daily.

Homoeopathy

- Baryta muriatica 6c, 3 times daily for 3 weeks.
- Proteus 30c, as needed during acute attacks.

Exercise

- walking is the best exercise for this condition. Try to do at least 1 hour daily. Walk until you feel moderate discomfort in the legs, then stop for a rest. Keep repeating the walk-pain-rest cycle. After two or three months of daily exercise you will begin to get some results as bypass blood vessels develop in the legs to overcome blocked ones.
- if the weather does not permit walking, stationary indoor bicycling is an alternative. Follow the same routine as above.

Orthodox

- arterial reconstruction using various synthetic grafts is used in about ⅓ of cases and can be very effective and durable. The feet must be stringently cared for as infection or trauma can lead to gangrene.

Irritable Bladder

An irritable bladder manifests with the sudden uncontrollable urge to urinate. It is often a result of a bladder infection (see Cystitis), a bladder stone (see entry), or obstruction to the outflow of urine by an enlarged prostate gland (see Prostate, Enlarged). In many cases the cause cannot be found, but the following treatments may help.

Treatment

Practical Advice

- drink plenty of water, at least 2 litres daily.
- consult your doctor to see if you have a urinary tract infection (see entry).
- make sure you empty the bladder completely each time you urinate.
- women: always wipe yourself from front to back after going to the toilet.
- empty the bladder after intercourse.
- wear cotton underwear.

Homoeopathy

to be taken every 15 minutes for 4 doses during acute attacks:
- urge to urinate, but nothing comes: Nux vomica 6c.
- pain which is relieved if urination is postponed: Equisetum 6c.
- urine feels like scalding water; violently painful: Cantharis 6c.
- burning pain at the end of urination and afterwards: Sarsaparilla 6c.
- stinging pains better from cold bathing: Apis 6c.

Exercise

- for women: to strengthen pelvic floor muscles, try

stopping urination mid-flow and then restarting. The muscles which control this reflex may need to be strengthened. During the day contract and relax these pelvic floor muscles when you are not urinating. The more often you do it, the stronger the muscles will become (see 'Exercise' under Incontinence, Urinary).

Orthodox

• urodynamic studies are useful in that they measure the flow and volume of urine passed through the bladder. They can diagnose problems in the bladder itself and in the urethra — the tube that leads from the bladder to the outside — so that accurate and precise treatment can be planned. Treatment may include drugs to suppress the nervous impulse to the bladder or to relax the bladder muscles.

Irritable Bowel Syndrome

Also known as spastic colon, symptoms include cramp-like stomach pains, swollen abdomen and alternating phases of constipation, hard stools and diarrhoea, often accompanied by gas. The cause is not fully understood, but it is thought that the symptoms result from improper functioning of the muscular contractions of the large intestine. Stress is often thought to contribute to the severity of the illness. Women are more susceptible to it than men.

Treatment

Dietary

• studies show that increasing intake of fibre is one of the most effective cures for this condition. Vegetables, fruit, oat bran, guar gum, cooked dried beans and peas are good sources of fibre. The effect is not immediate, and symptoms may worsen during the first 2 weeks of treatment. However, within 4 months of increasing fibre intake you should see an improvement.

- some people with irritable bowel syndrome have a lactose intolerance, which prevents them from digesting milk. It may be worth abstaining from all dairy products for two weeks to see if symptoms are relieved. See Lactose Intolerance for more details.
- different foods and food combinations bring irritable bowel syndrome in different people. Keeping a diary and noting everything you eat, including the circumstances in which you eat and your mood, may reveal what is upsetting you.
- eat plenty of natural unsweetened 'live' yoghurt (one large carton a day) to ensure the gut has a necessary supply of the healthy bacteria that are essential to digestion.
- if you cannot tolerate yoghurt, take non–dairy supplements of *Lactobacillus acidophilus*. Take 1 teaspoon of *Lactobacillus acidophilus*, 1 teaspoon of *Bifidobacteria* powder, and ½ teaspoon of *Lactobacillus bulgaricus* (available from health food stores) in a glass of spring water, 3 times daily.

Aromatherapy

- massaging the abdomen with relaxing and antispasmodic essential oils helps to relax any tension in the muscles and enhances digestion. Using 3 drops each of essential oil of peppermint and black pepper mixed with 20 ml of carrier oil or lotion, massage the abdomen very gently, using the following routine:
- put one hand over the other and gently knead the stomach, using small circular motions. Start at the right bottom corner, moving upwards to the right of the lower ribs, across the abdomen to the left lower ribs, down to the left bottom corner, and back across to the right.

Herbal

- peppermint infusion relieves intestinal spasm and gas: pour a cup of boiling water onto a heaped teaspoonful of the dried herb and infuse for 10 minutes. Try to replace tea, coffee and carbonated beverages with peppermint infusion.

Homoeopathy

to be taken every 15 minutes for 4 doses and repeat if necessary:
- sudden spasms with ineffectual urge to move bowels: Nux vomica 6c.
- colic with exhausting diarrhoea and much gas; voiding gas provides little relief: China 6c.
- profuse diarrhoea accompanied by burning and colicky stomach, restlessness, anxiety and chilliness: Arsenicum album 6c.
- burning in the rectum and anus with uncontrollable diarrhoea: Aloe 6c.
- greenish painless diarrhoea with gurgling and stomach cramps, worse early morning: Podophyllum 6c.

Chinese Medicine

- dandelion is recommended, along with magnolia bark, to ease the bloated sensation. Rhubarb and Chinese angelica prevent constipation, while poria aids diarrhoea.

Relaxation

- stress contributes to the severity of this condition. Yoga, meditation or biofeedback have been seen to reduce symptoms.

Orthodox

- antispasmodic drugs are given to relieve stomach pain

and sometimes antidiarrhoeal drugs to prevent long-
term diarrhoea.

Itching

Intense irritation or tickling which may be felt all over
the body, or in one particular place. It may be a sign of
skin disease, such as dandruff, eczema, or psoriasis (see
relevant entries). Anal itching may be caused by
haemorrhoids (see Anal Itching; Haemorrhoids). Vaginal
itching may be due to a yeast infection (see Thrush).
More generalized itching, which affects the whole body,
may be a sign of diabetes (see entry). Often itching is
caused by cosmetics, bath products, detergents, too
much washing or rough clothing. It is particularly
common in the elderly. The following treatments are for
itching which has no apparent underlying disease.

Treatment

Practical Advice

- try not to scratch, as this aggravates the irritation.
  Keep your nails short, so that you cannot break the
  skin and infect it. Apply a cool wet compress to the
  area when the urge to scratch occurs.
- soap irritates itchy skin, so use as little as possible.
  Mild cleansing lotions can substitute soap, or simply
  use water and a face cloth to wash.
- avoid talcs and scented bath products.
- wear loose, soft clothing, and cotton underwear.
  Avoid itchy fabrics.

Herbal

- add a strong infusion of chickweed to the bath. Pour
  3 cups of boiling water on 10 teaspoons of the dried
  herb, infuse for 15 minutes, add to bath water and
  soak in it to relieve itchy skin.

Chinese Medicine

- dittnay bark or broom cypress fruit are recommended.

Hydrotherapy

- ground oatmeal is a soothing agent. Add 2 cups to a warm bath and soak in it.

Orthodox

- antihistamine tablets, liquid or injections may be recommended and also soothing lotions, creams or ointments. Calamine is effective, and probably the safest of all these. Hydrocortisone or stronger steroid creams may be used in severe cases under supervision.

Jaundice

Yellowing of the skin and whites of the eyes as a result of an underlying liver disorder which leads to an accumulation of bile products in the body. This may be due to hepatitis (see entry), cirrhosis (see entry), blockage of the bile duct by a stone or tumour, or the abnormal destruction of red blood cells which leads to the release of red pigment into the blood.

Treatment

To be carried out in consultation with your doctor.

Dietary

- eat fruit, raw vegetables and vegetable protein (soya, dried, cooked beans, peas, wholegrain cereals and potatoes). Drink lemon juice and carrot juice every day. Reduce intake of all fats, including nuts and seeds. Avoid alcohol, caffeine and smoking.

Herbal

- dandelion root decoction is a gentle liver tonic: put 3 teaspoons of the root into a cup of water, boil then simmer for 10 minutes. Drink 3 times daily.

Homoeopathy

- persistent jaundice in newborns: Chamomilla 6c, 2 times daily.

- if Chamomilla doesn't help within 48 hours take Lycopodium 6c, 2 times daily for up to 3 days.

Chinese Medicine

- traditional Chinese Medicine relates jaundice to dampness in the liver and gallbladder. Oriental wormwood and gardenia fruit or corktree bark may be recommended to clear the dampness.

Professional Help

- in jaundice caused by haemolytic anaemia (when the red blood cells are broken down more quickly than they are replaced), professional homoeopathic treatment may be helpful.

Orthodox

- a blood test is necessary to confirm diagnosis. Treatment is aimed at the underlying cause.

Jellyfish Stings

Jellyfish stings generally result in a mildly itchy or painful rash. Occasionally they may cause more severe symptoms of vomiting, sweating and breathing difficulties which require immediate medical attention.

Treatment

First Aid

- do not rub the sting, but rinse it immediately with salt water.
- if fragments of the tentacle remain in the skin, apply vinegar or alcohol to inactivate them. Do not touch them, but try to scrape them off using a knife, a razor, the edge of a credit card, a towel or sand.
- keep the affected skin cool.

Homoeopathy

- Medusa 30c (a remedy prepared from jellyfish sting) take 1 dose as soon as possible and then hourly for as long as necessary.

Orthodox

- painkillers, antihistamines, or hydrocortisone cream will be offered to reduce the inflammation. A tetanus injection may be recommended.

Jet Lag

Disruption of normal sleep and wake cycles by flying across different time zones. Symptoms include fatigue, irritability, lack of concentration, disorientation, and sleep and appetite disturbances.

Treatment

Practical Advice

- get plenty of sleep in the few days before the flight.
- fly by day and arrive in the evening or at night.
- avoid alcohol during the flight, but drink plenty of other fluids to prevent dehydration.
- eat light meals during the flight.

Dietary

- the following jet lag diet was devised by American scientist, Dr Charles Ehret, and has been shown to help reset body clocks and prevent symptoms.
  - determine breakfast time at destination on day of arrival.
  - three days before departure day keep to the following routine:
  - day 1: eat a high protein breakfast and lunch, and a

carbohydrate dinner. No coffee, tea or cola except between 3 and 5 pm.

- day 2: fast on light meals of salads, soups, fruits and juices. No coffee, tea or cola except between 3 and 5 pm.
- day 3: do the same as day 1.
- day 4: fast on light meals; if you drink coffee, drink only in the morning when travelling west; or in the evening if travelling east. During the flight do not drink alcohol; sleep until breakfast time if possible. Break the fast at destination breakfast time, and eat a high protein meal. Stay awake and active and continue meals according to the meal times at the destination.
- another possibility is the following: for one week before departure and for two days after arrive, take Aminoplex amino acids, 2 capsules daily, and magnesium ascorbate vitamin C, 2 grams daily.

Aromatherapy

- some airlines are now using aromatherapy to help relax travellers. Lavender is recommended to encourage relaxation, rosemary and/or lemon to refresh and keep you alert.

Homoeopathy

- Arnica 6c: take every 3 hours during the flight and then twice daily for 3 days after landing.
- Cocculus 6c: take 3 times daily for 3 days after landing where there has been a significant change of time zones.

Jock Itch *see* Fungal Infection

Kidney Stones

Also known as urinary tract calculi, these are hard deposits of salts which collect in the kidney ducts or pass into the ureter, the tube leading down to the bladder. Stones which remain in the kidney may give mild pain in the back above the waist on one side. Stones which get stuck in the ureter produce excruciating and unmistakable pains which cause you to double up and render you helpless. Mild cases of this condition can be helped by the recommendations below, though it is advisable to consult a health professional.

Treatment

Dietary

- drink at least 3 litres of water daily.
- reduce intake of animal protein; increase intake of vegetables and wholegrain cereals.
- kidney stones are generally an accumulation of excess deposits of calcium phosphate or calcium oxalate. To prevent stones occurring, reduce your intake of calcium-rich foods (milk, cheese, butter and other dairy products); reduce intake of oxalate-rich foods (chocolate, celery, grapes, green peppers, beans, parsley, spinach, strawberries, blueberries, beetroot, tea).
- increase intake of vitamin A, essential to the health of the lining of the urinary system. Vitamin A-rich foods are: liver, kidney, egg yolk, fortified margarine, cod

liver oil, dark green yellow and orange vegetables (broccoli, carrots, sweet potatoes).
- daily supplements of vitamin B6 (10 mg a day) and magnesium (not magnesium carbonate) (300 mg a day) have been shown to prevent recurrence of kidney stones.
- use 2 tablespoons extra virgin olive oil daily in cooking or salad dressings.
- increase intake of magnesium-rich foods (nuts, cooked dried beans and peas, wholegrain breads and cereals, soya beans, dark green leafy vegetables, milk and seafood).

Herbal

- some herbal remedies are thought to help ease the stones out of the system. Herbalist David Hoffman recommends a combination of stone root, parsley piert, gravel root, and pellitory-of-the-wall. Put a teaspoon of each herb in a cup of water, simmer for 15 minutes and drink 3 times daily.
- decoction of stone root alone is also effective. Put 3 teaspoons of the dried root in a cup of water, simmer for 15 minutes and drink 3 times daily.
- aloe vera juice helps reduce the size of stones.

Exercise

- physical activity helps move calcium to the bones which need it. Inactivity tends to keep it in the kidney where it forms stones. Regular walking, swimming, running or cycling will help prevent kidney stones.

Orthodox

- although small gravelly stones may pass through the system on their own, larger stones in the ureter or bladder are generally broken up using shock wave treatment or a telescopic tube (ultrasonic lithotripsy).

Knee Pain

Knee pain can arise from a number of different conditions which may affect the bones themselves, the joint structures inside, or the muscles, ligaments and tendons outside. Knees are weight-bearing joints susceptible to a large amount of wear and tear and are a common site of pain. (See also Housemaid's Knee.)

Prevention

- do at least 15 minutes of warm up stretches prior to exercising.
- buy new running shoes regularly.
- run on soft rather than hard ground if possible.

Treatment For Pain Caused by Exercise or Strain

Dietary

- if you are overweight, you are putting more stress on the knees. Try to bring your weight down to the optimum level for your height.
- take evening primrose oil (6 x 500 mg daily).

Hydrotherapy

- pain and swelling can be eased by applying an ice pack or hot and cold treatments. Prepare an ice pack by wrapping ice cubes or a bag of frozen vegetables in kitchen towel. Prepare a hot water bottle and wrap it in a towel. Place the ice pack on the knee for 10 minutes, then do the same with the hot water bottle. Repeat the procedure 3 times, several times daily, while elevating the leg. Hot and cold packs encourage the circulation of blood through the knee, flushing out toxins and bringing fresh blood to promote healing. It is an extremely effective treatment for this condition.

Massage

- massage has a similar effect to hot and cold treatment: it increases circulation to the knee and helps flush out toxins. It also relaxes tense muscles and ligaments. Regular massage from a professional therapist is very helpful for this condition. Alternatively you can try the following routine:
- sit with your knee bent. Place your thumbs on the outside of your leg, rest your fingers and palms on the sides of your legs. Run your thumbs down the muscles, slowly exerting pressure until you reach the ankle bone. This is called stripping the muscle. Move your hands round to the inside of the ankle and massage up the inside leg. Finally, put your thumbs in front of and below the knee and your hands around the calf, with your fingers behind the knee, strip down the back of the calf with your fingers.

Acupressure

- massage of the points illustrated overleaf may be useful in many cases of knee pain.

Exercise

- the following exercises will help strengthen the muscles supporting the knee. They should only be done if they do not produce any pain in the knee. Try to do the exercises at least twice daily.
- sit on the floor with legs stretched out in front. Place a rolled towel under the sore knee. Tighten the muscles in your leg without moving the knee, hold for 30 seconds then relax. Repeat 20 times.
- sit with your back against a wall, legs stretched out in front. Raise the leg with the sore knee a few inches off the ground, hold for 5 seconds, then release. Do 20 lifts, then rest, then do another 20.
- lie on your stomach on the floor. Place the strap of a weighted bag over your ankles and bend your knees,

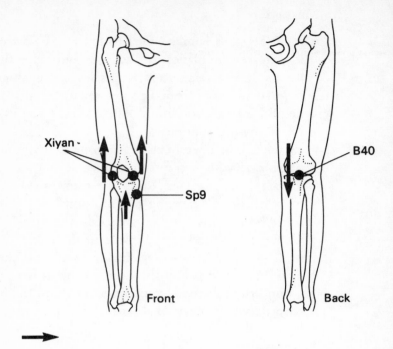

lifting your legs and the bag 20 times. Rest and
repeat.
- swimming and rowing are activities which do not put
  pressure on the knees yet will help strengthen leg
  muscles.

Professional Help

- an osteopath or chiropractor would recommend
  massage, ultrasound treatment, exercises, and possibly
  manipulation.
- acupuncture may be helpful in relieving pain.

Orthodox

- treatment depends on the cause of pain and can range
  from ice treatment (as above) to the prescription of
  anti-inflammatory drugs, physiotherapy or surgery.

Labour Pains

Most women experience pain before and during childbirth. There are many different ways of dealing with it which should be considered before the birth.

Practical Advice

- many women find that lying down increases the pain of contractions. Walking around has been found to increase the efficiency of contractions and shorten labour. Kneeling, standing or squatting often brings pain relief.
- the presence of people you know and trust helps create an atmosphere of security, allowing you to relax, which in turn reduces pain.

Aromatherapy

- essential oils of lavender and clary sage are the oils most commonly used in childbirth. Add between 4 and 6 drops to the bath or use in combination with a carrier oil or lotion for massage during labour (see below).

Homoeopathy

there are numerous remedies to help with labour pains, of which the following are the most common, to be repeated as often as the situation demands:
- sudden spasmodic pains with anger and impatience,

wants to open the bowels with every contraction:
Nux vomica 6c.
- hypersensitivity to all external stimuli — touch, light,
  slightest noise: Coffea 6c.
- hot and stuffy, weepy and needing reassurance:
  Pulsatilla 6c.
- frightened and panicky: Aconite 6c.

Hydrotherapy

- floating in water helps; some women also choose to
  deliver in water. Birthing pools can be hired privately
  or are available in some hospitals.

Massage

during labour it is the back and the buttocks which
need massaging: the following routine is helpful. When
carrying out massage, listen to the woman in labour and
do what she says. Use talc rather than oil.
- the mother-to-be can be squatting, supported over a
  large beanbag, or sitting, facing the back of a chair
  with pillow as support. She can have her head in her
  arms.
- between contractions the partner places the flat of
  his/her hands on her back and leaning towards her,
  performs slow firm strokes from the centre of the
  lower back out to the sides. Alternate with right and
  left hands, or work with both together, moving
  gradually up the back. Gentle neck stroking also
  helps.
- during contractions, do featherlight circular massage
  on the sacral triangle (see illustration) or just lean
  both hands gently across the lower spine and wait.
  Listen to the woman and do as she says.

Acupressure

learn these points before the delivery:
- bend your leg, and place your thumb between your

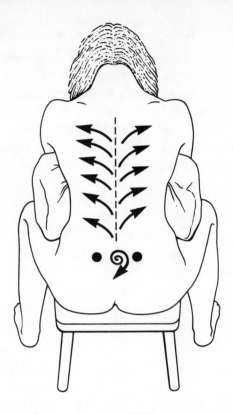

inner anklebone and the Achilles tendon. Massage deeply with the thumb for 1 minute, and repeat on the other side. Both points can be held simultaneously if you wish.

• Repeat on the other side.

Transcutaneous Electrical Nerve Stimulation (TENS)

• this technique is used more and more in delivery rooms. An adaption of traditional acupuncture techniques, it consists of a small battery-powered unit which sends out electrical stimuli to two electrodes attached to the skin. This 'blocks' the transmission of pain sensation along the nerves between the electrodes, reducing the pain sensation. It works immediately, is completely safe, and provides a moderate degree of pain relief.

Orthodox

- nitrous oxide gas and air (entonox) is breathed through a mouth piece bringing some pain relief. It may also make you lightheaded and sleepy. It does enter the baby's system, though the effects are unknown.
- epidural: a local anaesthetic is injected into the space between the spinal cord and the lumbar region of the backbone. It can give complete pain relief, and though it does enter the baby's system it is less harmful than pethidine (see below).
- pethidine: injection of a powerful painkilling narcotic drug into a vein or into the buttock muscle. It gives effective pain relief within 10 minutes, along with drowsiness, nausea and a drunken 'high'. These effects are sometimes seen on the baby, who is floppy, less responsive and likely to encounter breathing problems on delivery.

Lactose Intolerance

The inability to digest one of the sugars found in milk can lead to symptoms of bloating, gas, stomach cramps, vomiting and frothy diarrhoea. Symptoms often resemble colitis (see entry), and are sometimes mistaken for it. Lactose intolerance is especially common among those of African, Mediterranean or Oriental origin.

Treatment

Dietary

- if you think you may be unable to digest milk, test your tolerance level by giving up all milk products and foods containing milk for at least 2 weeks. If your symptoms disappear, it is likely you have a lactose intolerance. You may find, however, that you are able to tolerate small quantities of milk. Gradually introduce dairy products back into your diet in small quantities, noticing how much it takes to set off a reaction. You can organize your diet according to what you can tolerate.

- milk contains important sources of calcium. If you reduce or give up milk, ensure you eat plenty of other calcium-rich foods such as: canned fish (sardines or salmon), tofu, dark green leafy vegetables, cooked dried beans, dried apricots, sesame seed products.
- you may find you can eat live yoghurt, which contains the enzyme needed to digest milk and is rich in calcium.
- replace milky drinks with soya milk or dairy-free milk/whiteners. Buttermilk or goat's milk may be more digestible than ordinary cow's milk.
- lactase, the enzyme which digests milk in the stomach, is available from health food stores in bottles. When dropped into the milk and left overnight, it digests the lactose and the milk will no longer cause problems.

Orthodox

- doctors advise replacing lactose-containing products with soya-based produce. Often a child 'grows out of' lactose intolerance and can resume dairy produce by the age of 10–12 years.

Laryngitis

Inflammation of the larynx (voice box) generally caused by a virus, bacteria or straining the voice. Symptoms include pain, coughing and hoarseness. In children laryngitis may manifest as croup (see entry). If voice loss persists for more than two weeks, consult your doctor.

Treatment

Practical Advice

- avoid alcohol and smoking.

Aromatherapy

- essential oils of sandalwood and lavender are soothing and can be used in a gargle by adding 1 drop of each to half a glass of warm water. Add 2 drops of lemon or peppermint if you have an infection.

Herbal

- decoction of echinacea is effective against viral and bacterial attacks of laryngitis: put 2 teaspoons of the root in a cup of water, bring to the boil and simmer for 15 minutes. Drink 3 times daily.

Homoeopathy

to be taken hourly for 4 doses and repeated if necessary:
- barking cough, with burning and irritation in the larynx, after getting chilled: Aconite 6c.
- stringy yellow catarrh, metallic sounding cough and husky voice with raw pain: Kali bichromicum 6c.
- burning pain, tightness in the chest and hoarseness eased by eating ice cream: Phosphorus 6c.
- laryngitis from overuse of the voice, splinter-like pains on swallowing: Argentum nitricum 6c.

Chinese Medicine

- this condition is seen to result from heat and poison in the lungs. Treatment would be with honeysuckle flowers, peppermint and liquorice.

Hydrotherapy

- steam inhalations will help soothe inflamed mucous

membranes in the larynx. Fill a basin with boiling water and sit or stand with your head over it and a towel over your head to trap the steam, inhale deeply.

Orthodox

- antibiotics to reduce infection and steam inhalations are the mainstay of treatment. Long-term hoarseness (more than 4 weeks) requires examination by a specialist to rule out more serious abnormalities.

Lead Poisoning

Swallowing or inhaling lead can cause impaired mental development in children, anaemia and damage to the nervous and digestive systems. It can also bring subtle symptoms of weakness, lethargy and lack of coordination. The most common sources of lead poisoning are licking or eating old paint with high lead content, inhaling traffic exhaust fumes, drinking water from old lead pipes or storing food in lead-glazed pottery.

Prevention

- avoid canned food; a lead solder is often used in canning.
- do not eat food grown in industrial or urban areas exposed to exhaust fumes.
- do not buy fruit and vegetables from roadside vendors.
- if living in an old building, check your plumbing to ensure that lead is not used in the system. If in doubt, always run the water for a few minutes before drinking, and if possible arrange an alternative drinking water supply.
- pregnant women should avoid exposure to heavy traffic fumes; children should not play near busy roads.

Treatment

Dietary

- calcium prevents the accumulation of lead in the body. Increase your intake of low fat dairy products, tinned sardines and salmon, green leafy vegetables, and sesame seed products (tahini, halva, hummus).
- vitamin C helps to neutralize lead. Increase your intake of fresh fruit and vegetables, particularly citrus fruits, and/or take supplements.
- zinc and magnesium also help in the removal of lead. If you are buying supplements over the counter, follow the instructions on the packet; otherwise consult a naturopath or nutritionist.
- kelp contains sodium alginate, which combines with lead, allowing it to be excreted from the body. Take kelp tablets, or sprinkle the powder on your food. Use dried seaweed in cooking.
- the amino acid glutathione is effective in removing lead from the body. 1–3 g should be taken daily.

Aromatherapy

- to help the lethargy, weakness and lack of coordination use 2 drops each of grapefruit, rosemary and lemon essential oils in a daily bath.

Orthodox

- diagnosis of lead poisoning is generally made through a blood test. Calcium EDTA or dimercaprol are given to remove excess lead from the body.

Leg Ulcer

Also known as a varicose ulcer, this is a sore on the leg which fails to heal. It often occurs in elderly people with poor circulation or varicose veins, which prevents the supply of fresh blood reaching the wound and allowing it to heal. Leg ulcers are typically pale and weepy in the centre and red and itchy around the edge.

Treatment

Dietary

- oral supplements of vitamin E (400 to 800 iu daily), and zinc (30 mg daily) stimulate the circulation and encourage healing.

Aromatherapy

- bathe the ulcer with a solution of 1 cup of distilled water and 2 drops each of essential oil of clove and geranium.

Homoeopathy

- Gunpowder 6x is a wonderful blood-purifier and will assist healing by internal cleansing in addition to the topical applications mentioned. Take 3 times daily for up to 7 days.

Orthodox

- treatment consists of eradicating the infection (which prevents healing) and improving circulation. Dressings, leg elevation and removal of varicose veins are recommended.

Lice

Infestation with blood-sucking parasites, which live in the hair, causing itching and redness of the scalp. You may be able to diagnose lice through the sight of white or yellowish eggs (nits) attached to the hair. The parasites are often passed between schoolchildren. For pubic lice see Sexually Transmitted Diseases.

Prevention

Practical Advice

- regularly check the hair for nits or lice.

Aromatherapy

- use the rinse below if there is an outbreak of lice at your child's school, for example.
- comb the hair with a comb left in a mug of water with 10 drops red thyme between combings.

Homoeopathy

- Psorinum 30c: one single dose for children who are recurrently prone to lice.

Treatment

Practical Advice

- if a child has lice, all the family should be treated and school authorities should be alerted. A shampoo or scalp lotion containing malathion is the best way of killing the lice. After using the product, comb the hair with a fine-toothed comb. Wash clothing, and all brushes and combs. Inspect the hair with a fine comb every day to ensure there is not a reinfestation.

Aromatherapy

- after shampooing, rinse the hair slowly with 1 pint of water containing 6 drops each of sweet thyme and rosemary, stirring well before use. Towel dry and allow to finish drying naturally. Comb with a fine-toothed comb.

Longsightedness *see* Eyesight Problems

Low Blood Sugar *see* Blood Sugar, Low

Lower Back Pain

More commonly known as lumbago, lower back pain can result from an exaggerated inward curvature of the lower spine, known as lordosis or swayback. It may also be caused by poor posture, muscle strain from lifting, being overweight, having weak stomach muscles, or arthritis. Lower back pain can also result from degenerative diseases such as arthritis or from an infection in the bones themselves. It is advisable to consult a professional before attempting self help treatment.

Treatment For Lordosis or Muscular Strain

Bach Flower Remedies

- difficulty relaxing and sleeping: Agrimony.
- weariness of mind and body: Hornbeam.

Massage

- general back massage, concentrating particularly on the lower back and the buttock muscles, helps reduce muscle tension and pain, and restore lost mobility. Do not massage over the vertebrae, but either side, working upwards and outwards with stroking movements. If you find areas of tension or 'knots', spend a little more time using small circular movements to relax the muscles.

Acupressure

- massage the points illustrated using deep thumb pressure for at least one minute.

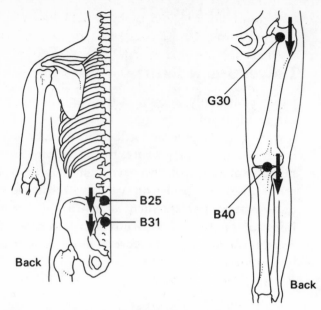

➡ Direction of acupressure massage

Exercise

the following exercises help strengthen the stomach
muscles, taking strain off the lower back. Stop if they
produce pain.

- pelvic tilt: lie on your back on the floor, place one
  hand under the small of the back, then try to squash
  the hand by pressing the small of the back
  downwards to the floor. Hold for 10 seconds then
  relax. Repeat 15 times.
- abdominal scrunches: lie on your back with your
  knees bent, slowly raise your head and chest a couple
  of inches off the floor, pointing your outstretched
  hands towards your knees. Hold for 3 seconds and
  relax. Repeat 10 times.
- lumbar stretch: lie on your back, draw both knees up
  to your chest and clasp your hands around them,
  pulling them inwards to your chest. Hold for 5—10
  seconds, relax and repeat 10 times.
- bring your legs into your chest again, but this time

make a wide circle with the tops of the knees. Repeat
5 times clockwise, 5 times anticlockwise.
- lumbar roll: lie on your back, bend your knees so
that your feet rest near to the buttocks. Keeping the
knees together let them fall over to the left side, while
keeping your shoulders and feet flat on the floor.
Repeat 3 times in each direction.

Relaxation

- the following routine may help reduce the pain. Lie
on your back and support the knees with a pillow or
bolster. It may also help to put a thin pillow or
rolled-up hand towel under the small of the back.
Experiment with the position until you are
comfortable.
- try to let go of your pain. Close your eyes and
become aware of how your body feels. Focus your
attention on each part of your body, starting with the
tips of the toes, and finishing with your face and eyes.
Consciously try to relax every part in turn. The
whole procedure should take at least 10 minutes.
- if you are unable to relax, try using relaxation tapes,
learn meditation or biofeedback.

Professional Help

- osteopathy and chiropractic provides effective
treatment through massage, ultrasound, and
manipulation. Exercises may also be recommended.
- the Alexander Technique will help improve posture
and is highly recommended for this condition.
- acupuncture is effective in reducing pain.

Orthodox

- anti-inflammatory drugs and muscle relaxants will
probably be recommended, along with physiotherapy.

Lumbago *see* Lower Back Pain

Lupus Erythematosus

An auto-immune disorder whereby the white blood
cells, which usually attack foreign invaders, instead turn
on the body's connective tissue, causing severe
inflammation, a red blotchy rash which appears on the
cheeks and bridge of the nose, nausea, fatigue, fever,
joint pain and weight loss. Sometimes lupus can lead to
problems with internal organs — lungs, liver and heart
— therefore, all treatment should be carried out in
collaboration with a doctor.

Treatment

Practical Advice

- some drugs can trigger lupus: talk to your doctor if
  you are taking medication.

Dietary

- a change in dietary fat intake and type has been
  shown to reduce inflammation caused by lupus.
  Instead of meat and dairy products, eat more fish,
  particularly herring, mackerel, sardines and salmon.
  The vital ingredient found in fish is called
  eicosapentaenoic acid (EPA), which is also found in
  supplement form, available in health food stores.
- studies have shown that vitamin E supplements can
  help relieve this disorder. Take up to 800 iu daily in
  supplement form. Apply vitamin E oil or cream to
  the rash.
- increased intake of vitamin B5 (pantothenic acid)
  helps this condition. The vitamin is found in its
  natural form in liver, fish, chicken, cheese, wholegrain
  breads and cereals, avocados, cauliflower, cooked dried

peas and beans, nuts, dates and potatoes.
- people with lupus often find they have food allergies or sensitivities. See Allergies — Food.
- increase intake of selenium, found in whole wheat, brown rice, oatmeal, poultry, lean meat, organ meats and fish.

Orthodox

- your doctor will prescribe non-steroidal anti-inflammatory drugs to relieve joint pain, antimalarial drugs for the rash and corticosteroid drugs for fever.

Lyme Disease

A disease which is transmitted by tick bites. The first sign is an area of redness surrounding a tick bite, followed by fever, headache, lethargy, muscle aches and swollen joints. If the disease is not treated early, the heart and nervous system can also be affected.

Prevention

- cover yourself up when outside in grass, woodland, scrub or caves. Wear shoes, socks, long trousers, a shirt and a hat.
- use an insect repellent, particularly around the ankles.
- check yourself for ticks before going inside. Wearing light clothing will help you see them, brush them off any clothing.
- when inside inspect the skin, scalp and pubic hair area for ticks, tiny specks which cling to the skin. Inspect children daily during the summer.
- put a tick collar on pets to prevent the parasite entering the house.

Treatment

- if you find a tick on your body do not try to pull it out or scrub it off, as its mouthpart may remain in your flesh. Instead hold a glowing match on the tick and it will drop off. Wash the bite with soap and water.
- keep an eye on the bite in the next few weeks. If you see redness developing around the area, consult your doctor immediately.

Orthodox

- if diagnosed before joint swelling occurs, antibiotics will clear up Lyme disease. If inflammation has set in, your doctor will recommend non-steroidal anti-inflammatory drugs and sometimes corticosteroids.

Manic Depression

A mental disorder, characterized by extreme mood swings. These may be recurrent periods of depression, or alternating phases of mania and depression. During the 'highs' a sufferer may be overly enthusiastic, self confident, hyperactive and sometimes reckless. During the depressive phase he/she is unable to see the positive side of life, and is consumed by anxiety and guilt. Treatment should be in consultation with a doctor.

Treatment

Practical Advice

- talking therapy: counselling, psychotherapy or psychoanalysis are extremely helpful in dealing with the symptoms and implications of this illness. See Appendix 1 for useful addresses.
- support and help from others in a similar situation can also help. See Appendix 2 for details of support groups.

Dietary

- a number of nutritional imbalances have been shown to contribute to depression. Your diet should be one which balances wholegrain cereals with plenty of fresh fruit and vegetables (raw if possible), and low fat meat, fish and dairy produce.
- dietary supplements which may help include:

- vitamin C: 1 g daily.
- vitamin B complex: 2 tablets daily.
- magnesium: 500 mg daily.
- amino acids: DLPA (D,L-phenylalanine) 400 mg daily, or L-phenylalanine 100—500 mg daily.
- **caution**: not to be taken if you suffer from high blood pressure.
- the Pill can interfere with nutrient absorption; therefore, naturopaths recommend finding an alternative means of contraception.
- avoid caffeine (tea, coffee, chocolate, cola drinks) and alcohol.
- some naturopaths carry out biochemical tests to determine mineral deficiencies which may contribute to depression.

Herbal

- St John's Wort has been shown to relieve symptoms of anxiety, depression and low self esteem. It also helps improve quality of sleep: take 1—4 ml of the tincture in water 3 times daily.

Exercise

- studies have shown that exercise can have a tremendously beneficial effect on mood disorders, particularly in alleviating depression. A regular exercise programme of at least 30 minutes of aerobic activity 3 times a week is recommended.

Relaxation

- techniques to reduce stress, such as massage, yoga, meditation, aromatherapy, and acupressure are helpful in alleviating the anxiety common to this illness.

Professional Help

- hypnosis can sometimes relieve tension and anxiety.
- homoeopathic treatment can also help.

Orthodox

- depression is generally treated with antidepressant drugs. Mania is often controlled with lithium, a specific anti-manic drug which reduces nervous activity in the brain. Long-term use produces side effects, including stomach upsets, tremor, drowsiness, and sometimes kidney damage.

Mastitis

Sometimes occurs while breast feeding. One or both breasts become painful and inflamed, and fever and flu-like symptoms occur. Bacteria may enter cracked or sore nipples, leading to infection and the development of an abscess.

Prevention

- mastitis often occurs as a result of painful breast feeding. According to La Leche League, this can be prevented by positioning your baby correctly. He/she should be facing you entirely, the head should be in the crook of your elbow, the buttocks in your hand. Support your breast with the other hand. Make sure the baby has your nipple deep inside his/her mouth, so that the nipple does not move and get irritated and sore.
- when you begin feeding, limit the time on each nipple to avoid soreness.
- be sure to insert your finger into the baby's mouth to break the suction, before removing the nipple.
- avoid using soap on your nipple, as this will dry out the skin.
- ensure you dry your nipples well (a hair dryer will help to remove all moisture) before covering them.
- rubbing a little of your own milk into sore nipples will help them to heal.

Treatment

Practical Advice

- expelling excess milk brings relief: hold a warm cloth on the breasts to encourage the flow of milk.
- apply vitamin E cream to heal cracked nipples.

Homoeopathy

take every 15 minutes for 4 doses and repeat if needed:
- when there is excessive milk production and high fever, with red streaks on breasts: Belladonna 6c.
- when breast are hot, hard and painful: Bryonia 6c.
- nipple cracked and infected: Silicea 6c.
- when pain radiates all over the body and the breast is engorged and purple: Phytolacca 6c.

Chinese Medicine

- a poultice made from powdered dried rhubarb root mixed with olive oil is applied to the breasts to ease pain. Madder root, peony bark, and dandelion are also prescribed.

Orthodox

- barrier sprays and antiseptic solutions are sometimes used to protect and prepare the nipples for lactation. Once mastitis has set in, antibiotic drugs are recommended, along with painkillers. If there is no infection, breast feeding can continue. If an abscess occurs it will be drained (see Abscess).

ME (Myalgic Encephalomyelitis)

Also known as post-viral fatigue syndrome, or chronic fatigue syndrome, this condition is characterized by extreme exhaustion, muscle aches and weakness, headaches, digestive problems, visual disturbances, mood swings, and difficulty concentrating and speaking. Doctor are unclear what causes the illness, though it sometimes occurs after a major viral infection.

Treatment

Dietary

- eat regular meals of wholegrain cereals, plenty of fruit and vegetables, and quality protein at least twice daily.
- avoid caffeine and alcohol.
- reduce intake of sugar and junk food.
- keep a supply of high energy snacks available for times when you cannot prepare meals (soup, fruit, nuts, cereals and juices are good).
- some ME sufferers are unable to digest milk (see Lactose Intolerance). Substituting milk with other non-dairy calcium-rich foods often helps clear up digestive problems associated with this illness.
- food allergy may be a factor in ME. See Allergies — Food for further details.
- some physicians and naturopaths believe that symptoms of diarrhoea, bloating and stomach pain in ME result from chronic yeast infection (see entry on Fungal Infection).
- B complex supplements may be helpful: 2 x 50 g daily.

Herbal

- evening primrose oil is sometimes helpful, though the supplement must be taken over at least 3 months to see the effects. 2—3 g daily is the recommended dose.

Homoeopathy

- professional homoeopathic treatment has shown good results with ME.

Exercise

• some exercise can help, but the key is not to overdo
  it, as this may bring a relapse. Walking or a short
  swim in a warm pool may be possible, but be aware
  when your body is telling you it has had enough.

Relaxation

• physical and mental rest is one of the most important
  factors in treating ME.
• accept that your commitments, activities and
  expectations will change as a result of your illness.
• plan every single day to ensure activities are organized
  to allow sufficient rest in between.
• plan for a period of bed rest in the afternoon; listen
  to the radio or a tape if you do not want to sleep.
• rest in a quiet place; do not answer the phone or
  doorbell.
• if you feel tired at different times during the day, rest;
  there is no point in continuing if you feel bad.
• relaxation tapes, biofeedback or autogenic training
  will help you to relax. A gentle yoga class can also be
  useful. Many ME sufferers also find that learning to
  meditate improves their physical and psychological
  condition.

Orthodox

• your doctor may prescribe antidepressants to treat
  depression, sleep disturbances and pain. ME sufferers
  often experience increased sensitivity to many drugs,
  so medication should be taken with caution.

Measles

A viral illness which generally occurs around the age of
1–3 years. The first signs are cold-like symptoms,
followed by a rash behind the ears, spreading over the

body; the eyes are often red and sensitive to light. The child may have a high fever, and a cough. Stomach pains, vomiting and diarrhoea may also occur. In some complicated cases of measles, chest and ear infections can occur, and in rare cases, inflammation of the brain tissue.

Treatment

Practical Advice

- put the child to bed, in a dimmed room. Try not to let him/her watch television or read. Instead, spend time with the child, keeping him/her calm.

Dietary

- during the fever stage give the child plenty of fluids, including fruit and vegetable juices.
- once the fever has gone down, introduce simple foods, such as cereals and vegetable soup.

Herbal

- yarrow infusion helps reduce the fever. It should be used during the first stages of the illness. Pour a cup of boiling water over 2 teaspoons of the dried herb, infuse for 15 minutes, and drink hot 3 times daily.
- echinacea decoction will combat the virus, ease out the rash and help clear catarrh. It should be used once the fever has started to come down. Put 2 teaspoons of the root in a cup of water, simmer for 15 minutes and drink 3 times daily.

Homoeopathy

take 1 tablet every hour for up to 4 doses and repeat if needed:
- sudden onset with fever, restlessness and intense dislike of light: Aconite 6c.
- burning bright red skin, hot head and cold

extremities, feverish and delirious: Belladonna 6c.
- mildly feverish, weepy and clingy, creamy yellow discharge from the eyes and nose: Pulsatilla 6c.
- hot acrid discharge from the eyes with a bland discharge from the nose: Euphrasia 6c.
- professional advice should be sought *immediately* if the rash is slow to develop or suddenly disappears.

Chinese Medicine

- the body is encouraged to detoxify and the rash to come out by giving safflowers, peppermint and honeysuckle.

Hydrotherapy

- to soothe the rash, take warm baths to which 3 tablespoons of baking soda have been added.

Orthodox

- many doctors recommend immunization of children against the measles virus. In the USA, proof of immunization is required before the child can attend school. The vaccine should not be given to children under the age of 1, or those who have a history of seizures, or epilepsy in the family.

Memory Problems

Memory loss, also known as amnesia, is the inability to recall or memorize information. Short-term memory loss is certainly part of the ageing process. It can also result from anxiety, depression, stress, poor nutrition, inadequate sleep or lack of brain stimulation. When memory loss is accompanied by confusion, lack of concentration, or a change in behaviour, it is usually an indication of a medical disorder and requires professional help.

Treatment

Practical Advice

- some drugs can sometimes cause memory problems. If you are taking medication, discuss alternatives with your doctor.
- the more you exercise your brain, the longer and the better it will serve you. Try to do activities which stimulate the brain: reading, crossword puzzles, games and classes which require mental concentration and learning. From time to time, test your memory by trying to memorize poetry or lines from a novel or play.
- if you find you are forgetting a name, a date, an event or a word, try to make associations which will bring it back. For example, if you forget a person's name, try to remember what they look like, where you met them, what they were wearing, etc. In your mind, try to find everything you can associate with the forgotten issue, eventually the links will lead you to remember what has been forgotten.
- if you find you are constantly losing things, take mental photographs when you put things down. Sometimes even holding up an imaginary camera and taking a picture will help you to remember.
- writing things down can help improve your memory. Make lists of things you have to remember. Put up notes in prominent places, if you are likely to forget to look at the list.

Dietary

- nerve cells require acetylcholine for healthy functioning. Acetylcholine is formed in the body from lecithin, found in eggs, sunflower oil, and soya bean oil. Lecithin can also be bought in granule form from most health stores. To be effective it must contain phosphatidyl choline. Studies have shown that taking supplements of up to 70 g of lecithin daily improves memory skills.

- increase intake of protein: the amino acids present in protein are vital to brain functioning. You could also take a supplement which combines all 22 free-form amino acids.
- ensure your diet is high in wholegrain cereals, vegetables and fruits and low fat protein. A multivitamin and mineral supplement taken once daily will ensure adequate intake of other nutrients essential to good mental functioning.

Chinese Medicine

- memory loss caused by stress or fatigue is treated with herbs such as Chinese wolfberry, Chinese fleeceflower root and black ginger seed. Acupuncture would also be recommended.

Orthodox

- investigations are made into the cause of severe memory loss, particularly if there are signs of other mental problems. Treatment will depend on the diagnosis.

Ménière's Disease

This is a disorder of the inner ear where an increase in the fluids of the inner canals leads to hearing and balance problems. Typical symptoms are ringing or buzzing in one or both ears, bouts of nausea, hearing loss and dizziness.

Treatment

Practical Advice

- stop smoking.

Dietary

- naturopaths recommend a salt-free, wholefood diet, high in raw and cooked vegetables, seaweed, seeds, nuts, beans, low fat yoghurt and fish. Avoid caffeine (coffee, tea, cola, chocolate), fried foods, alcohol and food additives and preservatives.
- reduce intake of fluids, except water which helps to detoxify the system.

Aromatherapy

- essential oils of lavender, geranium and/or sandalwood added to a bath help relieve stress.

Homoeopathy

- Ménière's disease responds well to professional treatment.

Exercise

- take regular daily exercise to increase blood circulation. Walking, swimming, cycling or jogging are all suitable activities.

Relaxation

- stress and tension play a large part in triggering attacks of Ménière's disease.
- one way to relieve the stress of this condition is to meet other sufferers by joining a support group (see Appendix 2).
- attend a yoga class, or learn to meditate.
- have a regular massage from a professional therapist, or exchange massages with a friend or family member.
- allow yourself to do things you enjoy. This may be developing a hobby, or sport, or simply taking some time off to do nothing in particular (have a bath, read a magazine, listen to music, etc.).

- if you are unable to determine the cause of stress, or have problems you are unable to resolve, talking to a counsellor or psychotherapist may help.

Reflexology

- massage the ear point, located where the little toe joins the sole of the left foot.
- massage the eustachian tube area, located in between the third and fourth toe, where they join the sole of the left foot.
- massage the sinuses, located on the pad of all toes except the big one.

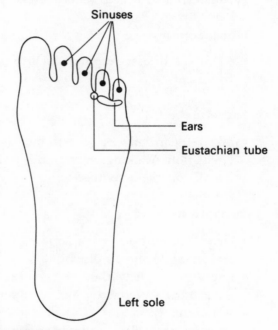

The reflex areas

Orthodox

- anti-sickness drugs may be prescribed. As a last resort surgery can be undertaken, but this results in hearing loss. Ultrasonic radiation may enable vertigo to be treated without permanent hearing loss.

Menopausal Problems

Menopause literally means the end of menstrual periods. It typically occurs during the late 40s and early 50s. Many women sail through the menopause without any problems. Some experience varying degrees of symptoms; the most common ones are listed below.

- hot flushes.
- night sweats, often leading to sleep disturbance.
- vaginal dryness which results in painful sexual intercourse.
- dry skin and brittle hair.
- psychological problems: poor concentration, anxiety, depression, tearfulness.
- brittle bones (see Osteoporosis), leading to frequent fractures which may be slow to heal.
- varicose veins (see entry).
- rheumatic symptoms (see Rheumatoid Arthritis).
- constipation (see entry).
- irregular bleeding.

Treatment

Treatment for many of the symptoms listed above are described in detail in other sections of this book. The following recommendations are general treatments to ease you through the menopause.

Dietary

- sound nutrition throughout life is one of the best ways of preventing problems with the menopause. Dietary changes made at the onset of symptoms can also help.
- eat wholegrain cereals, plenty of fruit and vegetables, and low fat protein. Avoid coffee, alcohol, sugar, chocolate and refined or processed foods.
- research has shown that increased intake of vitamin E relieves many of the symptoms of the menopause.

Vitamin E is found in vegetable oils, seeds, wheatgerm and nuts, avocados, peaches, wholegrain cereals, spinach, broccoli, asparagus and dried prunes. It can also be taken as a supplement: 400 iu daily is the recommended dosage, and this can be built up gradually to 800 iu. If you are diabetic or suffer from high blood pressure or rheumatic heart disease, consult a professional before increasing intake of vitamin E.

- psychological problems associated with the menopause are often helped by increasing intake of the B vitamins. The richest natural source of vitamin B complex is wheatgerm. Eat 3 dessertspoons daily with fruit and cereal and take one B complex supplement daily.

- calcium is a vital nutrient both before and during the menopause to counteract brittle bones. It is also said to reduce stress and nervous disorders, and may help relieve hot flushes. To ensure adequate intake of calcium, eat at least 3 servings of calcium-rich foods daily. These include: low fat milk, cheese, or yoghurt, dark green leafy vegetables, cooked dried beans, wholegrain cereals. If you do not eat dairy products it is essential to eat dark green leafy vegetables such as broccoli, kale, and mustard greens every day.

Herbal

- ginseng contains substances with the ability to regulate hormones. Clinical trials have shown that 400–1200 mg of Siberian ginseng daily relieved hot flushes, vaginal dryness, sweats and anxiety.

Chinese Medicine

- acupuncture can help. Herbs commonly recommended include Chinese angelica, romania, peony root and thorowax root.

Exercise

- studies have shown that regular exercise is highly beneficial in counteracting menopausal problems. Aerobic exercise which also includes stretching, muscle strengthening and relaxation is the best. Walking, jogging, swimming or aerobics classes are suitable. Combine one of these with a weekly yoga class to aid relaxation.

Orthodox

- Hormone replacement therapy (HRT) is often offered to women with menopausal problems. It provides oestrogen and progesterone in the form of vaginal cream, pills, skin implants or a slow release skin patch. It relieves hot flushes and vaginal dryness, and prevents brittle bones. However, the side effects of long-term use of hormone therapy are not clear, and some studies suggest they may increase the likelihood of developing breast or endometrial cancer.

Migraine

A throbbing headache usually on one side of the head, accompanied by visual problems and sometimes nausea or vomiting. A migraine can be an individual attack or a recurrent problem triggered by anxiety, anger, excitement, depression, shock, overexertion, or changes in diet, climate or routine. An attack can last for between 2 hours to two days.

Treatment

Dietary

- migraine is sometimes triggered by low blood sugar (see Blood Sugar, Low).
- specific foods which are thought to trigger migraines

in children include cow's milk, egg, chocolate, orange, wheat, cheese, tomato, rye, benzoic acid, tartrazine, fish, beef, pork, soya, bacon, coffee, yeast, peanuts. In adults: cheese, red wine, monosodium glutamate, nitrates and chocolate. To identify foods which may be a problem, check labels on foods scrupulously and keep a record of everything you eat, noting also any symptoms that appear. After a few months you may become aware which foods trigger a migraine. If you think you have identified a trigger, avoid the food for at least 1 month. During this time note down your symptoms, along with other foods eaten. If the migraine symptoms decrease, avoid the food group for another 3 months. After this you may find you can tolerate small amounts of it (once or twice a week only). However, if symptoms return, avoid the food altogether. You may have to carry out this process with many different foods to find the culprit.

Aromatherapy

• inhalations, baths or massages using essential oil of true melissa or rosemary and sweet marjoram.
• an aromatherapy massage is very relaxing.

Herbal

• medical studies have shown that feverfew (*Tanacetum parthenium*) is an effective remedy for reducing the intensity and frequency of migraine attacks. Take two or three small leaves of feverfew daily, chopped up in a sandwich (a sprinkling of sugar helps to disguise the bitter taste). Feverfew tablets are available from pharmacies and health food shops — follow the dosage instructions on the packaging. The results may take 2—3 months to become apparent.

Homoeopathy

to be taken every 15 minutes for up to 6 doses and repeated if needed:

- for hammering pain which comes and goes with the sun accompanied by visual disturbances and preceded by numbness and tingling in the lips: Natrum muriaticum 6c.
- visual disturbances with vomiting and burning in the gut: Iris versicolor 6c.
- preceded by visual disturbances which ease as the headache begins: Kali bichromicum 6c.
- pain spreads from the base of the skull to the right eye accompanied by flushes of heat: Sanguinaria 6c.
- severe pain round the left eye and down the left side of the face with tears from the affected eye and severely aggravated by tobacco smoke: Spigelia 6c.

Chinese Medicine

- acupressure and acupuncture carried out by a professional can be very effective.

Acupressure

- massage your head as if you were shampooing your hair.
- place your thumbs underneath the base of the skull on either side of the spinal column. Tilt your head back slightly and press upwards for 2 minutes while breathing deeply.
- it can be very helpful to massage the points illustrated overleaf. Use deep thumb pressure for at least one minute.

Exercise

- regular aerobic exercise has been shown to reduce attacks of migraine. Swimming, walking or running for 30 minutes three times a week is recommended. Yoga stretches help ease mental and physical tension.

Relaxation

- migraine is often triggered by stress. Learning how to

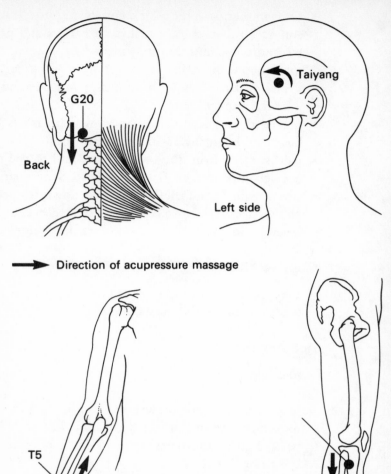

Direction of acupressure massage

anticipate and deal with stressful situations may
reduce attacks:
• learn to identify what your fears and concerns are;
  making a list can sometimes help.
• learn to deal with these problems one by one; talking
  to a friend, relative or health care practitioner, a
  counsellor or psychotherapist will help.

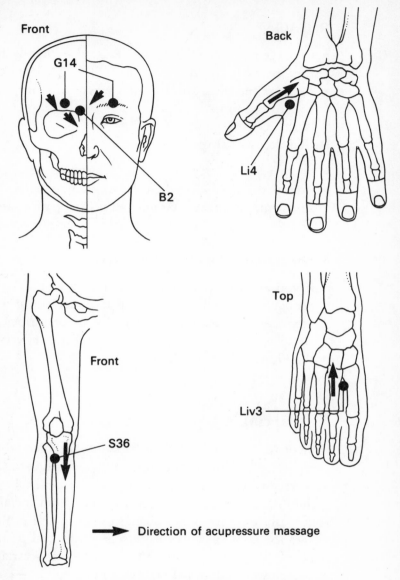

Front

G14

B2

Back

Li4

Front

S36

Top

Liv3

→ Direction of acupressure massage

- if possible avoid creating unnecessary stress; for example, always give yourself plenty of time, so that you don't have to rush to appointments; try not to take on more work or activities than you can handle; learn to say 'no'.
- attend a yoga or meditation class, take regular exercise or develop a hobby to help you relax.

Reflexology

- massage the area relating to the head, which is all the toes, particularly the big toes.
- massage the neck area, located where the toes join the sole of the foot.

Professional Help

- applied kinesiology is used to detect allergies.
- osteopathy can help when the migraine is related to a spinal misalignment. Craniosacral osteopathy can help when it is related to facial or jaw misalignment.

Orthodox

- if you are taking the Pill, your doctor would probably recommend an alternative method of contraception. Painkillers may also be prescribed, along with drugs which have a stabilizing effect on the blood vessels of the head.

Miscarriage

Loss of the baby before the pregnancy has come to term is relatively common: one in six pregnancies ends in miscarriage. There is often no specific cause; however, it is thought that most miscarriages result from foetal abnormalities, hormonal imbalances, structural problems in the uterus, weak cervical muscles, industrial or environmental toxins, or a fall. Signs of a miscarriage include lower abdominal cramps and bleeding — contact your doctor immediately if these symptoms occur.

Treatment After a Miscarriage

If you have had a miscarriage, it is advisable to delay the subsequent conception for 3 months. Spend this time bringing your health up to peak with the following guidelines.

Dietary

- eat 2—4 servings of protein rich foods (fish, poultry, eggs, beans peas, nuts, seeds) daily.
- eat plenty of wholegrain cereals (bread, rice, pasta).
- eat 5—7 portions of vegetables or fruit daily.
- eat a minimum of 3 portions of calcium-rich foods: dairy products or green leafy vegetables.
- drink spring water, fruit juices, herbal teas, and milk drinks, avoid caffeine (coffee, chocolate, tea, cola), alcohol, and cigarettes.
- avoid raw meat and fish, and uncooked vegetables which you have not thoroughly washed yourself.

Homoeopathy

take every 15 minutes for 6 doses:
- where there is a risk of miscarriage after an accident or shock: Arnica 6c.
- where there is a risk of a miscarriage caused by amniocentesis: Hypericum 6c.

Bach Flower Remedies

- Rock Rose, 4 times daily.

Exercise

- gentle stretching, swimming or yoga helps strengthen the body in preparation for childbirth. It also relaxes the mind and alleviates stress.

Professional Help

- osteopathy can help to minimize structural stress on supporting ligaments in the pelvic area and improve blood circulation and mobility.
- homoeopathy: professional treatment after a

miscarriage is often helpful and it can help where there is a history of recurrent miscarriages.

Orthodox

- consult your doctor if you have any bleeding in pregnancy. If your doctor does diagnose a threatened miscarriage it certainly does not necessarily mean that miscarriage will follow. Bed rest may be recommended, though there is no hard evidence that this prevents miscarriage. If a miscarriage does occur, dilatation and curettage (D and C) is carried out to remove any fragments from the uterus which might get infected or cause irregular bleeding or pain. In cases of recurrent miscarriage (three or more) a new type of treatment known as immunotherapy is available in some hospitals.

Mononucleosis, Infectious *see* Glandular Fever

Morning Sickness

Despite its title, morning sickness commonly occurs at any time of the day or night. About 50 per cent of pregnant women experience nausea and vomiting in early pregnancy as a result of changing hormonal levels. Despite the discomfort, this is not usually a sign of an unhealthy pregnancy.

Treatment

Dietary

- start the day with herbal tea, such as chamomile, and a few dry crackers.
- avoid fried and fatty foods.
- pineapple juice or fruit relieves nausea.
- eat small meals often. If you do not feel like eating,

maintain your blood sugar level with orange juice, fruit, milk drinks, soup or nuts.
- keep some nourishing snacks to nibble on: almonds are particularly nutritious.

Aromatherapy

- essential oils of mandarin and lavender help in a bath. Alternatively, sniff 2 drops each of peppermint and sandalwood placed on a tissue, or add them to 10 ml carrier oil and massage into the chest and stomach in a clockwise direction.

Herbal

- ginger is effective in reducing nausea: pour a cup of boiling water on 1 teaspoon of the freshly grated root, and infuse for 5 minutes. Drink when needed.

Homoeopathy

every hour for up to 4 doses and repeat if needed:
- feeling nauseous at the thought or smell of food or from travelling, but better after eating: Sepia 6c.
- nausea made better by vomiting: Nux vomica 6c.
- nausea relieved by eating with profuse salivation and a history of anaemia: Lactic acid 6c.
- nausea and vomiting relieved by keeping the abdomen uncovered: Tabacum 6c.

Chinese Medicine

- 'hot' foods, such as ginger, green and red peppers, chicken, cinnamon twigs and onions would be recommended. 'Cold' foods, such as bananas, grapefruit, lettuce and watermelon, should be avoided.

Acupressure

- place your right thumb on the inside of your left wrist, two thumb breadths from the centre of the wrist joint towards the elbow. Massage with the thumb using a deep circular motion for one minute, taking deep breaths. Do the same on the other wrist.

Orthodox

- generally, doctors avoid giving drugs during pregnancy. However, if you are vomiting all your food, and at risk of dehydration, antacids and certain antihistamines may be prescribed.

Mosquito Bites *see* Insect Bites and Stings

Mountain Sickness

Also known as altitude sickness, this affects climbers, walkers or skiers who rapidly reach heights above 8,000 feet. The reduced atmospheric pressure and oxygen at these heights lowers levels of oxygen in the blood, bringing symptoms of headache, nausea, dizziness and impaired concentration. Severe cases of mountain sickness result in a buildup of fluids in the lungs, leading to breathlessness, coughing and the production of frothy phlegm. Seizures may follow and sometimes coma.

Prevention

- make your ascent gradually, stopping for regular rests. Once you are above 8,000 feet you should stop for a few days every 2,000 feet to acclimatize.
- if you experience symptoms of mountain sickness, come down and do not climb higher until they have subsided.
- high altitudes can sometimes cause headaches. Taking 3,000 to 5,000 mg of vitamin C before the ascent can help prevent this.

Treatment

First Aid

- bring the victim down from the mountain as quickly as possible and seek emergency medical help. A delay may result in permanent brain damage.

Orthodox

- oxygen and powerful steroids are administered.

Mouth Ulcers

White, grey or yellow spots, which occur singly or in clusters in the mouth. Often they are inflamed with a red border and are extremely painful. Sometimes mouth ulcers result from injury (biting the side of the mouth or wearing a sharp brace, for example); they can be a sign of digestive disorders, or a physical response to stress or a virus. Any ulcer that fails to heal within 3 or 4 weeks should be reported to your doctor.

Treatment

Dietary

- naturopaths recommend a purifying diet of fruit juices, fruit and vegetables for two days. Follow this with a wholegrain diet with plenty of raw and cooked vegetables (if your mouth is too sore to eat rough food, liquidize the vegetables). Avoid foods which may cause allergies (see Allergies — Food).
- take daily supplements of vitamin A (750 mcg), vitamin E (250 mg) and vitamin B2 (10 mg).
- vitamin E oil (squeezed from a pierced capsule) can be applied directly to the ulcers.

Aromatherapy

- mix 1 drop of essential oil of geranium and lavender to half a cup of water. Use as a mouthwash 3 or 4 times a day.

Herbal

- myrrh is an effective antimicrobial agent, recommended specifically for mouth ulcers. Add 4 ml of the tincture to a cup of warm water and use as a mouth wash 3 times daily.
- alternatively, use the tincture neat as a mouth wash. It will sting a little, but is effective.
- if the ulcers result from injury, rub a little aloe vera gel on them.

Homoeopathy

to be taken every 2 hours on the first day, followed by 3 times daily for 2—3 days:
- when ulcers are on the edges of the tongue, with burning pain: Arsenicum album 6c.
- yellowish indented ulcers which feel firm and thick, with stinging pain: Kali bichromicum 6c.
- ulcers on the palate or tongue, yellowish and spongy, with gums which bleed easily: Mercurius solubilis 6c.

Orthodox

- antiseptic mouth rinses can be used on a short-term basis. Soluble hydrocortisone pellets or oral pastes are also prescribed.

Multiple Sclerosis

A disease of the central nervous system, where the myelin sheaths covering nerve fibres in the brain and spinal cord are gradually destroyed. There is a wide range of symptoms include tingling, pins and needles or numbness, difficulty walking, foot dragging, loss of coordination, distorted sensation, blurred vision, slurred speech, fatigue, and incontinence.

Treatment

Dietary

- avoid foods high in saturated fat: meat, dairy produce, hard fats, shop-bought pastries and snacks. (You can make your own pastries from wholemeal flour and polyunsaturated margarine.)
- increase intake of essential fatty acids, found in polyunsaturated margarines and oils (sunflower, safflower, soya, sesame, cotton seed, corn, rapeseed), nuts and beans (avoid coconuts and peanuts), liver, and green leafy vegetables.
- food sensitivities may enhance your symptoms. See Allergies — Food. Milk is a common allergy in MS sufferers. Applied kinesiology can be useful in detecting food sensitivities.
- avoid junk and processed foods, eat wholegrain cereals, plenty of fresh fruit and vegetables, avoid sugar.
- the following dietary supplements have been shown to be helpful:
  - 3 capsules of 500 mg of evening primrose oil 3 times daily with meals.
  - 1,000 mg fish oil in capsules or cod liver oil supplement daily.
  - 100 iu of vitamin E, 3 times daily.
  - 1 vitamin B complex tablet daily.
  - 50 mg of vitamin B6, daily.
  - 1 g of vitamin C, 3 times daily.
  - 15 mg of elemental zinc daily.
  - 50 mg of magnesium daily.

Massage

- regular massage increases blood circulation, prevents stiffness, enhances mobility and improves general well-being. Learn to do massage by attending a class, or exchanging treatments with a friend or family member.

Exercise

- gentle daily swimming, dancing, walking, trampolining and gentle stretching and aerobics are all helpful in maintaining mobility. However, do not allow yourself to become fatigued by exercise.

Yoga

- studies have shown that regular yoga helps prevent deterioration. There are special classes for people with MS, run by the Yoga For Health Foundation (see Appendix 1).

Professional Help

- osteopathy helps to maintain mobility. The Alexander Technique helps postural problems, coordination and movement.
- homoeopathic treatment helps in some cases.

Orthodox

- physiotherapy is very important to maintain the use of limbs. Hyperbaric oxygen treatment, where pressurized oxygen is introduced into the body, has been shown to help some people. Short courses of steroids are prescribed for acute attacks.

Mumps

A viral illness which causes infection and swelling of the glands, particularly the salivary glands and the parotids, situated below and in front of the ears. The infection, which is highly contagious, usually occurs in children between the ages of 3 and 10. Symptoms include mild sickness and discomfort and swelling in each of the glands in turn. Fever, headache and difficulty swallowing may follow. If mumps occurs in male teenagers and adults it can cause inflammation of the testes.

Treatment

Practical Advice

- the child does not have to stay in bed, unless the fever is high, but should be kept warm and quiet. He/she may be infectious to others until the swelling totally subsides.

Dietary

- eat light foods, such as soups, juices, fruit and vegetables.
- avoid dairy products, eggs, sugar and red meat.
- drink plenty of fluids.

Herbal

- poke root decoction is effective in detoxifying the glands and removing phlegm: put ¼ of a teaspoon of the root in a cup of water, simmer gently for 10 minutes, drink three times daily.

Homoeopathy

3 times daily for 3—4 days:
- child is flushed and hot, with throbbing pain in the glands worse on the right side: Belladonna 6c.

- pain worse on the left side with difficulty in swallowing liquids and intolerance of any covering of the throat: Lachesis 6c.
- stiff neck from swollen glands, profuse and offensive salivation: Mercurius solubilis 6c.

Orthodox

- a child in much pain will be given painkillers. In male adolescents or men, corticosteroid drugs will be given to reduce inflammation in the testes which can lead to infertility. A mumps vaccination is available, and is usually given in combination with measles and rubella vaccines. It should not be given to children under a year old.

Nail Problems

Healthy nails should be strong, smooth and flesh-coloured. Common problems include nail biting, nails which split or flake, the development of ridges, fungal infections and stunted nail growth.

Treatment

Practical Advice

- keep nails well manicured. File down any rough points or edges which you may be tempted to bite. Keep the cuticles soft and ease them back every time you wash your hands.
- for nail biters, paint the nails with bitter aloes, available from most herbalists. It makes the nails taste unpleasant and discourages biting.
- for fragile nails: damaged nails and cuticles can stunt growth. Keep cuticles pushed back by gentle massaging with cream after a bath or shower —with your fingertips, never with anything sharp.
- keep the nails in shape with gentle filing with an emery board.

Dietary

- iron deficiency (see Anaemia) can lead to nail problems. The most common sign is nails which grow to be spoon-shaped. Iron deficiency also causes brittle nails which crack easily. To increase iron intake

eat red meats, fish and poultry, and green leafy
vegetables. Vitamin C increases iron absorption, so
incorporate oranges, grapefruits or their juice into
your meals. Avoid drinking tea before, during or after
a meal, as this inhibits iron absorption.

- splitting and breaking can also be caused by lack of
vitamin A and protein. Incorporate liver, cod liver oil
and carrot juice into your daily diet.

- fungal infections and infections of the skin fold at the
base of the nail (paronychia) can be helped by
increasing intake of the B complex vitamins, found in
brewer's yeast (take one teaspoon in a drink 3 times
daily). Eat plenty of 'live' yoghurt every day or take
supplements of *Lactobacillus acidophilus*. Take 1
teaspoon of *Lactobacillus acidophilus*, 1 teaspoon of
Bifidobacteria powder, and ½ teaspoon of *Lactobacillus
bulgaricus* (available from health food stores) in a glass
of spring water, 3 times daily.

- white spots on the nails may be a sign of zinc and
vitamin B6 deficiency. This can be remedied by
increasing intake of poultry and fish, wholegrain
cereals, brewer's yeast and wheatgerm.

Biochemic Tissue Salts

- Silica up to 4 times a day will encourage healthy nail
growth.

Exercise

- exercising the fingers (typing, playing the piano,
doing craft work) speeds up the growth of nail tissue.
Regular massaging to keep the cuticles back will also
help.

Orthodox

- treatment consists of correction of any underlying
nutritional deficiency, or any causative medical
disorder, such as a fungal infection, psoriasis, thyroid
disease or respiratory condition.

Nappy Rash

Redness and soreness of the skin around the nappy area. It often results when the baby's delicate skin is irritated by prolonged contact with damp urine and stools.

Treatment

Practical Advice

- change the nappy as soon as it is dirty. Clean the skin gently and thoroughly and allow the nappy area to air. Try to let the baby go without a nappy for a period each day. Cloth nappies may be gentler to the skin than disposable ones.
- use the minimum amount of detergent possible for washing nappies, and rinse well to avoid irritants.

Dietary

- acidic urine and strong-smelling stools are often signs of digestive disturbances which bring nappy rash.
- supplementing the baby's food with Natren's *Bifidobacteria infantis*, also known as 'Lifestart', helps resolve nappy rash caused by a yeast infection.
- limit intake of rich and spicy foods. If you are breast feeding, avoid spicy foods, red meat, and alcohol.
- if the baby is not breast fed, give easily digestible foods and allow at least 2 hours between feeds.
- if the weather is hot and the baby perspires more than normal, increase the baby's intake of water.

Aromatherapy

- add 8 drops of essential oil of tea tree to the final rinse when washing nappies (diapers) to help disinfect them.
- to alleviate the rash make up 20 ml carrier lotion with 2 drops each of sandalwood, peppermint and lavender, and apply to the area.

Herbal

- apply calendula cream to the rash.
- make a strong infusion of chickweed by adding a cup of boiling water to 3 teaspoons of the dried herb, infuse for 10 minutes and add to the bath water to relieve pain and itching and use when cleaning the baby during each nappy change.

Homoeopathy

- give the baby 1 dose 4 times daily for up to 5 days. If breast feeding, the mother can take the remedy.
- red, dry, and hot rash: Sulphur 6c.
- accompanied by green-yellow diarrhoea in angry and irritable babies: Chamomilla 6c.

Orthodox

- barrier creams and emollients along with soothing antifungal agents are recommended. In severe cases, corticosteroid drugs or creams may be prescribed to suppress inflammation.

Nausea

Feeling sick, with or without vomiting. Nausea can result from eating rich foods (see Indigestion), drinking too much alcohol (see Hangover), food poisoning (see entry), shock, experiencing unpleasant smells, sights or tastes, migraine (see entry), stress (see entry), or as a reaction to a mild or serious disease. It may be caused by motion (see Travel Sickness), and some drugs can also cause nausea. If you are pregnant, see also Morning Sickness.

Treatment

Dietary

for food-induced nausea:
- if you are able to eat, take easily digestible wholegrain cereals, vegetable soups or steamed vegetables.
- drink plenty of fluids, particularly water.
- nibbling dry biscuits can help relieve nausea.

Aromatherapy

- nausea caused by stress or emotional disturbances is best treated with essential oils of sandalwood or lavender: add 4 drops of each to a warm bath.

Herbal

- black horehound infusion is an effective remedy for nausea caused by stress or nervousness: pour a cup of boiling water on 2 teaspoons of the dried herb, infuse for 10 minutes and drink 3 times daily.
- chamomile infusion soothes the stomach. Tea bags are widely available.
- ginger is also an effective remedy for most types of nausea: place a teaspoon of fresh grated root in a cup of boiling water, infuse for 5 minutes, strain and drink when needed.

Homoeopathy

- feeling nauseous at the thought or smell of food or from travelling, but better after eating: Sepia 6c.
- nausea made better by vomiting: Nux vomica 6c.
- nausea relieved by eating with profuse salivation and a history of anaemia: Lactic acid 6c.
- nausea and vomiting relieved by keeping the abdomen uncovered: Tabacum 6c.

Acupressure

- place your right thumb on the inside of your wrist at
  the point 3 fingers' width down your arm from the
  wrist crease. Press firmly for 1 minute. Then move
  the thumb to the point 2 fingers' width from the
  crease, press for a further 1 minute. Repeat on the
  other wrist.

Orthodox

- persistent and unexplained nausea lasting more than
  48 hours should be reported to your doctor. Once the
  cause has been established, antiemetic drugs which
  relieve nausea by suppressing the vomiting reflex in
  the brain may be prescribed.

Neck Pain and Stiffness

Usually, neck pain is a result of muscle spasm
originating in fatigue, tension, bad posture, long hours
spent at a desk or driving. It can also result from a
strain or injury (see Whiplash Injury). If neck pain is
accompanied by a severe headache, nausea, and
intolerance of light, consult your doctor immediately.
See also Fibrositis and Torticollis.

Prevention

Practical Advice

to reduce neck pain caused by bad posture:
- make sure your chair is the right height for your
  desk: your feet should be flat on the ground, and
  your back upright. You should not have to hunch to
  do your work.
- do not hold the phone between your shoulder and
  ear.
- get up and walk around every hour or so to change

position. Go out for a walk at lunch time and get some exercise before or after work.
- try to sleep on your back or side, not your front.

Yoga

these movements can be carried out at any time. They can be used as a preventive measure, or to relieve neck pain and strain. Do each movement at least 3 times, twice daily.
- let your head slowly drop forward as far as it will go towards your chest. Hold this position for 20 seconds. Lift your head and let it fall back as far as it will go, hold for 30 seconds.
- turn your head to the right as far as it will go without straining; hold for 20 seconds. Turn back to centre and drop your chin to your chest. Lift your chin and turn the head to the left as far as you can go; hold for 20 seconds and bring the head back to the centre and drop forward again.
- let your head fall to the side so that your ear approaches your shoulder; hold for 20 seconds. Repeat on the other side.
- if the neck and shoulder muscles are stiff, stand facing a wall with your feet about three feet from the base. Place your hands flat on the wall above your head and at shoulder width. Keeping your arms and legs straight, let your head and shoulders fall between your arms towards the wall. Hold the position for up to 20 seconds.

Treatment

Hydrotherapy

- to reduce neck pain and inflammation, prepare an ice pack by wrapping a bag of frozen peas in kitchen paper. Also prepare a hot water bottle wrapped in a towel. Apply the ice pack to the painful area for ten minutes, then apply the hot water bottle for

10 minutes. Repeat the procedure, and carry out
morning and night.

Massage

- turn your head to the left side, and place the ends of
  the fingers of your right hand at the top of the large
  muscle which runs from the back of the right hand
  side of your head to the collar bone
  (sternocleidomastoid muscle). Massage the length of
  the muscle with firm stripping movements. Do the
  same on the other side. (See illustration.)

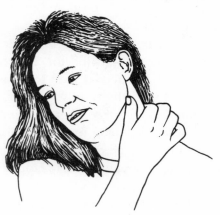

- hook the fingers of both hands over your shoulders,
  and squeeze the muscles lying between the neck and
  the shoulder joints.
- if you regularly suffer neck pain, it is worth having a
  regular massage from a therapist. Alternatively, learn
  to do massage with a friend and exchange treatments.

Acupressure

- massage the points illustrated with deep thumb
  pressure for one minute.

Relaxation

- neck pain is often a sign of fatigue and/or stress. Try
  to recognize its onset and adjust your schedule to

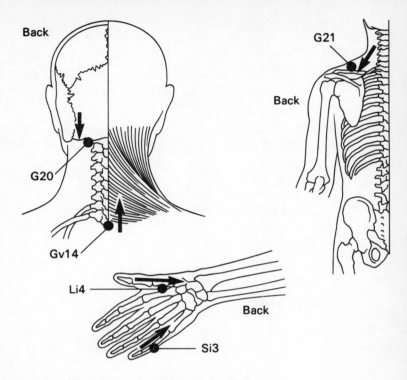

Back

G20

Gv14

Li4

Si3

G21

Back

Back

➤ Direction of acupressure massage

allow less tension and more sleep. See Stress.
- make a neck rest by putting 2 tennis balls in a sock and tying the end. Lie down on the floor, putting the sock under your neck. The balls should be on either side of the spine. Relax in this position for between 5 and 10 minutes daily.

Reflexology

if the neck is too sensitive to move or massage, reflexology can help.
- massage the neck area, located where the big toe joins the foot on the sole of the left foot.
- massage the cervical spine area, located along the inner side of both feet, along the joint of the big toe.
- rotate the big toe.

Professional Help

- if symptoms persist, consult an osteopath or chiropractor: treatment usually consists of massage and gentle manipulation. If there is underlying disease you will be referred to a GP or specialist for an x-ray.
- the Alexander Technique is very useful in correcting postural problems relating to neck pain and stiffness.

Orthodox

- painkillers and non-steroidal anti-inflammatory agents are useful in severe cases, but freezing sprays and/or deep heat should be tried first.

Neuralgia

Pain caused by injury to and/or inflammation of a nerve. Symptoms may include a shooting pain, tingling, numbness or bouts of pain. It can also be a burning sensation that occurs after an attack of herpes or shingles. If the nerves of the face are affected it is known as trigeminal neuralgia. If the nerves at the back of the leg are affected it is known as sciatica (see entry). Sometimes the back of the tongue and throat are affected, and is referred to as glossopharyngeal neuralgia.

Treatment

Dietary

B vitamins are important for the normal functioning of nerve cells:
- increase intake of vitamin B1, found in pork, green peas, oranges, dried beans and peas, wheatgerm and brewer's yeast.
- increase intake of vitamin B2, found in milk, green

leafy vegetables, mushrooms, asparagus, avocados, broccoli.
- increase intake of vitamin B7 (biotin) found in liver, oatmeal, egg yolk, soya beans, mushrooms, bananas, peanuts and brewer's yeast.
- take a vitamin B complex supplement daily.

Aromatherapy

- add 2 drops each of essential oil of lavender and basil to inhalations, baths or massage oils to relax the nervous system. One drop of valerian will enhance the effectiveness.

Herbal

- St John's Wort has sedating and painkilling properties. Make an infusion by pouring a cup of boiling water on 2 teaspoons of the dried herb, infuse for 10 minutes and drink 3 times daily.
- valerian infusion reduces tension and aids sleep. Add one cup of boiling water to 2 teaspoons of the root, infuse for 15 minutes and drink when needed.

Homoeopathy

every 15 minutes for up to 4 doses and repeat if necessary:
- pain after exposure to cold wind: Aconite 6c.
- shooting pain after an injury or spinal injection: Hypericum 6c.

Hydrotherapy

- prepare an ice pack by wrapping a bag of frozen peas in kitchen paper. Hold the ice pack to the affected area for 10 minutes. Wait 10 minutes then apply again for a further 10 minutes. Carry out the procedure twice daily.

Professional Help

- osteopathy or chiropractic should be your first step in seeking therapy. An osteopath who specializes in craniosacral techniques would be helpful.
- Chinese medicine would use acupuncture and herbs to treat this condition.
- hypnotherapy can be useful in treating this condition.
- transcutaneous electrical nerve stimulation (TENS), available in many hospitals, works in the same way as acupuncture without using needles: electrodes block electrical pain impulses to the brain and stimulate the release of endorphins, the body's own pain relief hormones.

Orthodox

- your doctor would try to identify and resolve the source of nerve irritation. This may involve surgery. If the problem cannot be resolved, pain relief and nerve tissue stabilizers, such as carbamazepine, are often recommended.

Nightmares/Night Terror

Vivid and unpleasant dreams which often bring a sense of suffocation. Nightmares are common in children aged 8 to 10, particularly if the child is unwell or anxious. In adults, anxiety, trauma or drugs are often the cause of bad dreams and night terror, thought the latter is more common in children aged 4 to 7. They do not wake up, but become agitated and start screaming, often within the first 3 hours of falling asleep, and are unable to recognize familiar faces. The child usually calms down after a while and does not remember the event the next day.

Treatment

Practical Advice

- limit evening television watching in children: some of the programmes may be unsuitable and cause fright; the flickering screen may also stimulate the child.

Homoeopathy

to be taken at night every 5 minutes until calmed:
- with a terrible fear of the dark: Stramonium 30c.
- hallucinations during sleep, wakes glassy eyed: Belladonna 30c.
- highly impressionable and imaginative, frightened of ghosts and thunderstorms: Phosphorus 30c.

Bach Flower Remedies

- nightmares, for those who wake in fear and panic, afraid to go back to sleep: Aspen.
- a child who wakes screaming from a nightmare: sip Rock Rose in water.

Orthodox

- no medication is given; in fact, drugs could make the problem worse. Doctors recommend parents to give gentle reassurance to children who wake up with nightmares. It is not necessary to talk about the content of the nightmare, but better to distract the child onto another 'comfortable' topic.

Nits *see* Lice

Nonspecific Urethritis *see* Sexually Transmitted Diseases

Nosebleed

Nosebleeds are common in children, and are not generally a cause for concern. They sometimes occur as a result of something hitting the nose, which damages delicate blood vessels, or during or after a cold or nasal infection. If a nosebleed occurs after a head injury, and is accompanied by drowsiness, vomiting or headache, or if the bleeding does not stop within 10 minutes, seek emergency help.

Treatment

Practical Advice

- sit up: do not lie down, as this forces the blood down the throat.
- blow your nose once to remove the clot which may be keeping the blood vessels open.
- pinch the nose with thumb and forefinger along the sides of the bony prominence in the middle of the nose.
- wet a piece of cotton wool with cold water, and plug up the bleeding nostril.

Dietary

- for persistent nosebleeds, take 2 g vitamin C complex daily and/or beetroot concentrate — this is rich in bioflavonoids which strengthen blood vessels. Also increase vitamin C and bioflavonoid-rich foods, especially citrus fruits.

Herbal

- nettle infusion should be taken if nosebleeds occur frequently for no apparent reason: pour a cup of boiling water onto 3 teaspoons of the dried herb, infuse for 10 minutes, drink 3 times daily.

Homoeopathy

to be taken every 10 minutes for 4 doses and repeated if necessary.
- when nosebleed results from a blow or injury: Arnica 6c.
- bright red blood which is slow to clot: Phosphorus 6c.
- nosebleeds during sleep: Sulphur 6c.
- dark, black and stringy discharge during the summer: Crocus sativa 6c.

Acupressure

- press the spot between the tip of the nose and the lip for 30–60 seconds.

Orthodox

- if heavy bleeding continues after 10 minutes, or if blood is being swallowed down the back of the throat, then it is advisable to seek emergency help at hospital. In severe cases, pressure packs within the nose are used, or diathermy, a procedure to shrivel up the bleeding blood vessels.

Obesity

Obesity is generally defined as being at least 20 per cent over the optimum desired weight for the person's height. The reasons why it occurs are unclear, though often it is a case of unconscious overeating and lack of activity, which may be combined with emotional conflicts and problems. Some believe that obese people have an unusually slow metabolism. It may also result from hormonal imbalances.

Treatment

Practical Advice

- keep a record of what you eat, when and where. This will make you more aware of your eating habits and how much you consume.
- always sit at a table to eat and be conscious of what you are doing. Don't eat while walking, reading, talking on the phone, watching television, etc.
- eat slowly and chew the food well.
- when you go food shopping buy only wholegrain cereals, low fat protein and dairy products, and fruit and vegetables. By limiting yourself to these foods you will avoid the temptation of other more calorific and less nutritious items.
- if you have a tendency to use food as a means of rewarding or comforting yourself, try to think of other ways you can do this: for example, an occasional massage or aromatherapy session can

provide a real treat, and give more long-term physical and mental enjoyment than the temporary pleasure and subsequent guilt and remorse brought by overeating.

- it is always easier to make dietary and lifestyle changes if you are motivated by others engaged in the same struggle. Join a local group where you can compare notes to make weight loss easier and more enjoyable.

Dietary

- crash dieting may bring temporary weight loss, but it rarely has a permanent effect. Moreover, it often leads to nutritional deficiencies, demoralization and unhealthy eating habits. Instead, the following guidelines help establish long-term balanced eating habits which will maintain optimum weight.
- gradually replace all refined foods with wholegrain foods (wholemeal bread, rice, pasta, oatmeal) and fresh fruit and vegetables. You will find you need less of this food to satisfy your appetite than if you eat refined foods.
- eat moderate amounts of low fat protein (chicken with skin removed, and fish) and vegetable protein, such as soya products, dried cooked beans and peas.
- eat moderate amounts of low fat dairy products.
- avoid all junk and snack food, sugar and sugar-containing foods.
- limit intake of alcohol.
- eat four small meals a day.
- try not to eat in between meals, but if you are hungry eat a piece of fruit.
- drink at least 6 glasses of water daily.
- bee pollen, available in health food stores, is said to stimulate the metabolism and suppress the appetite. Start with a few granules to ensure you are not allergic to it. Gradually build up to 1 teaspoon daily.
- brewer's yeast is helpful in reducing the craving for

sweet foods. Take 1—2 teaspoons in fruit juice before each meal.

- the amino acid phenylalanine has been shown to help weight reduction: 100 mg to 500 mg daily is recommended, taken on an empty stomach at night.
- the Hay diet has helped many people — the basic premise is not eating starch and protein at the same meal (see Appendix 4). *The Food Combining Diet* by Kathryn Marsden (Thorsons) is based on an adaptation of the Hay Diet for the purposes of weight loss.

Homoeopathy

- Phytolacca berry tincture, 3 drops in water, 3 times daily regulates appetite.
- Fucus 3x, 3 times daily when obesity may be thyroid-related.

Exercise

- exercise is essential to any weight loss programme. It helps speed up metabolism and burn calories; in most cases it also reduces appetite. Start off slowly and gradually increase the exertion and time spent exercising, so that excess strain, fatigue and stiffness are avoided. Moderate aerobic activity, which is sufficient to bring mild breathlessness and an increased pulse rate, should be carried out for at least 20 minutes three times a week. Walking, running, skipping, cycling, aerobics, dance and swimming are all suitable.

Professional Help

- Chinese medicine considers obesity to result from problems in the spleen and kidney. Acupuncture and herbal treatment are used to strengthen these organs.
- counselling or psychotherapy help resolve emotional conflicts and problems.

Orthodox

- treatment of obesity is very controversial. Some
  physicians recommend dietary changes and exercise.
  Others suggest appetite suppressant drugs under close
  supervision; however, these often have significant and
  unpleasant side effects. The prescribing of diuretics,
  thyroid hormones and amphetamines is potentially
  dangerous. Surgery is sometimes suggested and
  ranges from jaw wiring to stomach stapling.
  Undoubtedly, natural means of weight loss are far
  superior to any of these techniques.

Oral Thrush

A fungal infection of the mouth and throat which
generally affects the very young, the elderly, or those
whose immunity is compromised. The infection, known
as *Candida albicans*, thrives in warm moist areas where
the natural healthy bacteria have been disrupted by
illness, taking antibiotics or oral corticosteroids.
Symptoms include white patches in the mouth, which
peel off to reveal sore, reddened areas beneath.

Treatment

Dietary

- *Candida albicans* thrives on sugar, so avoid all sugar-
  containing foods, including fruit, fruit juices, honey
  and maple syrup.
- avoid coffee, tea, chocolate, vinegar, mushrooms and
  cheese.
- avoid fermented foods: alcohol, soya sauce.
- eat at least 3 cartons daily of 'live' yoghurt.
- olive oil acts to prevent the conversion of yeast into
  fungus, and should be incorporated into your diet as
  much as possible.

- take 1 teaspoon of *Lactobacillus acidophilus*, 1 teaspoon of *Bifidobacteria* powder, and ½ teaspoon of *Lactobacillus bulgaricus* (available from health food stores) in a glass of spring water, 3 times daily. This restores healthy bacteria to the body and helps fight candida.

Herbal

- garlic is an effective antifungal agent: incorporate plenty of the raw herb into your diet, or take garlic supplements: three capsules, 3 times daily.
- aloe vera mouthwash, available from herbalists and pharmacies, has an antifungal effect.
- studies have shown barberry to prevent the growth of candida, while stimulating the immune system. Take 1 teaspoon of the tincture in water 3 times daily.
  - **caution**: not to be taken during pregnancy.
- caprylic acid is an extract of coconuts which is a powerful antifungal agent. Take 3 capsules with each meal.

Homoeopathy

to be taken 4 times daily for up to 5 days:
- when the first signs start: Borax 6c.
- hot, sore patches in the mouth, made worse by cold water: Capsicum 6c.
- oral thrush with mouth ulcers: Arsenicum album 6c.

Orthodox

- treatment consists of antifungal agents, such as nystatin, in lozenges or mouthwash form.

Osteoarthritis

The most common type of arthritis, resulting from general wear and tear on the joints. The cartilage lining the joints typically degenerates and bony outgrowths may form. Symptoms include pain, stiffness, inflammation and sometimes loss of function.

Treatment

Dietary

- osteoarthritis has been seen to improve when intake of the following nutrients is increased:
  - magnesium: found in Brazil nuts, wholemeal flour, plain chocolate, lentils, parsley.
  - selenium: found in wholegrain cereals (wholemeal bread, rice, oatmeal), poultry, lean meat and fish.
  - zinc: found in lean meat, poultry, fish, liver and wholegrain cereals.
  - vitamin E: the best source is wheatgerm, which can be liberally sprinkled over food.
- excess weight increases the discomfort of osteoarthritis. If you are overweight try following the recommendations under Obesity.
- a vegetarian diet has been seen to help osteoarthritis and also helps in weight reduction.
- increasing the intake of oily fish such as mackerel and herring is also advised.

Chinese Medicine

- if it is treated in the early stages, warming herbs can help: pubescent angelica root, ledebouriellua root, timospora stem and cinnamon twigs are recommended. Acupuncture may also be recommended.

Hydrotherapy

- providing your general health and circulation is good, a cold compress can be used to relieve pain and inflammation: soak a piece of cotton material large enough to wrap around the joint in cold water, wring it out, place over the joint and cover it with 2 thicknesses of flannel or woollen material, pinned in

place. Leave the compress on for between 4 and
8 hours. It will draw the heat out of the joint and
become warm. Use the compress on alternate days.
- swimming is an excellent way to loosen stiff joints
and to stop muscles becoming weak. Many hospitals
or physiotherapy units have specially heated pools
where you can swim regularly in a safe environment.

Massage

- massaging the osteoarthritic joint will improve
circulation and reduce swelling and pain. Using a
little cream or oil, lightly stroke the muscles and flesh
around the joints in the direction of the heart, using
your fingertips or the heel of your hand. If you can't
use your hands, roll a clean tennis ball over the area
to provide a similar effect.

Orthodox

- the doctor will probably prescribe painkillers to
reduce discomfort and non-steroidal anti-
inflammatory drugs to reduce swelling. Physical
therapy is recommended, including exercises and heat
treatment. Joint replacement surgery is carried out in
severe cases.

Osteomalacia

Softening and subsequent weakening of the bones due
to calcium or vitamin D deficiency. In children the
disease is known as rickets. Early symptoms include
pain in the bones, particularly the neck, legs, hips and
ribs. Children with rickets typically have bowed legs or
knock knees, malformed teeth and, in babies, an
enlarged head.

Treatment

Osteomalacia is rare in those who are well nourished, active and get plenty of fresh air and sunlight. It is generally found in women who have multiple pregnancies, a poor diet, or the elderly who tend not to go outside (sunshine is an important source of vitamin D).

Treatment

Dietary

- increase intake of calcium found in low fat dairy products: milk, butter, yoghurt, green leafy vegetables and sesame seed products, such as tahini and halva.
- increase intake of vitamin D: get outside for moderate periods of sunshine, eat plenty of vitamin D-rich food: milk, lean meats, chicken and fish.
- take a multivitamin and mineral supplement which contains vitamin D and calcium.

Biochemic Tissue Salts

- Calc Phos, taken 4 times daily, promotes the uptake of calcium and phosphorus from the diet.

Orthodox

- if kidney disease or resistance to vitamin D is a problem, higher doses of vitamin D are recommended. Childhood rickets results in permanent bone deformity or lack of growth which cannot be remedied.

Osteoporosis

A thinning of the bones and loss of density as a result of loss of calcium. The bones become fragile and brittle, causing frequent fractures. Women who have reached the menopause are more susceptible to osteoporosis because their bodies stop producing oestrogen, which helps maintain bone mass.

Prevention

Little can be done once the bone tissue is lost, but much can be done early in life to prevent osteoporosis.

Practical Advice

- stop smoking, as nicotine lowers calcium absorption.

Dietary

- ensure you are getting adequate calcium. The best sources are low fat milk, yoghurt, canned fish, green leafy vegetables, dried, cooked beans and peas. You should have at least 3 daily servings of dairy products, along with a variety of other calcium-rich foods throughout the day. For those who do not eat dairy products, increase intake of dark green leafy vegetables, such as mustard greens, beet greens, kale and broccoli, and calcium-fortified soya milk.
- vitamin D is essential to calcium absorption. It is found in enriched dairy products and fish oil. It is also processed in the skin on exposure to sunlight.
- eating complex carbohydrates is though to help prevent osteoporosis. These are foods such as bread, rice, pasta and potatoes. Try always to eat wholegrain cereals.
- the following supplements help prevent osteoporosis and are useful if you have a low calcium diet:
  - calcium citrate: 1 g daily.
  - magnesium citrate: 500 mg daily.
  - vitamin B6: 100 mg daily.
  - folic acid: 1 mg daily.
- reduce intake of caffeine, as it inhibits absorption of calcium.
- reduce intake of alcohol, which accelerates bone loss.

Chinese Medicine

- herbal treatment can help this condition if it is caught in the early stages. Angelica sinensis, Chinese liquorice, cibote rhizome and eucomia bark are recommended.

Exercise

- bone loss occurs more rapidly if you do not exercise. Weight-bearing exercise increases and sustains calcium content in the bones. Walking, running, aerobics or racquet sports are the best types of activities and should be done for 30 minutes at least 3 times a week.

Orthodox

- hormone replacement therapy is prescribed for menopausal women to substitute reduced oestrogen production. However, it does have side effects (see Menopausal Problems). Disodium etifronate has been shown to reverse osteoporotic changes in menopausal women and may help reduce the likelihood of fractures.

Ovarian Cyst

Fluid-filled or solid sacs of tissue which grow on or near the ovaries. Usually cysts bring no symptoms, though they may sometimes disrupt menstrual cycles or, if they are large, press on another structure causing pain, discomfort or swelling.

Treatment

Dietary

- some research points to the fact that women with ovarian cysts frequently suffer from thyroid deficiency (see Hypothyroidism). You can find out if this is the case by taking your temperature first thing every morning; if on average you have a temperature lower than 97.6 degrees F (36.4 degrees C) you are likely to be thyroid deficient. The following recommendations will help resolve this:

- increase intake of fresh saltwater fish and shellfish, and ensure you use iodized salt.
- take a thyroid gland extract, available in health food stores.
- vitamin E is helpful in eliminating cysts. The best natural sources are vegetable oils, seeds, wheatgerm and nuts. A supplement of 800 iu is recommended daily.

- some naturopaths believe that cysts are the body's mechanism of ridding itself of toxins. To aid the purification process, they advise following a diet based of the following guidelines:
  - drink at least 8 glasses of spring water daily.
  - eat organically produced food and free-range meat.
  - eliminate sugar, coffee, tea, carbonated drinks and refined foods.
  - vitamin B complex is helpful in detoxifying the body: take 50—100 mg daily.

Homoeopathy

take 1 tablet 3 times daily for up to 2 weeks:
- left ovary gives pain, worse in morning, less during menstrual period: Lachesis 6c.
- right ovary gives stinging pain with painful periods: Apis 6c.

Exercise

- vigorous exercise is recommended to increase circulation and elimination.

Orthodox

- small benign cysts which result from changes occurring during the menstrual cycle are usually left alone. Large cysts are usually surgically removed, sometimes along with the ovary.

Ovulation Pain

In menstruating women, the reproductive system releases an egg between the 10th and 17th day of the cycle. This is known as ovulation and is felt by some women as a cramp or pain, which can occur on one side of the lower abdomen or both.

Prevention

Aromatherapy

- massage 4 drops each of basil, sweet marjoram and lavender in 30 ml carrier oil or lotion into the abdomen, in a clockwise direction on the 8th–12th day of your cycle.

Treatment

Dietary

- throughout the month, take evening primrose oil 6 x 500 mg daily and B complex, one daily.

Herbal

- pennyroyal infusion helps promote the menstrual process and strengthen uterine contractions: add 2 teaspoons of the dried herb to a cup of cold water, leave for 15 minutes and drink 3 times daily. It should be avoided if you are trying to conceive.

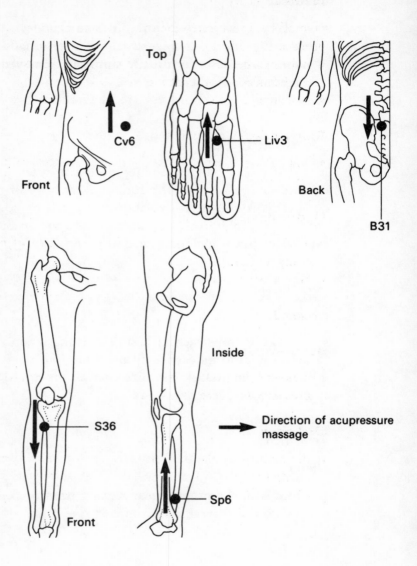

Homoeopathy

take every 15 minutes for up to 4 doses and repeat if needed:
- pain relieved by warmth and doubling up, often more on left side: Colocynth 6c.
- pain made better for stretching back: Dioscorea 6c.

Biochemic Tissue Salts

- Mag Phos: 2 tablets dissolved in a little warm water and sipped frequently.

Hydrotherapy

- a warm hot water bottle placed on the area of pain brings relief.
- take a warm bath, to which 4 drops each of essential oil of sweet marjoram and clary sage have been added.

Acupressure

- massage the points illustrated, using deep thumb pressure, for at least a minute.

Orthodox

- the pain of ovulation is usually mild and represents a normal physiological process, therefore only mild painkillers, if anything, are recommended.

P

Pain

A sensation that can range from mild discomfort to an excruciating experience. Initially, pain acts as a warning signal that something is wrong which requires treatment. Ongoing chronic pain is defined as pain that lasts, despite treatment, for more than 6 months.

Treatment For Ongoing Chronic Pain

Practical Advice

- one of the problems with pain that does not have a specific cause or reason is identifying and accepting it. One of the first steps in treatment is to come to terms with the fact that your pain really exists as a condition, and that you are taking control in dealing with it. Accepting your pain allows you to negotiate a realistic future offering happier and healthier options.
- join a support group. Shared experience helps understand and accept pain (see Appendix 2).
- try to continue with activities or hobbies you did before the pain set in; develop other new interests too.
- really try to talk and think less about your pain.

Dietary

- research has shown that the amino acid D,L–phenylalanine (DLPA), provides significant pain relief. Two 375 mg tablets are recommended 3 times daily prior to meals. If there is no improvement, double the

dose. If there is still no improvement, the treatment
should be discontinued. Relief is usually apparent
within 7 days, after which the dosage can be
gradually reduced until you achieve a minimum
maintenance dose.
* where the pain results from inflammation, evening
primrose oil, 6 x 500 mg daily and B complex,
1 daily may help.

Aromatherapy

* aromatherapy massage promotes relaxation. You can
also use essential oils yourself to help you relax.
Lavender has been shown to have relaxing and
sedating properties. Put a few drops in a bath, or on
a handkerchief and sniff regularly.

Massage

* having a massage from a friend or family member or
a massage therapist promotes deep relaxation. It is
extremely beneficial for many types of pain. However,
consult your doctor first to ensure that the treatment
is appropriate for your condition.

Acupressure

* the points for general pain relief are as illustrated
overleaf. Use deep pressure, preferably with the
thumb, for at least a minute.

Exercise

* exercise helps release endorphins, the body's natural
painkillers, as well as providing distraction from the
pain. Consult your doctor before embarking on any
of the following programmes.
* daily walking on flat ground: go as far as is
comfortable for the first week. If you experience a
flare-up of pain, cut back the exercise until the pain
settles. Increase your programme gradually.

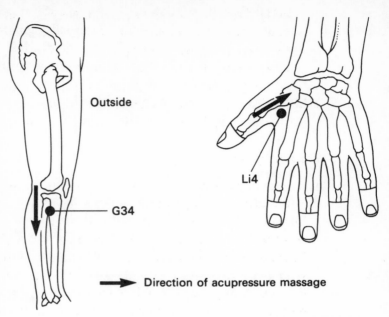

Outside

G34

Li4

➤ Direction of acupressure massage

- swimming often provides all-round pain relief, while exercising the muscles. Special hydrotherapy pools at physiotherapy units are specially heated for pain sufferers.

Relaxation

- relaxation promotes the release of stress-reducing endorphins, which in turn relieves pain.
- set aside a period of time each day to rest. Sit or lie in a comfortable position, do not answer the phone or door, and tell others not to disturb you. Listen to music or a relaxation tape.
- if you find your mind is constantly going over concerns and anxieties, make a list of the problems in their order of priority on the left side of a piece of paper; on the right list the potential solutions. Take 2 minutes for each problem, then put the paper aside and start your relaxation.
- the following routine can be carried out to help achieve relaxation:
  - close your eyes and become aware of how your

body feels. Focus your attention on each part of
your body in turn, starting with the tips of the
toes and finishing with your face and eyes.
Consciously try to relax every part in turn. The
whole procedure should take at least 10 minutes.
- biofeedback, attending a yoga class or learning
meditation can help with relaxation.

Visualization

- take time each day to do this. In a quiet room, settle
as comfortably as possible, close your eyes and
imagine the colour and shape of your pain. It may be
an object or symbol or a more abstract vision.
Imagine what colour or shape will soothe or relieve
your pain. Imagine asking the pain if it has a message
for you, how would it like you to treat it. Try to
remain with your visualization for at least 10 minutes.
Gradually increase the time day by day.

Professional Help

- acupuncture can be very effective in relieving pain.
- hypnosis can also help.
- transcutaneous electrical nerve stimulation (TENS),
available in many hospitals, works like acupuncture
without the needles. Ask your doctor for more
details, or enquire at your local hospital.
- spiritual healing has helped many people.

Orthodox

- painkilling drugs, muscle relaxants, non-steroidal anti-
inflammatory drugs, local anaesthetic (sprays,
injections or drops) are all possible treatments.
Neurosurgery is occasionally used to sever the nerves
causing pain.

Palpitations

A sensation that the heart is beating fast or irregularly. This usually occurs after hard exercise, a shock, or anger, but it may also be a symptom of heart disease (see Coronary Heart Disease), an overactive thyroid gland (see Hyperthyroidism), a food allergy (see Allergies — Food) or taking too much caffeine. If palpitations continue for several hours or recur over several days, or if they are accompanied by dizziness, shortness of breath, nausea or chest pain, consult your doctor.

Treatment

Practical Advice

• nicotine stimulates the heart, so do not smoke.

Dietary

• avoid caffeine (coffee, tea, chocolate, cola).
• if palpitations are related to heart disease, see dietary recommendations under Coronary Heart Disease.
• take magnesium supplements: 30—60 mg *elemental* weight daily with food. (Elemental weight should be shown on the label. It tells you how much of the mineral the body is expected to absorb.) This usually gives relief within 48—72 hours. Do not use magnesium oxide or magnesium carbonate.

Aromatherapy

• when the cause of palpitations is emotional, use calming essential oils such as lavender, mandarin and ylang ylang. Relax in a bath to which 6 drops of one of these oils have been added or dab a few drops on a tissue and inhale the odour regularly. An aromatherapy massage will greatly assist in reducing stress-induced palpitations.

Herbal

- for palpitations brought by stress or anxiety, infusion of motherwort is effective: add 1 cup of water to 2 teaspoons of dried herb, infuse for 15 minutes and drink 3 times daily.

Homoeopathy

to be taken every 5 minutes for up to 6 doses during palpitations:
- palpitations after a shock or a fright: Aconite 6c.
- palpitations after rich food, alcohol, coffee or stress: Nux vomica 6c.
- palpitations after sudden excitement or a pleasant surprise: Coffea 6c.
- palpitations which are worse lying on the left side and improved by lying on the right side: Phosphorus 6c.

Chinese Medicine

- herbs to nourish the heart and the blood are recommended, such as lilyturf root, asparagus root and wild jujube seeds.

Massage

- regular massage is also very helpful in promoting relaxation and lowering blood pressure.

Acupressure

- massage the two points illustrated overleaf, using deep thumb pressure, for at least one minute.

Relaxation

- whatever the cause of palpitations, regular relaxation will be generally beneficial. Carry out the following routine morning and evening.

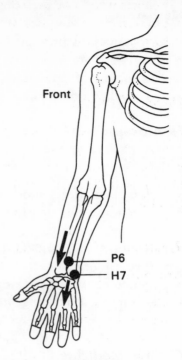

Front

P6
H7

━━▶ Direction of acupressure massage

- lie on a firm surface, close your eyes and become aware of how your body feels. Focus your attention on each part of your body in turn, starting with the tips of the toes, and finishing with your face and eyes. Consciously try to relax every part in turn. The whole procedure should take at least 10 minutes.
- attend a yoga class or learn meditation. Biofeedback is also helpful in learning to relax.

Orthodox

- an electrocardiograph (ECG) is taken to record the electrical impulses of the heart. If the palpitations are intermittent, yet significant, an ambulatory ECG (where the patient wears a portable recording machine for a full 24 hours) may be necessary. Simple abnormalities can be treated with medications, but physical disorders may very occasionally require surgical intervention.

Panic Attack

An attack of intense anxiety and/or fear which usually comes on unexpectedly, but can be triggered by a pattern of situations or events. Symptoms include breathing difficulties, chest pains, palpitations, dizziness, trembling and faintness.

Treatment For Immediate Relief

Aromatherapy

• essential oil of lavender has been shown in studies to relieve anxiety and reduce stress: keep a small bottle of the oil with you, or sprinkle it on your handkerchief and inhale during stressful moments. Rosewood and sweet marjoram are also effective.

Herbal

• valerian tea helps reduce tension and anxiety: pour a cup of boiling water over 1–2 teaspoons of the root and infuse for 15 minutes. Drink when needed.

Homoeopathy

to be taken every few minutes for up to 6 doses:
• after a sudden shock with chest pains and fear of dying: Aconite 6c.
• hysterical changes of mood, gasping for breath; Ignatia 6c.

Bach Flower Remedies

• Rock Rose: for extreme terror and panic nearing hysteria.

- Red Chestnut: for excessive fear for others, especially loved ones.

Long-term Treatment

Dietary

increase intake of B vitamins:
- increase intake of vitamin B1, found in pork, green peas, oranges, dried beans and peas, wheatgerm and brewer's yeast.
- increase intake of vitamin B2, found in milk, green leafy vegetables, mushrooms, asparagus, avocados, broccoli.
- increase intake of vitamin B7 (biotin) found in liver, oatmeal, egg yolk, soya beans, mushrooms, bananas, peanuts and brewer's yeast.
- take a vitamin B complex supplement daily.

Relaxation

a yoga or meditation class will help you relax, reducing anxiety and incidence of panic attacks. The following routine should be carried out at least once daily and before potentially stressful situations.
- lie on a firm surface, close your eyes and become aware of how your body feels. Focus your attention on each part of your body, starting with the tips of the toes, and finishing with your face and eyes; consciously try to relax every part in turn. The whole procedure should take at least 10 minutes.

Professional Help

- hypnotherapy can help.

Orthodox

- psychotherapy or counselling is recommended.

Parkinson's Disease

A degenerative disease which affects a small part of the brain, causing muscle tremor, stiffness and loss of physical coordination and movement. Typical symptoms are shakiness, rigid posture and a shuffling unsteady walk.

Treatment

All treatment should be carried out in consultation with your doctor. Natural therapies may complement orthodox treatment, but should not be substituted for medication.

Dietary

- eat nutritious food: wholegrain cereals, fruit and vegetables, low fat protein to provide energy.
- eat plenty of fibre to prevent constipation.
- some Parkinson's sufferers find spicy food or high protein meals make their symptoms worse.
  A vegetarian diet may be beneficial.
- fresh broad beans/fava beans (*Vicia fava*) contain levodopa, the drug used to treat Parkinson's disease. Studies have shown that patients felt relief of symptoms after eating these beans.

Chinese Medicine

- treatment given in the early stages can help, especially younger people. Acupuncture would be combined with herbal remedies (fleeceflower root, wolfberry root and umcaria stem).

Reflexology

- practitioners recommend massaging the head area, located at the tips of the toes on the right and left soles; the whole of both big toes; the spine area,

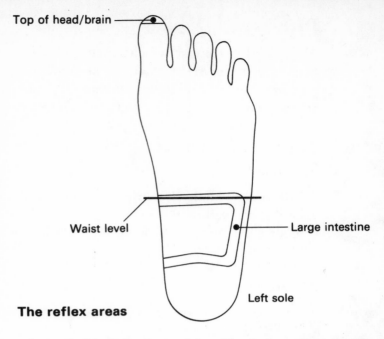

Top of head/brain

Waist level

Large intestine

Left sole

The reflex areas

located along the inner side of both feet; the adrenal glands, and the large intestine (see illustration).

Exercise

- regular exercise can help increase mobility and improve balance and coordination. Gentle walking, and simple stretching which mobilizes all the major joints, are recommended. However, be careful not to overdo it. If you feel tired, stop; if you have a bad day, do not exercise.

Professional Help

- minerals are often deficient in Parkinson's sufferers. Consult a dietitian or a naturopath for advice on mineral status testing.

Orthodox

- levodopa is the most commonly used drug. It replaces the brain chemicals that are missing and minimizes symptoms. It cannot, however, halt the degeneration of the brain cells. Sometimes brain surgery may be carried out to reduce tremor and rigidity. New advances are being developed, including foetal tissue implants, which have had some success.

Pelvic Inflammatory Disease

Also known as salpingitis, this is an infection of the female reproductive organs. The infection may not have any obvious cause, though sometimes it results from a sexually transmitted disease such as chlamydia (see entry). Pelvic inflammatory disease may also occur after childbirth, abortion or miscarriage. Symptoms include pelvic pain, fever, and foul-smelling discharge.

Prevention

If left untreated, pelvic inflammatory disease can cause infertility. Orthodox treatment with antibiotics is the only way to ensure you clear up the infection. Complementary treatments, however, can greatly assist in preventing a recurrence.

- get any vaginal discharge or pelvic pain checked out by your doctor immediately.
- if you or your partner also have intercourse with other people, protect yourself from sexually transmitted diseases by always using a condom.
- when you go to the toilet always wipe from front to back, to prevent bacteria from the anus entering the vagina.
- avoid anal sex.
- do not use intrauterine devices (IUDs) for birth control.

Treatment

Treatment with antibiotics is necessary (see above). The following complementary measures can be used in addition.

Dietary

• strengthen the immune system by ensuring you eat plenty of vitamin C, found in citrus fruits and vegetables; vitamin A, found in liver, egg yolk and dairy products, vitamin D, found in fortified milk and exposure to sunlight. Eat wholegrain cereals, lean meats or fish and plenty of green leafy vegetables. Eat 'live' yoghurt 3 times daily to prevent thrush, which often occurs after taking antibiotics.

Herbal

• garlic is an effective antimicrobial. Incorporate raw garlic into your diet as much as possible, or take garlic capsules (3 capsules 3 times daily). A tried and tested remedy is to peel a clove of garlic and wrap it in sterile gauze, tie the end with a long piece of thread or dental floss and insert into the vagina, using it like a tampon with the string outside the body. Change it daily, for up to 4 days.

Hydrotherapy

• for pain relief, take hot baths and place a hot water bottle on your stomach. This will encourage the circulation of blood through the infected area, helping to fight and flush away the infection.

Professional Help

• professional homoeopathic treatment is recommended to reduce recurrence of infections.

Orthodox

- antibiotic drugs would be given for at least 2—6 weeks. Painkillers may also be recommended. An intrauterine device would be removed, as it is a foreign body and could perpetuate any infection.

Peptic Ulcer

A raw area which develops in the mucous membrane of the digestive tract where it is irritated further by acidic digestive juices. Ulcers may be caused by excessive secretion of acid, resulting from eating the wrong foods, long-term stress, drugs or alcohol. Symptoms include burning pain in the stomach, loss of appetite, gas, nausea and vomiting.

Treatment

Practical Advice

- stop smoking.

Dietary

- ulcers are made worse by foods which stimulate acid secretion. Eliminate fatty foods, spices, especially pepper, fruit juices, coffee, tea, cocoa, cola, and alcohol,
- protein also stimulates acid secretion: avoid meat for the first 2 weeks of treating an ulcer. Instead of meat, eat 2 oz of cheese daily. This will give the system a rest and a chance to start healing.
- ensure that 80 per cent of your food is alkaline (fruit and vegetables), and only 20 per cent acidic (meat, fish, eggs, cheese, bread, concentrated starches and sugary foods).
- only eat when you are relaxed, and take your time.

Herbal

- liquorice has a soothing action on the mucous membranes, and is used in orthodox drugs for ulcers. A herbalist would recommend liquorice decoctions 3 times daily: put 1 teaspoon of liquorice root in a cup of water, and simmer for 15 minutes. When using this treatment, eat plenty of fresh fruit and vegetables to ensure adequate intake of potassium.
- marshmallow root decoction is also an effective treatment: prepare as above.

Homoeopathy

to be taken 3 times daily for up to 14 days and repeated if necessary:
- when the pain is worse immediately after eating, relieved 2 hours later: Nux vomica 6c.
- pain relieved immediately after eating: Anacardium 6c.
- pain in a small and precise spot: Kali bichromicum 6c.
- burning pains and vomiting, better temporarily for cold drinks: Phosphorus 6c.
- stomach feels like a stone and is very sensitive to touch: Bryonia 6c.

Chinese Medicine

- 'cold' foods, such as salads, bananas and grapefruit, should be avoided. Burning pain can be relieved by dandelion or dandelion juice. Noto ginseng is recommended to heal the ulcer.

Massage

- regular massage can help with relaxation.

Relaxation

- stress increases acid production in the digestive system and there is a high probability that it greatly contributes to the development of ulcers. Learning how to relax through yoga, meditation, biofeedback or relaxation tapes will help you to make it a regular part of your daily routine.

Orthodox

- antacids relieve mild symptoms. H_2-receptor antagonists are more effective in inhibiting stomach acid production and promoting healing. Surgery is used as a last resort, when the ulcer has perforated the stomach.

Period Pain

Period pain, also known as dysmenorrhoea, is categorized by doctors into 2 types: primary dysmenorrhoea, which tends to occur in young women when they begin their periods, and results from the contractions of the uterus; secondary dysmenorrhoea is more common later in life, and brings stomach cramps 1 or 2 weeks before the period starts, along with other premenstrual symptoms (see Premenstrual Syndrome). Secondary dysmenorrhoea may result from pelvic infections (see Pelvic Inflammatory Disease), endometriosis (see entry), fibroids (see entry) polyps (see entry), or other gynaecological abnormalities.

Treatment

Practical Advice

- hold a hot water bottle against the abdomen.
- take a warm bath.

Dietary

- take vitamin B6: 50 g, 2 times daily, and a daily B complex tablet.

Aromatherapy

- use 3 drops each of essential oils of chamomile and sweet marjoram, combined with 10 ml of carrier oil or lotion in the massage below.
- soaking in a warm bath to which these oils have been added also reduces discomfort.

Herbal

- cramp bark decoction is effective in relaxing muscular tension and spasm: put 2 teaspoons of the dried bark in a cup of water, simmer for 15 minutes and drink hot 3 times daily.
- ginger infusion is a common remedy: add a cup of hot water to 1 teaspoon of grated fresh root, infuse for 10 minutes and drink when needed.

Homoeopathy

every 2—4 hours as needed:
- cramping pain, better from hard pressure and bending double: Colocynth 6c.
- waves of labour-like pains: Chamomilla 6c.
- heavy bearing-down pains with tiredness and irritability: Sepia 6c.
- bright blood with dark clots and pain stretching from sacrum to pubes: Sabina 6c.

Biochemic Tissue Salts

- Mag Phos: 2 tablets dissolved in warm water and sipped frequently.

Massage

- massage of the lower abdomen, the sacrum, the lower back and the legs relieves period pain. Start with the routine below then, with a partner, work on the legs and back, using large, stroking, upward movements.

- direct massage of the uterus, just above the pubic hair, helps relieve spasm and encourages blood flow.
- lie on the floor or a bed with your knees bent. Place your right palm on the lower right side of your abdomen and place your left hand on top of it. Press in with the fingers of both hands, and make small circular movements. Gradually move your hands up the right of the abdomen to the waist, across under the ribs and back down, and across the lower abdomen above the pubic hair.

Acupressure

- lie on your front on a firm surface and ask a friend or family member to press with the flat of the thumb on either side of the spinal column from the tail bone to the waist (see illustration).

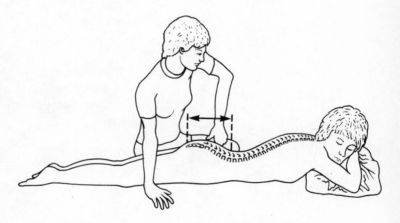

- massage the other points illustrated overleaf, using deep pressure, for at least a minute.

Yoga

period pain can be exacerbated by stress and unexpressed emotions. Regular yoga practice helps reduce stress and in turn pain:
- sit on the floor with your back straight, your knees bent and the soles of your feet together so your knees

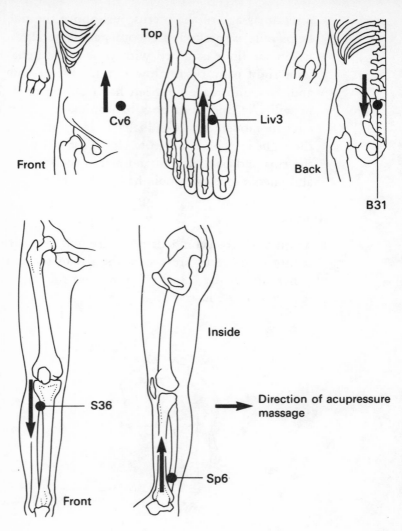

fall outward. Clasp your feet in your hands, and gently bounce your knees up and down. Gently lean forward, bending from the hips as far as you can comfortably go. Hold the position for several minutes and relax.

Professional Help

- Chinese medicine: acupuncture and moxibustion are very helpful in treating this problem.

- period pain can often be relieved by osteopathic treatment of the pelvis, spine and abdomen.
- homoeopathy can help where period pains are a recurrent problem.

Orthodox

- for primary dysmenorrhoea, doctors advise aspirin to relax the muscles of the uterus, and drugs which inhibit uterine contractions. The Pill is sometimes recommended. Low dose danazol is also effective, although not without side effects, such as unwanted hair growth. Treatment of secondary dysmenorrhoea depends on the underlying cause.

Periods, Heavy

The amount of blood lost during menstruation differs from woman to woman. However, if you experience abnormally heavy periods which last more than 7 days, produce large clots and saturate sanitary protection within minutes, it is advisable to consult your doctor.

Heavy periods may result from hormonal imbalances, fibroids (see entry), endometriosis (see entry), polyps (see entry), using an intrauterine device, stress and occasionally cancer. If there is no sign of underlying disease, the following treatments can help.

Treatment

Dietary

increase intake of the following nutrients:
- iron and zinc: found in red meat, poultry, fish and green leafy vegetables. Eat or drink citrus fruits and juices with meals to enhance iron absorption.
- vitamin B6, found in lean meats, wheatgerm, and brewer's yeast. Take 50 mg twice daily and a daily B complex tablet.
- vitamin A, found in liver, kidney, egg yolk, butter, whole milk and cod liver oil.
- citrus bioflavonoids, found in the pith of citrus fruits, can help balance hormonal levels and regulate menstruation.

Herbal

- herbalists recommend a decoction of either American cranesbill or greater periwinkle for excessive blood loss during menstruation. Pour a cup of boiling water on 1 teaspoon of either herb, infuse for 15 minutes and drink 3 times daily.

Homoeopathy

start dosage just before period is due; every 8 hours for 10 doses:
- spasmodic bleeding, producing dark clots with cramps, faintness, and pallor: China 6c.
- bright red blood, abdominal pains, throbbing headache: Belladonna 6c.
- heavy bleeding, bright red blood, with nausea: Ipecac 6c.

- pain bearing down, as if internal organs are going to 'drop out': Sepia 6c.

Orthodox

- heavy periods caused by hormonal imbalances are often treated by prescribing the Pill, or doses of progesterone during the later stages of each menstrual cycle. Other treatments will depend on the cause of the bleeding. Iron supplements may be given to prevent anaemia.

Periods, Irregular or Absent

The most obvious reasons for absent or irregular periods are pregnancy or the onset of the menopause. For women who have never had a period by the age of 18 it is advisable to seek medical advice. For those who experience irregular periods or a lapse in menstruation, the cause could relate to weight problems (either obesity or low body weight as a result of dieting or an eating disorder, see Anorexia Nervosa), hormonal imbalances, stress, or excessive exercising.

Treatment

Once a medical examination has ruled out pregnancy, structural abnormalities or disease, the following therapies may aid in regulating menstruation.

Dietary

- research has shown that deficiency of zinc and vitamin B6 can often result in absence of periods. Foods rich in vitamin B6 include lean meat, wheatgerm and brewer's yeast. Alternatively you could take a 25 g supplement of vitamin B6 daily with 1 vitamin B complex supplement. Foods rich in zinc include lean meat, poultry, fish and organ meats.

Herbal

- for delayed onset of periods in adolescent girls, blue cohosh decoction is prescribed: put 1 teaspoon of the dried root in a cup of water, simmer for 10 minutes and drink 3 times daily.
- chasteberry infusion helps regulate hormonal function; pour a cup of boiling water on 1 teaspoon of the ripe berries, infuse for 15 minutes and drink 3 times daily.

Homoeopathy

to be taken every 12 hours for 2 weeks:
- periods stop after an emotional shock: Aconite 6c.
- periods stop after grief or loss: Ignatia 6c.

Chinese Medicine

- Chinese medicine suggests eating warming foods to encourage regular menstruation: ginger tea, spiced dishes, and soups are recommended.

Exercise

- women who are underweight or who are under rigorous training schedules often experience irregular or absent periods. It is important to maintain a minimum amount of body fat for menstruation to occur.

Professional Help

- sometimes periods can stop as a result of an emotional shock, grief, sexual trauma or other psychological problems. Help from a counsellor or psychotherapist with experience of such problems may restore ovarian function.

Orthodox

- once psychological problems have been ruled out, and

the problem does not resolve itself spontaneously within a few months, hormonal correction using drugs such as clomiphene may be prescribed.

Pharyngitis

Inflammation of the pharynx (the part of the throat which lies between the tonsils and the voice box), resulting in a sore throat. Pharyngitis can result from a virus or a bacterial infection, and is commonly associated with a cold or flu.

Treatment

Practical Advice

- avoid alcohol and smoking, as both will irritate the pharynx.
- rest the voice as much as possible.

Dietary

the following nutrients help fight infection:
- vitamin C, found in fresh vegetables and fruits, particularly citrus fruits and juices.
- zinc, found in lean meat, fish and organ meats.
- gargle with cider vinegar and honey 4 times daily.

Aromatherapy

- a gargle made up of 2 drops of essential oils of both sandalwood and lavender in water helps soothe the throat.
- steam inhalations using any of the above essential oils are very beneficial: add 1—2 drops to a bowl of boiling water, lean over the bowl, with a towel over your head to trap the steam, close your eyes, and inhale deeply for 2—5 minutes.

Herbal

- decoction of echinacea is an effective remedy for both bacterial and viral infections: add 2 teaspoons of the root to a cup of water, simmer for 15 minutes and drink 3 times daily.

Homoeopathy

to be taken hourly for 4 doses and repeated if necessary:
- barking cough, with burning and irritation, after getting chilled: Aconite 6c.
- stringy yellow catarrh, metallic sounding cough and husky voice with raw pain: Kali bichromicum 6c.
- burning pain, tightness in the chest and hoarseness eased by eating ice cream: Phosphorus 6c.

Orthodox

- gargling with salt water is recommended, along with painkillers. Particularly severe cases may require antibiotics.

Phobia

An irrational and disabling fear of a specific object or situation. Phobias may result from past bad experiences or may be learnt from parents or siblings. Common phobias are fear of going outside (agoraphobia) and terror of being enclosed (claustrophobia). Symptoms include extreme anxiety and fear: rapid breathing, sweating and panic on exposure to the situation or object. This may be accompanied by general depression, and sometimes drug or alcohol abuse.

Treatment

Phobias are difficult to treat alone. The following self

help therapies will ease the way, but should be used in conjunction with the professional help listed below.

Dietary

- a naturopath would carry out a complete assessment of the diet, recommending high potency vitamin B complex and vitamin C supplementation.
- research has shown that people who suffer phobias experience similar symptoms to people with low blood sugar. Ensuring blood sugar levels remain stable may help prevent attacks:
  - eat many small meals over the day.
  - eat complex carbohydrates (potatoes, wholegrain breads and cereals, rice and pasta); avoid simple carbohydrates (sugar, sweets/candy, cakes, biscuits).
  - keep a snack with you at all times: nuts, fresh or dried fruit is best.

Aromatherapy

- essential oil of lavender has been shown in studies to provide immediate relief for anxiety and stress: keep a small bottle of the oil with you, or sprinkle it on your handkerchief to inhale at stressful moments. Sandalwood and sweet marjoram will help reduce the fear.

Herbal

- valerian tea helps reduce tension and anxiety: pour a cup of boiling water over 1–2 teaspoons of the root and infuse for 15 minutes. Drink when needed.

Bach Flower Remedies

- Rock Rose: for extreme terror and panic nearing hysteria.
- Rescue Remedy if the above is not appropriate.

Relaxation

- a yoga or meditation class will help you relax, reducing anxiety and incidence of phobic attacks. Learning biofeedback will greatly assist in relaxation.

Professional Help

- hypnotherapy can help.
- behavioural psychotherapy uses techniques which allow gradual exposure to the feared object or situation, accompanied by reassurance, relaxation techniques, and visualization helping to overcome the phobia.

Orthodox

- psychotherapy is recommended, and sometimes tranquillizers or antidepressants.

Piles *see* Haemorrhoids

Pimples *see* Spots and Pimples; Acne

Pinkeye *see* Conjunctivitis

Pneumonia

Infection of one or both lungs by a virus or bacteria. Symptoms include fever, chills, breathlessness, chest pain, a cough which produces yellow or green phlegm and sometimes blood. In young, healthy people, pneumonia may be mild; in the elderly, or those with weakened immune systems, it can be life-threatening.

Treatment

The following treatments should be used in collaboration with your doctor.

Dietary

- a naturopath would recommend plenty of fluids and small nutritious wholefood meals. Eat and drink plenty of fruits and vegetable juices, particularly those containing vitamin C (citrus fruits and tomatoes).

Herbal

- coltsfoot infusion has a soothing effect on coughs and helps fight chest infection: pour a cup of boiling water on 2 teaspoons of the dried flowers or leaves and infuse for 10 minutes. Drink 3 times daily.
- incorporate as much raw garlic into the diet as possible to fight infection, or take 3 garlic capsules 3 times daily.

Homoeopathy

to be taken every hour for 4 doses and repeated if necessary.
- when the illness has a rapid onset and brings a high fever: Aconite 6c.
- brings sharp stitching pain, made worse by coughing: Bryonia 6c.
- pale and weak with bloody phlegm and nosebleeds: Ferrum phosphoricum 6c.

Hydrotherapy

- steam inhalations help relieve a painful chest and facilitate breathing. Add a few drops of essential oil of eucalyptus to a bowl of boiling water, lean over the bowl with a towel over your head to trap the steam, close your eyes and inhale for 2–5 minutes.

Massage

- massaging the muscles of the upper back using an oil
  or lotion carrier with a few drops of essential oil of
  eucalyptus eases chest congestion and facilitates the
  release of phlegm. You should lie face down while
  massage is being carried out. Cover up the areas not
  being treated with towels and a warm blanket.
  Kneeling at your side, your partner can place the
  heels of the hands on the muscle running along the
  opposite side of the spine and push them gently away
  from him/her.
- cupping the hands, your partner can do a gentle,
  loose clapping stroke with alternate hands all over the
  upper back, particularly around the rib cage, avoiding
  the spine itself.

Orthodox

- antibiotics are given either orally or by injection.
  Sometimes chest physiotherapy to remove mucus and
  phlegm may also be recommended.

Polyp

A non-cancerous growth which projects out of a
mucous membrane, often in the nose, the cervical canal,
or the intestine. Nasal polyps can develop as a result of
allergies, and cause difficulty breathing, nosebleeds and
diminished sense of smell; cervical polyps can cause
watery bleeding after intercourse, or between periods.
Intestinal polyps are usually small and harmless, though
larger ones can cause obstructions.

Treatment

Professional Help

- acupuncture or Chinese herbs can be used.

- hypnotherapy or autogenic training may also help.
- there are a number of homoeopathic remedies which have been found to be helpful.

Orthodox

- small polyps do not necessarily require treatment. Regular examinations are recommended for cervical polyps; however, they rarely become cancerous. Removal is a relatively easy surgical procedure if the polyp is large or obstructive.

Postnatal Depression

Postnatal depression can range from a few days of mild sadness to serious bouts of depression. Common symptoms include feelings of loneliness, inadequacy, loss of interest in life, tearfulness, bouts of crying, guilt, and extreme fatigue, suicidal thoughts and inability to function or care for the child.

Treatment

Dietary

research has shown that postnatal depression can result from a deficiency in certain nutrients:
- take a vitamin B complex tablet daily.
- increase intake of zinc, found in lean meat, poultry, fish, organ meats and wholegrain bread. A supplement of 25 mg can be taken daily to ensure adequate intake.
- increase intake of magnesium, found in nuts, cooked dried beans, wholegrain cereals, soya beans, dark green leafy vegetables and seafood. A supplement of 300 mg can be taken daily to ensure adequate intake.
- increase intake of vitamin B2 (riboflavin), found in dairy products, brewer's yeast, meat and wheat.
- increase intake of vitamin B6, found in lean meat,

fish, brewer's yeast, wheatgerm, soya beans, cooked
dried beans and peas.
- the amino acid phenylalanine has been shown in a
  number of studies to relieve depression. The dosage is
  best determined by a naturopath.
- maintain blood sugar levels by eating a complex
  carbohydrate food every 3 hours, such as wholegrain
  bread or other cereal.

Herbal

- skullcap infusion is prescribed for exhaustion and
  depression. It helps relax the body, while reviving the
  nervous system: pour a cup of boiling water on
  2 teaspoons of the dried herb, infuse for 15 minutes
  and drink 3 times daily.
- take supplements of evening primrose oil: 500 mg,
  3 times daily.

Homoeopathy

take 4 times daily for 3 days and repeat if needed:
- lack of interest in life and former pleasures, feeling
  tired, irritable, end of one's tether: Sepia 6c.
- tearful, needing company, hugs and reassurance:
  Pulsatilla 6c.
- unsociable, reluctant to share one's feelings: Natrum
  muriaticum 6c.

Professional Help

- cranial osteopathy can often help by releasing strain
  patterns caused by childbirth, which are thought to
  impair hormonal function.
- Chinese medicine: acupuncture and moxibustion have
  been shown to help balance the body.

Orthodox

- antidepressant drugs, hormonal drugs and sometimes
  counselling or psychotherapy are recommended. In

severe cases when the child's well-being is at risk, the mother is admitted to hospital.

Pre-Eclampsia

Also known as toxaemia, this is a life-threatening illness in which high blood pressure, water retention and protein in the urine develop during the later stages of pregnancy. Symptoms include headaches, visual problems, swollen ankles, nausea and abdominal pain. If left untreated, convulsions and loss of consciousness can occur, threatening the life of the mother and child.

Treatment

Pre-eclampsia is a condition which requires emergency medical attention. Complementary treatments can be used to help prevent pre-eclampsia and as an adjunct to orthodox treatment; it is advisable to tell your doctor of any therapies you are using.

Prevention

Practical Advice

- prenatal care is vital; ensure you have regular checkups so that if you develop pre-eclampsia it is diagnosed early.
- reduce stress as much as possible (see under Stress for guidelines).
- ensure you get plenty of sleep.

Dietary

- some studies show that a deficiency in protein may contribute to pre-eclampsia. During pregnancy eat plenty of lean meat and fish, eggs, dried cooked beans, wholegrain cereals, and low fat dairy products, along with lightly steamed vegetables and fruit.

- if you are a vegetarian or vegan, ensure you get sufficient protein by combining foods which complement each other: pulses (legumes) with grains, pulses with seeds or nuts or, for non-vegans, grains with milk products.

Treatment

Dietary

- avoid dairy foods, spices and alcohol.
- eat plenty of fresh vegetables and fruit, especially onions, celery and garlic, which strengthen the blood vessel walls and improve circulation.
- eat plenty of potassium-rich foods, such as lean meat, potatoes, avocados, bananas, apricots, orange juice and other fruits.

Herbal

- dandelion leaves are helpful in reducing swelling caused by water retention: add the fresh leaves to salads, or prepare a decoction by putting 2 teaspoons of the root in a cup of water and simmering gently for 15 minutes. Drink 3 times daily.

Professional Help

- Chinese medicine offers herbs to reduce high blood pressure. Acupuncture can also be helpful in treating this condition.
- professional homoeopathic treatment is recommended.

Orthodox

- in mild cases your doctor will recommend bed rest and give drugs to reduce blood pressure and correct salt and water imbalances in the body. If you are nearing the end of the pregnancy the birth may be induced, as symptoms rapidly improve after delivery.

Pregnancy Problems

The following are some common problems experienced in pregnancy and how to treat them using gentle techniques.

Oedema

Puffiness of the flesh, especially in the feet, ankles, fingers and face, caused by an increase in fluid volume, and made worse by heat, standing, and fatigue. The condition may be linked to high blood pressure, and it is advisable to consult your doctor immediately.

Prevention

- avoid overeating, and overexertion.
- eat a wholegrain diet which includes plenty of fibre (to absorb fluids): cereals, fruit and vegetables, dried fruit, oat bran.

Treatment

- reduce fluid intake to 6 cups daily.
- practical advice: rest with your feet up as much as possible.
- herbalism: dandelion tea is an effective diuretic: put 2 teaspoons of the root into a cup of water, bring to the boil and simmer for 10 minutes, drink once daily.
- biochemic tissue salts: Nat mur 6x, 3 times daily for one week.
- massage helps improve circulation and drainage of fluids.
- exercise: gentle exercise, particularly walking, has the same effect as massage.

Muscle Pain

As the baby grows, the body adapts to accommodate it. This can sometimes lead to muscular discomfort,

particularly neck and back pain, and sometimes
headaches resulting from hormonal changes. If, however,
you experience severe or persistent pain, consult your
doctor.

Prevention

- pay attention to your posture.
- avoid lifting heavy objects. If you have to lift, squat
  down rather than bending forward.
- do not stand for long periods.
- take regular exercise: swimming is particularly good
  because the buoyancy of the water provides support.

Treatment

- aromatherapy: for headaches, soak a handkerchief in
  water with a few drops of lavender and place on the
  forehead; relax in a quiet, dimmed place.
- aromatherapy for muscle pain: ask your partner to
  rub the area gently with 2 drops Roman chamomile
  and 2 drops sweet marjoram in 10 ml carrier oil or
  lotion.
- gentle massage from a friend or partner can be very
  helpful in treating back, shoulder and neck pain. If it
  can be done by the person who will accompany you
  at the birth, this is even better, as they will learn how
  to relieve the pain of contractions. The pregnant
  woman can sit leaning over the back of a chair with
  her head on her arms. The massager uses long
  sweeping strokes from the base of the back, up and
  outwards. Do not massage over the spine itself, but
  across all the surrounding muscles. The giver should
  listen to what the woman wants him or her to do.
- yoga is very effective: there are many classes
  specifically for pregnant women (see Appendix 1).
- osteopathic and chiropractic treatment relieves pain
  caused by misalignments in the spine, which often
  occur during pregnancy.

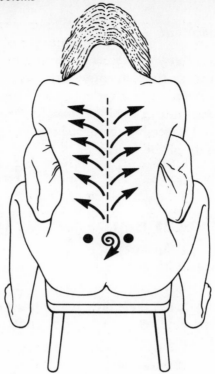

Nausea *see* Morning Sickness; Nausea

Constipation *see* entry

Heartburn

Hormonal changes during pregnancy often result in food and gastric acid backing up the oesophagus, giving pain and a sense of burning in the chest. As the foetus grows, pressure is put on the stomach, leading to indigestion.

Prevention

- eat small meals often.
- do not eat late at night.
- avoid spicy, greasy, sugary, and acidic foods.
- take a cup of chamomile, peppermint or fennel infusion after the meal.

Treatment

- yoghurt or milk ease the burning sensation.
- papaya supplements contain digestive enzymes.
- combine foods carefully: avoid eating carbohydrate and protein together, instead eat either carbohydrates and vegetables or protein and vegetables. Eat fruit only in the morning.
- see Acid Stomach and Indigestion for further advice.

Premenstrual Syndrome (PMS)

A collection of symptoms, both physical and emotional, which generally occur in women during the week or two before their period starts. The most common signs of PMS are irritability, tension, depression, fatigue, thirst, fluid retention, breast tenderness, head, back and stomach aches.

Treatment

Dietary

- the following nutrients are thought to be helpful in preventing and relieving PMS.
- vitamin B6: taken in doses of 50 mg daily throughout the whole month, it has been shown to reduce symptoms.
- vitamin E: breast tenderness is often relieved by taking supplements of 100—600 iu daily.
- magnesium: for breast tenderness, tension and weight gain, take 200—300 mg daily.
- the following dietary recommendations should be followed:
  - avoid alcohol, coffee, tea, cola and chocolate, which tend to aggravate symptoms.
  - eat regular nutritious meals to maintain blood sugar level (see Blood Sugar, Low for guidelines).
  - eat plenty of fibre to avoid constipation.

- studies have shown evening primrose oil to be an
effective treatment for women suffering breast
discomfort, irritability, and depression. Take six
500 mg capsules daily throughout your cycle. This
treatment usually takes around three months for
results to be noticed.

Homoeopathy

to be taken morning, noon and night for up to
3 days, starting 24 hours prior to the expected start
of symptoms:
- oversensitive to the slightest criticism with tearfulness:
Pulsatilla 6c.
- flies off the handle at the stupidity of others: Nux
vomica 6c.
- overtired, under-appreciated, worn out and snappy:
Sepia 6c.

Chinese Medicine

- acupuncture can greatly help. Herbs, such as Chinese
angelica, white peony, skullcap and poria, may be
recommended.

Exercise

- moderate exercise relaxes the muscles, improves blood
flow and prevents fluid retention. It also stimulates
the production of the body's endorphins which
improve your mood.
- try to exercise regularly throughout the month, but
increase your activity in the week or two before your
period starts.

Relaxation

- stress is thought to contribute to symptoms of PMS.
Attending a yoga or meditation class helps reduce
stress.
- try to plan your life in such a way that you can take

some time in the week before your period to relax
and get more sleep (see also Stress).

Orthodox

- vitamin B6 (100 mg 2 times daily) is commonly
  recommended, and the Pill is sometimes prescribed to
  suppress ovulation. Progesterone supplements are
  sometimes given for several days in the second half of
  the menstrual cycle to correct hormonal imbalances.

Presbyopia *see* Eyesight Problems

Prickly Heat

An itchy skin rash which generally occurs when people
unaccustomed to high temperatures experience extreme
heat. It is thought to be caused by the blockage of
sweat glands. Symptoms include red itchy spots, and
inflamed areas of skin, particularly around the waist,
upper trunk, armpits and insides of the elbows.

Treatment/Prevention

- some cases of prickly heat are made worse by a
  hypersensitivity to sunlight. Use a high protection
  factor sun cream as a preventative measure and cover
  yourself up.

Practical Advice

- take frequent cold showers or sponge down the skin
  with cool water.
- wear loose clothing to allow sweat to evaporate
  quickly.

Dietary

- increase intake of vitamin C, found in citrus fruits and juices, blackcurrants, green peppers, parsley and broccoli. Research has shown that daily supplements of 500 mg of vitamin C clear up itching and the rash.

Aromatherapy

- as a soothing lotion or oil: add essential oils of sandalwood (1 drop) and lavender (4 drops) to 1 fl oz (30 ml) of calendula carrier oil or lotion.

Herbal

- chickweed ointment helps soothe the rash. Simmer 2 tablespoons of chickweed in 220 g of Vaseline for 10 minutes, stirring well, strain through a fine gauze and pour into a container, allow to cool and apply when needed. You might prefer to keep an old pan specially for herbal preparations.
- chickweed infusion is also a soothing application: pour a cup of boiling water onto 4 teaspoons of dried chickweed, infuse for 15 minutes and allow to cool, dab on the rash when needed.

Homoeopathy

every 15 minutes for up to 4 doses and repeat if necessary:
- stinging itchy rash: Urtica urens 6c.
- burning and itching rash: Rhus toxicodendron 6c.
- dusky pink rash with swelling of lips, eyelids or throat: Apis 6c.

Orthodox

- calamine lotion (available over the counter) relieves the prickly itching. In severe cases, antihistamines are given orally, although these can cause allergy and should be avoided if possible.

Prostate, Enlarged

Also known as benign prostatic hypertrophy,
enlargement of the prostate gland generally only afflicts
men over the age of 50. As the gland grows it presses
on the urethra, interfering with the flow of urine. First
symptoms are an increased desire to urinate day and
night, difficulty starting urination, a weak urine stream,
and finally incontinence. Back pain and pain between
the legs may also be present. (See also Prostatitis.)

Treatment

Dietary

- studies have shown deficiency of zinc to be related to
  enlarged prostate. Increasing intake of zinc has also
  been shown to decrease the size of the prostate and
  reduce symptoms. Zinc is found in oysters, herrings,
  clams, wheat bran, whole oatmeal, pumpkin and
  sunflower seeds. To ensure sufficient intake, a zinc
  orotate supplement of 100 mg can be taken every
  other day.
- cholesterol in the blood accumulates in the prostate,
  damaging cells which can lead to cancer. Lower
  cholesterol levels by avoiding saturated fats: substitute
  red meat for chicken and fish, and reduce intake of
  high fat dairy products (see Cholesterol, High for
  further details).
- sufferers are often deficient in essential fatty acids:
  supplement your diet with 4 capsules of MaxEPA fish
  oil daily and 4 x 500 mg capsules of evening
  primrose oil.
- eat plenty of lean protein, vegetables and fruit with
  moderate intake of wholegrain carbohydrates. Fibre is
  important to prevent constipation and straining.

Herbal

- saw palmetto is an effective remedy for reducing

inflammation of the prostate: take the liposterolic extract of saw palmetto berries, 160 mg daily.
- flower pollen is also widely used.

Chinese Medicine

- the herbal remedy panax ginseng is recommended: take 2—4 g of the dried root, 3 times daily.

Hydrotherapy

- sitting in contrast sitz baths, which alternate hot and cold water, stimulates blood circulation in the pelvic area and tones the muscles. Run a hot bath, around 105—115 degrees F (40—46 degrees C), and prepare a plastic basin of cold water, around 55—85 degrees F (12—29 degrees C). Sit for 30 seconds in the hot, then 3 seconds in the cold, repeat 3 times, finishing with the cold. Carry out this treatment every other day. Ensure the rest of the body is well covered.

Yoga

- the following exercise improves circulation to the enlarged prostate, and helps reduce inflammation:
- supine butterfly: lie on your back, bend your knees, bring the soles of the feet together and bring the feet

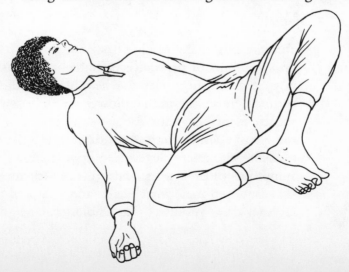

as close to your buttocks as possible. Relax your legs
letting the knees fall outwards towards the ground.
Hold this position for 5 minutes.

Orthodox

- the enlargement is palpated and assessed clinically by
  means of a rectal examination. A blood test is helpful
  in distinguishing between benign and malignant
  enlargement. In benign enlargement, if pressure on
  the urethra makes symptoms uncomfortable, part or
  all of the gland is surgically removed.

Prostatitis

Infection and inflammation of the prostate gland, usually
as a result of bacterial infection transmitted from the
urethra or bladder. The infection may also be sexually
transmitted. Symptoms include fever, flu-like aches and
pains, aching in the back, rectum and between the legs,
and considerable pain when going to the toilet.
Treatment of prostatitis is similar to that of enlarged
prostate (see Prostate, Enlarged).

Treatment

Dietary

- an increased intake of zinc has been shown to clear
  up symptoms of prostatitis effectively. Zinc is found
  in oysters, herrings, clams, wheat bran, whole
  oatmeal, pumpkin and sunflower seeds. To ensure
  sufficient intake, a zinc orotate supplement of 100 mg
  can also be taken every other day.
- reducing cholesterol levels also helps relieve
  symptoms of prostatitis, and prevent recurrent attacks:
  substitute red meat for chicken and fish, and avoid
  high fat dairy products (see Cholesterol, High).
- pollen, rich in essential fatty acids and protein, is also

a useful treatment. Take 4 Cernilton pollen tablets daily.

- sufferers are often deficient in essential fatty acids: supplement your diet with 4 capsules of MaxEPA fish oil daily and 4 x 500 mg capsules of evening primrose oil.

Herbal

- saw palmetto is an effective remedy for reducing inflammation and fighting infections of the prostate: take the liposterolic extract of saw palmetto berries, 160 mg daily.

Hydrotherapy

- sitting in contrast sitz baths, which alternate hot and cold water, stimulates blood circulation in the pelvic area and tones the muscles. Run a hot bath, around 105—115 degrees F (40—46 degrees C), and prepare a plastic basin of cold water, around 55—85 degrees F (12—29 degrees C). Sit for 30 seconds in the hot, then 3 seconds in the cold, repeat 3 times, finishing with the cold. Carry out this treatment every other day. Ensure the rest of the body is well covered.

Orthodox

- your doctor will prescribe drinking plenty of fluids and long-term antibiotics.

Psoriasis

A skin disease characterized by thick, red patches covered by a unique silvery scale, particularly around the elbows, knees, scalp, trunk and back. The skin does not usually itch badly, but is unsightly. The disease tends to run in families. One per cent of the population may develop psoriasis at some time in their lives; the condition tends to come and go.

Treatment

- reduce intake of meat, animal fats, sugar and alcohol.
- increase intake of fibre: wholegrain cereals, fruit, vegetables, cooked dried bean and peas.
- increase intake of oily fish.
- take 1—2 tablespoons of linseed oil daily.
- increase intake of fish, particularly mackerel, herring and salmon.
- the following supplements help:
  - zinc, 15—30 mg daily.
  - vitamin B complex, 100 mg morning and night.
  - vitamin A, 10,000 iu 3 times daily for 6 days a week.
- psoriasis is sometimes linked to food allergies, particularly citrus fruits and dairy products. See Allergies — Food.

Herbal

- burdock is one of the best remedies for dry, scaly skin: make a decoction by adding 1 teaspoon of the root to a cup of water, simmer for 15 minutes and drink 3 times daily. An ointment containing burdock will help relieve irritation and scaliness: simmer two tablespoons of the root in 220 g of Vaseline for 10 minutes, strain through a gauze and allow to cool, apply to the skin when needed. You may like to keep an old pan specifically for herbal preparations.

Hydrotherapy

- a hot Epsom salts bath stimulates circulation and helps eliminate toxins through the skin: add 1 lb of Epsom salts to a bath and soak in it for 15 minutes, preferably before going to bed. Not advised if you are weak or frail.
- an oatmeal bath helps soothe irritated skin. Put 2 lb of fine oatmeal in cheesecloth bags and place in a hot bath; soak for 15 minutes.

Exercise

- aerobic exercise helps improve circulation to the skin. Running, walking, swimming or exercises for 30 minutes, 3 times a week, will help.

Professional Help

- Chinese medicine: individually prescribed herbs can greatly assist this problem, as has been shown by a number of trials in British hospitals.
- homoeopathic treatment can help in some cases.

Orthodox

- psoriasis is sometimes helped by exposure to sunlight or an ultraviolet lamp. A coal tar or dithranol ointment may be recommended. In severe cases, corticosteroid drugs are prescribed.

Raynaud's Disease

A circulatory disorder where the blood vessels become hypersensitive to the cold and contract, preventing adequate blood flow to the fingers and toes. The affected areas become white, turning blue when warmed, then red. Tingling or numbness is also common.

Treatment
Practical Advice

- dress in layers to trap the heat.
- wear natural fabrics which absorb perspiration, the body's natural cooling agent.
- mittens keep you warmer than gloves.
- stop smoking; nicotine constricts the blood vessels.

Dietary

- ensure adequate intake of iron. The richest sources are lean red meat, poultry, fish, and leafy green vegetables. Drinking orange juice with meals helps increase iron absorption. Tea inhibits absorption, so do not drink tea immediately before, during or after meals.
- avoid coffee, which constricts blood vessels.

Aromatherapy

- essential oil of black pepper and rosemary help

improve circulation. Ask a friend or partner to give you a regular massage using these oils: mix 3 drops of each to 2 ½ teaspoons of carrier oil or lotion. Alternatively, add 3 drops of each oil to the bath water.

Herbal

- cayenne is useful in stimulating the circulatory system: pour a cup of boiling water on ¼ teaspoon of cayenne and infuse for 10 minutes; mix a tablespoon of the infusion with a glass of hot water and drink when needed.
- add grated fresh root ginger to your diet or drink an infusion when needed: add a cup of boiling water to 1 teaspoon of grated fresh root, infuse for 5 minutes.

Homoeopathy

to be taken every 30 minutes for up to 6 doses and repeated if necessary:
- burning sensation in fingers or toes, increased by heat, but the body is cold: Carbo vegetabilis 6c.
- heat or holding the fingers down increases discomfort: Pulsatilla 6c.
- swollen, burning, itching fingers and toes made worse by cold: Arsenicum album 6c.

Chinese Medicine

- professional treatment can be very effective. Cinnamon twigs and Chinese angelica are often prescribed.

Exercise

- any aerobic exercise (which raises the heart rate and exercises the lungs) is helpful for this condition: walking, running, cycling, swimming, or skipping.
- swing your arms in circular motion, as if throwing a ball over arm. Do twenty circles on each arm. Then,

with your arms outstretched, do twenty more small circles. Repeat morning and evening.

Orthodox

- vasodilator drugs are effective in relaxing and opening the blood vessel walls. Battery-heated gloves and socks and warmer pads containing a substance which heats up when activated are available.

Reiter's Syndrome

A disorder common in men, which produces a combination of arthritis (joint inflammation), urethritis (inflammation of the bladder outlet), and conjunctivitis (an eye infection). Reiter's syndrome is prompted by infection, but only occurs in those who are genetically predisposed. Symptoms include bladder discharge, painful stiff joints and fever.

Treatment

Practical Advice

- place cool wet tea bags on the eyes to soothe redness and itching.

Dietary

- drinking cranberry juice helps clear up urethritis. Drink 4 glasses daily.

Aromatherapy

- add 2 drops each of essential oil of juniper berry, eucalyptus and sandalwood to a warm bath, and sit in it for 10 minutes daily to relieve urethritis.

Herbal

- devil's claw decoction is an anti-inflammatory remedy. Add 1 teaspoon of the herb to a cup of water, simmer for 15 minutes and drink 3 times daily.
- for conjunctivitis, wash the eyes with eyebright tea. Add 1 teaspoon of the herb to a cup of boiling water, allow to cool and strain. With an eye cup, use the solution to rinse the eye.
- parsley and dandelion are useful in helping to flush infection from the bladder. Incorporate both herbs into your diet.

Hydrotherapy

- for inflamed and stiff joints, prepare a cold compress by soaking a piece of cotton material large enough to cover the joint in cold water, wring it out well and place over the painful joint. Wrap 2 thicknesses of woollen material around the cold compress and pin it securely. Leave on for 4–8 hours, or overnight. The compress should warm up and dry by the time it is taken off. If the compress does not warm up within 15 minutes, remove and try again, ensuring the material is well wrung out and insulated.

Massage

- gently stroke the muscles around painful joints in the direction of the heart. Use the fingertips to do gentle circular strokes in particularly stiff areas. A clean tennis or squash ball can also be rolled back and forth over the muscles if you cannot use your fingers well.

Orthodox

- painkillers and non-steroidal anti-inflammatory drugs are given to help relieve pain and inflammation.

Restless Legs

An aching, tickling, burning, or twitching in the muscles of the legs, which occurs particularly at night or when sitting for long periods. It is particularly common in pregnant and middle-aged women, smokers and those who drink lots of caffeine.

Treatment

Dietary

- increase intake of vitamin E, found in vegetable oils, seeds, wheatgerm and nuts. Take a supplement of 200 iu daily.
- increase intake of iron, found in lean red meat, poultry, fish, dried fruits, green leafy vegetables. Avoid drinking tea within 2 hours of eating.
- take a multivitamin and mineral supplement daily.
- avoid eating heavy meals late at night.
- cut down your intake of caffeine (coffee, tea, cola, chocolate).
- take a 60 mg vitamin B complex tablet daily.

Homoeopathy

- every 30 minutes for up to 6 doses.
- burning pain in the shins and crawling sensation on the skin, worse after drinking wine: Zinc metallicum 6c.
- involuntary reaction to music or bright colours: Tarantula hispanica 6c.
- restlessness worse from lying still and improved by walking around; worse during stormy weather: Rhus toxicodendron 6c.

Hydrotherapy

- bathe the legs alternately in hot and cold water to improve circulation.

Massage

to be done on the fleshy parts of the lower leg (avoid
pressure on the knees and any varicose veins):

- sit on a firm surface, bend one knee and place your
  foot flat on the ground. Place your thumbs on the
  muscle running along the outside of your shin bone,
  below the knee, and rest your fingers and palms on
  the sides of your legs for support. Applying pressure
  with your thumbs, run them slowly down the muscle
  as far as the ankle bone. Then move the hands around
  to the inside of the ankle and massage up the inside
  of the leg to the knee. Finally, place your hand on
  either side of the calf and squeeze with the thumbs in
  front and the fingers behind, kneading either side and
  the back of the leg (see illustration)

- repeat this procedure several times on both legs.

Exercise

- walking is one of the best ways to relieve this condition. An evening stroll can help prevent night discomfort.

Relaxation

- stress often makes this condition worse. Attending a regular yoga class will help you learn to relax, while providing some good stretching movements to help relieve symptoms. Biofeedback and meditation are also good methods of learning to relax.

Orthodox

- once more serious problems such as deep vein thrombosis or sciatica have been ruled out, mild muscle relaxants, or calcium supplements may be recommended.

Rheumatoid Arthritis

A type of arthritis in which the joints of the body (most commonly the fingers, wrists, knees and ankles) become painful, swollen, stiff and sometimes deformed. This is accompanied by mild fever and fatigue. Rheumatoid arthritis is an auto-immune disorder (where, for some unknown reason, the immune system attacks the body's own tissues).

Treatment

Dietary

- rheumatoid arthritis is rare in countries where a unrefined, low fat diet is consumed. Studies have indicated that adopting a diet which is high in wholegrain cereals, vegetables and fibre, and low in sugar, animal produce and refined carbohydrates helps

prevent and treat this condition.
- a vegetarian diet has been shown to reduce inflammation.
- substitute animal fats for vegetable oils and margarine. Eat oily fish: mackerel, herring sardines and salmon daily. These contain eicosapentaenoic acid (EPA), which helps to produce substances that reduce inflammation. An alternative to eating fish is a daily supplement of cod liver oil.
- increase intake of vitamin E, found in wheatgerm, nuts, seeds and seed oils and take a daily supplement of 400—1000 iu.
- sometimes rheumatoid arthritis can be triggered by food allergies (see Allergies — Food).
- take a daily supplement of 50—100 mg of selenium.
- bromelain is an extract of pineapple which has significant anti-inflammatory effects: take 600 mg daily in three doses away from meals.
- take a multivitamin and mineral supplement daily.

Herbal

- devil's claw decoction or tablets have been shown to help: add 1 teaspoon of the herb to a cup of water, simmer for 15 minutes and drink 3 times daily.

Homoeopathy

twice daily for up to 14 days; repeat if needed:
- worse from warm weather, inflamed joints, intolerant of touch and ill-humoured: Colchicum 6c.
- worse during stormy weather: Rhododendron 6c.
- when symptoms include pain and stiffness, made worse after rest and in cold, damp weather, symptoms improve with continued motion: Rhus toxicodendron 6c.
- stitching pain, made worse by any motion, eased by rest: Bryonia 6c.

Chinese Medicine

- bupleuri root, liquorice and Chinese skullcap are recommended for their powerful anti-inflammatory effects.

Hydrotherapy

- place a cold compress on the affected joint: wet a piece of cotton material in cold tap water, wring it out and wrap around the joint. Cover this with two layers of flannel or wool pinned in place. Leave in position for 4—8 hours. The compress should warm through. If it does not warm up within 15 minutes, remove it and try again.

Massage

- gentle self massage aids circulation and reduces inflammation: using a light cream or oil, lightly stroke the muscles and tissues around the area involved in the direction of the heart. Alternatively, roll a clean tennis or squash ball over the area, exerting pressure.

Exercise

- swimming in a heated pool helps keep joints mobile.

Professional Help

- osteopathy, chiropractic, homoeopathy and acupuncture may all be helpful.

Orthodox

- aspirin and non-steroidal anti-inflammatory drugs are generally recommended.

Rhinitis *see* Allergies — Hay Fever and Rhinitis

Rickets *see* Osteomalacia

Ringworm *see* Fungal Infection

Rosacea

A skin disorder where the forehead, nose and cheeks become abnormally red, due to minute blood vessels opening up near the surface of the skin. Sometimes redness is accompanied by pus-filled spots resembling acne. In elderly men the condition can develop into rhinophyma, a bulbous swelling of the nose.

Treatment

Dietary

- some studies have shown people with rosacea to be deficient in hydrochloric acid, a gastric secretion which digests the food in the stomach. Some naturopaths recommend taking hydrochloric acid capsules (10 grains) with every large meal. Start with 1 capsule, and increase the dose by one at every large meal, until you are taking 7 capsules, or you feel a warmth in your stomach. Once you have felt the warmth, decrease the dose by 1 capsule and keep taking that number at all meals of similar size (take a smaller dose at smaller meals). As your stomach begins to adapt, you will feel the warmth earlier and can gradually cut down the dosage.
- people with rosacea are often deficient in vitamin B: take 100 mg of vitamin B complex without niacin.
- the pancreatic enzyme lipase is also often deficient: take 1—2 tablets daily of pancreatin.
- avoid caffeine (coffee, tea, cola drinks, chocolate), alcohol, hot drinks, spicy foods and any other food or drink that causes flushing.

Homoeopathy

- hot, burning and itching skin: Sulphur 6c, 3 times daily.
- with a swollen, glazed appearance and stinging skin: Apis 6c, 3 times daily.

Relaxation

a reduction in hydrochloric acid production is often caused by stress, depression and anxiety. The following techniques may alleviate these symptoms:

- try to anticipate stressful situations, and prepare for them if possible.
- reduce your commitments. Learn to say 'no'.
- if you have a problem or concern, talk about it.
- take time out to do 'nothing'.
- develop a hobby, sport or interest which distracts you from your concerns and absorbs your attention while you are doing it.
- join a yoga class, or learn meditation or biofeedback.

Orthodox

- doctors generally recommend antibiotics. Surgery is offered to men with rhinophyma, allowing the thickened skin to be cut away.

Roseola Infantum

A viral infection common in children aged 6 months to 2 years. Symptoms include a high fever, swollen neck glands, and a pink rash on the chest, back and stomach, which lasts about 1 week.

Treatment

Dietary

- drink plenty of fluids, particularly fruit juices. Eat light nutritious meals of vegetable soups, broths and lightly cooked vegetables.

Herbal

- catmint infusion helps reduce fever: add a cup of boiling water to 1 teaspoon of the dried herb, infuse for 10 minutes and drink 3 times daily.

Homoeopathy

every hour for up to 4 doses and repeat if needed:
- high fever, eyes bright and staring, child delirious, neck glands sore: Belladonna 6c.
- child clingy and tearful, craving fresh air: Pulsatilla 6c.
- earache on swallowing, swollen glands, craving cold drinks: Phytolacca 6c.

Bach Flower Remedies

- keep a glass of water containing 1 or 2 drops of Rescue Remedy near the bed.

Orthodox

- paediatric paracetamol is given to reduce fever and tepid sponging is recommended.

Rubella

Also known as German measles, this infectious illness manifests as a slight fever, a mild rash and tender glands which usually last about 3—5 days. Rubella is very dangerous if contracted during pregnancy, as it can cause defects or death to the unborn baby. Women who have not had the illness are advised to seek immunization before becoming pregnant.

Treatment

Dietary

- ensure adequate intake of fresh fruit juices and vegetable soups, followed by a wholefood diet once the fever has gone.

Herbal

- infusion of yarrow: pour a cup of boiling water on 1 teaspoon of the dried herb, infuse for 10 minutes, drink hot 3 times daily.
- for children with a high fever, infusion of catmint: pour boiling water over 1 heaped teaspoon of the dried herb, infuse for 5 minutes and drink 3 times daily.

Homoeopathy

every hour for up to 6 doses. Repeat if necessary.
- child has a rash, red eyes, yellow mucus and is tearful: Pulsatilla 6c.
- bright red rash, hot red face, craving for lemons: Belladonna 6c.
- swollen glands and painful ears, alleviated by cold drinks: Phytolacca 6c.

Hydrotherapy

- cool sponging will help reduce fever and relieve discomfort caused by the rash.

Orthodox

- doctors recommend that children should be kept at home while they have a rash and for 3 days after the

spots have disappeared. If they have a high
temperature of over 38° Celsius, (98.6° Fahrenheit),
they should stay in bed. German measles is a mild
illness and does not usually warrant treatment;
however, fever should be monitored and treated
accordingly (see Fever).

Salpingitis *see* Pelvic Inflammatory Disease

Sand Fly Bites *see* Insect Bites and Stings

Scabies

An infectious skin condition brought by mites burrowing into the skin and laying eggs. Symptoms include an intensely itchy rash with red lumps, particularly around the trunk, between the fingers, the wrists and the genital area. The area above the neck is usually spared. Once scratched, the lumps develop into sores and scabs. See also Sexually Transmitted Diseases for scabies in the pubic area.

Treatment

Practical Advice

- thoroughly wash all clothes and bedding in the house in very hot water. If they cannot be washed, air them for several days; mites cannot survive for long without human contact.

Aromatherapy

- dab essential oil of lavender on the sores.

Homoeopathy

to be taken by all those living with the infected person:
• Sulphur 6c: every 8 hours for up to 3 days.

Orthodox

• your doctor will recommend applying an insecticide
  lotion to the entire body, which should be left on for
  24 hours before being washed off. A second
  application is advised. Skin irritation will continue for
  a few days as a result of residual foreign body
  material in the skin tissue.

Scar

A mark left on the skin after the tissue has healed
following an injury. Excess scar tissue, known as
hypertrophic scars or keloids, sometimes develop when
the injury is infected, or in people who have a genetic
tendency to produce excess scar tissue.

Treatment

Practical Advice

• ensure wounds heal properly: clean all cuts and
  scrapes properly and keep the wound slightly moist
  with vitamin E oil while it is healing.
• do not pick the scabs.

Dietary

- a well balanced diet is essential in encouraging healthy scar tissue to grow. Eat plenty of protein (lean meat, fish, low fat dairy products, dried cooked beans, soya beans), and incorporate plenty of zinc into your meals: found in lean meat, fish and organ meats, wholegrain breads and cereals, pumpkin and sunflower seeds, Brazil nuts, and peanuts.
- take vitamin E supplements: 100–400 iu daily.

Homoeopathy

- apply Calendula cream as soon as the wound starts to heal; use a fresh tube to ensure sterility.
- Thiosinaminum 6x, 4 times daily.

Massage

- massaging the scar area with vitamin E oil can be very successful.

Professional Help

- massage can soften the tissues and break down old scars.

Orthodox

- injections of steroids into thickened scar tissue can reduce the size and thickness.

Scarlet Fever

A bacterial infection most often found in small children. Symptoms include fever, a sore throat, swollen glands and a rash. The tongue is usually coated white with red spots which peel off to reveal a bright red ('strawberry') surface. Later, the skin on the body also peels.

Treatment

Dietary

- drink plenty of fluids, particularly citrus fruit juices (oranges, lemons, grapefruit).

Herbal

- catmint is effective in treating the fever. Take 20—30 drops of tincture in a glass of water 3 times daily.
- echinacea decoction will combat the virus, ease out the rash and help clear chest congestion. Put 2 teaspoons of the root in a cup of water, simmer for 15 minutes and drink 3 times daily.

Homoeopathy

- if a child has been in contact with others with scarlet fever, give Belladonna 6c twice daily for up to 10 days.

Biochemic Tissue Salts

four tablets, four times daily:
- in early stages, with sore throat and shivering: Ferr Phos.
- when there is a skin rash and white tongue: Kali Mur.

Hydrotherapy

- to soothe the rash, take lukewarm baths to which 3 tablespoons of baking soda have been added.

Orthodox

- scarlet fever itself is a relatively mild infection, but the bacteria that cause it can affect many other parts of the body in more serious ways if not treated. Therefore, painkillers and antibiotics may be prescribed to protect against heart, kidney and other complications which may arise.

Schizophrenia

A psychiatric illness which causes changes in personality and behaviour and a loss of touch with reality. The patient's thoughts are dissociated from the physical reality of his or her own body and surroundings. Sufferers often experience delusions, illusions, hallucinations and paranoia.

Treatment

Practical Advice

• recent research has shown that a caring, non-judgemental environment can help reduce the severity of this illness.

Dietary

• a number of nutritional deficiencies, particularly minerals, are thought to be linked to schizophrenia. Professional help from a naturopath or dietitian with a particular interest in this condition is recommended. The following guidelines indicate the type of treatment which may be proposed:
  • avoidance of gluten. Research studies have shown that eliminating gluten and milk from the diet sometimes helps schizophrenia. Gluten is found in all wheat and rye products and in smaller quantities in oats and barley. These cereals should be replaced by maize, millet, rice and potato products.
  • increase intake of niacin, found in protein-rich foods such as lean meat, chicken, fish, beans, peas, brewer's yeast, peanut butter, low fat milk and cheese, soya bean and nuts. Protein-rich foods should be eaten 3 times daily.

- take a vitamin B complex supplement daily to complement the niacin.
- avoid caffeine (coffee, tea, cola drinks and chocolate).
- avoid alcohol.
- megadoses of vitamins B3, B6, C and E may be recommended.
- supplements of amino acids may also be advised.
- food allergies can play a role in schizophrenia. For further information see Allergies — Food.

Orthodox

- drugs are used in oral or long-acting injection form to control excitable or violent states, as well as to reduce delusions and hallucinations. Electroconvulsive therapy is still sometimes used, especially where disorders of muscular control, known as catatonia, are present. Environmental stimulation, occupational therapy, rehabilitation and psychotherapy (individual and group) are all used as forms of supportive therapy.

Sciatica

Nerve pain which radiates through the buttock and often the back of the thigh, calf and sometimes down to the foot. Sciatica is usually a symptom of a structural problem in the lower back, where the nerve is pinched as it emerges from the spinal column and runs down the back of the leg. The pain can be accompanied by numbness or tingling.

Treatment

Practical Advice

- when sleeping or resting, lie on your side with a pillow between the knees to minimize pelvic strain.

Hydrotherapy

- to relieve pain and discomfort and reduce inflammation, prepare an ice pack by wrapping a bag of ice cubes or frozen peas in kitchen paper; also prepare a hot water bottle wrapped in a towel. Place each alternately on the site of pain for 10 minutes; repeat. This procedure should be done at least twice daily.

Massage

- place two tennis balls in a sock. Lie down on your back on the floor with knees bent and the sock under your lower back; one tennis ball should be either side of the spine. Relax for several minutes, letting your body sink down into the floor and the tennis balls.
- remove the balls and relax on the floor for a further 2 minutes, then place a tennis ball under each buttock, and repeat the procedure.

Acupressure

the following exercises help stimulate the pressure points related to sciatica:
- lie on your back on the floor with your knees bent; inhale and pull your knees up to your chest, keeping your lower back as flat as possible on the floor; hold your knees and hug them close to the chest and exhale; inhale and release your knees; exhale and hug them close to your chest again; repeat this action for several minutes.
- lying on your back with knees bent, place your hands, palms down, under your lower back. Taking deep breaths, rock your knees from side to side for several minutes. Bring your hands to the side, then raise your knees, steady them with your hands and continue rocking for several minutes.
- you can also massage the points illustrated, using deep thumb pressure, for at least a minute each.

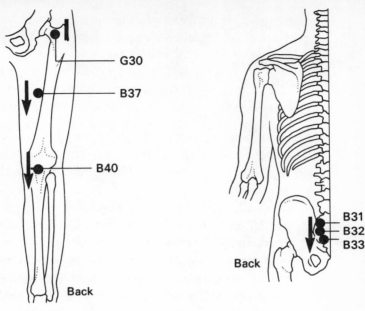

➤ Direction of acupressure massage

Professional Help

- osteopaths and chiropractors are specialized in dealing with sciatic pain.
- acupuncture can also be very helpful.

Orthodox

- anti-inflammatory tablets and muscle relaxants are generally prescribed. Surgery may be suggested if the pain results from a prolapsed disc (see Slipped Disc).

Seasickness *see* Travel Sickness

Seasonal Affective Disorder (SAD)

A syndrome which strikes during the winter months and is characterized by depression, fatigue and listlessness, along with the desire to eat more, and

subsequent weight gain. Symptoms generally begin in
September or October and are relieved in the Spring.

Treatment

Dietary

SAD sufferers have a tendency to binge on sweet,
fattening foods, leading to considerable weight gain
during the winter months. The following guidelines
help minimize food cravings:

- eat small, nutritious meals regularly: wholegrain
  cereals, lean meat, fish and low fat dairy produce,
  plenty of vegetables and fruit.
- incorporate a regular intake of complex carbohydrates
  into your diet (cereals, pasta, bread and potatoes).
  Avoid simple carbohydrates, such as sugar and foods
  containing sugar, as these are fattening and provide
  little nutritional value.
- avoid alcohol.
- keep nutritious snacks at hand for when you feel a
  slump in energy coming on: a sugar-free muesli bar, a
  slice of wholemeal bread with honey, fruit, and nuts.
- if you feel a craving, eat the food you want, but do it
  slowly and in small quantities. Put a small amount of
  the food on a plate, and go out of the kitchen to eat
  it. Eat slowly, have a drink, and allow yourself to
  digest the food. Then try to distract yourself from the
  craving by doing a calming activity: read, have a
  shower, call a friend.

Relaxation

- accept that you can do less in the winter.
- reserve stressful undertakings for the summer months
  when you have more energy.
- try to distract yourself when you become obsessed
  with a stressful thought: talk to others, try to
  rationalize your concerns by examining the possible
  outcomes of the problem realistically.

Phototherapy

- extensive research has shown light therapy to be an effective treatment for SAD. A high intensity light box (at least 2,500 lux) is required for treatment, available from some hospitals and specialist lighting manufacturers. 4—6 hours daily of light therapy is generally recommended, though this can vary from person to person depending on the type of light box used and the severity of the illness. A psychiatrist can help with initial treatment, or for further advice contact the association (see Appendix 2).
- introducing more natural daylight into your daily life will also help relieve symptoms. A 30-minute midday walk is recommended.

Orthodox

- light therapy is the accepted medical treatment. Antidepressant drugs are sometimes offered, particularly fluoxetine. Psychotherapy or counselling can also be helpful.

Septicaemia

More commonly known as blood poisoning, this is a potentially life-threatening condition, whereby large numbers of disease-causing bacteria invade the bloodstream. It generally occurs in people whose immune system is weakened, and results from bacteria escaping from an infected site, such as an abscess or pneumonia, into the blood. Symptoms include high fever, rapid breathing, headaches, nausea, low blood pressure and sometimes loss of consciousness. Immediate medical attention is necessary.

Treatment

Orthodox treatment with antibiotics, sometimes given by injection, is vital to prevent the multiplication of harmful bacteria in the body. The following treatments can complement the orthodox approach.

Aromatherapy

- oils which strengthen the immune system include bergamot, Roman chamomile and rosemary. Put 3 drops of two of these into a bath, or one drop of each in a vaporizer.

Herbal

- echinacea decoction is recommended for helping the body rid itself of microbial infections. Add 2 teaspoons of the root to a cup of water, bring to the boil and simmer for 15 minutes, drink 3 times daily.
- garlic also helps purify the blood: incorporate the raw herb into your diet as much as possible, or take 3 capsules, 3 times daily.

Homoeopathy

- delirious, aching and sore, disproportionately fast pulse: Pyrogen 30c, twice daily for 3 days.

Orthodox

- see above.

Sex Drive Problems

Lack of interest in sex can result from a number of factors: painful intercourse, vaginal dryness, erection difficulties and premature ejaculation are dealt with elsewhere in this book. Your sex life or your libido may also be affected by medication you are taking, so it is worth mentioning it to your doctor. More often, however, sexual problems are related to fatigue and decreased opportunity for sex (common in couples with children) or psychological factors: stress, anxiety, negative past experiences, insecurity and lack of communication and trust between partners can all contribute.

Treatment

If desire for sex is frequently overwhelmed by desire for sleep, or kept on hold by career or family worries, it is time to do something about it. The following therapies may help:

Practical Advice

give yourself time to relax in the evening by doing the following.
- avoid eating a heavy meal late at night.
- avoid excessive alcohol.
- start to wind down several hours before bedtime. Stop working and do an enjoyable activity: reading, yoga or meditation.
- avoid heavy discussions or arguments/avoid talking about work.
- have a warm bath, using essential oils of clary sage, rose or ylang ylang.
- give or receive a massage with your partner. You don't have to massage the whole body, but start with the neck and shoulders or the feet.

Aromatherapy

- essential oil of ylang ylang and clary sage are reputed to encourage relaxation and sensuality. Place 4 drops of each in the bath or in a vaporizer in the bedroom, or use in 20 ml of carrier oil or lotion in massage.

Acupressure

- pelvic and abdominal tension is thought to contribute to lack of sex drive. When the pelvic area is relaxed, pleasurable sensations and orgasm can be fully experienced.
- the following treatments help relax the pelvic area and stimulate sexual energy:
  - press lightly for 3 seconds on either side of each vertebrae, from the tailbone, up to the waist.
  - place the fingertips of one hand just above the centre of your pubic bone, and the fingers of the other hand between your navel and your pubic bone. Breathe deeply and apply deep pressure.
- also try the points illustrated, especially the ear point. (Massage this with the fingernail to get the exact point.)

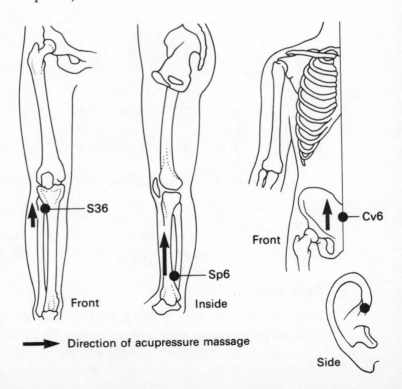

Direction of acupressure massage

Exercise

moderate exercise generally increases energy and relieves stress and fatigue. It also increases physical awareness and stimulates sexuality.

* adopt a regular exercise programme: running, walking, swimming, racquet or ball games and aerobics are all good. Pick something you enjoy and do it at least twice a week for 30 minutes.

Professional Help

* if lack of sexual desire results from inability to enjoy sex, lack of communication between partners, or anxiety about performance, it is advisable to seek help from a sex therapist or skilled counsellor.

Orthodox

* a common method taught to couples experiencing sexual difficulties is the sensate focus technique. The aim is to make each partner more aware of his or her pleasurable sensations, and those of the partner. First the couple give each other as much pleasure as possible without touching breasts or genitals. Secondly the breasts and genitals can be touched, stopping short of intercourse or orgasm. Thirdly intercourse occurs, but with an emphasis on enjoyment, not orgasm. By slowing down the procedure and increasing stimulation and enjoyment, this technique can be very successful.

Sexually Transmitted Diseases (STDs)

Infections or infestations which are typically, though not always exclusively, transmitted by sexual intercourse.

Prevention (General Advice)

- limit your number of sexual partners: STDs are more commonly diagnosed in people who have multiple partners.
- practise 'safe sex' (see AIDS).
- use a condom.
- if you discover symptoms such as a discharge from the vagina, urethra or penis, contact your doctor or a hospital STD clinic immediately for a checkup and abstain from sexual intercourse.
- if you develop an STD, it is advisable that your sexual partners be traced and treated to prevent spreading the infection further.

AIDS *see* entry

Chlamydia *see* entry

Genital Warts

Warts which appear anywhere around or inside the vagina, cervix or back passage. In men they may appear on the penis or under the foreskin. Genital warts are sexually transmitted and require immediate treatment, as there is some evidence of their link with cervical cancer in women.

Treatment

- for women who have had warts, or whose partner has them, frequent smear test are recommended.
- the warts are removed surgically or by painting them with podophyllin; however, they do tend to recur.

Gonorrhoea

More commonly known as 'the clap', this bacterial infection can be transmitted during sexual intercourse and oral or anal sex. It can also be passed from a mother to a child at birth. Symptoms in men and women include a green creamy discharge from the urethra, pain on passing water and sometimes abdominal pain and a fever. Men may experience swelling and pain in the testicles. If left untreated, gonorrhoea can lead to infertility and ultimately death.

Treatment

- antibiotics are essential, followed by medical checkups to ensure that the infection has not recurred. Sexual partners should be traced and treated.

Herpes, Genital see entry

Nonspecific Urethritis (NSU)

This is an extremely common sexually transmitted disease. The infection brings inflammation of the urethra, with a urethral discharge and often pain when passing water. It is more common in men but may cause infertility in women. Therefore, if you or your partner suspect NSU, consult a doctor immediately.

Prevention

- barrier methods of contraception help prevent transmission of NSU. Use a condom along with a spermicide; a diaphragm also provides some protection.
- both partners should wash before intercourse.
- both should go to the toilet and wash after intercourse.

Treatment

- your doctor will take a test to find the organism responsible for the infection and antibiotics will be given. Sexual partners should be traced and treated. Abstain from sexual intercourse until the infection has cleared up. See also Urinary Tract Infection.

Pubic Lice (Crabs)

Itching in the pubic area, particularly when warm in bed, may be caused by pubic lice (crabs) infestation. These are transmitted through close contact, though it does not have to be sexual (sharing clothes, towels, and bedding can pass on the parasites).

Treatment

- insecticide lotions are applied to the pubic area. It is advisable to treat all family members and sexual contacts.

Scabies

Itching in the pubic area may be caused by scabies. This may be transmitted by close contact, not necessarily sexual. See entry for details of treatment. Sexual contacts and other members of the family should also be treated.

Syphilis

Another common STD, this brings an extremely infectious ulcer on the shaft of the penis in men, or near the vagina in women. Syphilis may also cause swollen glands, and infection in other parts of the body.

Treatment

- antibiotics are effective, but must be taken in the early stages to prevent the infection spreading to other parts. Sexual partners should be traced and treated.

Thrush

This may be transmitted sexually. For details of treatment, see entry.

Trichomoniasis see entry

Shingles

Medically known as herpes zoster, this is caused by the chicken pox virus which lies dormant in a nerve root and re-emerges when the immune system is low. It begins with extreme sensitivity over an area of skin — usually the ribs, neck or upper half of the face. A rash follows which blisters and then turns to crusty scabs. Shingles can cause long-term nerve damage, so it is advisable to consult your doctor, particularly if the head or eyes are affected. The following complementary treatments will also help.

Treatment

Dietary

the following measures will help raise immunity and fight the virus:

- increase intake of vitamin C, found in fruit and vegetables, particularly citrus fruits, Brussels sprouts, parsley and strawberries. Take a supplement of 1000 mg, 4 times daily.
- take a vitamin B complex supplement daily to help build healthy nerve cells.
- eat a well balanced diet of lean meat, fish or vegetable protein, low fat dairy products, vegetables and fruit.
- studies have shown that supplementation with vitamin E can relieve the long-term symptoms associated with shingles. The recommended dosage is 1,400–1,600 iu of vitamin E daily, spread over three doses.
- vitamin E oil applied directly to the sores can also help.

Aromatherapy

- dab the sores with a solution of 1 cup of water with 2 drops each of essential oil of lemon and geranium.

Homoeopathy

to be taken every hour for up to 4 doses and repeated if
necessary:

- when symptoms improve with warm bathing and
  with movement: Rhus toxicodendron 6c.
- sharp pain worse at night, patient chilly, skin better
  for warmth: Arsenicum album 6c.
- skin burns and itches and is aggravated by warm
  bathing: Mezereum 6c.
- bluish tinge to the blisters; pain between the ribs:
  Ranunculus bulbosus 6c.
- **prevention:** if you have been in contact with
  someone suffering chicken pox or shingles:
  Variolinum 30c, once every 12 hours for 3 doses.

Chinese Medicine

- oriental wormwood and Chinese gentian are often
  recommended. Acupuncture helps long-term pain.

Orthodox

- antiviral drugs in liquid form to apply to the skin or
  in tablet form to swallow can reduce both the severity
  and duration of the attack. Antibiotics are only used
  if secondary bacterial infection is present.

Shortsightedness *see* Eyesight Problems

Sinusitis

Inflammation of the mucous membranes of the sinuses
(the air-filled cavities in the bones surrounding the
nose), caused by injury to the nose, bacterial or viral
infections, such as a cold, allergies (see entries), or
swimming. Symptoms include a blocked up nose, pain

in the nose and face area (including toothache and in the upper jaw), sometimes a fever, and the production of thick nasal discharge.

Treatment

Dietary

- recurrent attacks of sinusitis may indicate a food allergy. See Allergies — Food to identify and treat potential allergies.
- naturopaths recommend a diet free of dairy products, with limited carbohydrates and plenty of raw green vegetables and fruit.

Herbal

- golden seal infusion is an effective remedy: pour a cup of boiling water on 1 teaspoon of the powdered herb and infuse for 15 minutes, add 250 mg of bromelain (the proteolytic enzyme from pineapple, available in health food stores). Take every two hours during an acute attack.
  - **caution:** not to be used during pregnancy or by those with high blood pressure.
- garlic is also useful: include as much as possible of the raw herb in your cooking.

Homoeopathy

for recent symptoms: once hourly for up to 4 doses; for long-term symptoms: 3 times daily for up to 4 days:
- stinging pain in the cheekbone area or pressure on the bridge of the nose with thick stringy mucus: Kali bichromicum 6c.
- tearing facial pain, worse in the cold, teeth feel too long: Mercurius solubilis 6c.
- chronic sinusitis with no discharge, persistent stuffiness, feels as if floating when walking: Sticta pulmonaria 6c.

Hydrotherapy

- inhaling steam helps drain the sinuses:
  - take long, hot showers.
  - prepare a basin of boiling hot water and lean over it with a towel over the head, inhale deeply for 10 minutes.
  - use a humidifier in your bedroom.

Chinese Medicine

- the condition is seen as a deficiency of *qi* in the lungs. Peppermint, honeysuckle, fritillary bulb, tangerine peel and zanthium fruit are all helpful.

Acupressure

- place the thumb and index finger of your left hand on the indentation of the inner eyes, where the bridge of the nose meets the eyebrows; place your right hand behind the neck, grasping the muscles on either side of the spine with your fingers and the heel of your hand. Put pressure on all 4 points simultaneously for 1 minute while breathing deeply.

Orthodox

- doctors generally recommend antibiotics to fight the infection. Decongestant drops or sprays may be given for long-term problems. Surgery is sometimes carried out in extreme cases, to sterilize and dry out the sinus cavities.

Skin, Dry

Dry skin usually occurs when the sebaceous (oil) glands are inactive as a result of a hormonal imbalance or a nutritional deficiency. It can also be caused by exposure to harsh sun, wind or cold, indoor heat or air conditioning. Crash dieting sometimes results in changes to skin condition.

Treatment

Practical Advice

- use a water-in-oil moisturizer day and night to protect against water loss.
- avoid using detergents on the skin: use a lotion, not soap.
- add 2 cups of oatmeal to a lukewarm bath and soak in it to soften the skin. Pat yourself almost dry, and apply moisturiser to seal in the dampness.
- distribute bowls of water around your home and workplace during the winter or use a humidifier.
- keep the temperature in your home as low as possible.

Dietary

- increase intake of essential fatty acids, found in olive, sunflower or safflower oil.
- increase intake of vitamins A and D, found in fish liver oils, egg yolk, salmon, herring and mackerel, and carrots.
- increase intake of vitamin E, found in sunflower seeds, soya bean and olive oil. Rubbing vitamin E oil on the skin will also help.

Aromatherapy

- essential oil of geranium added to the bath, or used in a steam bath, helps balance the skin and regulate sebum secretion. Two drops each of sandalwood and rose otto in 20 ml carrier oil are excellent at night.

Orthodox

- in severe cases, a low dose cortisone cream may be recommended for itchy, very dry or eczematous skin (see Eczema).

Skin, Oily

Overactivity of the oil-producing glands in the face often occurs as a result of hormonal imbalances. It commonly occurs during pregnancy or when taking the Pill. Stress, poor diet and using the wrong cosmetics can also contribute.

Treatment

Practical Advice

- oily skin requires gentle treatment: avoid using soap, instead wash with a mild oil-in-water lotion cleanser which does not contain drying agents. Rub it onto the skin with your fingers and wipe it off with tissues, then rinse the face with cold water.
- use a water-in-oil moisturizer and water-based cosmetics.
- once a week make up a face mask with 1 teaspoon of brewer's yeast with enough water or plain/natural yoghurt to make a paste. Apply the mask after cleansing the face, allow it to dry completely, then rinse with warm water.

Dietary

- avoid fatty food, eat plenty of fruit and raw and cooked vegetables.
- vitamin B complex is important for healthy skin. It is found in wholegrain cereals and liver; brewer's yeast is also an excellent source: take 1 tablespoon in drinks 3 times daily.
- zinc helps regulate the oil-producing glands of the skin: it is found in lean meat, poultry, fish, organ meats and wholegrain cereals.

Aromatherapy

- after cleansing morning and night, dab the face with a solution made of the following: 4 drops of essential oil of lavender with 4 drops of essential oil of bergamot or lemon, well mixed with 100 ml of spring water.

Herbal

- calendula is one of the best remedies for skin problems: pour a cup of boiling water on 2 teaspoons of the petals, infuse for 15 minutes and drink 3 times daily.

Orthodox

- benzoyl peroxide creams or lotions are recommended. Antibiotic lotions are prescribed when the glands become infected. In severe cases, hormonally acting agents can be effective.

Slipped Disc

This term is often used incorrectly to refer to general backache (see Backache). Discs do not slip, but sometimes rupture, allowing part of their soft core to bulge out, which puts pressure on surrounding nerves and tissue. This may be caused by wear and tear of the discs, or by a sudden strain or fall. The result is excruciating pain in the back, which sometimes radiates down the legs. A more correct term for slipped disc is prolapsed or herniated disc.

Treatment

A prolapsed disc brings severe and incapacitating pain. Only 15 per cent of severe backaches are due to a prolapsed disc. For general advice on back pain see Backache. If you suspect you have a prolapse seek professional help. An x-ray will confirm diagnosis.

Practical Advice

- if you suspect you have a prolapsed disc, lie down to take pressure off the disc. Sometimes lying on your side with the knees bent is more comfortable than flat on your back. Placing a pillow between your knees can also help. If you experience weakness, tingling in the limbs or loss of bladder or bowel control, get immediate emergency help.

Homoeopathy

- Arnica 6c: to be taken every 30 minutes for up to 6 doses, then every 4 hours for up to five days.

Bach Flower Remedies

- Rescue Remedy will help deal with the shock of severe pain.

Hydrotherapy

- ask a friend or family member to use hot and cold treatment for pain relief. Prepare an ice pack by wrapping a bag of frozen peas in kitchen towel, place on the area of the most pain for 10 minutes, then place a hot water bottle wrapped in a towel on the area. Continue alternating hot and cold for 40 minutes.

Acupressure

- massage the points illustrated, using deep thumb pressure, for at least one minute.

Professional Help

- osteopathy or chiropractic are successful in treating moderate prolapses through manipulation.
- acupuncture is helpful in relieving acute pain.

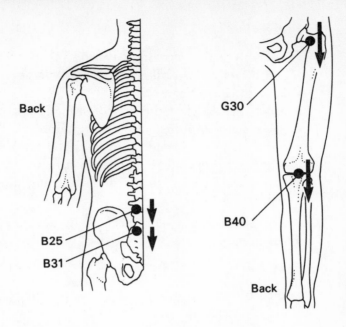

Back

G30

B25

B31

B40

Back

➤ Direction of acupressure massage

Orthodox

- painkillers, anti-inflammatory drugs and muscle relaxants are recommended, along with physiotherapy, including traction, to pull the vertebrae apart and allow the prolapsed part of the disc to move back into place. Surgery is used in severe cases to open up the vertebrae and relieve pressure on the nerve.

Snake Bite

Symptoms of a snake bite include an immediate burning pain at the site of the bite, which may be followed by dizziness, nausea and pallor. The bite can also affect the blood pressure, the heart rate and the nervous system, bringing symptoms of thirst, headache, slurred speech and double vision. Always try and remember the colour and markings of a snake that bites you, in case specific anti-venom is needed.

Prevention

- wear protective clothing covering the legs and ankles and boots when walking in overgrown areas.
- keep to cleared pathways.
- use a stick to clear the way of stones, logs, or brush.
- never sleep unprotected on the ground.
- put food in bags, tied up in trees and burn rubbish which attracts rodents, which in turn attract snakes.
- if you see a snake, do not disturb it, but move quietly away.

Treatment

First Aid

- keep the victim still; do not raise the injured area.
- place a sterile dressing on the bite.
- bandage the area firmly.
- start mouth to mouth resuscitation if the victim has stopped breathing.
- get medical help, but do not leave the victim alone.

Homoeopathy

- Golondrina 30c, every 30 minutes for up to 4 doses, until professional help can be obtained.

Orthodox

- antibiotics and tetanus antitoxin injections are given for all snake bites. For a severely poisonous bite, a serum injection containing antibodies against the venom will be given. Such treatment generally provides complete recovery if administered in time.

Sore Throat

A rough or raw sensation at the back of the throat which often is the first sign of a cold (see entry), influenza (see Flu), tonsillitis, laryngitis or pharyngitis (see entries). Sore throats are generally caused by viruses, but they can sometimes result from the *Streptococcus* bacteria, which produces a sore throat along with high fever and a more generalized feeling of illness, known as strep throat. Strep throat can sometimes lead to more serious problems such as rheumatic fever and rheumatic heart disease, so it is advisable to consult your doctor.

Treatment

Dietary

- drink plenty of fluids, particularly fruit juices.
- avoid milky drinks.
- increase intake of vitamin C, found in citrus fruits and vegetables.
- increase intake of zinc, found in lean meat and fish: freshly made chicken and vegetable soup is an excellent food for anyone with a sore throat.

Aromatherapy

- make up a gargle using 2 drops each of essential oil of lemon and sandalwood to a glass of warm water, stir well and gargle with the mixture 3 times daily.
- add 2 drops each of eucalyptus and peppermint to 10 ml of carrier oil or lotion and apply to the chest and throat area.

Herbal

- garlic is effective in attacking viral and bacterial infections. Incorporate as much raw garlic into your diet as possible or take 3 garlic oil capsules 3 times daily.
- red sage, used as a gargle, helps soothe an inflamed and sore throat: pour a cup of boiling water on 2 teaspoons of the leaves, infuse for 10 minutes and use hot as a gargle for 10 minutes twice daily.

- golden seal is particularly good for strep throat: add a
  cup of boiling water to 1 teaspoon of the powdered
  herb, infuse for 10 minutes and drink 3 times daily.
  - **caution:** not to be taken during pregnancy or by
    those with high blood pressure.

Homoeopathy

every 30 minutes for up to 4 doses and repeat as
necessary:
- strawberry red appearance with flushed face and fever:
  Belladonna 6c.
- pain in neck and ears, swallowing painful, feeling
  exhausted and weak: Gelsemium 6c.
- sudden sore throat made worse by cold wind, tonsils
  swollen, throat burning, everything tastes bitter:
  Aconite 6c.
- worse right side with purplish appearance and a
  swollen uvula, better from cold drinks: Apis 6c.
- worse left side, intolerant of any constriction, pain
  worse from swallowing saliva and better from
  swallowing food: Lachesis 6c.

Orthodox

- gargling with salt water is recommended, along with
  painkillers. Antibiotics may be recommended for
  severe cases of strep throat.

Spots and Pimples

Inflamed swellings either on or under the surface of the
skin, which are often red and pus-filled, are common in
adolescence and generally more or less clear up once the
hormonal changes of puberty have settled down. Severe
and unsightly spots on the face, neck and back are likely
to be acne (see entry). In adults spots occur as a result
of the hormonal changes of menstruation or pregnancy
or, some believe, as a result of inadequate elimination,

which allows toxins to build up in the body. They may also spring up as a result of fatigue or being 'run down'. Some people respond to food allergies with rashes or spots (see Allergies — Food).

Prevention

- ensure you get plenty of rest.
- practise stress reduction techniques.
- eat a wholefood diet, with whole grains, plenty of fresh fruit and vegetables and low fat protein. Avoid fats, sugars, refined and junk foods.
- drink plenty of water, at least 8 glasses daily.
- keep your skin clean by washing morning and night with an oil-free cleanser or mild soap. Rinse well with water.
- take regular exercise: this aids circulation and elimination.
- use deodorants rather than antiperspirants, as the latter sometimes inhibit elimination by blocking the sweat glands.

Treatment

Practical Advice

- the best way to deal with a spot is to leave it alone to take its course. Do not squeeze or pick it, as this may lead to infection and scarring.

Aromatherapy

- essential oil of tea tree is useful as an antiseptic. Dab it on the spot at regular intervals.

Herbal

- echinacea decoction helps detoxify the system: place 2 teaspoons of the root in a cup of water, bring to the boil and simmer for 10 minutes. Drink 3 times daily.

Chinese Medicine

- traditional Chinese doctors believe that spots are generated by excessive heat in the body. Chrysanthemum, honeysuckle or dandelion tea are recommended to reduce heat. A popular remedy is to cleanse the skin with watermelon or cucumber.

Acupressure

- massage the points illustrated, using deep thumb pressure, for at least a minute several times a week.

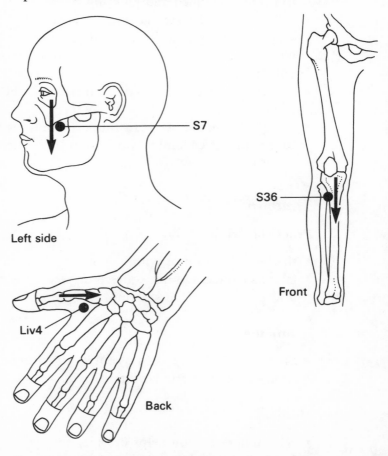

S7

S36

Left side

Liv4

Front

Back

➤ **Direction of acupressure massage**

Phototherapy

- sunlight and fresh air help clear up spots.

Orthodox

- normally, spots are left to take their own course. For treatment of severe cases, see Acne.

Sprains

Sprains result from overstretching ligaments that attach the bones of a joint to each other. They bring painful swelling and muscle spasm around the joint along with pain on movement. Being rope-like and fibrous, ligaments have a poor blood supply and generally take a long time to heal.

Treatment

Aromatherapy

- sweet marjoram and rosemary help dull the pain: add 4 drops of both essential oil of sweet marjoram and rosemary to a bowl containing enough cold water to cover the joint. Soak the joint for at least 10 minutes.
- at night make up a cold compress with the above mixture: soak a clean cotton cloth in the solution, wring out and wrap around the sprain. Wrap with a piece of dry cotton and cling film. Leave on for at least an hour before bedtime.

Homoeopathy

- Arnica 6c: every 30 minutes for up to 4 doses.
- apply cold compresses with Arnica solution twice daily to help reduce swelling.
- Ruta graveolens 6c, 3 times daily for 1 week.

Hydrotherapy

- apply an ice pack to the area as soon as possible: use ice cubes or a packet of frozen vegetables wrapped in kitchen paper. Place on the joint or muscles for 10 minutes, take it off for 10 minutes then reapply for 10 minutes. If no ice is available apply a cold compress (a clean cloth soaked in cold water and wrung out) for 30 minutes. If you have a sprained ankle or wrist, a light bandage may be used to support the joint. Rest with the joint elevated.

Massage

- massage can help once the swelling has subsided. Do not work directly on the joint, but on the muscles around it. For example, if it is a knee strain, work on the muscles from the knee up the thigh, and the muscles from the ankle to the knee. Use long upward sweeping strokes. As the injury heals, you can begin to work with careful kneading and friction strokes around the joint.

Professional Help

- osteopathy or chiropractic is helpful.
- acupuncture helps relieve pain.

Orthodox

- physiotherapy may be recommended. Heat treatment, infrared and laser treatment may be used to improve the blood supply, strapping (to support the joint) or, as a last resort, surgery for entirely ruptured ligaments.

Squint

Also known as strabismus, this is a condition where there is abnormal deviation of one eye in relation to the other.

The squint may be convergent (crosseye), where one eye is directed too far inward, or divergent (walleye), where the eye is directed outward. Sometimes an eye can be directed up or down — this is known as vertical strabismus. Squints can cause permanent visual problems in children and should be treated by a professional.

Treatment

Yoga

yoga may be beneficial by helping to relax the eye muscles:

- sit comfortably at a table, place your elbows on the table and rub the palms of your hands together. Cup your hands over your closed eyes, sealing out all light. Relax in this position for 20 seconds. Repeat as often as you like, but at least twice daily.
- sit comfortably at a table. Place a lighted candle at eye height about 3 feet away and gaze at the flame (without blinking, if possible) for 10 seconds. Then do the above palming exercise for 30 seconds. Then gaze at the candle with one eye for 10 seconds, then with both eyes for 10 seconds, then with the other eye for 10 seconds, repeat the palming. Carry out this procedure 3 times.

Professional Help

- the Bates Method: minor squints often disappear within a short time of starting this training. More established or severe squints may take longer.

Orthodox

depending on the severity of the squint, any of the following treatments might be employed:

- refraction: correction of a weak or lazy eye using glasses or contact lenses.
- occlusion: blocking off the good eye to force the lazy one to work harder.
- orthoptic training: a form of ocular physiotherapy to activate the lazy eye.
- surgery: to lengthen or shorten the muscles which control the movements of the eyes. Surgery must be undertaken at a young age if useful vision in the squinting eye is to be preserved.

Stiffness

Rigid and painful muscles may be caused by physical overexertion, osteoarthritis (see entry) or rheumatoid arthritis (see entry). The following treatments are for stiffness following overuse of muscles.

Prevention

Practical Advice

- when taking part in any sport or exercise, make sure you warm up properly and stretch before you begin. After exercising, 'warm down' thoroughly and stretch the muscles — this prevents the buildup of lactic acid, which is the main cause of stiffness. Consult a sport or exercise trainer if you are unsure of how to do this.

Treatment

Homoeopathy

- Arnica 6c, taken hourly for 4 doses, is often helpful in preventing stiffness after unaccustomed exertion.

Hydrotherapy

- soaking in a hot bath, a shower or a sauna immediately after exercising helps relax the muscles and prevent stiffness.

Massage

- massage is one of the best ways to relieve stiffness. It helps increase circulation to the muscles which in turn flushes out the waste products produced during exercise which cause stiffness. Add a soothing essential oil to the massage oil or lotion, such as eucalyptus or lavender.

Exercise

- take some gentle exercise while the stiffness lasts. Try walking or swimming.

Yoga

- salutations to the sun are an excellent way to loosen up stiff muscles on awakening:
  - stand erect with feet and palms together.
  - inhale, raise your arms above your head, and bend back arching your head, shoulders and back.
  - exhale, lean forward, letting your arms and head hang down by your legs and feet (as far as is comfortable).
  - inhale, bend your knees and put your palms flat on the ground beside your feet. Take your right leg back as far as you can with the knee resting on the floor, keep the arms straight, look up and push your hips forward.
  - take the left foot back to the right, raise the abdomen, making an arch, keeping the feet flat on the floor. Exhale.
  - lower the body slowly to the floor.
  - inhale and lift the chest and shoulders off the floor, look up.

- exhale, bring the chest and shoulders down, bring right foot forward, leaving the left knee on the ground, look up.
- inhale, bring left knee up and stand, as in position 3.
- exhale and return to position 1.
- repeat this procedure several times daily.

Orthodox

- heat treatment, exercise and massage are all
  recommended.

Stings *see* Insect Bites and Stings; Jellyfish Stings

Stomach Ache

Stomach pain can result from a number of different
causes which are dealt with elsewhere in this book. The
most common ones are listed below:

- indigestion: overeating or drinking or eating the
  wrong food (see entry).
- in women: period pain (see entry), ovulation pain (see
  entry) or gynaecological disorders, such as
  endometriosis (see entry).
- urinary infection/cystitis (see Urinary Tract Infection
  and Cystitis).
- stress or anxiety (common in children).
- colic (see entry).
- an ulcer (see Peptic Ulcer).
- a tumour.
- appendicitis (see entry).

Treatment

If pain lasts for more than 6 hours, or is accompanied
by feelings of dizziness, sweating and pallor or vomiting
blood, consult your doctor immediately. For specific
advice on the conditions listed above, refer to the
appropriate entry. The following treatments are for nonspecific stomach pain.

Practical Advice

- lie down with a hot water bottle or heated pad on the stomach.

Dietary

- eat a wholefood diet high in whole grains, fibre, fruit and vegetables, low in fat, caffeine and alcohol.

Herbal

- chamomile or peppermint tea helps soothe indigestion and relax muscular spasm.
- slippery elm soothes the mucous membrane of the digestive tract: use 1 part of the powdered bark to 8 parts of water, simmer for 10 minutes and drink ½ a cup 3 times daily.

Homoeopathy

take 1 tablet every 15 minutes for up to 4 doses and repeat if needed:
- after rich foods, with gas and rancid belching: Carbo vegetabilis 6c.
- after spicy food, caffeine, alcohol: Nux vomica 6c.
- burning pain, worse in the small hours of the morning: Arsenicum album 6c.
- burning pains and vomiting, better temporarily for cold drinks: Phosphorus 6c.
- stomach feels like a stone and is very sensitive to touch: Bryonia 6c.
- pain is better from eating but starts again 2 hours later: Anacardium 6c.

Acupressure

- massage the points illustrated, using deep thumb pressure, for at least one minute.

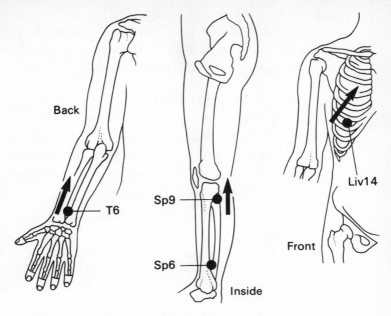

Back

T6

Sp9

Sp6

Inside

Liv14

Front

➤ Direction of acupressure massage

Relaxation

- practising yoga, or learning to meditate, helps relieve stress-related stomach ache in adults. Relaxation tapes and biofeedback can also help.
- psychotherapy or counselling may be helpful in learning to cope with stress.
- for children, Bach Flower Remedy: Aspen.

Orthodox

- Treatment depends on the cause of stomach ache. Antacids are commonly prescribed for digestive problems.

Stress

The stress reaction is a natural response to fear. It prepares the body for 'fight or flight' by tensing the muscles and constricting the blood vessels. However, most of the stressful experiences we encounter today do not require us to fight or flee, and therefore the body is left in a state of physical tension, which can result in a lowering of immunity, rendering us more susceptible to disease.

Common signs of stress are: recurrent headaches, dizziness, rashes, colds and infections, panic attacks or anxiety, palpitations, sexual problems, indigestion, aches and pains in neck, shoulder or back, loss of appetite, compulsive eating, irritability, fatigue, tearfulness, sleep problems, lack of concentration.

Treatment

There are many ways to tackle stress, and most complementary therapies will help, so it is a question of finding out which is best for you. The ones listed below are most commonly used.

Dietary

- how well you handle stress can be related to how well you are nourished. People who eat a diet high in wholegrain breads and cereals, fruit and vegetables, and low in refined carbohydrates, sugar and caffeine show greater ability to cope with stress.

Aromatherapy

- essential oil of lavender has been shown in studies to reduce stress. Use 5 or 6 drops in a bath, or on a handkerchief.

Chinese Medicine

- acupuncture brings deep relaxation. Herbs such as thorowax root, peony root and schizandra fruit may be prescribed.

Massage

- massage relieves many of the physical symptoms of stress: tense muscles, aching neck, shoulders and back, headaches. By relaxing the muscles and improving blood circulation, it also relaxes the mind.

Exercise

- exercise is what the body instinctively wants to do under stress, and it is extremely beneficial in relaxing the mind and body. Regular running, walking, cycling, swimming or any other aerobic exercise, ideally carried out for at least 30 minutes, 3 times a week, is helpful. Even a walk around the block can help let off steam or reduce anxiety.

Relaxation

- yoga: attending a yoga class and practising yoga yourself at home will divert your mind from stress, relax muscle tension through stretching, and teach you to breathe more completely.
- meditation: takes you into a deep state of relaxation. It is generally learnt with a teacher, but can then be practised at home.
- biofeedback: teaches you how to relax mentally and physically. Once you have learnt how to do this, it can be applied to everyday life.

Affirmations

- keep a list of affirmations to say to yourself when under stress: Chanting simple phrases, such as 'I can handle this', 'I know what I'm doing', 'I'm the best' and so on, can divert the stress response.

Orthodox

- your doctor would try to identify the cause of stress and help find ways of avoiding or dealing with it.

Counselling may be recommended. Tranquillizers and alcohol should be avoided at all costs.

Stretch Marks

Also known as striae, stretch marks are commonly found on the stomach, thighs, and breasts of pregnant women as a result of the loss of elasticity in the skin when it is extended over a long period of time. They also occur in women who are overweight. The marks first appear as red raised lines, which become purple, and then flatten into silvery streaks.

Treatment

Dietary

- increase intake of vitamin E, found in vegetable oils, seeds, wheatgerm, nuts, avocados, peaches, wholegrain cereals, spinach, broccoli, asparagus and dried prunes. Massage vitamin E oil into the skin during the pregnancy.
- ensure you get adequate zinc, found in lean meat, poultry and fish.
- increase intake of vitamin B6, by taking a vitamin B complex supplement daily.

Aromatherapy

- essential oils of lavender and myrrh can be used both to prevent and treat stretch marks. Aromatherapist Shirley Price recommends an anti-stretch mark concoction of 3 drops of both frankincense and myrrh, 6 drops of lavender, 4 drops of geranium and 2 fl oz of calendula carrier oil. This mixture should be applied to the breasts, stomach, buttocks, and thighs regularly every morning and night, starting in the fourth month of pregnancy.

Biochemic Tissue Salts

- Calc Fluor: take 3 tablets, 3 times daily for 5 days a week for up to 3 months.

Orthodox

- doctors recommend avoiding being overweight during pregnancy. Cosmetic surgery which cuts out the widest stretch marks is sometimes offered, though some scar will be visible and no absolute guarantee of reducing stretch marks is given.

Stroke

The interruption of blood supply and oxygen to the brain due to a blood clot or haemorrhage, which causes permanent damage to the cells of the affected area. Symptoms include differing degrees of paralysis, speech impairment and loss of function, depending on the area of the brain affected.

Prevention

- a poor diet, excessive alcohol and drug use, obesity and lack of exercise are all factors which contribute to a weakening of the arteries of the brain, leading to blood clots and strokes:
- reduce intake of saturated fats (found in red meat and dairy products)
- eat plenty of wholegrain cereals, fresh fruit and vegetables, dried cooked beans and lean protein (fish and poultry).
- stop smoking.
- limit alcohol intake.
- take aerobic exercise (such as walking, cycling or swimming) three times a week for at least 30 minutes, ideally.

Treatment

Dietary

- reduce intake of fatty meats and high fat dairy foods.
- increase intake of fresh fruit and vegetables, fish, poultry, wholegrain cereals and breads.
- as a preventive measure and a treatment, the following daily supplements are recommended:
  - vitamin E: 400 iu.
  - vitamin C: 500 mg.
  - evening primrose oil 6 x 500 mg capsules.
  - lecithin 5—10 g.
  - fish oils 3 g.

Herbal

- as part of a general health programme, yarrow infusion is recommended to improve circulation and tone the blood vessels: pour a cup of boiling water on 2 teaspoons of the dried herb and infuse for 15 minutes. Drink hot 3 times daily.

Homoeopathy

- take Arnica 200c as soon as possible after the stroke.
- Arnica 6c and the biochemic tissue salt Kali mur 6x twice daily for 1 month will help to dissolve blood clots.

Hydrotherapy

- swimming in a heated pool under the supervision of a physiotherapist is often helpful in restoring physical strength and movement.

Exercise

- gentle exercise is recommended as soon as possible after a stroke, to prevent the muscles contracting and becoming stiff. This is best carried out with the help of a physiotherapist.

Professional Help

- Chinese medicine: lovage tuber is often prescribed to dissolve or prevent blood clots. Acupuncture can be very helpful after a stroke in treating paralysis. The earlier it is given the better.
- osteopathy, chiropractic and massage all have a place in helping to maintain muscle function and prevent stiffness.

Orthodox

- treatment is aimed at improving quality of life, with occupational therapy, physiotherapy, home adjustments and walking aids. Psychotherapy or counselling are also invaluable. Drugs to prevent blood clotting and to regulate the heart are often prescribed.

Stye

A small abscess near the eyelash caused by infection of the hair follicle.

Treatment

Dietary

recurrent styes indicate that immunity is low. The following recommendations will help improve your resistance to infection:
- increase intake of zinc, found in lean meat, poultry and fish. Take a supplement of 30 mg twice daily.
- increase intake of vitamin C, found in fresh fruit and vegetables.
- eat a well-balanced diet of lean proteins, wholegrain cereals and plenty of raw and lightly cooked vegetables and fruit.

Homoeopathy

every 4 hours for up to 4 doses and repeat if needed:

- itching and weeping in the eye with a sensation as if the eyeball were covered by a film: Pulsatilla 6c.
- smarting and cutting pains, eyes feel dry: Staphysagria 6c.

Hydrotherapy

- make up a warm solution of water with a few drops of calendula tincture. Soak a compress in the solution and hold over the eye for a few minutes, to help discharge any pus. Do not squeeze the stye, as this may further infect the area.

Folk Remedies

- cold tea makes a soothing eye wash. Soak cotton wool in cold tea and hold over the eye. Alternatively place a cold, used teabag over the eye.

Orthodox

- plucking the offending eyelash sometimes does the trick, but in long-standing chronic or recurrent styes, treatment with an antibiotic ointment is recommended.

Sunburn

Redness, heat and sometimes blistering can easily occur on exposure to the sun if you are not used to it. The long-term effects of sunburn are premature ageing of the skin and skin cancer. Fair skin and young skin are most susceptible; however, even dark skin loses its elasticity with repeated and prolonged exposure to the sun.

Prevention

- limit your exposure to the sun: avoid going out in the sun during the hottest time of the day (10 a.m. to 4 p.m.).
- always wear a sunscreen.
- if you are exposed to the sun, wear protective clothing and a hat which shades the face.
- if you want to acquire a tan, do so gradually: use a high protection factor sunscreen, and limit yourself to 15 minutes' sunbathing per day until a tan is built up.

Treatment

Practical Advice

- stay out of the sun for at least a week after sunburn, as your skin will be very sensitive.

Herbal

- use aloe vera gel on the burned areas to soothe and heal. This can be bought in health food stores, or you can cut open a fresh leaf and smear the gel onto the skin.

Hydrotherapy

- a cool shower or bath is probably one of the best ways to relieve sunburn. You can add baking soda, fine oatmeal or vinegar to the water to soothe stinging skin.
- to soothe sore eyes, place a piece of cucumber on each eye and lie back and relax for 15 minutes.
- drink plenty of water or soft drinks, as you will probably be a little dehydrated. Avoid alcohol.

Orthodox

- calamine lotion or after-sun cream soothes the stinging. Painkillers may also be recommended, along with antihistamine preparations in severe cases. Blistering requires the application of sterile dressing and medical supervision to prevent and treat infection.

Sunstroke

Dry skin, restlessness, headaches, feeling hot, dizzy or being semiconscious after being in the sun for long periods are all symptoms of sunstroke. A raised temperature and rapid breathing and pulse rate may also occur. In the elderly and the very young, severe sunstroke can be very dangerous and requires medical aid.

Prevention

- limit the time spent outside to short periods, and gradually build up your exposure to the sun over a period of two weeks. Avoid the hottest period of the day (usually 10 a.m. to 4 p.m.). If you are outside, keep in the shade if possible and wear protective clothing: always cover the head and wear light coloured clothing which covers the skin. Drink plenty of fluids to avoid dehydration. Avoid alcohol.

Treatment

First Aid

- take the sufferer indoors to a cool environment if possible. Remove clothing. Lie in a semi-reclining but comfortable, supported position. Wrap a cold wet sheet around the sufferer. If a fan is available, blow the cool air in the direction of the sufferer. Give cool drinks and seek medical help.

Homoeopathy

every 15 minutes for up to 4 doses and repeat if necessary:
- hot red face, throbbing headache: Belladonna 6c.
- hot red face, throbbing headache and loss of sense of direction: Glonoine 6c.

Orthodox

- severe cases are admitted to hospital for supervised oral or intravenous hydration.

Syphilis *see* Sexually Transmitted Diseases

Tachycardia

An increase in the rate of heart beat. Most people's hearts beat at around 65–75 beats per minute at rest. Those with tachycardia have 100 or more beats per minute when resting. Rapid heart beat is sometimes accompanied by breathlessness, nausea and sweating or dizziness.

Prevention

- stress reduction and relaxation help prevent this ailment. Practising yoga, meditation or biofeedback are the best ways to reduce stress.
- some foods may trigger tachycardia; see the dietary recommendations below.

Treatment

Dietary

- avoid coffee, tea, chocolate, cola, alcohol, tobacco and other stimulants, as these activate the heart excessively.
- low blood sugar can trigger tachycardia: to stabilize blood sugar, eat regular meals of complex carbohydrates (pasta, potatoes, rice, bread), vegetables and fruit and moderate amounts of protein; avoid simple carbohydrates (foods containing sugar).
- increase intake of magnesium, found in nuts, cooked dried beans and peas, wholegrain breads and cereals,

soya beans, dark green leafy vegetables, milk and seafood.

Aromatherapy

- essential oil of lavender has been shown to reduce stress and lower blood pressure. Use in massage, or in the bath or place a few drops on a handkerchief and sniff when needed.

Homoeopathy

to be taken every 5 minutes for up to 6 doses and repeat if necessary:
- heart rate speeds up after a shock or a fright: Aconite 6c.
- heart rate speeds up after rich food, alcohol, coffee or stress: Nux vomica 6c.
- heart rate speeds up after sudden excitement or a pleasant surprise: Coffea 6c.
- worse lying on the left side and improved by lying on the right side: Phosphorus 6c.

Hydrotherapy

- plunging your face into a basin of cool water for 10–20 seconds sometimes helps stop an attack. Alternatively, try slowly drinking water or holding your breath.

Massage

- regular massage helps reduce stress and slow the heart beat.

Relaxation

- the best way to stop an attack of tachycardia is to slow down and rest for a while. The following exercise should be carried out if you feel an attack coming on:
- lie on a firm surface, close your eyes and become

aware of how your body feels. Focus your attention on each part of your body, starting with the tips of the toes, and finishing with your face and eyes; consciously try to relax every part in turn. The whole procedure should take at least 10 minutes.

Orthodox

- electrocardiograph (ECG) tracings are used to determine exactly the type of tachycardia responsible for the symptoms. For simple tachycardia, stimulation of the vagus nerve, which slows the heart beat, can be achieved by pressing on the eyeball or massaging the carotid sinus at the back of the neck. If this fails, then drug therapy or mild electric shock treatment under sedation is effective.

Tantrum

Temper tantrums are common in small children between the ages of 1 and 5. They occur particularly around the age of 2, when children feel frustrated at being unable to communicate their feelings and desires adequately through speech. Tantrums may also start when another child is born as a result of feelings of neglect. During a tantrum a child may scream, yell, cry, kick, bite, bang feet and fists, hold his/her breath, turn red or blue.

Treatment

Practical Advice

- try to understand the cause of the tantrum and explain it quietly and calmly to the child. Do not lose your temper. Allow the child to have the tantrum without paying too much attention, as long as he/she does not come to harm. Do not punish the child, but try to divert his/her attention away from the problem to a game or object. Most children grow out of tantrums as they learn to communicate more competently.

Dietary

naturopaths and practitioners of traditional Chinese medicine believe that dietary habits can affect children's behaviour and mood. They make the following recommendations:

- do not allow the child to overeat.
- give small regular meals.
- avoid rough wholemeal foods.
- reduce intake of milk.
- avoid toxins, such as artificial additives and preservatives, often found in processed and fast foods.
- sometimes food allergies can cause behavioural problems: see Allergies — Food for common allergies and how to deal with them.
- reduce intake of sugar.

Bach Flower Remedies

- Holly, Vine and Walnut are all suitable remedies for this condition.

Professional Help

- professional homoeopathic treatment may be helpful.

Orthodox

- when the child is particularly manipulative and behaves in a way which makes parental control difficult, family psychotherapy with a child psychologist may help by devising exercises designed to correct the problems.

Teething Problems

Most babies have problems when the teeth start to come through, starting at around 6 months and sometimes continuing until 3 years. The child will probably be irritable and clingy, have difficulty sleeping and cry more. A tendency to dribble more is also common.

Treatment

Dietary

digestive problems sometimes enhance teething problems:
- ensure you do not overfeed the baby.
- when weaning, give easily digested foods, such as baby rice or millet; raw vegetables and wholegrain cereals are too hard to digest.
- when allowed to eat on demand, some children eat too much, which may contribute to teething discomfort; establish regular feeding times once the child is on solid foods and feed him/her slowly.
- for toddlers, avoid rich foods, especially red meats, fats and wholegrain bread and raw vegetables.
- do not give the child too much to drink; he/she should have enough to moisten the food being eaten.
- burp your baby after feeding.

Herbal

- marshmallow root syrup helps soothe inflamed or sore gums: add 3 level teaspoons to the food or drink daily.

Homoeopathy

- Chamomilla Teething Granules (3x) dissolve easily and will help where there is one red cheek and the child is colicky and irritable. Give every 30 minutes until quiet.

Biochemic Tissue Salts

- Calc Phos: take 1 tablet every 30 minutes for up to 6 doses.

Acupressure

- spread the child's left thumb and index finger apart and gently massage between the thumb and the index finger. Do the same on the other hand.

Orthodox

- teething gels rubbed onto the gums can be helpful: they contain antiseptic and painkilling ingredients. Teething rings which the baby chews on can also resolve the problem (especially when they have been chilled in the refrigerator first). Paracetamol (120–240 mg every 6 hours for children between 1 to 6 years) or antihistamines are recommended for severe cases.

Temporomandibular Joint Syndrome (TMJ)

Pain which affects the head, jaw and face when the temporomandibular joint (connecting the jaw bone to the skull just below and beside the ear) and its surrounding muscles and ligaments do not function correctly. It is often caused by clenching or grinding the teeth. Symptoms include frequent headaches, pain around the ear and clicking noises when the mouth is opened or closed.

Treatment

Chinese Medicine

- teeth grinding would be treated with herbal teas of Chinese yam or skullcap.

Hydrotherapy

- the first course of treatment is to relax tight muscles in the jaw area by increasing the blood flow. This can be done with cold or hot treatment. Prepare an ice pack, using a bag of ice cubes or a packet of frozen peas wrapped in kitchen paper, and place it on the painful side of the jaw. Alternatively, use a heat pad or a hot water bottle wrapped in a towel. Keep the ice pack or the bottle in place for 10 minutes, then take it off for 10 minutes. Repeat several times.

Massage

- lay the tips of your fingers on the jaw muscles. You can locate these by clenching and unclenching the teeth, which activates the jaw muscles. Unclench the teeth and massage the area with small, firm circular movements, gradually easing away tension.

Acupressure

- place the heels of your hands between the upper and lower jaws, in front of the ear lobes, and gradually press inwards. Then clench your back teeth and you will feel a muscle pushing out into your hands. Press again on this muscle with the teeth apart for one minute. Take your hands away and move the jaw from left to right for a few seconds. Then place your fingertips on the same muscle and press firmly for another minute.
- other points which may be useful are shown in the illustration.

Professional Help

- osteopathic or chiropractic treatment can be most helpful in this condition.
- acupuncture can help relieve spasm and pain.
- hypnosis can also be effective.

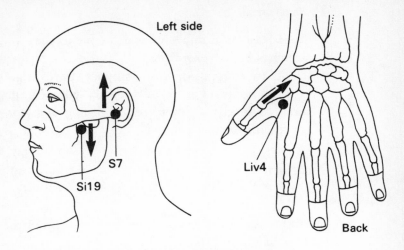

Left side

S7

Si19

Liv4

Back

Direction of acupressure massage

Orthodox

- muscle relaxant drugs may be recommended to relieve spasm. Your doctor may also offer a bite splint, a device which prevents teeth clenching at night. Cortisone injected directly into the joint can dramatically reduce inflammation and reduce symptoms.

Tendinitis

Inflammation of a tendon, the tissue which attaches muscle to bones. Usually this occurs as a result of an injury when the muscle is subjected to overuse, or overstretched. It is a common occurrence in those who exercise sporadically and vigorously without properly warming up. Symptoms include pain, tenderness and restricted movement. Often a feeling of 'creakiness' is also experienced on movement. The most commonly affected areas are the Achilles tendon at the back of the ankle, the front of the shoulder, the thumb, the knee and the inside of the foot.

Prevention

- do at least 15 minutes of warm-up exercises and stretches before exercising.
- if you are jogging or doing impact sports (e.g. aerobics, tennis, basketball), replace your running shoes regularly — don't keep the same ones for years.
- try to run on soft ground.

Treatment

Dietary

the following nutrients are thought to help aid the healing of injured tissue:
- vitamin C, found in high concentrations in citrus fruits, broccoli, parsley and green pepper.
- beta-carotene, found in green leafy vegetables and yellow vegetables.
- zinc, found in liver, meat, Cheddar cheese, lentils, haricot beans and wholemeal cereals.
- selenium, found in wholemeal flour, mackerel, port and eggs.
- vitamin E, found in wheatgerm, sunflower seeds and oil, olive oil, margarine.

Herbal

- turmeric is traditionally used as an anti-inflammatory in India and China. The extract of the turmeric root known as curcumin is the most effective. 250 mg is recommended, taken 3 times daily between meals.
- bromelain, an enzyme extracted from pineapples, is also an effective anti-inflammatory: take 250 mg, 3 times daily between meals.

Hydrotherapy

- immediately after exercise, carry out the following routine. Immediately rest the joint and apply an ice pack: wrap a packet of frozen peas in kitchen paper and apply to the joint for at least 10 minutes. Elevate the joint if possible. Remove the ice for 10 minutes then reapply for 10 minutes.

- an elastic bandage placed on the joint can sometimes help reduce swelling and internal bleeding.
- keep the injured part elevated as much as possible.

Professional Help

- osteopaths or chiropractors would probably treat this using massage, or with an ultrasound machine, which emits high frequency vibration that heats the area, increasing circulation and drainage.
- acupuncture helps relieve pain and may assist in healing.
- transcutaneous nerve stimulation (TENS), available in some physiotherapy units, helps control pain. It works in much the same way as acupuncture, without the needles.

Orthodox

- doctors prescribe non-steroidal anti-inflammatory drugs for this condition. Cortisone injections may be offered, but should never be injected directly into the tendon, but rather into the sheath surrounding the injured tendon.

Tennis Elbow

Inflammation of the muscles around the elbow joint often caused by straining the muscles and tendons around the elbow and lower arm. Racquet sports, gardening and home decorating are common activities which cause this ailment. Pain is felt on the outer edge of the elbow and the back of the lower part of the arm, and is often made worse by bending the arm or lifting a heavy object.

Treatment

Practical Advice

- rest the arm: this means no gripping, lifting or carrying heavy objects for several days. Try to keep the arm elevated when resting.

Chinese Medicine

- herbal teas of cinnamon twigs, mulberry twigs and ginger may be recommended.

Hydrotherapy

- prepare an ice pack using ice cubes in a plastic bag or a bag of frozen peas. Wrap the bag in kitchen paper and place on the elbow and lower arm for 5 minutes every hour for several hours during the first few days. If the elbow is very painful, alternate ice treatment with 10 minutes of warm treatment using a heat pad or a hot water bottle wrapped in a towel.

Massage

- after 2 or 3 days of hydrotherapy and rest, a partner can massage the arm and elbow. The patient should lie on his or her back and the person doing massage should be at his/her injured side. Start by kneading the upper arm, then the lower arm, by firmly squeezing all muscles. Then support the elbow on your knee and using small circular motions massage around the elbow joint with your thumbs. Finally, using deep thumb pressure, massage across the muscles of the lower arm, working upwards from the wrist to the elbow.

Acupressure

- massage the points illustrated, using deep thumb pressure, for at least a minute.

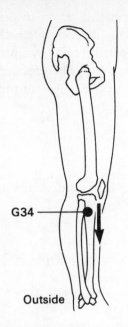 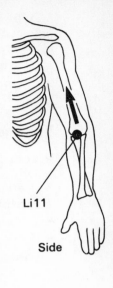

G34

Outside

Li11

Side

➡ Direction of acupressure massage

Professional Help

- osteopathy, chiropractic and professional massage would all be helpful.
- acupuncture and moxibustion are very effective.

Orthodox

- painkillers are recommended or a corticosteroid injection.

Thrombophlebitis

Inflammation of a vein, resulting from injury, infection and irritation of the vein walls and sometimes the formation of blood clots. The condition is most common in the superficial veins of the legs and in people with varicose veins. Symptoms include swelling and redness along the affected vein, sometimes

accompanied by fever. It is important to distinguish
between this condition and the deep vein thrombosis
(see entry) which produces different symptoms and is
potentially much more serious. Therefore, consult your
doctor before carrying out self help treatment.

Treatment

Practical Advice

- if you are taking the Pill, consider an alternative
  method of contraception.
- do not smoke.
- do not sit for long periods without taking breaks,
  particularly when travelling; in a plane, get up and
  walk around every 30 minutes.
- put your feet up when resting.
- wear support hosiery.

Herbal

- hawthorn is a good tonic for the circulatory system
  and the treatment of blood vessels: to make an
  infusion pour a cup of boiling water over 2 teaspoons
  of the berries and infuse for 20 minutes, drink
  3 times daily; it may take some time for effects to
  be seen.
- to help clear and prevent infection, take 3 garlic
  capsules 3 times daily.

Homoeopathy

to be taken 4 times daily for up to 7 days:
- if the condition follows an injury: Arnica 6c.
  If bruising persists: Hamamelis 6c.
- if the veins are worse in heat and when the limb is
  not elevated: Pulsatilla 6c.

Hydrotherapy

- contrasting temperatures help stimulate sluggish

circulation, which contributes to this condition. Spray the legs with first cold then hot water, for 5 minutes each. Repeat several times.

Exercise

- exercise helps pump blood around the body and stops it stagnating in the veins. Daily walking or swimming is particularly good for this condition.

Orthodox

- antibiotics are prescribed if the vein is infected, along with anti-inflammatory drugs and support bandages.

Thrombosis

A blood clot (thrombus) forms on the roughened walls of an injured blood vessel, gradually blocking the flow of blood. The clot may be caused by sluggish blood flow or an accumulation of fats in the blood. The blockage prevents blood and oxygen reaching part of the body, and a heart attack or stroke results. Generally there are no symptoms of thrombosis until the clot blocks the blood vessel.

Treatment/Prevention

Dietary

- the same dietary guidelines apply to thrombosis as for high cholesterol (see Cholesterol, High).
- fatty fish is known to reduce the stickiness of the blood platelets, making it more difficult for clots to form. Oily fish such as herring, kipper, mackerel, salmon, sardines and tuna are better than white fish, and should be eaten at least twice a week.
- linoleic acid, a fatty acid found in nuts, wheat germ and vegetable oils is thought to also help reduce

stickiness of blood platelets. A handful of nuts daily
is a good preventive measure.
- eat plenty of fresh garlic and onions, as these too help
prevent the formation of a thrombus.
- vitamin E is thought to both prevent the formation of
clots and dissolve any existing ones. If your blood
pressure is no higher than 160 systolic (ask your
doctor) take 300 mg of vitamin E daily; if your blood
pressure is higher than 160 systolic, take 200 mg
daily.

Herbal

- hawthorn is a good tonic for the circulatory system
and the treatment of blood vessels: to make an
infusion pour a cup of boiling water over 2 teaspoons
of the berries and infuse for 20 minutes, drink
3 times daily; it may take some time for effects to
be seen.

Orthodox

- a thrombus can be detected by x-rays of the blood
vessels after a radio-opaque substance is introduced to
the body. Treatment is with anticoagulant drugs to
prevent further clotting, along with anti-inflammatory
drugs to relieve the inflammation of the blood vessels.

Thrush

A yeast infection which usually affects the mouth or
vagina, producing a white coating or a cottage cheese
like discharge. The yeast organism (*Candida albicans*)
grows naturally in the body, but when the system is
upset its growth gets out of hand, causing a white
coating or an itchy, cottage cheese-like discharge.
Thrush occurs in the vagina when the immune system is
compromised or when the acid/alkali balance of the
vagina is upset by using douches, spermicides or bath

products. Excessive use of antibiotics can also trigger an attack, as can use of the Pill. For oral thrush, see separate entry. See also Fungal Infection.

Treatment

Dietary

- reduce intake of sugar, which encourages yeast growth; this includes fruit and alcohol.
- reduce foods containing yeast: bread, mushrooms, blue cheese, alcohol, soya sauce, foods containing monosodium glutamate, smoked fish and sausages, vinegar.
- thrush tends to occur when immunity is low. To increase immunity, ensure you are eating plenty of raw and lightly cooked vegetables, brown rice, lean meat or fish.
- incorporate plenty of olive oil and garlic into your meals.
- avoid coffee and tea, instead drink mineral water, rooibos tea and other herbal teas.
- eat plenty of 'live' yoghurt (at least one large carton daily).
- take supplements of *Lactobacillus acidophilus*. Take 1 teaspoon of *Lactobacillus acidophilus*, 1 teaspoon of *Bifidobacteria* powder, and ½ teaspoon of *Lactobacillus bulgaricus* (available from health food stores) in a glass of spring water, 3 times daily.

Aromatherapy

- take baths with 4 drops of essential oil of tea tree and 2 drops of myrrh added.
- use 4 drops tea tree in 1 litre of warm spring water in a douche or 1 drop tea tree on a tampon and insert overnight.

Douches

- douches help restore the acid/alkali balance of the vagina for vaginal thrush. (**Caution:** not to be used during pregnancy.) Buy a commercial douche, empty it out and rinse it thoroughly with bottled or boiled water. Make up a solution with 1 tablespoon of 'live' yoghurt or *Lactobacillus acidophilus* powder (found in health food stores) and 1 quart of warm boiled or bottled water. Place the solution in the douche and insert into the vagina twice daily, allowing it to flush out completely.
- an alternative douche can be made using 2 tablespoons of apple cider vinegar added to 1 quart of warm bottled or boiled water.

Orthodox

- antifungal agents are prescribed in cream, tablet, vaginal pessary, oral solution or tampon-impregnated form. Treatment is effective within a matter of days, but thrush is a condition which tends to recur, so it is worth resolving the cause. In vaginal thrush it is advisable for sexual partners to be treated simultaneously, as the infection can be passed back and forth.

Tinnitus

A ringing, buzzing, hissing or whistling sound in the ears, often worse when background noise is low. It is sometimes accompanied by hearing loss. Tinnitus may be caused by long-term exposure to loud noise, excessive wax in the ears, catarrh, sinusitis or damage to the nerves of the ear. Some drugs, particularly aspirin, may also contribute to the condition.

Treatment

Practical Advice

- removal of excess ear wax can sometimes bring relief. Your doctor can syringe the ears to remove wax. Some complementary practitioners use Hopi wax candles, a safe and natural method of drawing wax out of the ear. Another method is to place two drops of slightly warmed almond oil in the ear, keep the head on one side to prevent the oil running out, and insert a twist of soft cotton material gently into the ear to soak up the oil and remove the softened wax.

  - **caution:** never put match sticks or sharp instruments in the ear to remove wax.

Dietary

- naturopaths recommend a cleansing regime, which includes a 3-day vegetable juice fast every 6 weeks and a diet high in raw and cooked vegetables, grains, nuts, pulses and low fat yoghurt and fish. Coffee, alcohol, salt and fried food should be avoided.
- increasing intake of the following nutrients can sometimes help:
  - magnesium, found in Brazil nuts, soya flour, wholemeal flour, lentils, and parsley.
  - potassium, found in dried brewer's yeast, dried dates, mushrooms, cabbage, lean meats and bananas.
  - manganese, found in tea, wholemeal cereals, dried cooked beans and leafy vegetables.

Acupressure

- massage the points illustrated, using deep thumb pressure for at least a minute.

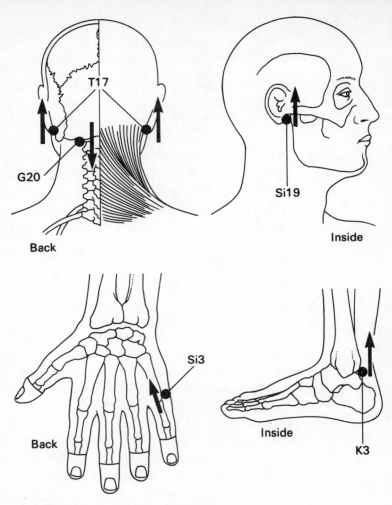

T17

G20

Back

Si19

Inside

Si3

Back

Inside

K3

Direction of acupressure massage

Exercise

- increasing the blood circulation to the head may help.
  Most vigorous exercise increases circulation; for
  example, running, fast walking, swimming or
  aerobics.

Yoga

- some postures are particularly good for increasing
  circulation to the head:

- to loosen the neck: keeping your chin tucked in, turn your head slowly to the left as far as it will comfortably go, hold for a few seconds, then turn to the right, hold again and come back to centre. Repeat 3 times.
- tilt your head forward, bringing your chin towards your chest, hold for a few seconds, then tilt your head backwards, keeping the chin tucked in, return to the starting position. Repeat 3 times.
- if you are comfortable doing the above postures, move on to the next: tilt your head forward, roll it to the right, so that your ear is close to your right shoulder, and very slowly roll your head back around to the left shoulder, and forward and back to centre.

Professional Help

- cranial osteopathy and acupuncture have been known to help.
- professional homoeopathic treatment may also be helpful.

Orthodox

- treatment is disappointing, though some success has been seen using maskers, battery operated gadgets like hearing aids which emit a constant noise of a different frequency to the one heard in the tinnitus. This provides a soothing effect, but is not a cure.

Tonsillitis

Inflammation and swelling of the tonsils, which are situated at the back of the throat. This condition usually occurs in children, who have enlarged, red tonsils, a sore throat, difficulty swallowing, a fever and sometimes a congested chest and nose.

Treatment

Dietary

naturopaths make the following recommendations:
- during the illness:
  - drink plenty of water and fresh fruit and vegetable juices.
  - eat lightly steamed vegetables or vegetable broths.
- to avoid recurrent attacks:
  - reduce intake of dairy produce: milk can be replaced with soya milk or goat's milk.
  - reduce intake of carbohydrates: particularly sweets, pastries and white bread. Instead eat wholegrain cereals in moderation and plenty of fresh fruit and vegetables and low fat protein.

Aromatherapy

- add 2 drops of essential oil of eucalyptus and 1 drop of peppermint to 5 ml (one teaspoon) of carrier lotion or oil and massage the chest, back and throat. Gently rub the oil or lotion into the throat too.

Herbal

- red sage infusion soothes the inflammation: put 2 teaspoons of the leaves in half a litre of water, bring to the boil, and stand for 15 minutes. Gargle with the warm tea for 5 minutes several times daily.

Homoeopathy

every 30 minutes for up to 4 doses and repeat as necessary:
- pain in neck and ears, swallowing painful, feeling exhausted and weak: Gelsemium 6c.
- sudden sore throat made worse by cold wind, tonsils swollen, throat burning, everything tastes bitter: Aconite 6c.
- worse right side with purplish appearance and a

swollen uvula, better from cold drinks: Apis 6c.
- worse left side, intolerant of any constriction, pain worse from swallowing saliva and better from swallowing food: Lachesis 6c.
- stitching pain like a fish bone which extends to the ears when swallowing; cheesy exudate on the tonsils: Hepar sulphuris 6c.
- moist flabby tongue and foul breath; swollen neck glands: Mercurius solubilis 6c.
- tonsils are as large as plums: Baryta muriatica 6c.

Chinese Medicine

- Honeysuckle flower tea is recommended and a salt gargle is helpful to soothe and sterilize the throat. Avoid spicy foods if you are prone to tonsillitis. Recurrent bouts may be helped by ear acupuncture.

Orthodox

- painkillers are usually given to provide relief. In severe cases antibiotics are also prescribed and/or surgery carried out.

Toothache

Pain in or around one tooth or several teeth and gums most commonly results from decay, and is a sign that dental treatment is needed. An abscess around the root of the tooth may also be a cause of pain (see Dental Abscess).

Treatment

The following remedies will help relieve discomfort while awaiting dental treatment.

Aromatherapy

- wet one finger with essential oil of clove and rub on the gum of the painful tooth. Dilute 2 drops in one teaspoon of carrier oil if the skin is sensitive.

Herbal

- tincture of myrrh can also be applied to the gum of the tooth to relieve pain.

Homoeopathy

to be taken every 5 minutes for up to 4 doses and repeated if necessary:
- pain made worse by hot food and drinks and soothed by cold drinks: Coffea 6c.
- pain made worse by cold air, along with the tendency to produce a lot of saliva: Plantago 6c.
- pain made worse by cold air, food and drinks: Calcarea carbonica 6c.
- pain after dental treatment: Arnica 6c.

Chinese Medicine

- if there is no apparent dental problem, traditional Chinese doctors may suggest that a toothache is linked with a stomach or liver problem: herbs such as gypsum are recommended with rhubarb for the stomach and Chinese ginseng for the liver.

Acupressure

- apply deep pressure to the area between the thumb and the index finger to relieve pain. Stimulating this point can also reduce pain during dental treatment.
- another point which may be helpful is on the top of the foot, about a centimetre towards the ankle from the point where the second and third toes join.

Orthodox

- painkillers may be recommended for temporary relief until you are able to see your dentist. If you suspect an abscess (severe continuous pain, swelling around the gum, and tenderness of the tooth), make an emergency appointment.

Torticollis

Also known as wry neck, this is a twisting of the neck, causing the head to be rotated and tilted to one side, bringing pain and stiffness. Torticollis can result from an injury, sleeping in an awkward position, or stress. It can also occur at birth.

Treatment

Hydrotherapy

- use hot and cold treatment for torticollis which follows an injury, awkward sleeping position or stress: make an ice pack by filling a plastic bag with ice cubes, or use a bag of frozen peas, wrap in kitchen paper and place on the tense muscle for 10 minutes. Then place a hot water bottle wrapped in a towel on the muscles for a further 10 minutes. Alternate hot and cold several times morning and night.

Massage

- if you are able, turn your head to the left side and place the ends of the fingers of your right hand at the top of the large muscle which runs from the back of the right hand side of your head to the collar bone (sternocleidomastoid muscle). Massage deeply the length of the muscle with your thumb. Do the same on the other side.
- hook the fingers of both hands over your shoulders

and squeeze the muscles lying between the neck and the shoulder joints.

Reflexology

if the neck is too sensitive to move or touch, reflexology may help:
- massage the point where the big toe joins the foot on the sole of the left foot.
- massage the cervical spine area: along on the inner side of both feet, along the joint of the big toe.
- rotate the big toes.

Relaxation

- to relieve stress and relax tense muscles, make a head rest by putting 2 tennis balls in a sock and tying the end. Lie down on the floor on your back, using the balls as a rest under the neck. Each ball should be on either side of the spine. Relax in this position for 10 minutes daily.

Professional Help

- an osteopath or chiropractor is specialized in dealing with this problem.
- acupuncture helps if the neck is very painful.
- the Alexander Technique corrects postural problems which may lead to torticollis.

Orthodox

- heat treatment and physiotherapy are recommended. Sometimes an orthopaedic collar is used to immobilize the neck. Occasionally surgery will be carried out.

Toxoplasmosis

An infection found in animals, birds and reptiles which is passed on to humans through eating infected meat or touching animals or their litter. Usually the body's immune system protects us against the infection. However, in pregnant women toxoplasmosis can be transmitted to the foetus, causing miscarriage or stillbirth. A routine blood test should be carried out during pregnancy to ensure women do not have toxoplasmosis.

Prevention

- avoid handling cat litter.
- wash your hands thoroughly after touching pets.
- do not allow pets to lick you.
- use separate utensils for animals' food and wash them separately from your own.
- always wash your hands before eating or preparing food.
- avoid raw meat or fish during pregnancy.
- wash all raw vegetables thoroughly — avoid eating raw vegetables in restaurants.

Treatment

Orthodox

- if you suspect toxoplasmosis, a blood test can be taken to make a diagnosis. Most patients have a mild form of the disease and no treatment is required. In immune-compromised patients and where there is severe disease, antibiotics, such as pyrimethamine and sulphadiazine, are given. In pregnancy, spiramycin is used instead of pyrimethamine and steroids can be useful if the eyes are affected by the disease.

Travel Sickness

A feeling of uneasiness, headache, sweating and salivation, pallor, nausea and vomiting while travelling by car. It is caused by the effect of movement on the organs of balance in the inner ear. Anxiety, lack of oxygen, a full stomach, or the sight of food, reading or focusing on nearby objects often make symptoms worse.

Prevention

Sea Travel

- try to stay outside on deck, where you can see the horizon. Enclosed spaces increase feelings of nausea.
- heavy meals during travelling are best avoided, though a light snack may help.
- lie down if possible.
- don't read or play games which require focusing on moving objects or words.
- stay in the mid-line of the boat, as this part oscillates less than the sides.

Road/Rail Travel

- try to travel in the front seat; focusing on the road ahead helps stabilize the balance system.
- do not eat or drink just before travelling.
- do not allow smokers in the car.
- sit still.
- do not read or play games which require focusing on moving objects or words or stationary objects inside the car.

Treatment

Aromatherapy

- add 4 drops of essential oils of peppermint and ginger to a carrier oil or lotion. Massage this into the chest before travelling. Sprinkle a little of the same mixture on a handkerchief and sniff it if you feel nauseous.

Herbal

- ginger root is warming and helps prevent sickness. Take two ginger root capsules 30 minutes before travelling, or chew a piece of fresh, peeled root ginger.

Homoeopathy

to be taken hourly as soon as symptoms begin:
- nausea made worse by the smell of food, made better by eating: Sepia 6c.
- nausea with a metallic taste in the mouth and feeling very giddy: Cocculus 6c.
- when overtired and irritable: Arnica 6c.
- chilly with the sensation you would feel better for vomiting: Nux vom 6c.
- angry and frustrated: Staphysagria 6c.

Bach Flower Remedies

- Scleranthus and Rescue Remedy are recommended before and during travelling as needed.

Acupressure

- place your right thumb on the inside of your left wrist, 3 finger widths from the centre of the wrist crease. Massage with the thumb using a deep circular motion for one minute, taking deep breaths. Then do the same on the other side.
- the same treatment can be obtained by wearing acupressure wrist bands, available in many pharmacies, supermarkets, and travel goods shops. The bands have a small ball attached which, when placed on the pressure point described above, exerts continuous pressure while the band is worn.

Orthodox

- antihistamine drugs such as dimenhydrinate or
  cinnarizine are recommended. To be taken 30 minutes
  to 1 hour before travelling. Myoscine is useful too
  and can be used in the form of a skin patch giving a
  slow release formulation.

Trichomoniasis

An parasitic infection of the vagina which is often
sexually transmitted, or contracted from a towel,
clothing or face cloth carrying the infection. Symptoms
include inflammation and itching of the vaginal area,
frothy, yellowish discharge and sometimes a burning
sensation when passing water and pain during
intercourse.

Prevention

- do not share towels, swimsuits or clothing.
- avoid using washcloths or sponges to wash the genital
  area, these may harbour germs.
- always wipe from front to back when going to the
  toilet to prevent bacteria from the anus entering the
  vagina.
- remove your swimsuit immediately after swimming.
- in those prone to infection it is advisable for both
  partners to wash before and after intercourse.

Treatment

Dietary

- drink plenty of unsweetened cranberry juice every
  day, to acidify the system.
- eat 'live' yoghurt daily and take a *Lactobacillus
  acidophilus* supplement: 1 teaspoon in a glass of water
  3 times daily, with 1 teaspoon of *Bifidobacteria*.

- the following supplements help promote healing and boost immunity:
  - vitamin A: 10,000 iu daily.
  - vitamin C: found in fresh fruit and vegetables. Also take a daily supplement of 1,000 mg 3 times daily.
  - vitamin E: 800 iu daily.
  - zinc: 50 mg daily.

Douches

- the parasite thrives in an alkaline environment, so use one of the following douches to acidify the vagina once a day during the infection.
  - (**Caution:** not to be used during pregnancy.)
- vinegar douche: add one teaspoon of vinegar to a quart of warm water, place in a douche bag or in an infant syringe (available from most pharmacies). Use the douche while lying in a warm bath: insert into the vagina and remain horizontal for a while to allow the solution to remain inside. When you stand up it will flush out of the vagina.
- 'live' yoghurt or a solution of *Lactobacillus acidophilus* (½ teaspoon of powder to a cup of water) helps reintroduce healthy bacteria into the vagina. Mix either ingredient with the strained juice of one lemon to introduce acidity and using an infant syringe, place in the vagina, remain horizontal for a few moments and rinse off, using a sanitary towel to catch any drips over the next few hours.

Orthodox

- antibiotics, such as metronidazole, are generally prescribed for this condition. However, the drug should be used with caution, as it has been shown to cause birth defects and cancer in animal studies.

Urinary Tract Infection

The symptoms of a urinary tract infection include burning when passing water, a frequent urge to urinate, abdominal pain and sometimes a mild fever. The infection can occur anywhere along the urinary tract. The most common types are:

- urethritis, inflammation of the urethra, the tube which excretes urine from the bladder.
- cystitis, inflammation of the bladder (see entry).
- pyelonephritis, inflammation of the kidneys.

Urethritis may result from structural problems or from an infection which is often a sexually transmitted disease, such as gonorrhoea or nonspecific urethritis (see Sexually Transmitted Diseases). Most other urinary tract infections result from bacterial infections spreading from the rectum. Women are more susceptible due to the shortness of the urethra. In men urinary infections may be a sign of an enlarged prostate (see Prostate, Enlarged). It is important to consult your doctor if you experience symptoms of a urinary tract infection to identify the source, and receive treatment, particularly if the infection is sexually transmitted.

Prevention

- ensure you pass water regularly; do not delay going to the toilet.
- always urinate after intercourse.

- women: always wipe the genital area from front to back.

Treatment

Dietary

- naturopaths advise building up immunity to fight infection. Eat plenty of raw and lightly cooked vegetables, wholegrain cereals, and low-fat protein.
- drink plenty of water, at least 8 glasses a day, to help flush the infection out of the system.
- vitamin A helps build healthy mucous membranes. It is found in liver, egg yolk, butter, fortified margarine, cheese and cod liver oil.
- it is likely that you will be given antibiotics for the infection. To restore healthy bacteria destroyed by the drugs, eat plenty of live unsweetened yoghurt, at least one 5 oz carton daily, for at least one month.

Aromatherapy

- add 2 drops of essential oil each of juniper berry, eucalyptus and sandal wood to a warm bath and sit in it for 10 minutes to relieve symptoms.

Herbal

- buchu helps to clear infection. Take as a tea 3 times a day: use a large teaspoon of leaves per cup.

Homoeopathy

to be taken every 30 minutes for up to 5 doses and repeated if necessary:
- urine feels like scalding water; violently painful: Cantharis 6c.
- burning pain at the end of urination and afterwards: Sarsaparilla 6c.
- stinging pains better from cold bathing: Apis 6c.

- violently painful with blood in the urine: Mercurius corrosivus 6c.
- Berberis mother tincture: 3 drops in a little water twice daily act as a general support and tonic during treatment.

Orthodox
Urine tests are carried out to identify the micro-organism responsible for the infection. Antibiotics are generally recommended. If the infection is sexually transmitted, sexual partners should be traced and treated.

Urticaria *see* Hives

Uterine Prolapse

A condition in which the uterus drops down into the vagina, usually as a result of weakening of the ligaments during childbirth. Symptoms are few, though there may be a dragging sensation in the pelvis, backache and difficulty passing water or motions.

Treatment

Dietary

- if you are heavier than your recommended weight, try to lose weight (see Obesity).

Exercise

- strengthening the pelvic floor muscles through exercise helps hold the uterus in place. To locate these muscles, try stopping and starting the flow of urine when you pass water. Practise tightening and relaxing these muscles throughout the day: start with

5 contractions 10 times daily, then build this up to 10 contractions 10 times daily.
- your doctor can provide small weights which are designed to be held inside the vagina, making the pelvic floor muscles work.

Professional Help

- professional homoeopathic treatment can be helpful.

Orthodox

- passive exercises for the muscles using an electric current is sometimes recommended. A pessary which fits around the cervix and holds the uterus up and back provides relief for a mild prolapse, but the pessary has to be enlarged every 3—6 months to reduce the possibility of infection. As a last resort, surgery is used to tighten the ligaments.

Vaginal Irritation

Also known as vaginitis, this is inflammation of the vagina which can be caused by infection (see Thrush), drugs, allergy, hormonal problems or a foreign body, such as a forgotten tampon. Post-menopausal women are particularly susceptible. Symptoms include irritation, redness and intense itching, and sometimes odour, discharge and pain during intercourse.

Prevention

- wash the genital area regularly and pat dry with a clean towel. Avoid talc, vaginal deodorants and scented soaps.
- wear cotton underpants and avoid tight clothes.
- always wipe from front to back when going to the toilet.
- always wash the genital area (both partners) before intercourse.
- use a lubrication such as KY jelly during intercourse.

Treatment

Dietary

- reduce intake of coffee and sugar, as these can upset the acid/alkali balance of the vagina and increase the likelihood of infection.
- if symptoms are caused by a fungal infection (see Thrush), avoid all sugars for at least one month. Eat

plenty of fresh vegetables, wholegrain cereals and lean meat and fish. Eat at least one carton of 'live' yoghurt a day and take ½ teaspoon of *Lactobacillus acidophilus* in a glass of water 3 times daily, with ½ teaspoon *Bifidobacteria*.

Aromatherapy

- essential oil of tea tree and myrrh are both effective when added to a warm bath.
- apply 2 drops of tea tree oil to the top of a damp tampon and insert into vagina for 3 hours.
  - **caution:** not to be used during pregnancy.

Herbal

- golden seal—myrrh douche: simmer 1 tablespoon of each herb in 3 cups of water for 5 minutes and use as a douche once a week.
  - **caution:** not to be used during pregnancy.
- to relieve itching, bathe the vagina in chickweed infusion: pour a cup of boiling water on 2 teaspoons of the herb, leave to infuse for 5 minutes and allow to cool.
- garlic is an effective antifungal, so incorporate plenty into your diet or take capsules.

Orthodox

- after diagnosis of the micro-organism that is responsible by means of vaginal swabs, antibiotic treatment is usually prescribed to eradicate the infection.

Vaginismus

Painful spasm of the muscles surrounding the vaginal entrance which make sexual intercourse and the use of tampons painful and sometimes impossible. Sometimes the legs also straighten and come together involuntarily

during sex or a vaginal examination. The condition may
result from infection, fear of pain, past trauma, or
psychological causes relating to negative sexual
experiences or guilt.

Treatment

Professional help is recommended (see below), but the
following can be used as an adjunct to talking therapy:

Relaxation

- practising yoga and/or meditation provides mental and
  physical relaxation which facilitates talking therapy
  and relieves the stress brought by this condition.
  Aromatherapy and massage are also extremely helpful
  in providing deep relaxation, especially if carried out
  by your partner.

Professional Help

Vaginismus is very difficult to treat alone. The
vaginismus support group, Resolve (see Appendix 2),
recommends talking therapy as the most beneficial
treatment for this syndrome. Psychotherapy, counselling,
or simply talking with an understanding health
professional, friend or family member can be very
helpful. If you have a partner, it is a good idea to do
talking therapy together. The following are some of the
techniques used.

- behavioural therapy includes relaxation, visualization
  of the lovemaking situation, and the use of dilators or
  a cervical cap to insert into the vagina, thus
  presenting the fearful situation, and allowing the
  patient to overcome it in a safe and supportive
  environment.
- sex therapy: usually carried out in couples, this
  includes counselling, examination of the vagina,
  vaginal exercises (contracting and releasing the
  muscles which control urination), which demonstrate

control of the vagina, and visualization. Relaxation is also encouraged, and sometimes hypnosis. Dilators are sometimes used to accustom the woman to inserting something into the vagina. Sensate focusing is encouraged (where the focus of lovemaking is giving each other pleasure rather than penetration).
- as an adjunct to these treatments, professional homoeopathic treatment can be successful.

Orthodox

- talking therapy is recommended.

Vaginitis *see* Vaginal Irritation

Varicose Ulcer *see* Leg Ulcer

Varicose Veins

Blue, prominent and sometimes kinked veins just below the surface of the skin, most commonly in the legs, but also in the anus (see Haemorrhoids), and the testes, where they are commonly known as varicocele. Varicose veins occur when the valves which prevent blood draining backwards are weakened, and blood tends to pool and stagnate in the lower veins. The condition is often made worse by pregnancy, the menopause, obesity and long periods of standing.

Practical Advice

- the development of varicose veins is closely linked with constipation. Follow the advice given in the entry on Constipation and try to avoid straining at all times.
- if you are overweight, try to lose some weight (see Obesity).

- avoid wearing tight clothing.
- wear support hose if you have to stand for long periods.
- put your feet up whenever possible.

Dietary

- research has shown that varicose veins improve on taking 400 iu of vitamin E daily.
- increase intake of citrus fruits, apricots, blackberries, cherries, rosehips and buckwheat, all of which contain rutin, a valuable natural remedy for improving elasticity of the veins.
- take 500 mg of vitamin C with 100 mg of bioflavonoids daily.
- increase intake of raw beetroot.

Hydrotherapy

- for swollen veins apply alternate hot and cold compresses: using two basins, one with hot (but not boiling) water and one cold (with ice cubes in it). Soak towels in the water and wring out. First place the hot towel on the vein for one minute, then the cold for 30 seconds. Repeat the process 3 times, finishing with the cold pack.

Exercise

- in his book *Varicose Veins*, naturopath Leon Chaitow suggests the following daily stretches for the prevention and treatment of early varicose veins:
  - stand with feet apart and hands clasped behind your back. Bend forward from the hips as far as you can go, hold for 30 seconds, breathing slowly and deeply.
  - stand with feet 12—15 inches apart and slowly go into a squat position. If this is easy, hold out your arms in front of you; if you are losing your balance, hold onto a table or chair to stabilize you. Repeat 3—10 times.

- lie on the floor on your back, stretch your arms above your head and press the lower back to the floor. Keep the leg straight, lift one leg 15 inches off the floor, circle the foot 4 times each way, then do the same with the other leg.
- skipping, dancing or brisk walking are all good activities for varicose veins and should be done at least every other day.

Yoga

- the inverted corpse: lie near a wall and place the legs at an angle of 45 degrees against the wall. Remain in this position for 3 minutes daily.
- a regular yoga class will help improve your breathing, an important factor in the treatment of this condition.

Orthodox

- veins below the knees are injected with a sclerosing agent which fuses the walls of the vein together. Alternatively, surgery is used to strip out the vein from groin to ankle: this brings longer lasting results.

Verruca *see* Warts

Vomiting

There are many causes of vomiting, the most common of which are listed below.

- general illness, which can be trivial or serious, e.g. hepatitis, cancer, kidney disease, meningitis.
- drugs and medications, especially chemotherapy for cancer, but also non-steroidal anti-inflammatory drugs for arthritis.
- food poisoning: bacterial, viral or chemical, or toxins produced by bacteria which has entered the body.

This is the most common cause (see Food Poisoning
for treatment).

- travel sickness (see entry).
- ear infections (see Earache).
- emotional upset.
- smoking, recreational drugs, alcohol.
- migraines (see entry).
- stomach ulcer (see Peptic Ulcer).
- gall bladder disorders (see Gallstones).

The following treatments provide relief after an attack of
vomiting. However, they do not address the cause. An
episode of vomiting which lasts more than an hour or
two is unusual and should be brought to your doctor's
attention for diagnosis and treatment.

Treatment

Dietary

- to avoid dehydration from vomiting, drink plenty of
  fluids. Bottled or boiled cool water to which a little
  sugar and salt is added is the best (½ teaspoon of
  each to 1 litre of water). Avoid eating solids until
  nausea subsides, then introduce bland, non-fatty
  foods, such as yoghurt, bananas, toast.

Herbal

- ginger is an effective remedy for nausea: place a
  teaspoon of fresh grated root in a cup of boiling
  water, infuse for 5 minutes, strain and drink when
  needed.
- meadowsweet infusion soothes and protects the
  mucous membranes of the digestive system: pour a
  cup of boiling water on 1—2 teaspoons of the dried
  herb and infuse for 10—15 minutes. Drink 3 times
  daily.

Homoeopathy

take every 15 minutes for up to 4 doses and repeat if needed:
- vomiting with persistent nausea and an unusually clean tongue: Ipecac 6c.
- vomiting with pain and burning sensation in stomach, frightened of being sick: Arsenicum album 6c.
- nausea made better by vomiting: Nux vomica 6c.
- nausea and vomiting relieved by keeping the abdomen uncovered: Tabacum 6c.
- burning pains and vomiting, better temporarily for cold drinks: Phosphorus 6c.

Acupressure

- place your right thumb on the inside of your left wrist, two thumb breadths from the centre of the wrist joint towards the elbow. Massage with the thumb using a deep circular motion for one minute, taking deep breaths. Do the same on the other wrist.

Orthodox

- treatment depends on the cause of vomiting.

Warts

Harmless yet contagious growths which are spread by a virus and are commonly found on the hands, face, knees, scalp or feet (where they are known as verrucas or plantar warts). Usually warts are symptomless, though they may sometimes itch or be painful, particularly if on the soles of the feet. Genital warts, found around the vagina, anus, penis or scrotum, can lead to cervical cancer in women and should be reported to your doctor immediately. It is advisable to use a condom to prevent transmission of genital warts (see Sexually Transmitted Diseases).

Treatment

Warts often disappear after about a year without treatment. The following treatments may help stubborn cases.

Herbal

- rubbing a crushed garlic clove on the wart is said to help remove it. Eating plenty of raw garlic may also help.

Homoeopathy

professional treatment is strongly recommended though the following remedies may be tried initially, to be taken every 12 hours for up to 3 weeks:

- large jagged warts on the face, eyelids, fingertips which bleed easily: Causticum 6c.
- cauliflower-like warts, itchy, which bleed when washed: Nitric acid 6c.
- flat horny warts on the hands and soles of the feet: Antimonium crudum 6c.
- warts on the palms, when the hands tend to be sweaty: Natrum muriaticum 6c.
- Thuja mother tincture is a common remedy which is applied twice daily, then keep the wart covered.

Visualization

- spend 5 minutes each day relaxing with your eyes closed and visualizing your wart(s) shrinking and gradually disappearing.

Other Applications

- castor oil and baking powder mixed into a paste: apply at night and cover with a band aid/sticking plaster. Leave exposed to the air during the day.
- vitamin E oil: apply 3 times daily and cover.
- vitamin A oil: apply 3 times daily and cover.

Professional Help

- hypnotherapy can be effective.

Orthodox

- freezing or burning, sometimes surgery.

Wasp Stings *see* Insect Bites and Stings

Whiplash Injury

An injury to the joints and ligaments of the neck caused by the neck suddenly being thrown forward and then backward, or vice versa. This condition is common after a car accident and leads to symptoms of neck pain and stiffness which may be short-lived or long-term and are often accompanied by headaches, nausea, insomnia, numbness in the arms and fingers and ringing in the ears.

Treatment

Dietary

- stiffness can be relieved by taking a high dose supplement of calcium pantothenate: 2,000 mg daily. Reduce dose as stiffness wears off.

Aromatherapy

- essential oil of sweet marjoram and rosemary are effective in relieving pain. Add 2 drops of each to your bath, and the same to 10 ml of carrier oil or lotion and rub in night and morning.

Homoeopathy

- Arnica 6c every 5 minutes for up to 6 doses, then Hypericum 6c every 4 hours for up to 3 days.

Hydrotherapy

- immediately after injury, apply an ice pack to the painful area. Take a bag of frozen peas or a plastic bag of ice cubes, and wrap in kitchen paper. Hold on the painful area for 10 minutes. Then apply a hot water bottle wrapped in a towel for 10 minutes. Continue to alternate several times. Carry out this treatment morning and evening.

Acupressure

- place the fingers of both hands on the tops of your shoulders and apply firm pressure to the muscles near

the base of the neck. Hold for 1 minute, while taking slow deep breaths.
- shrug your shoulders up and hold for a few seconds and relax. Repeat several times.
- place the fingers of both hands on the muscles of your neck either side of the spine. Apply firm pressure while nodding your head slowly and breathing deeply for 1 minute. Repeat several times.

Professional Help

- a whiplash injury will almost certainly require professional treatment. An osteopath or chiropractor is specialized in diagnosing and resolving structural problems connected with bones, ligaments and nerves. A massage therapist will help restore movement and an acupuncturist can help combat pain. Long-term problems concerned with posture can be treated successfully by the Alexander Technique.

Orthodox

- painkilling drugs, muscle relaxants and sometimes the use of a collar to immobilize the neck. Physiotherapy may be recommended.

Whooping Cough

An infectious disease which mainly affects young children and results in fits of violent coughing with the characteristic 'whoop' as the child catches breath, often followed by vomiting. The illness brings extreme exhaustion and sometimes permanent lung damage. It can be life-threatening, particularly in babies.

Prevention

Many children are vaccinated against whooping cough. Although this does not guarantee immunity, it is recommended by doctors due to the severity of this illness.

Treatment

Practical Advice

- the child may become frightened by the violence of the coughing attacks. Reassure your child by remaining calm. Consider having the child sleep in your room during the illness for comfort at night.
- babies should be laid chest down with their head to one side to prevent choking.

Dietary

- avoid dairy products, excessive sugar and raw vegetables.
- give warm vegetable broth or soup every day.
- eat the main meal in the middle of the day; eat lightly in the evening to reduce night vomiting.

Aromatherapy

- place 2 drops of essential oil of lavender or rosemary on a tissue and place near the child to let him or her inhale it. Eucalyptus oil is also good but it is stronger, so use it in an electronic vaporizer.

Homoeopathy

- it is advisable to consult a professional homoeopath. The treatments listed under Cough may help during the first few days.

Orthodox

- if the illness is recognized early, antibiotics may be given. Once the coughing has started they are not particularly helpful. If a child becomes blue or keeps vomiting after coughing, call emergency help.

Wind *see* Flatulence

Worms

The most common type of worms to infest humans are the digestive parasites, threadworms (also called pinworms) and roundworms. They can be acquired by eating undercooked infected meat. They are particularly common in small children aged two to five, who tend to play on the ground and put things in their mouths: dirt can harbour eggs which are ingested and hatch in the intestine. The principal symptom of threadworms is itching around the anus at night. Roundworms produce few symptoms until they have multiplied when they cause stomach pain, diarrhoea and vomiting.

Prevention

- hygiene should be improved: ensure children always wash their hands after going to the toilet and before eating. Keep nails short and clean and discourage children from putting their fingers in their mouth.
- worm pets regularly.
- vacuum carpets regularly, particularly around and under beds.

Treatment

Herbal

- wormwood is an effective remedy. For appropriate dosages, consult a medical herbalist.
- take the equivalent of one clove of garlic daily, fresh or as capsules.

Homoeopathy

for threadworms: to be taken 3 times daily for 2 weeks, consult a professional if there is no improvement.
- itchy anus, child irritable, hungry, rings under eyes: Cina 6c.
- itchy anus and nose, worse in evening after going to bed: Teucrium 6c.

Orthodox

- anthelmintic drugs are given. They kill or paralyse the worms and allow them to be passed out in the faeces. They may produce side effects of nausea, vomiting and abdominal pain.

Wry Neck *see* Torticollis

X

Xanthomatosis

A condition in which fatty, yellow deposits accumulate in different parts of the body, particularly the skin, internal organs, blood vessels, eyes and brain. When the deposits occur only in the eyelids the condition is known as xanthelasma.

Prevention/Treatment

Aimed at reducing levels of fat and cholesterol in the body.

Dietary

- avoid saturated fat, found in animal products (meat and dairy produce). Replace red meat with poultry, fish and vegetable protein and use skimmed milk.
- eat moderate amounts of polyunsaturated fats, which lower blood cholesterol. They are found in most fats of plant origin (excepting coconut and palm oils): use olive oil for cooking and low fat vegetable spreads to replace butter.
- avoid ice cream (have sorbet instead), confectionery made with fat, savoury snacks and fried food.
- increase intake of wholegrain cereals, complex carbohydrates (potatoes, pasta, rice), cooked dried beans and peas and fresh fruit and vegetables.
- increase intake of oat bran and rice bran, which lower cholesterol.
- eat reasonable quantities of nuts, and avocados. These

contain monounsaturated fat, which is though to help lower cholesterol.
- eat plenty of fish, particularly salmon, tuna, trout, mackerel and sardines. Fish oil reduces cholesterol.

Herbal

- eat plenty of raw garlic, shown to reduce harmful blood fats.

Exercise

- aerobic exercise helps lower cholesterol. Any activity which raises the pulse and respiration rate significantly for more than 20 minutes is the most effective. Jogging, swimming, skipping and brisk walking are all good.

Relaxation

- studies have shown that relaxation also helps lower cholesterol levels. Learning to meditate, or attending a yoga class, will teach you deep relaxation. Relaxation tapes and biofeedback can also help.

Orthodox

- a low cholesterol and high polyunsaturated fat diet is recommended. Drugs are prescribed to reduce fats in the blood.

Y

Yeast Infection *see* Fungal Infection

Appendix 1:
Therapies—Associations

Most associations have a list of registered practitioners. Send a stamped addressed envelope. These addresses were correct at the time of going to press.

UK

Acupressure
Shiatsu Society
Foxcote
Wokingham
Berkshire
RG11 3PG

Acupuncture
British Acupuncture Association and Register
34 Alderney Street
London
SW1V 4EU

Traditional Acupuncture Society
1 The Ridgeway
Stratford-upon-Avon
Warwickshire
CV37 9JL

International College of Oriental Medicine
Green Hedges House
Green Hedges Lane
East Grinstead
West Sussex
RH19 1DZ

Alexander Technique
Society of Teachers of the Alexander Technique
20 London House
266 Fulham Road
London
SW10 9EL

Aromatherapy
International Federation of Aromatherapists
Dept Continuing Education
Royal Masonic Hospital
London
W6 0TN

International Society of Professional Aromatherapists
Hinckley and District Hospital and Health Centre
The Annexe
Mount Road
Hinckley
Leics
LE10 1AG

International Federation of Aromatherapists
Department of Continuing Education
The Royal Masonic Hospital
Ravenscourt Park
London
W6 0TN

Aromatherapy Organisations Council
3 Latymer Close
Braybrooke
Market Harborough
Leics
LE16 8LN

Bates Method
The Bates Association of Great Britain
11 Tarmount Lane
Shoreham by Sea
West Sussex
BN43 6RQ

Chinese Medicine
Register of Traditional Chinese Medicine
19 Trinity Road
London
N2 8JJ

Chiropractic
British Chiropractic Association
29 Whitley Street
Reading
RG2 0EG

Counselling and Psychotherapy
British Association for Counselling
1 Regent Place
Rugby
Warks
CV21 2PJ

British Association of Psychotherapists
37 Mapesbury Road
London
NW2 4HJ

Herbalism
General Council and Register of Consultant Herbalists
Grosvenor House
40 Sea Way
Middleton-on-Sea
West Sussex
PO22 7SA

National Institute of Medical Herbalists
9 Palace Gate
Exeter
EX1 1JA

Homoeopathy
British Homoeopathic Association
27a Devonshire Street
London
W1N 1RJ

Society of Homoeopaths
2 Artizan Road
Northampton
NN1 4HU

Hypnotherapy
National Council of Psychotherapists (and
    Hypnotherapy Register)
46 Oxhey Road
Oxhey
Watford
Hertfordshire
WD1 4QQ

The National Register of Hypnotherapists and
    Psychotherapists
12 Cross Street
Nelson
Lancashire

British Hypnosis Research
Southpoint
8 Paston Place
Brighton
BN2 1HA

Massage
London College of Massage
5 Newman Passage
London
W1P 3PF

Meditation
School of Meditation
158 Holland Park Avenue
London
W11 4UH

Naturopathy and Diet
General Council and Register of Naturopaths
Frazer House
6 Netherhall Gardens
London
NW3 5RR

Society for the Promotion of Nutritional Therapy
1st Floor
Enterprise Centre
Eastbourne
East Sussex
BN21 1BE

Institute of Optimum Nutrition
5 Jerdan Place
Fulham
London
SW6 1BE

Osteopathy
General Council and Register of Osteopaths
56 London Street
Reading
Berks
RG1 4SQ

Reflexology
Reflexologists' Society
General Secretary
44 Derby Hill
Forest Hill
London
SE23 3YD

Yoga
Iyengar Yoga Institute
223a Randolph Avenue
London
W9 1NL

Yoga for Health Foundation
Ickwell Bury
Biggleswade
Beds
SG18 9EF

Yoga Biomedical Trust Research and Information
PO Box 140
Cambridge
CB4 3SY

General Advice
British Holistic Medical Association
179 Gloucester Place
London
NW1 6DX

British Complementary Medicine Association
St Charles Hospital
Exmoor Street
London
W10 6DZ

Council for Complementary and Alternative Medicine
179 Gloucester Place
London
NW1 6DX

Institute for Complementary Medicine
PO Box 194
London
SE14 1QZ

Australia

For advice on various complementary therapies, contact
AFONTA
8 Thorp Road
2232 Woronara

Appendix 2:
Ailment Support Groups and Information

For many of the ailments listed in this book there is a support group or information centre which can provide vital advice and contact with other sufferers. Some are listed below. Because most of these groups are registered charities and operate on restricted funds, it is advisable to send a stamped addressed envelope for information.

UK

AIDS
Body Positive
51b Philbeach Gardens
London
SW5 9EB

Terrence Higgins Trust
52–54 Gray's Inn Road
London
WC1X 8JU

London Lighthouse
111–117 Lancaster Road
London
W11 1QT

Alcohol Abuse
Alcoholics Anonymous (AA)
General Service Office
PO Box 1
Stonebow House
Stonebow
York
YO1 2NJ

Women's Alcohol Centre
66 Drayton Park
London
N5 1ND

Allergies
Action Against Allergy
23—24 High Street
Hampton Hill
Middlesex
TW12 1PD

Food and Chemical Allergy Association
27 Ferringham Lane
Ferring by Sea
West Sussex
BN12 5NB

Breakspear Hospital (Allergy and Environmental
   Medicine)
High Street
Abbots Langley
Hertfordshire
WD4 9HT

Alzheimer's Disease
Alzheimer's Disease Society
Gordon House
158—160 Balham High Road
London
SW12 9BN

Amnesia
AMNASS, The Amnesia Association
Headway National Head Injuries Association
7 King Edward Court
King Edward Street
Nottingham
NG1 1EW

Anorexia Nervosa
Anorexia and Bulimia Nervosa Association
Tottenham Women's Health Centre
Annexe C
Tottenham Town Hall
Town Hall Approach
London
N15 4RX

Anxiety
Be Not Anxious
33 Broadway Avenue
Rainham
Kent
ME8 9DB

Relaxation for Living
29 Burwood Park Road
Walton-on-Thames
Surrey
KT12 5LH

Arthritis
Arthritis and Rheumatism Council
Faraday House
8–10 Charing Cross Road
London
WC2H 0HN

Arthritis Care
18 Stephenson Way
London
NW1 2HD

The Arthritic Association
Hill House
1 Little New Street
London
EC4A 3TR

Asthma
National Asthma Campaign
Providence House
Providence Place
London
N1 0NT

Backache
National Back Pain Association
31–33 Park Road
Teddington
Middlesex
TW11 0AB

Spinal Injuries Association
Newpoint House
76 St James's Lane
London
N10 3DF

Breast Feeding Problems
La Leche League of Great Britain
Box BM3424
London
WC1 6XX

Association of Breast Feeding Mothers
Sydenham Green Health Centre
Holmshaw Close
London
SE26 4TH

Burns
Helpline for Burns
22 Westwood Gardens
Chandlers Ford
Eastleigh
Hants
SO5 1FN

Caesarean Birth
Caesarean Support Group
81 Elizabeth Way
Cambridge
CB4 1BQ

Cancer
The Breast Care and Mastectomy Association
15–19 Britten Street
London
SW3 3TZ

The Bristol Cancer Help Centre
Grove House
Cornwallis Grove
Clifton
Bristol
BS8 4PG

Cancer Winners
Omega House
New Street
Margate
Kent
CT9 1EG

CancerLink
17 Britannia Street
London
WC1X 9JN

Coeliac Disease
Coeliac Society of the United Kingdom
PO Box 220
High Wycombe
Bucks
HP11 2HY

Colic
CRY-SIS Support Group (advice and help to parents of
    excessively crying babies or children who do not
    sleep)
BM Cry-sis
London
WC1N 3XX

Colitis/Crohn's Disease
National Association for Colitis and Crohn's Disease
98a London Road
St Albans
Herts
AL1 1NX

Coronary Heart Disease
British Heart Foundation
14 Fitzhardinge Street
London
W1H 4DH

Cystitis
Cystitis and Candida
75 Mortimer Road
London
N1 5AR

Deafness
National Association of Deafened People
103 Heath Road
Widnes
Cheshire
WA8 7NU

British Association of the Hard of Hearing
7—11 Armstrong Road
London
W3 7JL

Royal National Institute for the Deaf
105 Gower Street
London
WC1E 6AH

Depression
Depressives Anonymous
36 Chestnut Avenue
Beverley
North Humberside
HU17 9QU

Depressives Associated
PO Box 5
Castletown
Portland
Dorset
DT5 1BQ

MIND (National Association for Mental Heath)
22 Harley Street
London
W1N 2ED

Diabetes
Diabetes Foundation
177a Tennison Road
London
SE25 5NF

British Diabetic Association
10 Queen Anne Street
London
W1M 0BD

Eczema
National Eczema Society
4 Tavistock Place
London
WC1H 9RA

Endometriosis
Endometriosis Society
Unit F8A
Shakespeare Business Centre
245a Coldharbour Lane
London
SW9 8RR

Epilepsy
British Epilepsy Association
Anstey House
40 Hanover Square
Leeds
LS3 1BE

National Society for Epilepsy
Chalfont Centre for Epilepsy
Chalfont St Peter
Gerrards Cross
Bucks
SL9 0RJ

Glaucoma
International Glaucoma Association
c/o King's College Hopsital
Denmark Hill
London
SE5 9RS

Hair Problems
Hairline International (support group for alopecia and
    hair loss)
c/o Chantrey Vellacott
Post and Mail House
Colmore Circus
Birmingham
B4 6AT

FACE (support group for those with unwanted hair)
PO Box 484
Cambridge
CB4 3TF

British Association of Electroysists
18 Stokes End
Haddenham
Bucks
HP17 8DX

Hepatitis
Group B Hepatitis
Basement Flat
7a Fielding Road
London
W14 OLL

Herpes
Herpes Association
41 North Road
London
N7 9DP

Hyperactivity
Hyperactive Children's Support Group
71 Whyke Lane
Chichester
West Sussex
PO19 2LD

Hypothyroidism
Hypothyroidism Self Help
47 Crawford Avenue
Tyldersley
Manchester
M29 8ET

Incontinence
Incontinence Advisory Service
The Dene Centre
Castles Farm Road
Newcastle upon Tyne
NE3 1PH

Indigestion
British Digestive Foundation
3 St Andrew's Place
London
NW1 4LB

Infertility
British Association for Betterment of Infertility and
    Education (BABIE)
PO Box 4TS
London
W1A 4TS

ISSUE: The National Fertility Association
Birmingham Settlement
318 Summer Lane
Birmingham
B19 3RL

Kidney Disease
National Federation of Kidney Patients' Associations
Acorn Lodge
Woodsetts
nr Worksop
S81 8AT

Labour Pains
Active Birth Centre
55 Dartmouth Park Road
London
NW5 1SL

National Childbirth Trust (NCT)
Alexandra House
Oldham Terrace
London
W3 6NH

Lead Poisoning
CLEAR (Campaign for Lead-Free Air)
3 Endsleigh Street
London
WC1H ODD

Manic Depression
Manic Depression Fellowship IYQ
51 Sheen Road
Richmond
Surrey

ME (Myalgic Encephalomyelitis)
Myalgic Encephalomyelitis (ME) Association
PO Box 8
Stanford-le-Hope
Essex
SS17 8EX

ME Action Campaign
PO Box 1126
London
W3 0RY

Ménière's Disease
Ménière's Society
98 Maybury Road
Woking
Surrey
GU21 5HX

Migraine
British Migraine Association
178a High Road
Byfleet
West Byfleet
Surrey
KT14 7ED

The Migraine Trust
45 Great Ormond Street
London
WC1N 3HD

Miscarriage
Miscarriage Association
PO Box 24
Ossett
West Yorks
WF5 9XG

Stillbirth and Neonatal Death Society
28 Portland Place
London
S1N 4DE

Multiple Sclerosis
Action for Research into Multiple Sclerosis (ARMS)
4a Chapel Hill
Stansted
Essex
CM23 8AG

Multiple Sclerosis Society of Great Britain and Northern
  Ireland
25 Effie Road
London
SW6 1EE

Obesity
Eating Disorders Association
Sackville Place
44 Magdalen Street
Norwich NR3 1JE

Overeaters Anonymous
PO Box 19
Stretford
Manchester
M32 9EB

Weightwatchers UK Ltd. (head office — for details of
  local meetings)
Kidwells Park House
Kidwells Park Drive
Maidenhead
Berks
SL6 8YT

Osteoporosis
National Osteoporosis Society
PO Box 10
Radstock
Bath
Avon
BA3 3YB

Pain
Self Help In Pain (SHIP)
33 Kingsdown Park
Tankerton
Kent
CT5 2DT

Pelvic Inflammatory Disease
Pelvic Inflammatory Disease Support Network
WHRRIC
52 Featherstone Street
London
EC1Y 8RT

Phobias
Action on Phobias
8 The Avenue
Eastbourne
Sussex
BN21 3YA

Phobic Action
7 Court House Gardens
London
N3 1PU

PAX
4 Manorbrook
Blackheath
London
SE3 9AW

Post-Natal Depression
Association for Post Natal Illness
25 Jerdan Place
London
SW6 1BE

Pre-conceptual Care
Foresight
28 The Paddock
Godalming
Surrey
GU7 1XB

Pre-Eclampsia
Pre-Eclamptic Toxaemia Society (PETS)
'Ty lago'
High Street
Llanberis
Caernarfon
Gwynedd
LL55 4HB

Premenstrual Syndrome (PMS)
Premenstrual Society (PREMENSOC)
PO Box 102
London
SE1 7ES

Psoriasis
Psoriasis Association
7 Milton Street
Northampton
NN2 7JG

Raynaud's Disease
Raynaud's and Scleroderma Association
112 Crewe Road
Alsager
Cheshire
ST7 2JA

Schizophrenia
SANE (Schizophrenia — a National Emergency)
5th Floor
120 Regent Street
London
W1A 5FE

Schizophrenia Association of Great Britain
Bryn Hyfryd
The Crescent
Bangor
Gwynedd
LL57 2AG

Seasonal Affective Disorder
Seasonal Affective Disorder Association
51 Bracewell Road
London
W10 6AF

Stress
International Stress and Tension Control Society
The Priory Hospital
Priory Lane
London
SW15 5JJ

Stroke
Chest, Heart and Stroke Association
Tavistock House North
Tavistock Square
London
WC1H 9JE

Chest, Heart and Stroke Association Volunteer Stroke
    Scheme (CHSAVSS)
Manor Farm
Appleton
Abingdon
Oxon
OX13 4JR

Thrush
Cystitis and Candida
75 Mortimer Road
London
N1 5AR

Tinnitus
British Tinnitus Association
c/o Royal National Institute for the Deaf
105 Gower Street
London
WC1E 6AH

Vaginismus
Resolve
PO Box 820
London N10 3AW

Australia

AIDS Pastoral Care
PO Box 291
Belmont WA 6104

Agoraphobic Support
c/- Livingstone Foundation
2 Thorogood Street
Victoria Park WA 6100

Alcohol and Drug Information Service
PO Box 8165 Stirling Street
Perth WA 6849

Allergy Association of Australia
PO Box 214
North Beach WA 6020

Allergy Association of South Australia
PO Box 104
North Adelaide SA 5006

Alzheimer's Association
PO Box 1099
Subiaco WA 6008

Alzheimer's Society of Victoria
98 Riversdale Road
Hawthorn Vic 3122

Arthritis Foundation
PO Box 34
Wembley WA 6014

Australian Crohn's and Colitis Association Inc.
PO Box 201
Mooroolark Vic 3138

Breast Cancer Support Service
c/- Cancer Foundation of Western Australia
334 Rokeby Road
Subiaco WA 6008

Bulimia/Anorexia Nervosa Group
PO Box 794
Nedlands WA 6009

Cancer Support Association
80 Railway Street
Cottesloe WA 6011

Chronic Pain Support Group
16 Ashworth Street
Cloverdale WA 6105

Concern for the Infertile Couple
PO Box 412
Subiaco WA 6008

Depression Anonymous
PO Box 271
Wembley WA 6014

Endometriosis Association
PO Box 428
Melville WA 6156

Herpes Support
c/- WISH
80 Railway Street
Cottesloe WA 6011

Mid-life and Menopause Support Group
PO Box 1112
Subiaco WA 6008

Multiple Sclerosis Society of Western Australia
PO Box 1168
East Victoria Park WA 6101

Nursing Mothers Association of Australia
16 Dinsdale Place
Hamersley WA 6022

Pregnancy Problem House
114 Great Eastern Highway
Belmont WA 6104

True Grit Stroke Club
c/- A Kennedy
9 Burges Street
Geraldton WA 6530

West Australian Epilepsy Association
14 Bagot Road
Subiaco WA 6608

Appendix 3:
Distributors and Suppliers

Many complementary remedies can be found in good health food shops or pharmacies. If in doubt, ask a member of staff. The support groups in Appendix 2 may be able to advise you on suppliers.

UK
Homoeopathic Remedies
Ainsworths
38 New Cavendish Street
London
W1M 7LH

Galen Pharmacy
1 South Street
Dorchester
Dorset
DTT 1DE

Helios
97 Camden Road
Tunbridge Wells
Kent
TN1 2QR

Nelson's Pharmacies Limited
73 Duke Street
London
W1M 6BY

Weleda UK Limited
Heanor Road
Ilkeston
Derbyshire
DE7 8DR

Herbs
G. Baldwins
171–173 Walworth Road
London
SE17

Cathay of Bournemouth Ltd
32 Cleveland Road
Bournemouth
Dorset

Culpeper Ltd
21 Bruton Street
Berkeley Square
London
W1X 7DA

East West Herbs
Langston Priory Mews
Kingham
Oxon
OX7 6UP

Gerard House Ltd
475 Capability Green
Luton
LU1 3LU

The Herbal Apothecary
3 High Street
Syston
Leicester
LE7 8GQ

Napier and Sons
18 Bristo Place
Edinburgh
EH1 1EZ

Neals Yard Apothecary
Neals Yard
Covent Garden
London
WC2

Phyto Products
Tidebrook Manor Farm
Wadhurst
Sussex
TN5 6PD

Potters Herbal Suppliers Ltd
Douglas Works
Leyland Mill Lane
Wigan
Lancs
WN1 2JB

Frank Roberts (Herbal Dispensaries) Ltd
91 Newfoundland Road
Bristol
BS2 9LT

Flower Remedies
Dr Edward Bach Centre
Mount Vernon
Sotwell
Wallingford
Oxon
OX10 OPZ

Flower Essence Association
Anubis House
Cresswell Drive
Ravenstone
Leicestershire
LE6 2AG

Appendix 4:
Further Reading

The books in this list are merely suggestions: you will find many more books on these subjects. Some of them have different publishers in the US and the UK. If you are unable to find any of them in your local library or bookshop, ask the librarian or shop assistant, as they may be able to order them.

Acupressure
Acupressure's Potent Points, Michael Reed Gach, Bantam Books.
Acupuncture Without Needles, J.V. Cerney, Reward Books.
The Healing Benefits of Acupressure, F.C. Houston, D.C., Keats.

Acupuncture
Acupuncture – The Illustrated Guide, Peter Firebrace B.Ac., Harmony Books.
The Healing Power of Acupuncture, Michael Nightingale, Javelin Books.

Alexander Technique
Alexander Technique, Bill Connington and Judith Leibowitz, HarperCollins.
Alexander Technique: Learning to use your body for total energy, Sarah Barker, Bantam.

Applied Kinesiology
Applied Kinesiology, Tom Valentine and Carol Valentine, Inner Traditions.

Applied Kinesiology, Clayne R. Jensen and Gordon M. Schulz, McGraw.

Aromatherapy
Aromatherapy to Heal and Tend the Body, Robert Tisserand, Lotus Light.
Aromatherapy for Common Ailments, Shirley Price, Fireside.
Aromatherapy: an A to Z, Patricia Davis, C.W. Daniel.
Practical Aromatherapy, Shirley Price, Thorsons.
The Power of Holistic Aromatherapy, Christine Stead, Javelin.

Biochemic Tissue Salts
Biochemic Handbook, Colin B. Lessell, Thorsons.
The Biochemic Tissue Salts Handbook, J.S. Goodwin, Thorsons.

Chinese Medicine
Chinese Herbal Medicine, Daniel P. Reid, Shambhala.
Chinese Medicinal Herbs, Li Shih Chen, Georgetown Press.
The Chinese Art of Healing, Stephen Palos, Bantam Books.
Secrets of the Chinese Herbalists, Richard Lucus, Parker Publishing Company, Inc.

Chiropractic
Thorsons Introductory Guide to Chiropractic, M.B. Howitt-Wilson, Thorsons.

Flower Remedies
Bach Flower Therapy, Theory and Practice, Mechthild Scheffer, Thorsons.
Flower Remedies to the Rescue, Gregory Vlamis, Thorsons.
Dictionary of the Bach Flower Remedies, T.W. Hynne-Jones, C.W. Daniel.

Herbalism
The Dictionary of Modern Herbalism, Simon Y. Mills, Healing Arts Press.

Thorsons Guide to Medical Herbalism, David Hoffman, Thorsons.
A Woman's Herbal, Kitty Campion, Century.

Homoeopathy

The Complete Homoeopathy Handbook, Miranda Castro, Macmillan.
Homoeopathic First Aid, Dr Anne Clover, Thorsons.
Homoeopathy: Medicine for the 21st Century, Dana Ullman, Thorsons.
How To Use Homoeopathy Effectively, Christopher Hammond, Element Books.
Everyday Homoeopathy, David Gemmell, Beaconsfield.
Thorsons Introductory Guide to Homoeopathy, Dr Anne Clover, Thorsons.
The Family Guide to Homoeopathy, Dr Andrew Lockie, Prentice Hall Press.

Hypnotherapy

Hypnosis in Therapy, H.B. Gibson and M. Heap, Lawrence, Earlbaum Associates.
Hypnotherapy: Is it for you? Roger Sleet, Element Books.

Massage

Self Massage, Jacqueline Young, Thorsons.
Massage Cures, Nigel Dawes & Fiona Harrold, Thorsons.
Performance Massage, Robert K. King, Human Kinetics.
Massage for Common Ailments, Sara Thomas, Fireside.

Naturopathy and Diet

The A-Z of Nutritional Therapy, Adrienne Mayes Ph.D., Thorsons.
The Essential Guide to Vitamins and Minerals, Elizabeth Somer, M.A.,R.D., HarperPerennial.
Amino Acids in Therapy, Leon Chaitow D.O., N.D., Healing Arts Press.
Probiotics, Leon Chaitow N.D., D.O. and Natasha Trenev, Thorsons.
Naturopathic Medicine, Roger Newman Turner, Thorsons.

Food Combining for Health, Doris Grant and Jean Joice, Thorsons (The Hay Diet).

Osteopathy
Thorsons Introductory Guide to Osteopathy, Edward Triance, Thorsons.

Reflexology
Holistic Reflexology, Avi Grinberg, Thorsons.
Hand and Foot Reflexology, Kevin and Barbara Kunz, Thorsons.
Thorsons Introductory Guide to Reflexology, Nicola M. Hall, Thorsons.

Yoga
Office Yoga, Julie Friedeberger, Thorsons.
Yoga for Common Ailments, Dr Robin Monro, Dr Nagarathna, Dr Nagendra, Fireside.
The Yoga Book, Maxine Tobias and Mary Stewart, Pan Books.
Bodylife, Arthur Balaskas, Sidgwick and Jackson.
Yoga Self Taught, Andre von Lysebeth, Allen and Unwin.

Visualization
Creative Visualization, Shakti Gawain, Bantam.
Creative Visualization Workbook, Shakti Gawain, New World Library.

Women's Health
Essential Supplements for Women, Carolyn Reuben & Dr Joan Priestley, Thorsons.
Alternative Health Care for Women, Patsy Westcott, Thorsons.
The New Our Bodies Ourselves, The Boston Women's Health Book Collective, Touchstone.
The 35-plus Good Health Guide for Women, Jean Perry Spodnik and David P. Cogan, M.D., Harper and Row.
The Well Woman Handbook: A Guide for Women Throughout Their Lives, Suzie Hayman, Penguin.

General

The Practical Encyclopedia of Natural Healing, Mark Bricklin, Penguin.

The Alternative Dictionary of Symptoms and Cures, Dr Caroline Shreeve, Century Paperbacks.

Better Health Through Natural Healing, Ross Trattler N.D., D.O., Thorsons.

Encyclopedia of Natural Healing, Michael Murray, N.D. and Joseph Pizzorno, N.D., Prima.

Natural Medicine for Children, Julian Scott M.A., Ph.D., Unwin Paperbacks.

Specific Ailments

AIDS

Immune Power – Health and the Immune System, Jennifer Meek, Macdonald Optima.

Mind, Body and Immunity – How to Enhance Your Body's Natural Defences, Rachel Charles, Methuen.

Pathways to Wellness – Strategies for Self-Empowerment in the Age of AIDS, Paul Kent Froman, Penguin.

AIDS and the Healer Within, Nick Bamforth, Amethyst Books.

The Terrence Higgins Trust HIV/AIDS Book, Judy Tavanyar, Thorsons.

Allergies

Asthma and Hayfever (New Self Help Series), Leon Chaitow N.D., D.O., Thorsons.

All about Asthma & Allergy, Dr H. Morrow Brown, Harper & Row.

The Allergy Connection, Barbara Paterson, ––

The Allergy Handbook, Dr Keith Mumby, Thorsons.

Alzheimer's Disease

Alzheimer's Disease – Coping with a Living Death, Bob Woods, Souvenir Press.

Alzheimer's Disease, A Guide for Families, Lenore S. Powel Ed.D. with Katie Courtice, Addison Wesley.

The Alzheimer's Cope Book, R.E. Markin, Citadel Press.

Amnesia
Overcoming Memory Problems, Robert Erdmann Ph.D. and
  Meirion Jones, Thorsons.

Anorexia Nervosa and Bulimia
Coping with Bulimia, Barbara French, Thorsons.
Bodysize or the Hungry Self, Kim Chernin, Viking
  Penguin.
Surviving an Eating Disorder: strategies for family and friends,
  Siegel, Brisman and Weinshel, Harper and Row..
Anorexia Nervosa, R.L. Palmer, Penguin Books.
The Anorexic Experience, Marilyn Lawrence, Women's
  Press.
Fat is a Feminist Issue, Susie Orbach, Berkeley Pub.
Feeding the Hungry Heart, Geneen Roth, Grafton.

Arthritis
Arthritis (New Self Help Series), Leon Chaitow N.D.,
  D.O., Thorsons.

Back Pain
Back Pain, Roger Newman Turner, Thorsons.
Your Painful Neck and Back, J.W. Fisk, Arrow Books.

Blood Pressure, High
High Blood Pressure (New Self Help Series), Leon Chaitow
  N.D.,D.O., Thorsons.

Breast Feeding
The Womanly Art of Breastfeeding, La Leche League.
Nursing Your Baby, Karen Pryor and Gale Pryor, Pocket
  Books.
Bestfeeding: Getting Breast Feeding Right for You, Mary
  Renfrew, Chloe Fisher and Suzanne Arms, Celestial
  Arts.

Breast Problems
Breast Awareness, Cath Cirket, Thorsons.
Dr Susan Love's Breast Book, Dr Susan Love, Addison
  Wesley.

Cancer

The Bristol Programme: An Introduction to the Holistic Therapies Practised by the Bristol Cancer Help Centre, Penny Brohn, Century.

Always a Woman: A Practical Guide to Living with Breast Cancer, Carolyn Faulder, Thorsons.

Cancer: Your Life, Your Choice, Rachael Clyne, Thorsons.

Catarrh

Catarrh (New Self Help Series), Arthur White N.D., D.O., Thorsons.

Colitis

Colitis (New Self Help Series), Arthur White N.D., D.O., Thorsons.

Cystitis

Cystitis: a Complete Self Help Guide, Angela Kilmartin, Warner Books.

Cystitis, Caroline Shreeve, Inner Traditions/Thorsons.

Depression

Depression, The Way Out of Your Prison, Dorothy Rowe, Routledge.

Diverticulitis

Diverticulitis (New Self Help Series), Arthur White N.D., D.O., Thorsons.

Eczema

Eczema Relief, Christine Orton, Thorsons.

Endometriosis

Endometriosis, Dr Lyle Breitkopf and Marion Gordon Bakoulis, Thorsons.

Eye Problems

Improve Your Eyesight, Jonathan Barnes, Angus and Robertson.

Better Sight Without Glasses, Harry Benjamin, Thorsons.

Fatigue
Fatigue (New Self Help Series), Leon Chaitow N.D., D.O., Thorsons.

Headaches
Headaches and Migraine (New Self Help Series), Leon Chaitow, N.D., D.O., Thorsons.

Heart Problems
Heart Disease (New Self Help Series), Leonard Mervyn Ph.D., Thorsons.

Hiatus Hernia
Hiatus Hernia (New Self Help Series), Joan Lay N.D., Thorsons.

Hyperactivity
The Hyperactive Child – Handbook for Parents, Belinda Barnes and Irene Colquhoun, Thorsons, London.
Why Your Child is Hyperactive, B.F. Feingold, Random House, New York.

Incontinence
Overcoming Urinary Incontinence, Dr Richard J. Millard, Thorsons.

Infertility
Getting Pregnant, Robert Winston, Anaya Publishers.
The New Fertility and Conception, John J. Stangel, M.D, NAL Dutton.

Labour Pain/Childbirth
Mew Active Birth, Janet Balaskas, Thorsons.

ME
M.E. And You, A Survivor's Guide to Post-Viral Fatigue Syndrome, Steve Wilkinson, Thorsons.
Living With M.E.: A Self Help Guide, Dr Charles Shepherd, Heinemann Cedar.

M.E. Post-Viral Fatigue Syndrome: How to Live With It, Dr
Anne Macintyre, Thorsons.

Menopause
Overcoming the Menopause Naturally, Dr Caroline Shreeve,
Arrow.
Menopause – A Positive Approach, Rosetta Reitz.

Multiple Sclerosis
Multiple Sclerosis: A Self Help Guide To Its Management,
Judy Graham, Thorsons.

Osteoporosis
Understanding Osteoporosis, Wendy Cooper, Arrow Books.
Avoiding Osteoporosis, Dr Allan Dixon and Dr Anthony
Woolf, MacDonald Optima.

Pain
The Book of Pain Relief, Leon Chaitow, Thorsons

Period Pain
*Pain-free Periods – Natural Ways of Overcoming Menstrual
Problems*, Stella Weller, Thorsons.

Post-Natal Depression
*Depression after Childbirth: How to Recognise and Treat Post-
Natal Depression*, Katharina Dalton, Oxford University
Press.

Pregnancy
Eating Well For a Healthy Pregnancy, Dr Barbara Pickard,
Sheldon.

Premenstrual Syndrome
The Premenstrual Syndrome, Dr Caroline Shreeve,
Thorsons.
PMS Self Help Book: A Women's Guide, Susan M. Lark,
Celestial Arts.
Once a Month, Katharina Dalton, Borgo Press.

Prostate Problems

Prostate Problems, Jeremy Hamand, Thorsons.
Prostate Troubles (New Self Help Series), Leon Chaitow
    N.D., D.O., Thorsons.
The Prostate Book: Sound Advice on Symptoms and Treatment,
    Stephen Rous MD, W.W. Norton.
Men's Reproductive Health, edited by Janice M. Swanson
    and Katherine A. Forrest, Springer Publishing.

Psoriasis

Psoriasis, Sandra Gibbons, Thorsons.

Seasonal Affective Disorder

*Seasonal Affective Disorder, Who Gets It, What Causes It,
    How To Cure It*, Angela Smyth, Thorsons.

Stress

The Book of Stress Survival, Alix Kirsta, Allen & Unwin.
Coping with Stress: A Practical Self-help Guide for Women,
    Georgia Wikin-Lanoil, Sheldon.

Tinnitus

Tinnitus (New Self Help Series), Arthur White N.D., D.O.,
    Thorsons.

Ulcers

Stomach Ulcers and Acidity (New Self Help Series), Leonard
    Mervyn Ph.D., Thorsons.

Varicose Veins

Varicose Veins (New Self Help Series), Leon Chaitow N.D.,
    D.O., Thorsons.

Vaginismus

*When a Woman's Body Says No to Sex: Understanding and
    Overcoming Vaginismus*, Linda Valins, Penguin.